Communication Begins
with Children

LIFESPAN
COMMUNICATION
Children, Families, and Aging

Thomas J. Socha

GENERAL EDITOR

Vol. 8

The Lifespan Communication series
is part of the Peter Lang Media and Communication list.
Every volume is peer reviewed and meets
the highest quality standards for content and production.

PETER LANG
New York • Bern • Berlin
Brussels • Vienna • Oxford • Warsaw

Communication Begins with Children

A Lifespan Communication Sourcebook

Edited by Thomas J. Socha and Narissra Maria Punyanunt-Carter

PETER LANG
New York • Bern • Berlin
Brussels • Vienna • Oxford • Warsaw

Library of Congress Cataloging-in-Publication Data

Names: Socha, Thomas J., editor. | Punyanunt-Carter, Narissra M., editor.
Title: Communication begins with children: a lifespan communication
sourcebook / edited by Thomas J. Socha and
Narissra Maria Punyanunt-Carter.
Description: New York: Peter Lang, 2021.
Series: Lifespan communication: children, families, and aging; Vol. 8
ISSN 2166-6466 (print) | ISSN 2166-6474 (online)
Includes bibliographical references and indexes.
Identifiers: LCCN 2020033437 (print) | LCCN 2020033438 (ebook)
ISBN 978-1-4331-3149-3 (hardback) | ISBN 978-1-4331-6656-3 (paperback)
ISBN 978-1-4331-6657-0 (ebook pdf) | ISBN 978-1-4331-6658-7 (epub)
ISBN 978-1-4331-6659-4 (mobi)
Subjects: LCSH: Interpersonal communication in children. |
Communication in families. | Media literacy. | Social
interaction. | Language disorders in children.
Classification: LCC BF723.C57 C648 2021 (print) | LCC BF723.C57 (ebook) |
DDC 302.2 23—dc
LC record available at https://lccn.loc.gov/2020033437
LC ebook record available at https://lccn.loc.gov/2020033438
DOI 10.3726/b15276

Bibliographic information published by **Die Deutsche Nationalbibliothek**.
Die Deutsche Nationalbibliothek lists this publication in the "Deutsche
Nationalbibliografie"; detailed bibliographic data are available
on the Internet at http://dnb.d-nb.de/.

To my future grandchildren with all my love.

—TJS

To Ezra & Zavin Carter, I love you more than I could ever put into words.

—NPC

Table of Contents

Introduction

THOMAS J. SOCHA
Old Dominion University

NARISSRA M. PUNYANUNT-CARTER
Texas Tech University

June 2, 2020

As we complete work on this volume, we are experiencing an unprecedented global pandemic as well as national racial unrest in the US. Over the past few months (since March 2020), and likely for the foreseeable near future, the Covid-19 virus has radically changed the everyday life of the world's children. It has moved children out of their preschools, daycare centers, schools, playgrounds, sports fields, and recreational facilities and away from their care-givers, teachers, coaches, and adult leaders and into their homes and to their parents, along with expectations of continuing their development. Caught-off-guard educational systems are racing to speed-deliver make-shift digital classes into children's homes in hopes of satisfying students' and parents' needs for continuing knowledge, information, and formal education. Over-taxed supply chains and delivery systems are struggling to speed-deliver gro-ceries and prized toilet paper into homes, in an effort to keep children and families fed, sanitized, and safe. Taken-off-line broadcast media companies are also streaming archived content to bored children and families needing unprecedented lengths of diversion and escape. At the same time, families are celebrating graduations, birthdays, and more via Zoom, Google Meets, Skype, and other similar digital platforms.

While the global Covid-19 pandemic rages, the US is also coping with the murder of George Floyd by a police officer in Minneapolis, Minnesota, and the protests and riots that have followed this racial hate crime. Here too children are watching and listening along with their parents to news reports and social media postings about curfews, national guards, violent clashes and calls for peaceful justice. As the world struggles and changes, it is important that we not lose sight of the fact that the world's children are watching the grownups and learning (or not) about positive coping, wellness, caring (for themselves and others), resilience, and more as they communicate with their families and interact with media. And, many children are also afraid and need comforting and reassurance that they will be kept safe.

The global pandemic and unceasing racial struggles in the US are taking a massively devastating toll, economically, educationally, socially, and more on all in the world. In terms of this volume, the timing of these events again brings into stark relief a foundational and chronic problem that has long plagued the communication field: the neglect of children and their vital role in creating better futures. Twenty-one years ago, Socha and Diggs (1999) wrote about the role of communication in managing "race" at home where children play a key role in the development of better, brighter, and inclusive futures. A decade ago, Socha and Yingling (2010) wrote about children's communication development at home. And today, this volume argues, once again, that the field of communication can no longer afford to focus exclusively on studying the communication of what has been mostly white, young adults, along with preparing and delivering collegiate courses of study to what has been mostly white college students. Instead the field of communication must adopt a fully inclusive lifespan approach that places all the world's children at the beginning of communication research and education, as well as connects communication in each lifespan stage to the next. We cannot predict the future, but we can work in the present to increase the chances that tomorrow the world will be better for future generations by educating and communicating with our littlest communicators, today. It is in this spirit and hope that we offer this volume.

References

Socha, T. J., & Diggs, R. H. (Eds.). (1999). *Communication, race and family: Exploring communication in Black, White and Biracial families.* Mahwah, NJ: Erlbaum.

Socha, T. J., & Yingling, J. A. (2010). *Families communicating with children: Building positive developmental foundations.* Cambridge, UK: Polity.

Section One: Foundations

1. Comprehensive Communication Development during Childhood

First Steps in Positive Lifespan Communication

THOMAS J. SOCHA
Old Dominion University

NARISSRA M PUNYANUNT-CARTER
Texas Tech University

Children around the world are quarantined in their homes due to the coronavirus pandemic. As of July 8, 2020, Covid-19 infected 11,662,574 people and ended the lives of 539,057 others (Johns Hopkins Coronavirus Research Center, 2020). Proportionately, the elderly and African Americans are bearing the brunt of the Covid-19 virus, but children have not been immune including enduring the stressors of quarantine and more (Centers for Disease Control and Prevention, 2020). As the world has turned to connecting online and socially-distancing, we must also look to the horizon to a future time when our everyday communication lives will resurge, albeit in a new key. We must use this time productively to pause and take stock of our core values and beliefs, especially those related to the world's children and their futures. What are our hopes and beliefs for the world's children?

First, we believe that all the world's children should live long lives. According to the World Health Organization (WHO) (2018a), the world's average life expectancy at the time of birth is age-72. Life expectancy in the US is age-78 and by comparison in South Africa it is age-63 and in Chad it is age-54 (WHO, 2018a). Living a long life is dependent on myriad factors: communicative, cultural, economic, educational, environmental, familial, genetic, geographic, medical, military, political, relational, social, and more. Although desired, for most of us, making it to a ripe old age is not easy and trouble can start early. According to the US Central Intelligence Agency (2018), infant mortality in the US is 5.8 deaths per 1000 live births, in South Africa, it is 31 deaths per 1000, and in Chad, it is 81 deaths per 1000 (Central Intelligence Agency, 2018). And, many medical factors can affect infant mortality including: "infections (36%, which includes sepsis/ pneumonia, tetanus, and diarrhea), pre-term birth (28%), and birth asphyxia (23%)" (WHO, 2018b), as well as the quality of medical care. Mothers' education and medical support are also among the most critical factors affecting the neonatal quality of medical care.

According to WHO figures from August 2011, newborn deaths, that is deaths in the first four weeks of life (neonatal period), account for 41% of all child deaths before the age of five. That share grew from 37% over the last decade and is likely to increase. The first week of life is the riskiest for newborns, but many countries are just starting postnatal care programs to reach mothers and babies at this critical time (WHO, 2018b).

Second, we believe that all the world's children should live healthy lives. Unfortunately, here too children's health and wellness around the world varies widely and like adults, children face many health challenges. According to the World Health Organization (WHO) (2018c):

> In 2016, an estimated 41 million deaths occurred due to noncommunicable diseases (NCDs), accounting for 71% of the overall total of 57 million deaths. The majority of such deaths were caused by four main NCDs: cardiovascular disease (17.9 million deaths; accounting for 44% of all NCD deaths); cancer (9.0 million deaths; 22%); chronic respiratory disease (3.8 million deaths; 9%); and diabetes (1.6 million deaths; 4%)." NCD's are linked in part to "… tobacco use, air pollution, unhealthy diet, physical inactivity and harmful use of alcohol—as well as improved disease detection and treatment. (p. 7)

Of course, some health and wellness factors facing all of us are beyond our abilities to control such as inherited genetics, air quality, the availability and quality of water sources, pandemics, as well as access to safe and adequate food supplies and of course quality medical care. However, some health and wellness factors are controllable, manageable, and affected by education and individual choice, such as vaccinating children against communicable diseases, teaching children to exercise, avoid overeating, never smoke, never experiment with illegal drugs, avoid risky situations (e.g., dangerous stunts, underage drinking, unprotected sex), and so on. There are indeed many factors that affect children's health and wellness, but it is important to remember that many of these factors are under the control of the adults who care for them.

Finally, third, we believe that all the world's children should live happy lives. Like health and wellness, global happiness varies widely and does not come easy for most. According to the *World Happiness Report* (2018), a couple years back the happiest people in the world (ranked #1) live in Finland. By comparison, the US ranked #18, South Africa ranks at #105, and Chad at #131. The measurements used by Gallop to assess happiness are complex. They are linked to longevity and health and include GDP, life expectancy, social support, freedom to make life choices, generosity, perceptions of corruption, as well as daily perceptions of people's positive and negative affect. Although a combination of genetics (estimated to play a 50% role in personal happiness) and social/geographical circumstances (estimated to play a 10% role in happiness) contributes 60% to total happiness, individuals exert considerable direct control over as much as 40% of their personal happiness (Seligman, 2012). That is, what we do and what we say, especially to the world's children, can facilitate or inhibit individuals' happiness (Socha & Beck, 2015).

So, where are the world's people living the longest, the healthiest, and the happiest? Costa Rica, Loma Linda, California; Okinaw, and Sardinia are counted among the world's geographic areas where a relatively higher proportion of residents enjoy health and happiness beyond their 100th birthday. These areas are called "Blue Zones" (Buettner, 2008, 2010, 2015). And, what is making a difference in these zones that might account for long, healthy and happy living? Buettner (2008) identified nine qualities. Predictably, four blue-zone qualities involve diet and exercise (i.e., moderate physical activity, semi-vegetarian, eating moderately, and moderate alcohol intake). However, five blue-zone qualities are dependent upon positive communication: (1) having a sense of purpose, (2) effectively managing stress, (3) participating in spirituality/religion, (4) engaging in positive family living, and (5) engaging in positive social living. Although communication scholars have yet to undertake studies of everyday communication taking place in the Blue Zones, there is little doubt that people who are living long, healthy, and happy lives in the world's Blue Zones are using communication to help children and themselves satisfy their basic human needs of belonging, feeling loved, feeling safe and secure, self-actualizing, and more (see Socha & Beck, 2015, for an overview of positive communication and human values). And, consistent with findings in the Blue Zones, contemporary communication studies are also suggesting that communicating effectively, appropriately, and positively across the entire human lifespan can promote happiness (Socha & Pitts, 2012), facilitate health and wellness (Pitts & Socha, 2013), and may even add to longevity (e.g., Buettner, 2015; Nussbaum, 2015).

In addition to the blue-zone factors that depend on communication, communication qualities such as articulateness, eloquence, empathy, expressiveness, humor, persuasiveness, and synchrony also serve as important forms of social capital (Burleson, Delia, & Applegate, 1995) in commerce, education, entertainment, government, as well as at home (see Socha & Stoyneva, 2014, for a discussion of the upper bounds of positive communication). That is, in terms of communication, we value individuals who can dazzle us with their stories, make us laugh, share with us optimal choices that are in our best interest, and in general, communicate in ways that reassure us, and leave us happy.

Finally, as people face life's many, varied, challenging, and unavoidable problems, like Covid-19, their resilience depends in large measure on how well (or how poorly) they manage messages before, during, and after these episodes (see Beck & Socha, 2015; and see Elder, 1999, for a longitudinal study of children of the US's great depression). In sum, communicating effectively, appropriately, and positively from the start of life and throughout all of life's stages plays an important part in an individual, relational, organizational, and societal thriving, and, as suggested by evidence from Blue-Zone dwellers, may even help to extend human life.

Reaching the heights of communication development is a lifelong endeavor that encompasses continuously experiencing, learning, and refining communication in relationships, groups, organizations, cultures, publics, and media during each of life's stages. All human communication learning begins at birth. We first experience, acquire, and learn foundations of basic nonverbal communication and basic verbal communication from infancy through early childhood at home (Socha & Yingling, 2010). We first experience, acquire, and learn increasingly complex and varied forms of communication across contexts beyond the family (relational, group, organizational, cultural, digital) throughout childhood and adolescence. We then continue to experience these forms of communication, and some of us may refine and master some of them as well as experience, acquire, and learn new "grown-up" forms of communication. From middle childhood through middle adulthood we of course continue to experience some adult communication firsts and may even polish and master some of these early communication abilities as well as acquire and learn new ones. Finally, later in life, we experience and adapt (nor not) to the many communication challenges as senior citizens.

The developmental arc of some communication skills spans human lifetimes. For example, saying "no" is initially acquired in early childhood (around age-2 when children discover linguistic negation) and we continue to say "no" across the entire human lifespan. Saying "no" effectively and appropriately is an important lifespan communication skill because it can potentially play a lifesaving role as when children and adolescents face invitations to smoke, drink alcohol, take illegal drugs, abuse firearms, and/or engage in risky sexual behaviors (Hecht, Colby, & Miller-Day, 2010). Even at the very end of life, saying "no" can determine how one is treated during his/her final days.

Although individuals vary considerably in their levels of overall communication mastery, many of life's "adult" communication abilities are experienced, acquired, learned, and mastered (by some) by the close of adolescence (Socha & Yingling, 2010). That is, some individuals may continue to refine some of their communication abilities (e.g., take a public speaking course in college) and some individuals may even master some communication skills at very high levels of proficiency early on and maintain them. Indeed, many vital communication abilities, that is, those linked to longevity, wellness, and happiness, stretch across the entire human lifespan including creating moments of communication beauty (Baxter, Norwood, & Nebel, 2012), managing communication ethically (Socha & Eller, 2015), using communication in service of laughter (Socha & Kelly, 1994), managing communicative and cultural synchrony (Kim, 2012), and much more.

Communication researchers are only beginning to identify and understand which human communication skills might achieve blue-zone-like importance in supporting a lifetime of health, wellness, and happiness. However, a critical element in facilitating the development of effective, appropriate, and even eloquent communication across many contexts over the human lifespan is communication education (informal and formal). It is safe to say that without some form of communication education, individuals' communication skills across contexts could persist in a primitive state and may prove inadequate as they are plied across life's later stages (e.g., adults may exhibit child-like communication skills including displaying a childish sense of humor, throwing temper tantrums, etc.).

Because communication plays such a vital role in living long, healthy and happy lives, in human flourishing (Seligman, 2012), it is vitally important that all members of society learn to communicate effectively, appropriately, and even eloquently to meet the varied communication demands of all of life's stages. And because communication development commences in infancy and continues until the end of life, it is imperative that societies of the world provide high-quality, culturally appropriate, communication education systems (formal and informal) that can support achieving effective, appropriate, and eloquent lifelong communication at every stage of life.

The Consequences of Neglecting Children

To date, the communication discipline has primarily studied young adults (ages 18–34; see Miller-Day, Pezalla, & Chestnut, 2013) and developed formal communication education programs mostly for college students (and see Chapter 2, this volume). Thus, when viewed through a lifespan lens, in actuality, very little formal communication education is taking place in the U. S., other than in university classes offered by departments of communication. Of course, informal and indirect communication education is also taking place in grades K–12, as well as sporadic communication training of some adults in business and in some senior centers. Taking a closer look, even within universities, unless a student chooses to major or minor in Communication, his/her entire formal communication education might consist of a single college-level course in public speaking. In some states, this might also include a survey-of-communication course taken in high school or a perhaps a high school speech and debate class taken as an elective. Thus, today, in 2020, most US citizens under age 18, or over age 34, especially those who have not attended college and/or are not employed in communication-specific industries, are not receiving the benefits of formal, research-based, communication education programs delivered by communication-education professionals. Further, if formal communication education is to be comprehensive, to include the development of relational, group, organizational, cultural, and public communication competencies and, most importantly, digital media literacies, the current state of formal communication education in the US, especially given the rise of digital media, is alarmingly lacking.

Many reasons could be advanced to explain today's lack of formal communication education at any lifespan stage. Some may argue "most people have been doing OK without formal communication education and some are even doing well. K–12 curricula are jammed packed. So, even if we could add communication education, do we really need it?" Others may contend, "The folks in the Blue Zones have done pretty well without formal communication education. Would it make a difference for them?" The editors and authors of this volume collectively argue that although our system of informal communication education may have (arguably) provided many members of society with some sort of minimal levels of communication competencies and emerging digital literacy skills, as we go forward into increasingly complex, communication-dependent, and information-oriented futures, our past informal, ad hoc, delivery system of communication education is inadequate to equip all societal members with effective and appropriate, let alone eloquent, relational and digital competencies to levels that are necessary to manage society's ever-expanding communicative demands. And, although octogenarians who currently dwell in the Blue Zones may have been living well without the benefit of formal communication educations, going forward, the communication demands facing young Blue-Zone dwellers are far more complex, weightier, and certainly set a much higher bar for communication competencies and media literacies than the past.

In sum, we pose a large question that is motivating this volume. Are we as a society genuinely pleased with the current state of communication competencies and digital media literacies of our citizens of all ages? Or, do we envision room to improve the quality of relational communication, group communication, organizational communication, cultural communication, public communication as well as media production and consumption for people of all ages? Collectively, the editors and authors of this volume seek to sound a clear and clarion call that the quality of society's relational communication and media literacy—from first words to final conversations—requires high-quality, formal, lifespan communication education.

Purpose of the Volume

This volume has two primary purposes. First, the volume seeks to raise readers' awareness of the need for formal, comprehensive, lifelong communication education starting in early childhood. And, second, it offers an overview of children's communication, the methods used to study children, as well as some of the kinds of communication learning taking place during the critically important developmental period of childhood and early adolescence. The book not only shines a spotlight on some of the intricacies of children's communication and its development but also advocates for the critical need to develop formal, comprehensive, communication education systems starting with the world's preschoolers. Formal communication education in early childhood, backed up by informal communication education at home, is essential if the world is to build a solid foundation upon which the future development of relational communication competencies and digital media literacies can rest. Formal pre-K communication education should then be followed by formal communication education from Kindergarten through college. Undoubtedly, we are living in an information and communication age that demands that all the world's citizens possess increasingly sophisticated communication educations to be able to meet increasingly many and varied communication-centered societal goals. This can only happen if the world and the field of communication pay greater attention to childhood as the foundation of lifelong formal communication education.

Historically, from birth, humans have been learning how to communicate primarily by what can best be described as an informal, ad hoc, system of socialization. Young communicators learn primarily through mere exposure to the everyday communication episodes modeled by whomever they are exposed to including parents, siblings, significant adults, friends, media personalities, and cartoon figures (Bandura, 1986). These people and media figures, as sources of children's informal communication learning, vary in their levels of communication competency. Some individuals may skillfully model effective, appropriate, and eloquent communication. However, others may or may not even be cognizant of the myriad "communication lessons" they are conveying to their young audiences about what to say, to whom, when, and how, let alone how to do so effectively, appropriately, and positively (e.g., see Socha & Pitts, 2013; Socha & Yingling, 2010). And, at a more basic level, they may or may not even know whether or not their own messages to children (and others) are effective and appropriate. That is, they may not understand how to effectively and appropriately model an array of human communication skills for children of varying age-levels, as well as how to advance children's nonverbal, verbal, and media-related communicative abilities through skillful communication modeling. And, as for the myriad media persona to which children are exposed, their messages, driven largely by commercial interests, are more concerned with teaching children to be effective consumers, rather than modeling effective, appropriate, and eloquent communication.

Thus, unless adult communicators have formally studied communication (in college, or least high school), and/or the creators of commercial mass media programs have relied on communication education experts, they must draw upon on culturally-inherited, informally-taught folk understandings to inform and guide their communication with children. For example, from 1968 until 2001, the children's television show, *Mister Rogers' Neighborhood*, delivered 895 episodes presenting an exhaustive array of occupations and ways of earning a living (see *Mister Rogers' Neighborhood*, 2018; and see Rogers, 2001). Fred Rogers was graduate-educated in child development and carefully crafted every episode to teach children about myriad subjects including difficult ones like divorce, death, and inter-racial understandings. To the extent that the children who watched Mister Rogers' Neighborhood, and shows like it, can later recall the content of these shows, provides evidence that early childhood communication certainly can shape future communication behaviors far beyond an initial viewing. The stark reality is that the totality of many adults' communication educations—the communication legacies they will pass along to the next generation—rests upon their recollections of informal, historically-situated communication (from relational or electronic sources) that may, or may not, have been effectively and appropriately communicated to them in the first place, let alone mastered. Yet, these sources of informal communication learning continue to function as the world's primary and often sole source of children's communication education.

To be considered "educated," citizens typically require an understanding of arts, history, literature, math, science, (e.g., STEM, STREAM, etc.) and more. However, today it is abundantly clear that our everyday lives are also affected to a large extent by the quality of communication experienced at home, school, work, in social and mass media, and more. Thus, we argue that society needs to improve the quality and delivery of communication education (formal and informal) so that the world might benefit from the latest theories, research, and efficacy-tested communication practices, coupled with critical abilities necessary to communicate effectively, appropriately, and eloquently.

Some may also ask, are not children and young adults already being exposed informally to effective communication learning in schools modeled by their teachers and other similar adults as they communicate with them? Is that not enough? Why should it be formalized? It is true that many classroom teachers can and do model effective and appropriate communication and sometimes eloquence as they teach. However, this kind of communication learning is indirect, informal, and viewed as secondary to the lessons of math, science and so on. And, to the extent that not all teachers are award-winning communicators, the current arrangement perpetuates an ad hoc system where some children may get lucky and learn from teachers who communicate effectively while others will not. More importantly, when communication is not taught as a graded subject, classroom communication learning resides in the shadows with the added implicit message that communication is not all that important. For example, in elementary schools, interpersonal communication skills are taught, indirectly, as a component of a more general language-arts curriculum. And, digital literacy may be taught as a sub-unit in a computer education class. However, in both contexts, interpersonal skills and digital media literary are not assessed and hence do not count.

If children are not formally taught which particular communication practice to emulate, how will they ever hope to discern what effective communication even looks like? Some high-school students, in some states, for instance, may take a public speaking course as a graduation requirement or as an elective. While including such a class certainly moves formal communication education in a productive direction, a course about public speaking may not contain lessons about relational communication. And, similarly, although many college students may take a required course in public speaking (to fulfill an oral communication general-education requirement) that course too does not provide instruction in relational communication and group communication. Although public speaking is vitally important for professional success, practically-speaking, we spend more of our lives communicating in relationships and groups. And, how long with the learning in a single course last?

Ultimately, Emanuel (2011) concluded the current system of communication education (even at the college level) is inadequate:

> (1) Today's college students are not getting adequate oral communication education. (2) Oral communication education is being relegated to a "module" in another discipline-specific course. (3) When an oral communication course is included in the general education curriculum, that course tends to be narrow rather than broad in scope. (4) An increasing number of college faculty who teach oral communication courses do not have a graduate degree in the discipline. These concerns may be indicative of similar issues affecting oral communication education throughout the United States and beyond. (p. 1)

Simply stated, US students in grades Pre-K to 12 are not receiving an adequate formal education in relational and digital communication. Although we are now well into the 21st century, an age of communication and information, society continues to rely on an outdated system of informal, accidental, and incidental communication learning to prepare its members for the many and varied communication challenges they face at each of life's stages.

It is our contention that today, in 2020, most Americans (from kids to senior citizens), lacking an adequate formal education in relational communication and digital media literacy are, at worst, unprepared, and at best under-prepared to face many of life's communication situations and difficulties as they navigate increasingly complex educational, familial, occupational, and relational demands. Indeed, the cry of "failure to communicate" continues to be a common scapegoat upon which society heaps lots of blame for many of its ills. And an often-heard refrain is "If we could only communicate better, we would not have all these problems!" Furthermore, formal communication education is a key tool of resilience that empowers members of society to optimally manage what are inevitable problems (Beck & Socha, 2015). Thus, if educating societal members to communicate effectively and appropriately in relationships as well as digitally across the lifespan is to become a priority, there are several matters to consider.

Children Are the Beginning of Communication

First, because leaning the fundamentals of communication education begin at birth, the communication field must pay greater attention to early lifespan communication education during infancy and childhood. Currently, less than 4% of all the research articles published in the field of communication have studied children's communication (Miller-Day, Pezalla, & Chestnut, 2013). And even in outlets where readers might reasonably expect to find communication studies of children, like the *Journal of Family Communication*, studies of children make up less than 6% of the articles appearing in that journal (Miller-Day et al., 2013). Additionally, the most recent relational communication book focusing on children (other than the current volume) was published a decade ago (Socha & Yingling, 2010). And, a most-recent volume on children and media appeared in 2014 (Strasburger, Wilson, & Jordan, 2014) (see Chapter 2, this volume).

Second, the current adult-centric curricula of communication departments in American universities must be reimagined to include communicators from all stages of life. That is, Departments of Communication around the globe should adopt an age-inclusive lifespan communication approach as championed for decades by Penn State University Communication and Father of Lifespan Communication, Professor Jon Nussbaum (see Nussbaum, 2015). College courses in communication today are aimed almost exclusively at emerging adults, and communication departments in US universities offer few (if any) courses that specifically focus on children or adults in later life. Our informal online search found only nine US communication departments currently offer at least one college-level course on children's communication (whether relational, media, or a combination): Athabasca University, Bellarmine University, Humboldt State University, Old Dominion University, San Francisco State University, Stanford, University of California at San Diego, the University of Montana at Missoula; and the University of New Hampshire. Old Dominion University's Department of Communication & Theatre Arts does offer an undergraduate, age-inclusive, concentration in "lifespan communication" as well as a fully age-inclusive and communication medium-inclusive MA degree in Lifespan & Digital Communication.

Third, professional communication associations must assume active leadership roles and champion lifespan communication education. The communication of children and adolescents, as well as seniors, should become routine foci of papers presented at professional conferences across all divisions. Over twenty years ago, a group of members of the *National Communication Association* (NCA) developed a plan and a curriculum outline for K–12 communication education (that included standards and goals, see NCA, 1998). However, unfortunately, to date, that work went largely unnoticed by the mainstream communication field. And, at one-point NCA's website (under the tab K–12 resources) replaced this prior work with two items: a guide for middle and high school teachers on the first amendment and social media (Social Media, the Classroom and First Amendment, 2011) and the following endorsement:

> The College Board has published content standards for middle school and high school English Language Arts and Mathematics and Statistics. The College Board Standards for College Success define a developmental progression of rigorous learning objectives for six courses in middle school and high school that will lead all students to be prepared for AP or college-level work. NCA members Sherry Morreale, John Heineman, and Mary Bozik served on the writing team for the Communication Standards, which were endorsed by the Executive Committee as a replacement for NCA's K–12 Standards. (*National Communication Association*, 2016)

Fourth, because learning about relational communication undoubtedly begins at birth, communication researchers and educators must pay greater attention to early lifespan communication including the informal relational communication learning taking place during early childhood as well as formal communication learning in the nation's preschools. The context of "home" functions as our first informal communication "classroom" and our first communication "teachers" include parents, household members, welcomed and unwelcomed others, as well as media figures (Socha & Yingling, 2010; Strasburger, Wilson, & Jordan, 2014). Extending this metaphor, unlike formal communication education where an efficacy-tested communication curriculum is delivered by certified communication teachers, our first communication "curriculum"—the foundation for all future communication learning and development—is informal, anecdotal, ad hoc, and delivered by household members whose formal communication educations can vary from no formal communication education, to perhaps taking a public speaking class in high school, to taking one or more communication classes in college, to individuals holding undergraduate and graduate degrees in communication. Thus, the inherited communication skills of our early communication "teachers" comprise the totality of a communication-education legacy, or the available content of communication learning (informal and formal) that can be passed along from one generation of communication "teachers" (parents, caregivers) to the next generation of communication learners (who then become communication teachers). And, currently, an efficacy-tested curriculum of formal communication instruction for children ages 2–5 attending preschool in the US has yet to emerge.

Skeptics may ask, "Is informal communication learning taken place in early childhood at home and on the playground really all that bad?" Although hard data about the current state of informal communication education taking place in US households is not available, anecdotal data point towards conclusions that mirror the anemic state of formal K–12 communication education. That is, many adults in US households and preschools are not likely to be fully equipped with formal educations in communication that are sufficient to effectively instruct and coach children in both relational and digital-media communication competencies necessary to succeed in our communication-saturated worlds. A poll from ABC News offers an illustrative example.

> Sixty-five percent of Americans [adults] approve of spanking children, a rate that has been steady since 1990. But just 26 percent say grade-school teachers should be allowed to spank kids at school; 72 percent say it shouldn't be permitted, including eight in 10 parents of grade-schoolers (ABC News, 2015, November).

These conflicting opinions regarding corporal punishment fly in the face of extensive, research-based, and compelling evidence that argues against the use of corporal punishment entirely (see Straus, Douglas, & Medeiros, 2014; Wilson & North, 2012). According to the late Professor Murray Straus (2015), "more than 20 nations now prohibit spanking by parents. There is an emerging consensus that this is a fundamental human right for children. The United Nations is asking all nations to prohibit spanking." Professor Straus is joined by the United Nations Office of the High Commissioner for Human Rights (2013), the American Psychological Association (2012) and the American Academy of Pediatrics (2015a) who all argue that parents and caregivers should use verbal communication to direct children's behaviors (and for that matter the behaviors of all others) and not beat, hit, paddle, punch, or slap. Yet, some Americans continue to strike their children and believe that doing so is somehow good for their children.

Another example of the need for formal lifespan communication education can be found on the digital side of the communication field. Despite warnings from the American Academy of Pediatrics (AAP) (2015b) about exposing children under age-2 to screened-media and limiting exposure to digital media entertainment to no more than 30-minutes to 1-hour per day (e.g., by creating screen-free zones at home), examples of young children playing endlessly with iPads, smartphones, as well as interactive games on parents' laptops, and watching hours of television are commonplace. Some parents who purchase iPads for their 2-year-olds to play with are doing so on the assumption that they are doing a "good" thing. "Look. My two-year-old can operate an iPad better than me!" However, unless their pre-K curriculum (or home schooling) includes instruction in digital media literacy, children's digital media literacy instruction will continue to be learned by happenstance. That is, the development of contemporary digital media competencies that include being able to create, interpret, and manage messages (e.g., composing, uploading, interpreting) using various social media platforms (e.g., Twitter, Facebook, Instagram, Vine, etc.) are learned by a largely informal, ad hoc, and often self-taught system with the occasional assistance of knowledgeable household members (often older siblings), aided by You-Tube videos, and/or an occasional trip to an Apple store. During the current pandemic, and out of necessity, children in grades K–12 are being shifted to online learning where the short- and long-term effects of doing so are largely unstudied. Of course, moving to online assumes that a household owns or has access to the internet and adequate digital communication devices and technologies. Although such communication technologies are seemingly everywhere, globally, the digital divide persists (Livingstone & Helsper, 2007).

Thus, with the possible exceptions of children who attend a pre-school that may offer a some sort of formal pre-K curriculum (which may or may not specifically teach communication skills development) and/or children living in a home with communication-educated members, the curriculum and delivery system of early childhood communication education remains informal, ad hoc, and likely replicative of communication values of a households' members (often unrecognized and poorly understood). Further, because informal communication learning taking place today is based largely on what was learned decades earlier it is also likely to be outdated as well as driven by a poplar media culture that may not support prosocial communication values (e.g., see Socha & Stamp, 2009).

Besides learning relational communication competencies and digital communication literacies, children are also learning communication values, that is, preferences for which forms of communication are desirable and which are not. Although the content of today's mass media may run counter to this conjecture, experience suggests that, for example, polite communication continues to be valued by many members of society, and that teaching children politeness is a good thing to do. That is, if politeness is valued in a household, its members' message choices are likely to reflect politeness as they go about making simple requests, depicting others, and so on. However, given the coarseness of social media and mass media today, the extent to which politeness is valued and practiced in US households seems in doubt. For example, a CNN special report about social media use among a group of 13-year-olds (#*Being Thirteen: Inside the Secret World of Teens*, 2015) suggested that lessons about politeness may be lost on some teens. Examples of these teens' language choices, viewed in the episode, in their social media exchanges with their "friends" (real and virtual) were decidedly anti-social: "I'm going to whip the s**t out of you," "Most of these bitches at Rodney Thompson middle bru, goddamn, u dirty bitch, u dirty bitch, u dirty bitch," and "lemme hit" (referring to marijuana). Further, viewers of this CNN special learned about "TBR" (i.e., "to be rude"), where teens purposively post vulgar, shocking, and highly negative depictions of others (including their "friends") via social media for "fun." Although the teens professed to not use such messages at home or with adults, no evidence was presented to the contrary. Viewers of this broadcast are left with lingering doubts about the extent and depth to which these teens value politeness and prosocial communicative forms. Further, adults who use "polite" forms of discourse have also come under fire by those claiming that "polite" discourse somehow obscures "meaningful" communicative exchanges (a process labeled "political correctness"). Such claims are not supported by research and also illustrate a lack of understanding about the simultaneous relational communicative discourse occurring alongside the instrumental (Burgoon & Hale, 1984). Further, those advocating a disdain for, and avoidance of, speech labeled politically correct often contemporaneously value aggressive forms of communication (dark-side) over prosocial (positive). Of course, if a given communicative form is valued and modeled by adults at home, it follows that we will likely see similar patterns of use in children's and adolescents' discourse. Sadly, in the future, especially due to the high rates at which children and adults are participating in unrestricted social media, whether society will be collectively-embarrassed or jointly-proud when hearing F-bombs coming from 5-year-olds remains an open question.

On the positive side, Rasmussen et al. (2016) found that prosocial parent-child communication helps foster prosocial behaviors. If children are exposed to positive prosocial behaviors, they are more likely to emulate those behaviors, especially if the parent reinforces those behaviors. Further, his findings also suggest that although learning about prosocial skills benefits all children, there might be special added value for children from low-income families in learning and using prosocial discourse forms as they seek empowerment by increasing their social capital. Thus, how parents interact with their kids can significantly influence their children's future lives (e.g., Socha & Yingling, 2010).

Given the complexities of contemporary relational and digital communication, and the need for competent communicators in all sectors of society, this volume argues that the US and the Communication discipline can no longer afford to leave lifespan communication education to chance, and with all due speed should develop formal lifespan communication education systems starting with early-childhood education, following into elementary, high school, and collegiate contexts, as well as developing continuing education for adults extending into later life. In this volume, we have gathered together a group of early lifespan communication scholars who stand ready to help by offering a preliminary foundation upon which to build lifespan communication-education systems.

The Need to Take Development Seriously

Learning to communicate effectively is of course highly complex and multifaceted but it must be first acknowledged that all communication competencies (relational and digital) start at some point and develop over time (like saying "no," discussed earlier). That is, all communication processes have a developmental arc which extends across life's developmental stages. Second, communication processes change as individuals change and mature across the human lifespan. Communication can get better (become more effective and appropriate) or can also worsen over time. It should not be assumed that communication will automatically get better simply due to its frequency of use. And, third, as we change, the world is changing along with us and our communication should follow suit. Communicating with infants (around the world) in 1958 is not the same context as communicating with infants in 2020. Before the field of communication can begin to create and offer a lifespan communication curriculum, it must take a critical first step by acknowledging that all forms of communication must be studied developmentally and globally. Like the teaching and scholarship of lifespan developmental psychology, we need the teaching and scholarship of global lifespan developmental communication.

To illustrate why it is important to study communication developmentally let's consider humorous communication. Typically, for most of the world's children humorous communication learning begins very early in childhood as rudimentary nonverbal play sequences (e.g., peek-a-boo), transitions into playful sound exchanges (e.g., exchanges of silly noises), and with the acquisition of language morphs into simple verbal messages (e.g., simple riddles, simple jokes), and later evolves into increasingly complex humorous messages and message sequences (e.g., humor that involves contextualized surprise such as playing with language, timing, sequencing, meaning, and more; see Socha, 2012). Although some aspects of the developmental arc of humor communication may be universally invariant (i.e., paralleling typical communication development such as learning nonverbal humor occurs before learning linguistic humor), not all the developmental arcs of humor communication skills follow the same pattern for all individuals in all cultures. That is, although humor communication skills may universally start for all of us in early childhood, for some of us they may peak during middle childhood and may (or may not) continue relatively unchanged across the lifespan (e.g., some adult men may stand accused of having an adolescents' sense of humor, and see Shafer, 2015). It is clear that among adults there are wide-ranging individual differences in humor communication competencies such that some adults can effectively communicate in humorous ways (they can tell a joke) while others cannot.

Other communication skills, such as formal argumentation, may begin with the onset of negation (saying "no") around age 2 (Socha & Yingling, 2010), become more complex during early and middle childhood, and may (or may not) increase in sophistication during emerging adulthood and later life. Still, other communication skills may follow an oscillating pattern of elaboration and diminution both across and within lifespan-developmental stages (e.g., humorous communication skills might blossom during early childhood, be dulled by increasing seriousness through middle childhood, adolescence and on into emerging adulthood, and be rediscovered during early adulthood perhaps at a comedy workshop).

Although communication scholars will undoubtedly tacitly agree that communication does develop over time, for the most part, unfortunately, they are likely to continue to study communication statically, where communication's past development will be ignored, and its future development taken for granted (Socha & Yingling, 2009 chapter 2). In short, unless development is fully included in communication thinking, communication scholars will continue to ignore the development of communication before age-18 and assume, erroneously, that all communication skills from age-18 onwards continue invariantly through our final conversations.

What might explain why the field of Communication has ignored (and continues to ignore) individuals from birth-to-age 18 and those beyond age 26? First, some communication scholars complain that they do not study children because of cumbersome Institutional Review Board (IRB) policies and procedures that apply when studying children. Although, in practice, seeing a children's communication study through an IRB review can pose challenges, on the positive side doing so compels researchers to fully consider participants' needs and to closely examine the fit of their methods and approach to their participants. Great care must be taken to do no harm, especially to children, and working with parents to secure their permission can be challenging (see Socha, Chapter 3, this volume). However, the benefits of doing so far outweigh the costs.

Second, others blame the lack of children's communication studies on the overuse of samples of convenience (i.e., white, college-age folks). Admittedly, it is more difficult and costlier to recruit beyond the classroom, but those researchers who can do so, should. And, finally, some communication scholars and educators say they do not study children because their undergraduate and graduate communication educations ignored childhood (and later life), and they profess to lack knowledge about communication's early developmental stages. Instead, they prefer to leave the study of children to other communication specialists. Unfortunately, the choice to leave the business of studying children's communication to specialized others has reached a crisis point. Today, there are so few "specialized" others in the field of communication who study children (see Socha, Chapter 2, this volume) that unless our call to adopt a lifespan approach and to bring the study of children to forefront of the communication field is successful, the field of communication will continue to take a back seat to the fields of developmental psychology and education when it comes to early lifespan communication, or worse, it will become completely irrelevant when it comes to having something to say about children, adolescence, and communicators in later life.

Indeed, children have been studied in the communication field (albeit mostly in media studies) but unfortunately this work has largely gone unnoticed in the broader communication field due in part to the communication field's adult-centric, white, masculine hegemony (see Socha, Chapter 2, this volume). And, as you will read in the next chapter what research has been undertaken about children has not been inclusive, that is, it has largely focused on white, heterosexual children. The current volume seeks to begin to offer at least a partial remedy to the exclusion of those under age-18 by presenting a primer of what is known about children's communication as well as a issue a call to adopt an age-inclusive, lifespan communication agenda featuring all the world's children.

It is our collective hope that readers of this volume will begin to view children as an integral part of everyone's communication past and everyone's communication futures and become more aware of issues pertaining to children as well as more informed about this area of communication study and education. We hope to inspire and motivate communication scholars young and old to expand their vision and understanding of communication by including children, to provide information that will be helpful and meaningful for communication scholars interested in the study of children, as well as to put children's formal communication education on the map within the general field of childhood education and child development. Communication begins with children.

Overview of the Chapters

Nest in section one, "Foundations," a chapter that highlights some of the harms communication's neglect has caused children and a critical-experiential review of children's communication research is offered (Socha, Chapter 2, this volume). This is followed by a chapter that gives an overview of research methods used to study children (Socha, Chapter 3, this volume). The second section of the book. "Relational Communication Development," examines children's communication in children's personal and social relationships. Gary Beck and Kristen Carr (Chapter 4) lead the section with a discussion of resilience and fostering children's in communication between children and parents. Malinda Colwell and Elizbeth Trejos-Castillo then explain socio-emotional development in Chapter 5. Closing the first section, Paula Tompkins (Chapter 6) presents the latest update about moral development and children.

The third section of the book covers children's digital communication development. Alexis Lauricella, Fashnia Alde, and Ellen Wartella (Chapter 7) present the latest findings about children and technology. Robin Duffee, Sydney Cox, and Narissra Punyanunt-Carter (Chapter 8) discuss parasocial relationships and children and Andrea McCourt and Jillian Yarbrough (Chapter 9) examine how media consumption affects body image and eating behaviors. Then in Chapter 10, Danyella Jones examines the contested boundaries of childhood by focusing on the portrayal of gay marriage in the children's educational television show, *Arthur*. Ronda Scantlin (Chapter 11) closes the section with an overview of media literacy.

The fourth and final section of the book looks at some of the developmental communication challenges children face. John Chetro-Szivoc, Marit Eikaas Haavimb, and Kimberly Pearce (Chapter 12) use Coordinated Management of Meaning theory (CMM) in an educational program to help kids make better social worlds. Jenna LAFreniere (Chapter 13) examines communication, children, and lingering issues of divorce. Jason Wrench and Wendy Bower (Chapter 14) discuss the social (pragmatic) impairment of communication development. And, finally, Michelle Miller-Day (Chapter 15) close the section with a discussion about children's wellness and prevention programs for children.

We then close the volume with a Coda where we pose an urgent call for a global, inclusive, and comprehensive approach to the study of communication the recognizes children are the beginning and the foundation.

Conclusion

Communication Begins with Children: A Lifespan Communication Sourcebook proposes a radical departure from the communication field's past by calling for acceptance of the fact that communication begins with children. The volume begins a necessary and important conversation about comprehensive communication development, beginning with children's relational communication and digital media (infancy through adolescence) with an emphasis on optimal communication development. This book features well-known veteran scholars who are either working on or have researched communication behaviors with children as well as newcomers who are studying the latest in children's comprehensive communication development. Indeed, the volume is foundational in Peter Lang's *Lifespan Communication: Children, Families, and Aging* book series, as it focuses our collective attention on the very beginnings and the very foundations upon which a lifetime of communication is built.

References

ABC News. (2015, November). *Poll: Most approve of spanking*. Retrieved on December 11, 2015, from http://abcnews.go.com/US/story?id=90406&page=1

American Academy of Pediatrics. (2015a). *Where we stand: Spanking*. Retrieved from https://www.healthychildren.org/English/family-life/family-dynamics/communi-cation-discipline/Pages/Where-We-Stand-Spanking.aspx

American Academy of Pediatrics. (2015b). Media and children. https://www.aap.org/en-us/advocacy-and-policy/AAP-health-initiatives/pages/media-and-children.aspx

American Psychological Association. (2012). *The case against spanking: Physical discipline is slowly declining as some studies reveal lasting harms for children*. Retrieved from http://www.apa.org/monitor/2012/04/spanking.asp

Bandura, A. (1986). *Social foundations of thought and action*. Englewood Cliffs, NJ: Prentice-Hall.

Baxter, L. A., Norwood, K. M., & Nebel, S. (2012). Aesthetic relating. In T. J. Socha & M. J. Pitts (Eds.), *The positive side of interpersonal communication* (pp. 19–38). New York: Peter Lang.

#*Being Thirteen: Inside the Secret World of Teens*. (2015). A CNN special report retrieved from http://go.cnn.com/?type=episode&id=2072696.

Buettner, D. (2008). *The blue zones: Lessons for living longer from the people who live the longest*. Washington, DC: National Geographic Society.

Buettner, D. (2010). *Thrive: Finding happiness in the blue zone way*. Washington, DC: National Geographic Society.

Buettner, D. (2015). *The blue zones solution: Eating and living like the world's healthiest people*. Washington, DC: National Geographic Society.

Burgoon, J. K., & Hale, J. L. (1984). The fundamental topoi of relational communication. *Communication Monographs, 51*, 193–214.

Burleson, B., Delia, J., & Applegate, J. (1995). The socialization of person-centered communication: Parents' contributions to their children's social-cognitive and communication skills. In A. Vangelisti & M. A. Fitzpatrick (Eds.), *Explaining family interactions* (Chapter 2), Thousand Oaks, CA: Sage.

Centers for Disease Control and Prevention. (2020). *Keep children healthy during the Covid-19 outbreak.* Retrieved from https://www.cdc.gov/coronavirus/2019-ncov/daily-life-coping/children.html

Central Intelligence Agency. (2018). *The world factbook.* Retrieved from https://www.cia.gov/library/publications/the-world-factbook/rankorder/2102rank.html

Elder, G. H., Jr. (1999). *Children of the great depression: Social changes in life experience.* Boulder, CO: Westview Press.

Emanuel, R. (2011). Critical concerns for oral communication education in Alabama and beyond. *Education Research International* [Article ID 948138], 1–12. Available at doi:10.1155/2011/948138.

Hecht, M. L., Colby, M., & Miller-Day, M. (2010). The Dissemination of keepin' it REAL Through D.A.R.E. America: A lesson in disseminating health messages. *Health Communication, 25*(6/7), 585–586. doi:10.1080/10410236.2010.496826.

Johns Hopkins Coronavirus Research Center. (2020). Retrieved from https://coronavirus.jhu.edu

Kim, Y. Y. (2012). Being in concert: An explication of synchrony in positive intercultural communication. In T. J. Socha & M. J. Pitts (Eds.), *The positive side of interpersonal communication* (pp. 39–56). New York: Peter Lang.

Livingstone, S., & Helsper, E. (2007). Gradations in digital inclusion: Children, young people, and the digital divide. *New Media & Society, 9*(4), 671–696.

Miller-Day, M., Pezalla, A., & Chestnut, R. (2013). Children are in families too!: The presence of children in communication research. *Journal of Family Communication, 13*(2), 150–165.

Mister Rogers' Neighborhood. (2018). Retrieved from IMDB, https://www.imdb.com/title/tt0062588/

National Communication Association. (1998). K–12 speaking, listening, and media literacy standards and competency statements. Retrieved on May 30, 2016, from http://www.natcom.org/uploadedFiles/About_NCA/Leadership_and_Governance/Public_Policy_Platform/K-12Standards.pdf.

Nussbaum, J. F. (Ed.). (2015). *The handbook of lifespan communication.* New York: Peter Lang.

Pitts, M. J., & Socha, T. J. (Eds.). *Positive communication in health and wellness.* New York: Peter Lang.

Rasmussen, E. E., Shafer, A., Colwell, M. J., White, S., Punyanunt-Carter, N., Densley, R. L., & Wright, H. (2016). The relation between active mediation, exposure to *Daniel Tiger's Neighborhood*, and US preschoolers' social and emotional development. *Journal of Children and Media, 10*, 1–19.

Rogers, F. (2001). A point of view: Family communication, television, and Mister Rogers' Neighborhood. *Journal of Family Communication, 1,* 71–73.

Seligman, M. E. P. (2012). *Flourish: A visionary new understanding of happiness and well-being.* New York: Atria Books.

Shafer, J. (2015, August 13). Donald Trump talks like a third grader. *Politico.* Retrieved on June 2, 2016, from http://www.politico.com/magazine/story/2015/08/donald-trump-talks-like-a-third-grader-121340

Socha, T. J. (2012). Children's humor: Foundations of laughter across the lifespan. In R. DiCioccio (Ed.), *Humor: Theory, impact, and outcomes* (Chapter 9). Dubuque, IA: Kendal Hunt.

Socha, T. J., & Beck, G. A. (2015). Positive communication and human needs: A review and proposed organizing conceptual framework. *Review of Communication, 15,* 173–199.

Socha, T. J., & Eller, A. (2015). Parent/caregiver-child communication and moral development: Toward a conceptual foundation of an ecological model of lifespan communication and good relationships. In V. Waldron & D. Kelley (Eds.). *Moral talk across the lifespan: Creating good relationships* (pp. 15–34). New York: Peter Lang.

Socha, T. J., & Kelly, B. (1994). Children making "fun": Humorous communication, impression management, and moral development. *Child Study Journal, 24,* 237–252.

Socha, T. J., & Pitts, M. J. (Eds.). (2012). The positive side of interpersonal communication. New York: Peter Lang.

Socha, T. J., & Pitts, M. J. (2013). Apples and positive messages: Towards healthy communication habits and wellness. In M. J. Pitts & T. J. Socha (Eds.), *Positive communication in health and wellness* (pp. 301–306). New York: Peter Lang.

Socha, T. J., & Stoyneva, I. (2014). Positive communication: Towards a new normal. In L. Turner & R. West (Eds.), *The Sage handbook of family communication* (Chapter 25). Thousand Oaks, CA: Sage.

Socha, T. J., & Yingling, J. A. (2010). *Families communicating with children.* Cambridge, UK: Polity.

Strasburger, V. C., Wilson, B. J., & Jordon, A. B. (2014). *Children, adolescents, and the media* (3rd ed.). Thousand Oaks, CA: Sage.

Straus, M. (2015). *The case against spanking: New book by renowned researcher offers definitive study.* Retrieved from http://www.unh.edu/unhtoday/Murray-Straus

Straus, M., Douglas, E. M., Medeiros, R. A. (2014). *The primordial violence: Spanking children, psychological development, violence, and crime.* New York: Routledge.

United Nations Office of the High Commissioner for Human Rights. (2013, January). Ending corporal punishment of children. Retrieved from http://www.ohchr.org/EN/NewsEvents/Pages/CorporalPunishment.aspx

Wilson, S. R., & North, P. E. (2012). Nurturing children as assets: A positive approach to preventing child maltreatment and promoting healthy youth development. In T. Socha & M. Pitts (Eds.), *The positive side of interpersonal communication* (pp. 277–296). New York, NY: Peter Lang.

World Health Organization (2018a). *Life expectancy.* http://www.who.int/gho/mortality_burden_disease/life_tables/situation_trends/en/

World Health Organization. (2018b). *Newborn death and illness.* Retrieved from http://www.who.int/pmnch/media/press_materials/fs/fs_newborndealth_illness/en/

World Health Organization. (2018c). *World health statistics-2018: Monitoring health for sustainable development goals.* Retrieved from http://apps.who.int/iris/bitstream/handle/10665/272596/9789241565585-eng.pdf?ua=

2. End the Neglect of Children and Transform the Field of Communication

A Critical-Experiential Review and Research Agenda

Thomas J. Socha
Old Dominion University

This chapter, like this lifespan communication sourcebook, is offered as a touchstone for all who wish to transform the field of communication by repositioning children to its beginnings and its foundation. The chapter opens by framing the historic invisibility of children in the field of communication as a problem of symbolic "child neglect" attributed at least in part to white, male privilege. Next, the chapter offers a critical-experiential review of the past 40+ years of communication literature about children that covers the highlights and points out the costs of child neglect not only for this literature but for the entire communication field. Finally, building on the review, I argue that going forward the field of communication should adopt a comprehensive, functional, lifespan (CFL) meta-theoretical approach to communication theorizing, research, and education that has the potential to give the field of communication a second chance at becoming a more comprehensive, inclusive, and developmental field of study that champions all communicators.

Communication's Neglect of Children

Throughout my 36-year career as a professor of communication, I have argued for the inclusion of children in communication theorizing, research, and education, especially in family communication (e.g., see Socha & Stamp, 1995; Socha & Yingling, 2010). Unfortunately, while it is universally acknowledged that children do in fact communicate, and with the exceptions of those whose work is reviewed in this chapter and cited in this volume, as well as the work of members of the Children, Adolescents and Media Division of the International Communication Asociation, children remain largely invisible in the larger field of communication. Why is this? My charitable response is that the literature of children's communication has failed to capture the imagination of all communication scholars. Over the years, I have heard communication colleagues acknowledge that although studies of children are "interesting," they fail to see how this work is relevant to their own. Other colleagues find children's communication research to be too specialized as well as dull and boring. And, still, other colleagues find the extra steps needed to get a children's communication study through an IRB review to be burdensome. And, even those who profess to work under the banner of lifespan communication have shared with me that they focus mostly on later-life communication in part because it is easier to recruit and study senior adult participants.

So, why is it that children have yet to capture the communication-field-at-large's imagination? My honest, albeit disquieting response is that, again, with the exception of members of the Children, Adolescents and Media division of the International Communication Association, as a result of historic white, male privilege in the field of communication (e.g., see Chakravartty, Kuo, Grubbs, & McIlwain, 2018), along with its neglect of women and people of color, the broad field of communication is guilty of child neglect.

I can appreciate that sometimes reading publications about syntax acquisition of young children can require specialized knowledge and may be dull. And, yes, there are more IRB obstacles to studying children than studying senior citizens. However, the communication field's systematic and ongoing neglect of children is indicative of a deeper and far more serious problem. Failing to consider children and communication development in its theory-building, research, and pedagogy, failing to prioritize the study of children's communication, failing to fully share its existing understandings about children's communication (however limited) for the benefit of the world's children, and failing to fully use the power of the communication field to prevent the harming of the world's children (although for important exceptions see Wilson, Shi, Tirmenstein, Norris, & Combs, 2006; Wilson & Whipple, 1995), the field of communication is responsible, at least symbolically, for child neglect. Although it certainly cannot be claimed, nor is there any supporting evidence that the field of communication has been abusing children, there is abundant evidence that it certainly has been neglecting them. Of course, outside of academia real "child neglect" is a crime. Here is the technical framing of the concept of child abuse and child neglect (i.e., failure to act):

> The Federal Child Abuse Prevention and Treatment Act (CAPTA), as amended and reauthorized by the CAPTA Reauthorization Act of 2010, defines child abuse and neglect as, at a minimum, "any recent act or *failure to act* on the part of a parent or caretaker which results in death, serious physical or emotional harm, sexual abuse or exploitation (including sexual abuse as determined under section 111), or an act or *failure to act* which presents an imminent risk of serious harm" (42 U.S.C. 5101 note, § 3). (Child Welfare, 2019, p. 2, italics added)

Certainly, some readers will push back. "You cannot be serious! How can the field of communication be held responsible for damaging children because it failed to fully include them in its theory-building, research, and education? Is the field of communication really responsible for the world's children?" My response: Communication is a fundamental part of the human condition and the field of communication is morally and ethically obligated to study and educate *all communicators.* However, historically, the field of communication has been selectively choosing to study and educate mostly college-aged adults in universities. Some might say, "OK, so what if the communication field has not been studying or educating children about communication? What real harms, if any, have resulted from not doing so?" My response: There is no way to fully ascertain the extent of harm the field of communication has caused children due to its neglect. However, in order to bring the problem of communication's neglect of children into relief, let's consider how many children are being abused and the potential role of communication in their abuse as well as neglect. According to DoSomething.org (2019), "Approximately 5 children die every day because of child abuse … [and] 2.9 million cases of child abuse are reported every year in the United States." Further, child neglect and child abuse take a toll on children's lifespans. "Children who experience child abuse and neglect are 59% more likely to be arrested as a juvenile, 28% more likely to be arrested as an adult, and 30% more likely to commit violent crime" (Dosomething.org, 2019). Thus, because communication is integral in all humans' development (e.g., Socha & Yingling, 2010; Socha & Beck, 2015), it is not a stretch to conclude that the world's children would be better off today had the communication field, from its very beginning, joined numerous other academic fields and helped to care for, protect, educate, and empower children through its research and communication education.

And, why blame white, male privilege for communication's neglect of children? Although I am a white, cishet male, white males have been at the editorial helm of the field's books and journal publications throughout most of the communication field's intellectual history. They have been deciding and limiting what the field should read. And, how do I know that such limiting has been happening with respect to children? Beside studies that empirically demonstrate that the literature about children comprises a very small part of the total communication literature (Miller-Day, Pezalla, & Chestnut, 2013), I know this because I have experienced it professionally.

Years ago, I sought to publish a study about children's humorous communication development (in grades K–8) only to have it systematically rejected by most of the communication field's journals. Like all scholars, I am used to rejection. I appreciate and am happy to work with reviewers' feedback to improve a work's quality. And, I am also able to admit when a study is a bust and should not see the light of day. However, what was telling with this particular manuscript was that all of the white, cishet, editors gave the exact same reason for rejecting the manuscript (sometimes without sending it out for review). They wrote that the study was "interesting," well-executed, and when there were reviews, they were mostly positive. However, all the editors, uniformly, concluded that the manuscript would not be a good "fit" to publish in their respective communication journal. Rather, the manuscript would be a better "fit" to publish elsewhere, specifically in a child development journal, and they urged me to send it there. One editor even wrote that the readers of "their" journal would have zero interest in the topic of children's humorous communication and their moral development. Ultimately, the manuscript was later accepted, *without revision*, and published in a child development journal (Socha & Kelly, 1994). This is not an isolated case. Other communication scholars who study children have shared similar stories with me. My then-department chair also commented that he was glad I had finally found the "right audience" for the study. I assumed this to mean people who cared about children. Although my anecdotal evidence is nowhere near as systematic as "disciplining the feminine" (Blair, Brown, & Baxter, 1994), it does offer similar evidence of white, male, privilege supportive of the larger argument that "children" do not seem to have been in the province, purview, or interest of many white, males in positions of editorial power in communication. A sad conclusion that I am certain will resonate with women and people of color who have experienced far worse for far longer.

Over the years, I have remained and will continue to remain resolute in my beliefs. Communication is inherent in the universal human condition. Communication is a lifespan process (e.g., Nussbaum, 2015). Communication matters in all humans' survival and thriving (Socha & Beck, 2015). And, all communication occurring during childhood (or early lifespan) is consequential to the development of subsequent communication taking place during all of life's stages (e.g., Socha, & Yingling, 2010). For better or worse, we all bring our communication pasts forward into the future, and unless we are mindful, our pasts can ride roughshod on our present. Finally, as the title of this volume asserts, lifespan communication absolutely and unequivocally begins with children's first words and ends at the close of their final conversation.

Thus, it is high time to hit the reset button and give the communication field a second chance to reposition children at the beginning of communication theorizing and research, to make children a valued and integral part of the consciousness of mainstream communication theorizing, and not a topic that "other people" should care about. We are all responsible for children's communication because like us all they are communicators too and so goes our communication, so goes theirs.

In the next section, I offer a critical-experiential review of the children's communication literature. I add the term experiential because I have professionally and personally lived and contributed to these works. And, as I review these works, I will endeavor to point out the highlights as well as some of the costs of communication's neglect of children. The purpose of the review is also to acquaint, or reacquaint, readers with what I regard as the pioneering shadow-work taking place in the communication field concerning children. That is, as the hard and essential work of everyday childcare continues to take place in societal shadows, the work of children's communication scholars has also been taking place in the shadows of the field.

A Critical-Experiential Review of Children's Communication

Before I begin the review, I must again fully and openly acknowledge my privileged status as a white, cishet, male. I fully acknowledge that I did, and do, benefit from white, male privilege. Yet throughout my career, I have also honestly valued inclusion and have consciously tried to walk the talk as a cultural ally, to all, in all of my scholarly pursuits. I did not enjoy economic privilege during my childhood. I was raised in a lower-middle-class family in an inner-city neighborhood that was home to immigrant neighbors of Puerto Rican as well as Polish descent. I had to pay for my higher education entirely on my own (through the Ph.D.). During school, I worked year-round (manual labor, office work, and summer farm work) and am ever grateful to have been supported by essential scholarships and graduate assistantships that made my higher education possible. I understand and continue to admire those working their way through school as I did.

First, I will examine the communication field's books about children. Second, I provide an overview of some of the published review essays about some of the understudied topics concerning children. Finally, I close the section by identifying key topics that are missing from this work. Throughout this review, where relevant, I will also interject experiential insights from my professional experiences and my own communication education.

Children's Communication Books

Figure 2.1 displays a chronological list of 23 books about children's communication written and edited by scholars in the field of communication. Although I have attempted to be comprehensive, I chose these volumes primarily because they are among the key works in my education, research, and teaching concerning children. To my understanding, it is a fairly complete list of the field's major books about children, although, I may have missed a particular work.

Let me begin by pointing out a few general patterns that characterize these 23 works.

First, the academic field of communication began in 1914 with the founding of what today is the *National Communication Association* (NCA, 2019). Yet, the field of communication did not publish a book about children's communication until over six decades later when the first children's communication book appeared in 1976, Barbara S. Wood's (1976), *Children and Communication: Verbal and Nonverbal Language Development* (see reviews by Higginbotham, 1976; O'Keefe, 1976). I first read this book in the early 1980s when I was an MA student in Professor Wood's children's communication class at the University of Illinois at Chicago.

Second, the communication field's books about children can be organized into at least three conceptual groups (arranged chronologically): (a) children's communication development, (b) children's television (media), and (c) children's communication at home. And, third, these three conceptual groups have developed independently of each other. They rarely, if ever, cite or mention work from another conceptual group (i.e., volumes about children's TV do not cite volumes about children's relational communication and vice versa). There has also been little formal connection between these three groups inside the communication field and fields of outside the field of communication such as: developmental psychology, educational psychology, and juvenile justice studies, other than these communication volumes cite the work of these allied fields.

Figure 2.1 Books Published about Children in the Field of Communication (in Chronological Order)

1. Wood, B. S. (1976). Children and communication: Verbal and nonverbal language development. New York: Prentice-Hall.
2. Sypher, H. E., & Applegate, J. L. (Eds.). (1984). *Communication by children and adults: Social cognitive and strategic processes.* Beverly Hills, CA: Sage.
3. Bryant, J. (1983). *Children's understanding of television.* New York: Academic Press.
4. Naremore, R. & Hopper, R. (1990). Children learning language: Practical introduction to communication development (3rd ed.). New York: Harper & Row.
5. Stafford, L., & Bayer, C. L. (1993). *Interaction between parents and children.* Thousand Oaks, CA: Sage.
6. Zillman, D., Bryant, J., & Huston, A. C. (Eds.). (1994). *Media, children and the family.* Hillsdale, NJ: Lawrence Erlbaum.
7. Clifford, B., Gunter, B., & McAleer, J. (1995). *Television and children: Program evaluation, comprehension, and impact.* Hillsdale, NJ: Lawrence Erlbaum.
8. Socha, T. J., & Stamp, G. H. (Eds.) (1995). *Parents, children, and communication: Frontiers of theory and research.* Mahwah, NJ: Lawrence Erlbaum
9. Gunter, B., & McAleer, J. (1997). *Children and television.* London: Routledge.
10. Wartella, E. (Ed.) (1997). Children communicating: Media and development of thought, speech, understanding. Beverly Hills, CA: Sage
11. Haslett, B. B., & Samter, W. (1997). *Children communicating: The first five years.* Mahwah, NJ: Lawrence Erlbaum (Routledge).
12. Cantor, J. (1998). "Mommy, I'm scared." How TV and movies frighten children and what we can do to protect them. Boston: Houghton Mifflin.
13. Van Evra, J. (1998, 2004). *Television and child development* (2nd, 3rd eds.). Mahwah, NJ: Lawrence Erlbaum.
14. Jordan, A. B., & Hall Jamieson, K. (1998). Children and television. *The Annals of the American Academy of Political and Social Science, 557.* Thousand Oaks, CA: Sage.
15. Socha, T. J., & Diggs, R. H. (Eds.). (1999). Communication, race and family: Exploring communication in Black, White and Biracial families. Mahwah, NJ: Erlbaum.
16. Meyer, J. (2003). Kids talking. Learning relationships and culture with children. Lanham, MD: Rowman & Littlefield.
17. Cantor, J. (2004). *Teddy's TV troubles.* New York: Goblin Fern Publishing.
18. Bryant, A. (2006). (Eds.). *The children's television community.* New York: Routledge.

Continued

Figure 2.1 Continued

19. Calvert, S. L., & Wilson, B. J. (Eds.). (2008). *The handbook of children, media, and development.* New York: Wiley.
20. Socha, T. J., & Stamp, G. H. (Eds.). (2009). Parents & children communicating with society: Managing relationships outside of home. New York: Routledge.
21. Socha, T. J., & Yingling, J. A. (2010). *Families communicating with children: Building positive developmental foundations.* Cambridge, UK: Polity (John Wiley & Sons).
22. Pettigrew, J. (2014). *Stepfather-stepson communication: Social support in stepfamily worlds.* New York: Peter Lang. [Lifespan Communication Series: Book 3]
23. Strasburger, V. C., Wilson, B. J., & Jordon, A. B. (2014). *Children, adolescents, and the media* (3rd ed.). Thousand Oaks, CA: Sage

Fourth, most all of the communication scholars (that thankfully does not yet include me) who have authored and/or edited these volumes about children's communication have passed away, retired, or no longer write about children's communication. Today, in 2020, the field of communication is literally at a crisis point. If the study of children's communication is to advance, an immediate infusion of many more scholars is needed to join the authors of this volume and take up the study of early lifespan communication. Let's take a closer look at the topics covered in the volumes that span these three conceptual groups (discussed in the order in which these volumes appear historically).

Children's communication development. In the late 1970s and early 1980s, a few pioneering communication scholars, starting with Barbara S. Wood, recognized the need to study and write about children's communication. However, because white male privilege was assuredly at work during this time, and because the field of communication had no history of publishing books about children's communication, publishers and scholars alike were forced to accept that the primary market for children's communication development books was limited to women who were teaching in elementary schools. That is, children's communication development books sought to inform an almost exclusively female and largely white audience of early childhood and elementary school teachers about how to best communicate with the children in their classes as well as how to help the children in their charge to learn to communicate effectively. However, it is critically important to add that to date in the US. communication has yet to be taught to children as a stand-alone academic subject in pre-K or elementary school but does continue to be viewed as an important topic to include in teacher education and teacher training programs.

Experientially, when I took Professor Wood's children's communication course in the early 1980s, during my MA program in Communication at the University of Illinois at Chicago Circle campus (as it was called back then), I was one of a very few males enrolled in her course. Also, for the past 32 years, I have been teaching an undergraduate and beginning graduate-level course on children's communication that also continues to enroll mostly females as well as a handful of males. Similar to Professor Wood's students in her class, students who have been taking my children's communication classes are pursuing degrees in early childhood and elementary education, speech pathology, and counseling, as well as some undergraduate and graduate students pursuing degrees in communication. It is only during the past nine years that students have been taking this course as an integral elective in the lifespan communication graduate degree offered at Old Dominion University (that started in 2011).

Table 2.1 compares the content of the chapters in the communication field's first three books about children's communication development written by the field's pioneering children's communication scholars: Barbara S. Wood (1976), Rita Naremore and Robert Hopper (1990), and Beth Haslett and Wendy Samter (1997). Barbara Wood (retired) was a professor of communication at the University of Illinois at Chicago. Although Rita Naremore was a professor of speech and language sciences at Indiana University, she co-wrote this particular volume with the late communication professor, Robert Hopper (University of Texas at Austin). Finally, Beth Haslett (currently a Communication professor at the University of Delaware) once told me that she has been emphasizing organizational communication in her more recent work and no longer is active in researching children. Her co-author Wendy Samter (currently a Communication Professor and Dean at Bryant University) has been also working in administration. Further, it is important to note that Haslett and Samter's important volume was published 23-years ago. All three volumes are no longer in print.

Although the audiences for these three volumes do include communication scholars, they are primarily targeted for use as classroom textbooks in upper division communication courses. All three volumes provide similar overviews of children's communication development that include: the child as a developing communicator, communi-biological foundations of communication development, language development, verbal communication development, and contexts and individuals affecting verbal communication development that include families, parenting, and schools. Two of the

Table 2.1 Comparison of the Content of Three Foundational Children's Communication Books

Wood (1976)	Naremore & Hopper (1990)	Haslett & Samter (1997)
Child as a Communicator	Children's Eloquence	Basic Concepts
Intrapersonal Forces	Speech as a Biological Process	
Interpersonal Forces	Language-Learning Environments	Family influences
Language	Pre-Verbal	Language Development
Sounds	Sounds	
Words	Meanings	
Syntax	Syntax	
Semantics	Meanings	
Body		Nonverbal communication
Voice		
Space		
Communication Situations	Pragmatics	Verbal Communication Development
Communication Instruction	Learning to Communicate Teaching Communication to Children	Developing Communicative Knowledge Parenting
Analyzing Children's Communication		
Participating in Children's Communication		Doing Friendships Children's Friendship
	When Language goes awry Speech and Literacy Language Diversity	

volumes include nonverbal communication (Wood, 1976; Haslett & Samter, 1997) and one includes a chapter on speech and literacy, a chapter on communication problems, as well as a chapter on language diversity (Naremore & Hopper, 1990). For the most part, the chapters contained within these volumes are organized by developmental age and include age-related examples of communication development. They also offer age-related touchstones of communication development, or what communication looks like for children of varying ages (infancy through age 5). All of three of the volumes focus extensively on children's language development (with a heavy focus on pragmatics) and all three volumes draw upon the classics of developmental psycho-/sociolinguistics (e.g., Chomsky, Bruner, Piaget, Vygotsky, etc.). Professor Wood's ground-breaking volume does attempt to offer an integrative emphasis on how children develop their personal "communication power" throughout its chapters. That is, how we can equip children with the communication tools needed for them to thrive. The outline of Wood's volume also was somewhat duplicated in the two subsequent volumes in Table 2.1.

As to cultural inclusion, although Wood's volume explicitly argues that diversity does exist in the development of children's communication (e.g., acknowledging that children learn to communicate in a variety of contexts and with a variety of people), and she does mention ethnic culture, the volume offers few specifics about ethnic cultural diversity (similar to Haslett & Samter, 1997). And, although Naremore and Hopper (1990) devoted an entire chapter to "linguistic diversity," unfortunately they focused their discussion on learning, speaking, and correcting "non-standard dialects" (i.e., correcting Black speech and Hispanic speech that assumes White speech to be the "standard"). Not surprisingly, none of these volumes mentions LGBTQ children.

Back then, because communication was a newcomer to the field of children's studies, these three volumes also devoted considerable space to theories originating outside the communication field in order to discuss and explain children's communication. However, an important exception is the theoretical perspective of constructivism that was birthed by communication scholars at the University of Illinois (e.g., Professors Jesse Delia and Ruth Ann Clark). Constructivism emphasizes cognitive complexity's role in message production and message interpretation (e.g., see Burleson, Delia, & Applegate, 1995). Constructivist work is cited and discussed throughout Haslett and Samter's volume.

In addition, and in my opinion, Haslett and Samter (1997, pp. 4–13), articulated one of the most comprehensive definitions of communication to date. They included ten elements in their definition. And, of particular importance to children, all 10 elements are subject to learning and developmental forces. That is, communication is: (1) inferential, (2) intentional, (3) conventional, (4) jointly negotiated, varies by (5) context and (6) language user, (7) involves commonsense knowledge, (8) systematic, (9) interpretive, and (10) varies according to participants social relationships. These 10 elements appear throughout their volume. I continue to use their definition in all of the communication classes that I teach.

A related, but somewhat different volume also appearing in Figure 2.1 also requires mention in this section. It was co-edited by Purdue communication scholar, Howard Sypher and, constructivist, children's communication scholar, and current, Executive Director of the Illinois Board of Higher

Education, Dr. James Applegate (Sypher & Applegate, 1984). Although it is not a book about children's communication development per se, the volume is unique insofar as it compares and contrasts children's and adults' communication. It was organized into four sections (two devoted to children and two devoted to adults). With respect to children, the volume features chapters about (a) children's prosocial processes including prosocial cognition (Eisenberg & Silbereisen, 1984), perspective taking (Barnett, 1984), and comforting (Burleson, 1984, 1994), and (b) children's influence processes that include social reasoning and persuasion (Forbes & Lubin, 1984), conflicts of interest (Oden, Wheeler, & Herzberger, 1984), and sociability skills (Rubin & Borwick, 1984).

An important, primary, and a shared goal of all four of these volumes, although focused on early childhood and elementary-school years, was to explicitly connect communicators' ages and levels of cognitive, linguistic, and social development to the production and interpretation of messages. Such a goal should also be among the major objectives of all lifespan communication research (birth through end of life). That is, a major objective of the field of communication, as related to early lifespan, should be to understand and explain age-related communication and its development from birth until adolescence.

The three early volumes also aptly point out that human communication development begins with nonverbal communication, onto which is scaffolded language development (that features mostly the face-to-face medium, but may include digital media), as well as verbal communication development (communication pragmatics) into a continuously expanding array of communicators, contexts (in relationships, groups, organizations, and public), media, and situations.

All four of these books, however, are also communication-medium exclusive. That is, they all focus exclusively on face-to-face communication and make no mention of electronic media. An important point to make here is that today's introduction of digital screened media to pre-linguistic children is changing the "natural" course of human communication development and the consequences of doing so are not yet understood. However, based on what is known, the American Academy of Pediatrics cautions that children under the age of 2 should not be exposed to screens (AAP, 2019). Let's turn next to examine books about children's television and media that were also appearing at the same time as books about children's communication development.

Children's media. Unlike books about children's face-to-face communication development that confronted the problem of needing a specialized audience of women teachers (i.e., those who would purchase books about children development), books about children's TV seemed to have an easier time gaining attention and garnering a wider audience. Everyone watches TV, and among TV viewers, from the very beginning, children have been seen as vulnerable audience members requiring special protections. This framing sets the stage, paternalistically, for white males (and female allies) to not only be the inventors of new communication technologies but also to be the protectors of children from the allegedly numerous harms and ills caused by exposure to television and more recently digital media. An important and sharply contrasting note here is that none of the children's human communication development volumes (reviewed in the previous section) mention any harms that children can potentially encounter in their face-to-face interactions. Whereas, books about children's television and media focus heavily, and sometimes almost exclusively, on numerous harms that can arise from viewing television. It is certainly the case that children are at least equally likely, if not more likely, to be harmed, and harmed more severely and in more lasting ways, during their face-to-face communication with the people they live with, than from watching TV or playing a video game (a point I will take up later in this essay).

Because TV is ubiquitous, it is no surprise that volumes about children's television and media outnumber children's relational communication development. These volumes have been written and edited by the field's pioneering children's media scholars, like Ellen Wartella (Northwestern University, see Chapter 7, this volume) and the esteemed media scholar, Jennings Bryant (emeritus, University of Alabama). Most of the volumes about children's media appearing in Figure 2.1 focus on children and television (i.e., in chronological order, Bryant, 1983; Clifford, Gunter, & McAleer, 1995; Wartella, 1997; Canter, 1998; Jordan & Hall Jamieson, 1998; van Evra, 1998, 2004; Canter, 2004; and Bryant, 2006). Most of these volumes situate the child as a vulnerable member of TV audiences and examine how TV-viewing affects many aspects of children's development. For example, the volume by Gunter and McLear (1997) examined the effects of children viewing TV on children's knowledge, social roles, aggressive behaviors, good behaviors, consumer behaviors, health orientations, and school performance. Van Evra (1998, 2004) examined TV's impact on violence and aggression, cultural diversity, advertising, family relations, health, and social-emotional issues, while also considering how children process information from TV as well as how this affects children's language development, reading, and academic achievement. Another important topic appearing throughout these volumes is children's media literacy (see Scantlin, Chapter 11, this volume) and features intervention strategies that include use of program rating systems, technological aids, as well as parental mediation to manage what are considered to be TV's harmful effects on children. There is also a national professional association devoted to media literacy (see the Association for Media Literacy, http://www.aml.ca).

Other volumes appearing in Figure 2.1 include Zillman, Bryant, and Huston (1994), Calvert and Wilson (2008), and Strasberger, Wilson, and Jordon (2014) that all focus more comprehensively on children's media (as well as families), including the internet, video gaming, and much more. Indeed, the volume by Strasberger et al. (2014) is a most comprehensive volume to date about children's media and includes chapters on: children as unique members of media audiences; advertising; prosocial and educational media; media violence; sex, sexuality, and media; obesity, eating disorders and media; the internet; social media; video games; family and media; media literacy and media education; as well as children's media policy. An additional note is that similar to the communication-medium exclusive volumes focusing on children's relational communication (i.e., that do not mention media), these children's media volumes are also communication-medium exclusive, that is, they do not cite the literature of children's relational communication development (even in chapters that specifically focus on families).

Going forward, emerging topics in this conceptual group include the convergence of media onto narrowing digital platforms, a plurality of varied forms of electronic media (as seen in the Strasberger et al., 2014, volume), and the expanding use of mobile digital media (smartphones) in everyday relational communication (e.g., see Breuss, 2015). This suggests that in the future there is a need for greater communication-media inclusiveness (relational and digital) when studying children and indeed all forms of communication. I see the future of the field of communication as featuring the convergence of face-to-face, digital media, and cultures as central to the theorizing and research of lifespan communication development. To their credit, these children's media volumes do explicitly consider ethnic-cultural diversity when writing about audiences.

Regarding media-inclusiveness, experientially, I had my own professional struggles and offer the following anecdotes. In the mid-1990s, my then department Chair, Professor Gary Edgerton (a renowned media scholar and historian) communicated his appreciation for my children's communication course, but also urged me to include children's television. Until then, drawing upon my two graduate communication courses in children's communication (during my MA program from Barbara Wood at UIC and during my Ph.D. program from the late Dr. Julie Burke at University of Iowa), my children's communication course was primarily focused on children's relational communication development. As a part of Edgerton's efforts to convince me to include media, he treated me to a children's television conference held at Washington DC's National Press Club that was sponsored by the University of Pennsylvania's Annenberg School of Communication. At the time, I was reluctant to incorporate work on media alongside relational communication in part because there was no guiding model of how to do so. However, after attending the conference and later co-planning a children's film and media festival at ODU, I accepted the necessity to think more comprehensively about children's communication worlds and subsequently widened the focus of my course to include children's media. From that point on, I have been offering what I label a course about children's global and comprehensive communication development that includes the development of numerous communication competencies of children from around the world: nonverbal communication, language, verbal communication, relational and group communication, children's media, and media literacy.

Later, I attended a subsequent Annenberg Children's Television Conference (this time on my own). At the time I was beginning my tenure as the founding Editor of the *Journal of Family Communication*. The keynote speaker for the conference was Fred Rogers (Mister Roger's Neighborhood). It occurred to me as I listened to Fred's moving speech, what a cool idea it would be if he would write a point-of-view article about children, families, and television for the inaugural issue of *JFC*. It could help to garner interest in the journal but also serve as a potential bridge for those who studied family relational communication and those who studied family media. After Fred's speech, an incredibly long line cued to meet him. It took well over 45 minutes to work my way to him. We shook hands. I introduced myself, informed him of my new role as the Founding Editor of the *Journal of Family Communication*, and asked if I could call him later to talk about writing a journal article for JFC. Instead, Fred preferred to sit down at a nearby table and begin a conversation with me. Fred was especially excited by the name of the journal, saying that "family" was so central to his work with children that he named his television production business, Family Communication, Inc. He said that he had never written an academic journal article, but if I was open to helping him to learn how to do it, that he'd be happy to write it. Meeting Fred and briefly getting to work with a children's TV legend is an experience and memory I will always cherish. Not to mention that it cemented the idea that the field of communication should be more medium-inclusive in our teaching and research about children's communication. Thus, relational communication scholars/educators and digital media scholars/educators should play nice in the sandbox of early lifespan communication and across the lifespan as they have much to learn from each other.

Children's family communication. In 1982, the very first family communication book was published (Galvin & Brommel, 1982) and over a decade later this was followed by several books that focused on children's relational communication within families. Let's review these volumes about children that focus on family communication including: (a) communication between children and parents (in chronological order, Stafford & Bayer, 1993; Socha & Stamp, 1995, 2009; Socha & Yingling, 2010; Pettigrew, 2014), (b) children's ethnic-cultural communication at home (Socha & Diggs, 1999), and (c) communication in children's relationships at a daycare (Meyer, 2003).

The largest sub-area focuses on communication between children and parents. It is important to note that while all of the volumes and the chapters featured in this conceptual grouping are in some way significant in their own right, some of the chapters appearing in the parent-child communication volumes are truly ground-breaking and are counted as the very first publications in the family communication field about their respective topics. Further, many of these works stand as a testament to the field of family communication's commitment to inclusiveness (i.e., culturally and sexually). For example, a full twenty years before the legalization of same-sex marriage, Socha and Stamp (1995) included the communication field's first published work on gay/lesbian parent-child communication (West & Turner, 1995). Later Socha and Stamp (2009) featured the communication field's first chapter on gay and lesbian foster parental communication (Patrick & Palladino, 2009). And, although not solely focused on children (they appear throughout the volume and are the explicit focus of a few chapters), Socha and Diggs (1999) co-edited the communication field's first book on Black/White/Bi-Racial family communication that was not only co-edited by a African American female and a white male, but also features chapters co-authored by African American and European American Communication scholars. Further, Socha and Stamp's (2009) subsequent parent-child communication volume added to the complexities of the contexts of children's communication by focusing on parent-child communication in the contexts of education, health and wellness, media, and evolving child caregiving roles of grandparents and stepfamilies.

Summary

Collectively, the children's books in these three areas of inquiry offer a rich foundation upon which future work in early lifespan communication can be built. However, unless and until the content of these pioneering books about children is brought into the consciousness and imaginations of all contemporary communication researchers and educators, and most importantly shared with current students of communication, there is a danger that this work will be lost to history and that with the exception of children and media, the communication field will remain childless. I acknowledge and fully understand that much work lies ahead in making this shift. I also understand that some may argue that repositioning children to the start of the communication field is a far too daunting of a task, requiring far too much work, and perhaps it is better for the communication field to remain childless. I will counter that an inescapable fact is that as we communicate with children today, we are actively creating communication legacies for future generations who will one day become parents as well as our caretakers in later life. The quality of all of our futures depends heavily on having citizens with effective, appropriate, and optimal communication skills. It is therefore in all of our interests to ensure that the quality of early lifespan communication is as high as we can make it.

Widening the Lens on Children's Communication

These aforementioned books about children played an important role in staking out the field of early lifespan communication to include children's communication development, children's media and children's communication within families and friendships. However, today, the contemporary field of communication is far broader and includes, for example, group communication, organizational communication, intercultural communication, public communication, as well as persuasion that must also be considered in light of children. There are also many other important topics appearing in the children's literature in other fields that may also appear in the children's communication literature that deserve consideration. Therefore, we must reframe the study of early lifespan communication to also fully include all those areas that are a part of mainstream theorizing, research, and education of adults' communication. Towards this goal, I offer a selected list of overview essays of some of these topics. Second, I will discuss important areas needing further development that include: children in communication theory development, communicatively abusing children, informal and formal communication education, communicating with children of varying levels of abilities, as well as children in global cultures.

Selected overview essays. Figure 2.2 offers a selective list of publications that provide overviews of some of these topic areas that seek to connect children's communication to the work of adult communication. Like

Figure 2.2   Children's Communication: Selected Overview Essays

Children and bullying. Socha. T. J., & Sadler, R. (2019). A look at bullying communication in early childhood: Towards a lifespan developmental model. In R. West & C. S. Beck (Eds.), The Routledge Handbook of Communication and Bullying (pp. 188–197). New York: Routledge.

Children and family communication systems. Socha, T. J. (1999). Communication and family units: Studying the first "group". In L. Frey, M. S. Poole, & D. Gouran, (Eds.), *Handbook of Group Communication Theory & Research* (pp. 475–492). Thousand Oaks, CA: Sage.

Children's group communication. Socha, T. J., & Socha, D. M. (1994). Children's task group communication: Did we learn it all in kindergarten? In L. Frey (Ed.), Group communication in context: Studies of natural groups (pp. 227–246). Hillsdale, NJ: Lawrence Erlbaum.

Children's humor. Socha, T. J. (2012). Children's humor: Foundations of laughter across the lifespan. In R. DiCioccio (Ed.), *Humor: Theory, Impact, and Outcomes* (Chapter 9). Dubuque, IA: Kendal Hunt.

Children's communication and moral development. Socha, T. J. & Eller, A. (2015). Parent/caregiver-child communication and moral development: Towards a conceptual foundation of an ecological model of lifespan communication and good relationships. In V. Waldron & D. Kelley (Eds.), *Moral Communication across the Lifespan: Developing Good Relationships: (pp. 13–34).* New York: Peter Lang.

Communication and parental discipline. Socha, T. J. (2006). Orchestrating and directing domestic potential through communication: Towards a positive reframing of "discipline." In L. Turner & R. West (Eds.), *Family Communication: A Reference for Theory and Research (pp. 219–236).* Thousand Oaks, CA: Sage.

Children's Strategic Communication skills. Delia, J. G., & Clark, R. A. (1977). Cognitive complexity, social perception, and the development of listener adapted communication in Six-, Eight-, Ten-, and Twelve-year old boys. *Communication Monographs, 44,* 326–345.

Clark, R. A. & Delia, J. G. (1979). Topoi and rhetorical competence. *Quarterly Journal of Speech, 65,* 187–206.

Delia, J. G., Kline, S., & Burleson, B. (1979). The development of persuasive communication strategies in Kindergartners through twelfth graders. *Communication Monographs, 46,* 241–256.

---

this chapter, these entries are intended as a primer of readings about these topics for those seeking to learn more as well to those who wish to begin to merge the current "adult" communication literature with early lifespan. All of these works intentionally frame communication as occurring developmentally over the lifespan regardless of context. That is, as children communicate with families during dinners, as children make mistakes and engage in anti-social behaviors, as children communicate while playing team-sports, and as children communicate in social groups like scouting and church, they are also learning communication lessons that they will carry forward as they one day become parents who are communicating during family dinners, parents and caregivers orchestrating and implementing children's behavioral changes, coaches communicating during children's team sports, and leaders communicating with scouts and church members. Formal education must occur in these contexts as well as with communication development, media, and families.

Children in communication theory construction. At an NCA conference, the esteemed late communication professor, theorist, researcher and friend, Charles (Chuck) Berger (then retired) flagged me over to join him for a beverage. During that conversation, I asked him about the development of his Uncertainty Reduction Theory (URT). Had he ever thought about children in the URT's development? He admitted that he had not but was nevertheless delighted to think that his theory could be considered a lifespan theory. I believe he said something like, "You are right! We start out incredibly uncertain [expressed in my more polite terms] and we must battle uncertainty our entire lives. Who knows if we ever successfully manage it?" Similarly, like URT, it is my belief that most of the theories developed thus far in the field of communication have also not considered children, nor lifespan development, nor global culture, and that a sea change in thinking would take place if children and lifespan communication development were incorporated. Although admittedly radical, I believe that such a change is necessary to strengthen our field's already strong, albeit adult-centric theories.

Communicatively abusing children. During my own early lifespan (late 1950s and early 1960s), I recall hearing adults say, "Children should be seen but not heard." As a child, I recall understanding this expression to be an admonition to stop speaking and to refrain from speaking. It also served as a notice that whatever I had to say as a child was unimportant, irrelevant, and back then, a warning that physical punishment would follow if I continued to trespass into the adults' world. Given that children are largely invisible in communication, it seems to me that many in the field of communication may have also internalized a version of this unfortunate expression. As children communicate while at home, at school, on the playground, in the homes of friends and relatives, and while watching digital media they are likely to encounter messages from parents, teachers, relatives, and other children that will harm them as well as empower them. Works by Steve Wilson and colleagues (cited earlier) studying negative physical child abuse takes the lead here in helping us to understand communication processes and preventing physical child abuse. Back as a student when I read the children's relational communication literature and even today as a communication scholar working in this area, it seems as if no harms ever come to children through their relational communication. This, of course, runs contrary to my professional assessment of the state of children today as well as my personal experiences as a child. However, when I read the children's media literature, it seems that lots of harms (and little good) befall kids watching TV and playing video games. Going forward both the positive and dark sides of communication must be considered in studying children's communication regardless of communication-media (see Socha & Beck, 2015). And, it goes without saying that the communication field must work harder to prevent children from being physically as well as communicatively harmed, abused, and worse as they communicate with the adults charged with their care and development.

Children learning communication (informally and formally) at school. Although children in the US are not yet being taught using a *formal* communication education curriculum in grades K–12, nevertheless, they are *informally* being taught about communication. We need to learn more about what children are learning informally about communication while they are at school because these lessons will facilitate and/or inhibit their optimal communication development and will also form a lasting foundation for their future interactions. For better or worse, we all have stories of communication learning in early our lifespan that should be told, analyzed, and included as a part of lifespan communication learning that may or may not continue into college. I was fortunate that besides majoring in communication, earning a high school teaching certificate and teaching communication in high school, I also took two graduate-level communication courses that focused on children (with Barbara Wood at UIC and the late Dr. Julie Burke at the University of Iowa). Taking two graduate-level communication classes about children is unique because today most Ph.D.'s in communication graduate with no classes that focus on children, even among those who study families. Undoubtedly, our academic communication experiences (Kindergarten through graduate school) shape our understanding and love of communication as well as help to hone our communication abilities. All lifespan communication learning starts during early childhood and continues through adulthood: from show-n-tell in Kindergarten classrooms to "show-n-tell" (with PowerPoint) in classrooms and boardrooms. We all have communication education stories that need to be told so that we can begin to connect our pasts with our presents. And, more importantly, our informal communication education (and formal communication to the extent that it occurs) happens mostly by luck (or not luck) and by happenstance (i.e., We get what we get).

Children of varying communication (dis)abilities. In the commonly used database, *Communication and Mass Media Complete*, when entering the search terms "children" and "disabilities" and limiting the search to scholarly peer-reviewed journal articles 2876 entries appear. These articles, in general, focus on communicating with children of varying: sensory abilities (e.g., eyes, ears, touch), speech abilities (e.g., fluency, non-speaking), physical abilities (e.g., mobility, facial and mouth movement, body movement, hand movement, head movement), physical appearances (e.g., head shapes, facial features), intellectual abilities (e.g., cognitive, memory, learning), as well as multi-leveled and complex conditions (e.g., Autism, Asperger's, Down's Syndrome) and the intersections of race, ethnic culture, and varying levels of abilities. In truth, all children have varying levels of human abilities that can have wide bandwidths and variabilities. Some children have complex communication needs that require augmentation, support, therapies, and medical interventions, while others require less. It must be acknowledged that children with complex communication needs do require communicators with specialized training (e.g., American Sign Language or AMESLAN as a second language) and sometimes specialized equipment is necessary in order to be fully inclusive. Communication inclusiveness is also an important part of raising the consciousness of the field to include *all* children.

Children and global culture. It cannot be assumed that the material, societal, communicative, and geographic circumstances in which the world's children develop their communication are all the same. Both similarities and differences exist that should be considered as a part of global, comprehensive communication education. For example, many parents around the world sing their children to sleep (see *World Sings Goodnight*, 1993), but they are doing so in their native languages (that aid in teaching children the foundations of phonetics in their native tongue) and also with content that features their cultures' values, histories, and geographies. In an online newsletter, for example, Ralph (2015), highlighted at least 20 ways that parenting differs around the world, for example, allowing children to go hungry from time to time as a way to teach self-discipline (Korea), communicating between parents and children as equals (Sweden), leaving children unattended in strollers outside a restaurant while parents dine inside is OK (Denmark), getting paid by the government to parent (Germany), as well as having children care for children (Polynesia), and more. Of course, the experiences of children in rural, sub-Saharan Africa, for example, are not the same as children of rural southern USA. However, the field of communication has not yet tapped the cultural communication experiences of the world's children, but in doing so it would find that communication is, universally, a necessary force that has far-reaching consequences in terms of human development.

Communication and LGBT youth. Important research and an educational frontier for children's communication pertain to LGBT youth. It is essential to study this area if we are to develop a full and complex understanding of the development of human sexuality and identity. To date, doing so, unfortunately, has not been without dangers and controversy (see Chapter 11, for a discussion about the boundaries of sexuality in childhood focusing on a children's television show depicting a gay wedding). Going forward it is important for the field of communication to more fully examine relational and mediated communication in all of the contexts of LGBT youth's development and also to build on existing research from allied fields (e.g. see US Government, http://youth.gov; American Institutes of Research-LGBT Youth, https://www.air.org/topic/health/lgbtq-youth; and American Psychological Association-LGBT Youth Resources, https://www.apa.org/pi/lgbt/programs/safe-supportive/lgbt/).

Looking to the Future

Formal Lifespan Communication Education

Instead of leaving lifespan communication education to chance, if communication education is to become fully inclusive and fully comprehensive, the field's overall approach to lifespan communication education must start by becoming formal and systematic from the very beginning. That is, early lifespan must become a formal part of all communication education. Second, it follows that graduate and undergraduate communication curricula should include at least one early lifespan communication course in all graduate communication degree programs especially those focusing on families. Third, all introductory human communication texts for undergraduates in the US should include at least a chapter about early lifespan communication and should also integrate the topic of lifespan communication development into the fabric of their courses. Finally, as this review makes obvious, all early lifespan communication education must be far more ethnically and sexually inclusive than the predominantly cishet, whiteness that I experienced in my formal and informal communication development.

Towards Comprehensive Functional Lifespan Communication

In my opinion, the greatest potential to transform the field of communication lies first in incorporating a lifespan meta-theoretical approach to communication theory, research, and education—one that features and champions communication development at all stages but particularly early lifespan. Specifically, I propose that the field of lifespan communication return to consider a functional communication approach (Dance & Larsen, 1976) to develop a framework for comprehensive functional lifespan communication.

Communication scholars, Frank E. X. Dance and Carl Larson (1976) argued that communication has three primary functions: linking, mentation, and regulation. The linking communication function is how humans use communication to connect to the changing worlds of each other and their environment. It involves constructing, sharing, and accepting/rejecting the construal of selves. Mentation refers to the role of communication in higher mental processes and involves "memory, planning or foresight, intelligence or cognitive insight, thinking, judgment, and speech communication and its derivatives of reading and writing" (p. 93). It also involves decentering. "Whatever terms are used to describe this operation—it has assumed such labels as empathizing, role-taking, interpersonal understanding, and person perception—the concept of decentering takes us to the core of a unique phenomenon, interpersonal understanding" (p. 116). Lack of decentering is linked to interpersonal violence and interpersonal distrust. Finally, regulation refers to the use of communication to create, maintain, and change the beliefs, attitudes, behaviors, and routines of self and others. For example, it highlights work in the area of interpersonal persuasion (Wilson, 2002).

All three communication functions (linking, mentation, regulation) are subject to developmental forces (e.g., communi-biological, cognitive, emotional, relational) across the entire lifespan and are shaped by unique obstacles at all of life's stages [i.e., early lifespan (childhood), adolescence, early adulthood, adulthood, and later life]. For example, humor is a form of entertainment that functions to link people (e.g., see Chapter 1 this volume). Throughout the human lifespan, humor communication functions can change and develop (e.g., may flat-line, augment, or diminish) as communicators confront unique, historically situated individual, contextual, and relational communication conditions. Of course, communication functions all start in primitive forms. For example, a 3-year old might cry loudly and demand a cold drink on a hot day (regulation). Over time, individual development (cognitive, linguistic, communication) will take place accompanied by informal and formal communication education where communicators can learn to deploy a communication function with greater sophistication. For example, a 30-year old can mention that it is hot outside and suggest that perhaps a cold drink would be welcomed. Of course, sometimes communication's development can be arrested, and primitive forms (whether effective or not) may continue to be used. For example, a 30-year old can cry, loudly, and demand a cold drink on a hot day (regulation).

There are many conceptual and methodological advantages to a functional lifespan communication approach. First, it provides a way to integrate the study of communication at all of life's stages. That is, with some modification to measurement (see Chapter 3, this volume) we can study all of the communication's primary functions at all of life's stages using comparable metrics to chart lifespan development. We can ask important research questions like: Are adults communicating in ways that are more sophisticated than kindergartners? What does the developmental arc of a given communication function look like across the lifespan for individuals and what sorts of individual, relational, contextual, and historical qualities are making a difference in development? Can formally teaching positive communication skills to 3- and 4-year old children, for example, not only help to improve their communication during this time but does doing so also carry forward into primary education (K–3) and help to prevent and manage to bully? Across the lifespan how far can these early lessons be carried and what formal communication education is necessary along the way to keep them increasing in sophistication and complexity?

Second, this approach grounds foundational textbooks and classes in an integrative framework that includes contexts but does not tie the study of communication exclusively to contexts. That is, it focuses on what all those who study communication have in common (unifying) as well as the role communication functions play in many contexts (persuasion in relationships, groups, organizations, public). Contexts, of course, matter, but when imagined as a part of human communication development are viewed differently as when adopting Bronfenbrenner's bio-social ecological (Bronfenbrenner, 1979) model where varying spheres exert varying kinds and degrees of influence on proximal development.

Third, and finally, a functional approach allows for findings in the field of communication to link more readily with findings from education, developmental psychology, and more. For example, we can add to the literature about early lifespan education by more closely examining the unique contribution of early lifespan communication's role in facilitating and inhibiting early childhood learning (mentation function and regulation function) over and above socioeconomic status, and so on.

In summary, we must work to move the field of communication from being childless to child-centered, from being adult-centric to lifespan-focused, and from excluding some communicators to welcoming all communicators from their first words to their final conversations.

References

AAP. (2019). Retrieved from https://www.aap.org/en-us/about-the-aap/aap-press-room/Pages/American-Academy-of-Pediatrics-Announces-New-Recommendations-for-Childrens-Media-Use.aspx

Barnett, M. A. (1984). Perspective-taking and empathy in the child's prosocial behavior. In H. E. Sypher & J. L. Applegate (Eds.), *Communication by children and adults: Social cognitive and strategic processes* (pp. 43–62). Thousand Oaks, CA: Sage.

Blair, C., Brown, J. R., & Baxter, L. a. (1994). Disciplining the feminine. *Quarterly Journal of Speech, 80*, 383–409.

Breuss, C. J. (Ed.). (2015). *Family communication in the age of digital and social media.* New York: Peter Lang.

Bronfenbrenner, U. (1979). *The ecology of human development.* Cambridge, MA: Harvard University Press.

Bryant, J. (1983). *Children's understanding of television.* New York: Academic Press.

Bryant, A. (2006). (Ed.). *The children's television community.* New York: Routledge.

Burleson, B. R. (1984). Comforting communication. In H. E. Sypher & J. L. Applegate (Eds.). *Communication by children and adults: Social and strategic processes* (pp. 63–105). Thousand Oaks, CA: Sage.

Burleson, B. R. (1994). Comforting messages: Features, functions, and outcomes. In J. A. Daly & J. M. Wiemann (Eds.), *Strategic interpersonal communication* (pp. 135–161). Hillsdale, NJ: Lawrence Erlbaum.

Burleson, B. R., Delia, J. G., & Applegate, J. L. (1995). The socialization of person-centered communication: Parents' contributions to their children's social cognitive and communication skills. In M. A. Fitzpatrick & A. L. Vangelisti (Eds.), *Explaining family interactions* (pp. 34–76). Thousand Oaks, CA: Sage.

Calvert, S. L., & Wilson, B. J. (Eds.). (2008). *The handbook of children, media, and development.* New York: Wiley.

Cantor, J. (1998). *"Mommy, I'm scared." How TV and movies frighten children and what we can do to protect them.* Boston: Houghton Mifflin.

Cantor, J. (2004). *Teddy's TV troubles.* New York: Goblin Fern Publishing.

Chakravartty, P., Kuo, R., Grubbs, V., & McIlwain, C. (2018). #CommunicationSoWhite. *Journal of Communication, 68*, 254–266.

Child Welfare. (2019). What is child abuse and neglect? Recognizing the signs and symptoms. Retrieved from https://www.childwelfare.gov/pubPDFs/whatiscan.pdf#page=2&view=How%20is%20child%20abuse%20and%20neglect%20defined%20in%20Federal%20law

Clark, R. A., & Delia, J. G. (1979). Topoi and rhetorical competence. *Quarterly Journal of Speech, 65*, 187–206.

Clifford, B., Gunter, B., & McAleer, J. (1995). *Television and children: Program evaluation, comprehension, and impact.* Hillsdale, NJ: Lawrence Erlbaum.

Dance, F. E. X., & Larson, C. E. (1976). *The functions of human communication: A theoretical approach.* New York: Holt, Rinehart and Winston.

Delia, J. G., & Clark, R. A. (1977). Cognitive complexity, social perception, and the development of listener adapted communication in Six-, Eight-, Ten-, and Twelve-year old boys. *Communication Monographs, 44,* 326–345.

Delia, J. G., Kline, S., & Burleson, B. (1979). The development of persuasive communication strategies in Kindergartners through twelfth graders. *Communication Monographs, 46,* 241–256.

Dosomething.org. (2019). *Facts about child abuse.* Retrieved from https://www. dosomething.org/us/facts/11-facts-about-child-abuse

Eisenberg, N., & Silbereisen, R. (1984). The development of children's prosocial cognitions. In H. E. Sypher & J. L. Applegate (Eds.), *Communication by children and adults: Social cognitive and strategic processes* (pp. 16–42). Thousand Oaks, CA: Sage.

Forbes, D., & Lubin, D. (1984). Verbal social reasoning and observed persuasion strategies. In H. E. Sypher & J. L. Applegate (Eds.), *Communication by children and adults: Social cognitive and strategic processes* (pp. 106–128). Thousand Oaks, CA: Sage.

Galvin, K., & Brommel, B. (1982). *Family communication: Cohesion and change.* New York: Allyn & Bacon.

Gunter, B., & McAleer, J. (1997). *Children and television.* London: Routledge.

Haslett, B. B., & Samter, W. (1997). *Children communicating: The first five years.* Mahwah, NJ: Lawrence Erlbaum.

Higginbotham, D. (1976). Review of *Children and Communication* by B. S. Wood. *Communication Quarterly, 24,* 42.

Jordan, A. B., & Hall Jamieson, K. (1998). Children and television. *The Annals of the American Academy of Political and Social Science, 557.* Thousand Oaks, CA: Sage.

Meyer, J. (2003). *Kids talking. Learning relationships and culture with children.* Lanham, MD: Rowman & Littlefield.

Miller-Day, M., Pezalla, A., & Chestnut, R. (2013). Children are in families too!: The presence of children in communication research. *Journal of Family Communication, 13*(2), 150–165.

Naremore, R., & Hopper, R. (1990). *Children learning language: Practical introduction to communication development* (3rd ed.). New York: Harper & Row.

Nussbaum, J. F. (Ed.). (2015). *The handbook of lifespan communication.* New York: Peter Lang.

Oden, S., Wheeler, V. A., & Herzberger, S. D. (1984). Children's conversations within a conflict-of-interest situation. In H. E. Sypher & J. L. Applegate (Eds.), *Communication by children and adults: Social cognitive and strategic processes* (pp. 129–151). Thousand Oaks, CA: Sage.

O'Keefe, B. J. (1976). Review of *Children and communication* by B. S. Wood. *Quarterly Journal of Speech, 62*, 325–327.

Patrick, D., & Palladino, J. (2009). The community interactions of gay and lesbian foster parents. In T. J. Socha, & G. H. Stamp (Eds.), *Parents and children communicating with society: Managing relationships outside of the home* (pp. 323–342). New York: Routledge.

Pettigrew, J. (2014). *Stepfather-stepson communication: Social support in stepfamily worlds.* New York: Peter Lang.

Ralph. S. (2015, May 18). *20 ways that parenting styles differ around the world.* Retrieved from https://thenextfamily.com/2015/05/20-ways-that-parenting-styles-differ-around-the-world/

Rubin, K. H., & Borwick, D. (1984). Communicative skills and sociability. In H. E. Sypher & J. L. Applegate (Eds.), *Communication by children and adults: Social cognitive and strategic processes* (pp. 152–171). Thousand Oaks, CA: Sage.

Socha, T. J. (1999). Communication and family units: Studying the first "group". In L. Frey, M. S. Poole, & D. Gouran (Eds.), *Handbook of group communication theory & research* (pp. 475–492). Thousand Oaks, CA: Sage.

Socha, T. J. (2006). Orchestrating and directing domestic potential through communication: Towards a positive reframing of "discipline." In L. Turner & R. West (Eds.), *Family communication: A reference for theory and research* (pp. 219–236). Thousand Oaks, CA: Sage.

Socha, T. J. (2012). Children's humor: Foundations of laughter across the lifespan. In R. DiCioccio (Ed.), *Humor: Theory, impact, and outcomes* (Chapter 9). Dubuque, IA: Kendal Hunt.

Socha, T. J., & Beck, G. A. (2015). Positive communication and human needs: A review and proposed organizing conceptual framework. *Review of Communication, 15,* 173–199.

Socha, T. J., & Diggs, R. H. (Eds.). (1999). *Communication, race and family: Exploring communication in Black, White and Biracial families.* Mahwah, NJ: Erlbaum.

Socha, T. J., & Eller, A. (2015). Parent/caregiver-child communication and moral development: Towards a conceptual foundation of an ecological model of lifespan communication and good relationships. In V. Waldron & D. Kelley (Eds.), *Moral communication across the lifespan: Developing good relationships.* (pp. 13–34). New York: Peter Lang.

Socha, T. J., & Kelly, B. (1994). Children making fun: Humorous communication, impression management, and moral development. *Child Study Journal, 24,* 237–252.

Socha, T. J., & Sadler, R. (2019). A look at bullying communication in early childhood: Towards a lifespan developmental model. In R. West & C. S. Beck (Eds.), *The Routledge handbook of communication and bullying* (pp. 188–197). New York: Routledge.

Socha, T. J., & Socha, D. M. (1994). Children's task group communication: Did we learn it all in kindergarten? In L. Frey (Ed.), *Group communication in context: Studies of natural groups* (pp. 227–246). Hillsdale, NJ: Lawrence Erlbaum.

Socha, T. J., & Stamp, G. H. (Eds.). (1995). *Parents, children, and communication: Frontiers of theory and research.* Hillsdale, NJ: Erlbaum.

Socha, T. J., & Stamp, G. H. (Eds.). (2009). *Parents & children communicating with society: Managing relationships outside of home.* New York: Routledge.

Socha, T. J., & Yingling, J. A. (2010). *Families communicating with children: Building positive developmental foundations.* Cambridge, UK: Polity.

Stafford, L., & Bayer, C. L. (1993). *Interaction between parents and children.* Thousand Oaks, CA: Sage.

Strasburger, V. C., Wilson, B. J., & Jordon, A. B. (2014). *Children, adolescents, and the media* (3rd ed.). Thousand Oaks, CA: Sage.

Sypher, H. E., & Applegate, J. L. (Eds.). (1984). *Communication by children and adults: Social cognitive and strategic processes.* Beverly Hills, CA: Sage.

Van Evra, J. (1998). *Television and child development* (2nd ed.). Mahwah, NJ: Lawrence Erlbaum.

Van Evra, J. (2004). *Television and child development* (3rd ed.). Mahwah, NJ: Lawrence Erlbaum.

Wartella, E. (Ed.) (1997). *Children communicating: Media and development of thought, speech, understanding.* Beverly Hills, CA: Sage.

West, R., & Turner, L. (1995). Communication in lesbian and gay families: Building a descriptive base. In T. J. Socha & G. H. Stamp (Eds.), *Parents, children, & communication: Frontiers of theory and research* (pp. 147–170). Hillsdale, NJ: Lawrence Erlbaum.

Wilson, S. R. (2002). *Seeking and resisting compliance.* Thousand Oaks, CA: Sage.

Wilson, S. R., Shi, X., Tirmenstein, L., Norris, A., & Combs, J. (2006). Parental physical negative touch and child noncompliance in abusive, neglectful, and comparison families: A meta-analysis of observational studies. In L. Turner & R. West (Eds.), *Family communication: A reference for theory and research* (pp. 237–258). Newbury Park, CA: Sage.

Wilson, S. R., & Whipple, E. E. (1995). Communication, discipline, and physical child abuse. In T. Socha & G. Stamp (Eds.), *Parents, children, and communication: Frontiers in theory and research* (pp. 299–317). Hillsdale, NJ: Erlbaum.

Wood, B. S. (1976). *Children and communication: Verbal and nonverbal language development.* New York: Prentice Hall.

World Sings Goodnight (1993). Audio CD. Silver Wave. ASIN B000000POT.

Zillman, D., Bryant, J., & Huston, A. C. (Eds.). (1994). *Media, children and the family.* Hillsdale, NJ: Lawrence Erlbaum.

3. Studying Communication during the Early Lifespan

Rationale, Approaches, and Methods

Thomas J. Socha
Old Dominion University

Undergraduate and graduate courses in research methods are commonplace in today's communication curricula. For undergraduates majoring in communication it is often a single course (sometimes two) that provides students with foundational instruction in quantitative and qualitative social scientific methods as well as critical-rhetorical methods. For those students pursuing MA and Ph.D. degrees in communication, the research methods bar is naturally set higher and includes multiple quantitative, qualitative, and critical-rhetorical methods courses offered at advanced levels. Graduate courses in quantitative communication methods are often accompanied by a series of courses in advanced statistics. However, unfortunately, as discussed previously in Chapters 1 and 2, like all undergraduate and graduate courses in communication, courses in communication research methods are also adult-centric. That is, undergraduate and graduate courses in communication research methods as well as accompanying textbooks focus exclusively on how to study 18- to 26-year-old+ communicators. Undergraduates and graduates taking these courses receive little to no instruction in how to study communicators under age 18 especially those in early and middle childhood, or for that matter adult communicators in later life (see Harwood, 2007). Although a few scholars in the field of communication have recognized and acted on the need that methods courses become lifespan-inclusive (e.g., see Pitts & Hummert, 2014), most continue to focus on adults and exclude children. And, as discussed previously, this situation stands in stark contrast to fields like psychology and sociology that have long-studied children and developed sub-specialties such as developmental psychology featuring research methods specifically developed to study children.

Future Communication Research Must Change

There are pragmatic, important, and immediate reasons to include children in the communication field's research methods education. Starting in 2019, the National Institutes of Health (NIH) began to enforce a new policy—*Inclusion across the Lifespan*—that states the NIH will no longer fund research studies which are not explicitly focused on the human lifespan (NIH, 2018):

> The purpose of the *Inclusion Across the Lifespan Policy* is to ensure individuals are included in clinical research in a manner appropriate to the scientific question under study so that the knowledge gained from NIH-funded research is applicable to all those affected by the researched diseases/conditions. The policy expands the *Inclusion of Children as Participants in Clinical Research Policy* to include individuals of all ages. The policy also clarifies potential justifications for age-based exclusion criteria and requires participant age at enrollment to be provided in progress reports (NIH, 2018).

The rationale for the NIH policy argues that diseases, for example, are experienced across the lifespan, and by leaving out children, adolescents, and the aged, research studies testing the efficacy of treatments and cures based on adult-centric testing may result in ineffective interventions when offered to individuals other than adults. Further, one-size-fits-all (i.e., adult-centric) medical remedies and therapies may be toxic and harmful especially to younger populations.

By extension, the NIH's rationale applies aptly to all of the social and behavioral sciences including communication. That is, like one-size-fits-all adult-centric medical remedies and therapies seeking to respond to disease, one-size-fits-all adult-centric prescriptions, interventions, and educational curricula seeking to help communicators manage social, relational, and digital communication problems may be inappropriate for children and adolescents and could conceivably create additional harms and problems (especially given the absence of basic research backing up these choices). Thus, going forward it is critically important that the field of communication, like all social sciences, adopt an age-inclusive or lifespan communication framing for its future research studies (especially if researchers wish to seek NIH research funding). Also, by including children and adolescents, communication theorists will enrich and expand the field's understanding of its adult-derived, medium-exclusive, theories, conceptualizations, and methods.

This chapter seeks to begin to assist the communication field in a move towards greater lifespan-inclusiveness and media-inclusiveness by providing an outline of communication research methods as applied to children. The chapter concludes with a call to communication researchers and educators, especially those who administer undergraduate and graduate communication curricula, as well as authors of communication research methods textbooks, that all communication students at all educational levels should receive a lifespan-inclusive education in communication research methods that fully incorporates children and adolescents as well as seniors.

Researching Children Communicators

When researching children communicators there are at least five elements that require special consideration. These include: (1) understanding and accepting children's unique points of view, (2) developing an awareness of age-related verbal and non-verbal communication development, (3) properly adapting adult-centric research methods to fit children's attention spans and developmental levels, as well as (4) assessing children's changing communication abilities, and (5) protecting children's rights in the planning and executing of children's communication studies.

Understanding Children's Points of View

According to Heywood (2001), a historian, "childhood" is a socially-constructed period of human development where conceptions of "children" have varied widely at different points in history. For example, according to Heywood, in humans' early history (e.g., 1600–1700) children's points of view were considered "deviant" and required physical "disciplining" (i.e., us of the "rod") in order to become properly adult-like (and less like a spoiled child), a sad trend that persists today among those who use corporal punishment. And, for the greater part of the very early history in academia, it is also the case that children were not deemed worthy of serious academic study. It is only more recently (late 19th century) that the period of childhood has been conceptualized by civil society as a critically important time in human development. Not only one that is worthy of academic study, but also a critically important time in human development requiring extensive child protections (legally enforced) and specialized means of care. Developmental psychologist Miller (2007) concluded by asking an all too apparent question: "What could be more obvious than the need to study how people develop?" (p. 1).

Authors of developmental research methods textbooks outside the field of communication (e.g., see Miller, 2007) conceptualize children as autonomous agents, and have consistently emphasized that children's experiences should not be studied as derivative of adults' experiences, or as somehow less than adults, but rather as early, primary, and foundational links in what is a chain of lifespan human development. Following this line of reasoning, developmental scholars crafted research methods specifically to study children as children. For example, seeking to understand children's behavior on their own terms, Pellegrini (2009) developed a variety of methods to study naturally occurring play including an ethogram (a kind of socio-behavioral map) used, for example, to study children's playground behaviors. Based on hundreds of hours of direct observation, Pellegrini found that children's patterns of behavior often do not follow adult norms and their patterns may only make sense when seen from the points of view of children. That is, children may physically congregate by a jungle gym in part because of its proximity, but more so because they collectively agree to perceive it as a pretend "center" (e.g., rocket ship, space station) that organizes their play experiences. In another example, Socha and Socha (1994) compared the group decision-making communication of college-aged students to 6-year-old children using comparable and age-graded decision-making tasks (e.g., choosing what objects to bring to a picnic). Not surprisingly, college students played little during group decision making while the children played more (i.e., college students were found to be more task-oriented). However, the children reported to actually like their group's communication far more than their college-aged counterparts (who score higher in group hate, e.g., see Myers, & Goodboy, A. K., 2005). Socha and Socha accepted the premise that children will understand and approach processes like group decision making differently than adults, but this does not necessarily mean that children will be less effective at group decision-making tasks. Yet, another example of child-centeredness in the field of communication is John Meyer's (2003) extensive and rich research treatise that captures children's everyday communication from their point of view. Myer, a communication scholar, spent years in a daycare facility mapping communication behaviors and patterns of children and their adult caregivers. As readers might imagine the daycare center featured in his book is perceived differently when viewed from the day-to-day eyes of its children the adult staff members and the children's parents.

Thus, when studying children, their point of view matters. There is little doubt that children's points of view are indeed unique and are accompanied by varying levels of developmental communication abilities as well as potentialities (see Socha & Yingling, 2010). Of course, in order to capture children's unique views and ascertain their communication abilities in valid and reliable ways, not only are special research methods necessary but more fundamentally communication researchers must first understand children's lifespan-developmental communication abilities.

Increasing Awareness of Age-Related Communication Development

Socha and Yingling (2010), and before them Wood (1976), as well as Haslett and Samter (1997) collectively, argue that *all communication abilities are age-dependent*. It is obvious to adults, for example, that communicating with a 3-year-old is different than communicating with an 8-year old, or a 13-year-old, or a 60-year-old. In order to communicate effectively with children of any age, an understanding of their age-related communicating abilities is required. That is, what are children of varying ages capable of understanding and presenting? It is beyond the scope and space of this chapter to offer a comprehensive discussion of children's communication development (e.g., see Haslett & Samter, 1997; Socha & Yingling, 2010, and Chapter 2, this volume). However, a few key general features related to the selection and use of research methods in communication studies of children are discussed.

Nonverbal communication. Humans are born with innate nonverbal communication abilities (e.g., crying) to signal adults to help them to satisfy their needs. Language comes later. Thus, the study of communication of pre-linguistic children must focus exclusively on elemental forms of human nonverbal communication—hearing, touching, space-use, scents, and tasting, and a bit later seeing. But what are pre-linguistic children capable of encoding and decoding nonverbally? Socha and Yingling (2010, pp. 46–48) summarized some of these nonverbal developmental communication features (i.e., face, eyes, body, gesture, and space) from birth to age-4. For example, with regards to the development of facial communication, although infants may not realize that they are smiling, children can present a smile at age 6–8 weeks. They will continue to present a smile until around 3–6 months when they are capable of beginning to engage in mimicking the smiling of others in a kind of call and response pattern. At ages 6–12 months (along with the onset of language) smiling will develop into a primitive communicative response of emotion (e.g., signaling a positive affective state). Smiling, now as communication, continues through ages 2–4 and acquires adult-like qualities. Smiling will continue as communicative and for some may eventually include presenting and understanding more complex types of smiles such as the wry smile or the sarcastic smile, as well as forms of smiling that require advanced socio-cognitive abilities of perspective-taking and meta-communicating (which will occur during middle childhood ages 6–12). By age 12, although varied among individuals, many children will be able to present, engage in, and understand smiling just like adults. However, this does not mean that by age-12, or for that matter even among adults, that communicators have become fully competent smilers. Rather, it means that the developmental arc of smiling as a communicative process may peak (become fully adult-like) at a certain developmental point (e.g., during middle childhood). And, unless there is further education or training, smiling abilities will remain unchanged through the rest of their lives (unless a person should choose to work at Walt Disney World where smiling is a job requirement and, arguably, elevated to high art, e.g., see Bajgrowicz, 2018).

Methods used by developmental psychologists to study some aspects of the nonverbal communication of pre-linguistic children often feature indirect approaches to ascertain what children may be experiencing (see Schroeder, 2014, November). For example, the rate of sucking a pacifier (when differing from a base rate), as well as computer-assessed looking time (gauged by eye-tracking and pad touching), have been used to study infants' interest in a given stimulus. Northwestern University's Infant Cognition Lab (e.g., see https://sites.northwestern.edu/infantcognitionlab/our-research/) is one of many similar labs around the US employing these and many more methods to understand the world of the pre-linguistic child. Of course, communication studies should follow suit especially when it comes to addressing critically important questions such as the early prolonged exposure to screened media, interfacing of screened media and interpersonal communication skills development, and learning the foundations of interpersonal communication via screened media.

Language. "Reaching becomes pointing; sounds become words; words are combined syntactically to form sentences. This build-up of meaning occurs over about two years [ages 1–2]" (Socha & Yingling, 2010, p. 30). Assuming sensory and cognitive development is within normal ranges (e.g., see Olsson, 2004, concerning children with multiple disabilities), children will utter the first word (e.g., dada, mama, goggie or hi) around 9–12 months and then it is off to the linguistic races with rapid language acquisition and development. Ages 2–4, or the pre-school years, is a time of discovery of new vocabulary and learning communicative forms and routines where children are eager to try out their new and amazing abilities. And, as all adults who have ever cared for children in any capacity can attest, children will repeat everything they hear. Of course, the more often they hear something, the more likely it will be added to their vocabulary and, unless communication education intervenes, words, expressions, or routines will continue to be available to them for their communicative use (and often at the most inopportune moments).

Children are exposed to so many prosocial and antisocial communicative words, expressions, and routines (often for the first time) during the Pre-K years, it baffles us why communication theorists and researchers have almost completely ignored this pivotal period of communication firsts. Analogous to computer coding at the machine-level, for better or worse, the foundations of our lifespan communication processes and routines are laid down during early childhood. And, unless communication education (formal and informal) is successful at teaching children effective and appropriate communication during this time as well as throughout their educations, patterns that take hold may not only be undesirable but will also become increasingly difficult to unlearn and relearn later. For example, most parental advice websites (e.g., see the Australian parenting site: https://raisingchildren.net.au/preschoolers/ behaviour/common-concerns/swearing-toddlers-preschoolers) feature articles, blogs, and discussion boards about managing the problem of potty talk of children ages 3–5. Although perhaps surprising to those outside of early childhood education, many Pre-K and early elementary teachers have classroom stories about frustrated children lobbing F-bombs at their peers as they work on group projects. According to a *Washington Post* article (Wright, 2015) bad language seems to be starting earlier (age 3) and, is more commonplace than in the past due in part to children's increasing exposure to broadcast media (e.g., viewing primetime national speeches of a United States President freely using terms like "bullshit," see Nelson & Fredricks, 2020).

Because the field of communication has devoted such little time to studying communication during this developmental period it has yet to develop and formally test the efficacy of communication curricula for Pre-K students. Thus, a great deal of work lies ahead. But, on the plus side, this also means that the field of early childhood communication theory and research is wide open for inquiry and has tremendous potential to shape future communication development of generations to come.

When studying children's communication, whether verbal message production or message reception, communication researchers must carefully consider developmental linguistics and ask a critically important question: How many years of education are needed in order for a participant to a study or comprehend the words a communication researcher is using? Here, we extend the concept of understanding printed text (readability) to understanding oral speech and employ the *Gunning Fog Index of Readability* (Gunning, 1952, and see the free, online calculator see http://gunning-fog-index.com/index.html). This is a systematic method to assist communicators in language-level approximation as they communicate with children. Here is how it works. Consider the sentence: "The house is big." Submitting this sentence to the computer-based Gunning Fog Index, we find that 1.2 years of education (1st grade, second month) is needed to understand the sentence's semantic and syntactic meaning. However, in order to make sense of the parallel sentence,

"The domicile is of gargantuan proportions," 22.4 years of education (grad-uate-level) is needed. Why is this so? The *Gunning Fog Index* is based on the assumption that easy-to-comprehend sentences contain few words and simple words (1-syllable). Adding more words to a sentence (increasing syn-tactic complexity) and more complex words (i.e., three-or-more-syllables to increase semantic complexity), increases the education level needed in order to comprehend a given sentence. Thus, when adult communicators are speak-ing to children ages 5–6 (first grade), if he/she wants to be understood then he/she should take into account the general maxim that for these younger children, simple words used in short sentences have a better chance of being understood than bigger words used in longer sentences. This is especially an important insight for researchers to consider when seeking to empirically measure and systematically study children's communication, and to do so in such a way to yield valid and reliable results.

Communication researchers, especially those studying child-age partici-pants, must ask, are the study participants able to decode the linguistic mean-ings of any prompts, scales, and questions used in a study? This means that prior to a study, communication researchers should not only use the Gunning Fog Index on their instruments but should also consult with Pre-K and ele-mentary school teachers in order to check the overall approach as well the language of the instruments. And then they should also pre-test the measure with children of the targeted age to make sure that the approach and level of language will have a good chance of yielding valid and reliable results. Thus, lesson one of studying children's communication: Make sure they can under-stand you at a linguistic level.

Adapting Existing Research Methods for Children

Survey studies of communication using questionnaires that contain empir-ically derived measures are commonplace in adult communication studies. But can the same kinds of methodological approaches yield valid and reliable data when studying children? It is obvious that language-based approaches like survey methods cannot be used with pre-linguistic children. But what about children during early and middle childhood? Can children commu-nicate a valid and reliable response using a Likert scale? Research studies in psychology commonly show that children (ages 3–6) are capable of making and communicating valid and reliable dichotomous choices about concrete stimuli such as: yes/no, I like it/I don't like it, or smiley face/yuk face. In an important study, Mellor and Moore (2014) found that using numbers (rather than words) produced low concordance among children ages 6–13. That is, using words are better than using numbers, and further, the dichotomous response yields what they refer to as the gold standard of children's responses. Further, their ability to make concrete dichotomous judgments not only continues throughout the primary grades but can become refined over time. That is, as children's language skills advance (in middle grades 4–6) they become increasing able to also understand and report what "neutral" or "not sure" means and can make increasingly finer distinctions (very much, very little) that are a common feature of Likert scales.

The field of communication is certainly replete with adult-targeted, Likert-type measures of thousands of communication concepts that are integral to understanding, explaining, and predicting communication in a wide array of contexts and relationships. In order to move the communication field towards a lifespan approach, an admittedly massive task facing the field of communication (far larger than available space to be addressed adequately in this chapter) is to ascertain the extent to which any given communication measure used to study adults can be extended (at all or with modification) to study children. If the field of communication is to develop lifespan theories and explanations, a sine qua non is that it must develop methods to assess children's developing communication abilities as well as that of teens, young adults, and seniors.

Given what is already known from past research, it is safe to say that in early childhood most children can make gross, dichotomous judgments about communication stimuli (smiley or yuk). However, it is important to also conduct communication studies to ascertain children's message production abilities so they may be normed. For example, Socha and Kelly (1994) gathered humorous messages from children in grades K–8 and found that very young children (K–3) do have a primitive understanding of what sorts of messages they believe can potentially make other children laugh (e.g., making silly faces, fart sounds, etc.) and that the humor of some children can become increasingly sophisticated as they move into middle school. Unfortunately, their study also showed that not only can children (ages 6–12) tell jokes, but that some children (i.e., boys in about 4th grade) may also acquire adults' anti-social humor communication habits of racist, sexist, and ageist joking. We will have more to say about this agenda item later in the chapter.

Assessing the Changing Communication Abilities of Children

When studying children, researchers must also attend to another measurement problem that is often hidden when studying the communication of adults. That is, communication is constantly developing and changing. During adulthood, communication changes often take place over long periods of time making changes less noticeable. Whereas during childhood, changes take place in far shorter periods of time and are often far more dramatic. For example, at the start of first grade (ages 5–6), most children enter as emergent readers, yet after less than one year, most will leave first grade able to read and comprehend 2nd and 3rd-grade level texts, as well as compose sentences (along with performing lots of mathematical operations and more). We know from past research that development of any sort does not necessarily follow a straight line. It may cycle through stages of progression and regression that include learning, unlearning, and relearning. An example that will resonate with those teaching at the college level is that all college students write their very first grammatically-correct sentences in 1st grade and continue to write sentences throughout K–12 education. Yet, an often-heard complaint of those teaching writing to first-year college students (age-18) is that their students cannot write grammatically correct sentences! Children's communication abilities might even change for the better within the course of participating in a research study but any gains may also disappear quickly if they are not reinforced.

The field of communication is replete with one shot, short-term studies, but lags far behind other fields in studying communication over time. For example, it is useful to empirically demonstrate that a given educational intervention is effective at immediately changing a communication skill or habit, but without longitudinal studies (over years) whether or not the effect can be sustained is left open to serious question, whether studying children or adults. Here too the field of communication lags far behind other fields in studying communication over time. We will also have more to say about this as an agenda item at the close of the chapter.

Planning and Executing Children's Communication Studies

An often-heard complaint (used as an excuse to avoid studying children) heard from researchers is "I don't have access to children," or accessing children is far more difficult than working with college students. There are of course good reasons for this. No parent wants strangers to have access to their offspring. Educators do not want day-to-day educational processes disrupted by a researcher and his/her study, especially if the educational benefit to children in doing so is unclear. Sadly, trusted others who have had access to children have taken advantage of this trust and harmed them, such that today everyone who works with children are now screened for criminal backgrounds. So, yes, it is more difficult today to conduct research about children's communication than in years past. But this does not mean children should be completely abandoned. Rather, researchers should work with children's organizations, institutions, groups and individuals to understand how they can become partners and allies of children and assist in advancing children's development with these organizations and demonstrate that we in the field of communication do have something to share that is of mutual benefit. Researchers should not enter the worlds of children seeking only to benefit themselves but rather should partner with those working with children for the mutual benefit of all. But how should this be done?

First, communication researchers seeking to study children must become better friends with childcare workers, child educators, child professionals, and administrators of children's programs and understand their needs and concerns. For example, when invited, I have provided my services as a guest speaker to local pre-schools, elementary and middle schools, as well as organizations that support schools, including a large annual conference for school nurses run by a local medical school and children's hospital as well as local groups of fathers. At these events, I have shared research findings and best practices from the communication literature as well as my recent studies about smartphone use and children. I have also given talks to parents about an array of topics such as positive communication development, media literacy, talking about sexuality, and more. I have taught online classes for an organization that helps to provide continuing education for pre-K teachers (at no cost) as well as afterschool talks for a parent education program for Pre-K parents. My wife is also a primary grade teacher and administrator. I have learned that there are many needs in education that the communication field can help those in education to meet and there is a willingness to partner and share resources if partnerships are the primary goal and not simply data collection.

Second, today, after-care and before-care child programs are commonplace. Children arrive early to school and stay late after school before heading home. During after-care and once homework is done, children are afforded free time until their pick-up time. This free time can range from 30 minutes to a couple of hours. It is during free time that communication researchers would stand a good chance to be granted access by parents and program administration to work with children in grades Pre-K to 5th or depending on the school PreK to 8. The reasoning here is that participation in a research study during what otherwise would be downtime can be viewed as a learning experience that will not detract from any of the children's other learning experiences during the regular school day. And, because children's school days are complex with lots of moving parts, it is far easier to work with parents and what is often a single aftercare program administrator than several school officials and teachers.

Third, during the summer, when children are out of school, they are often enrolled in day camps of many kinds. Similar to the regular school year, summer camps may also include a before camp and after camp care component. Many camps often span 5 days that will include inevitable unscheduled times. Communication researchers can partner with parents and day camp directors to include children's participation in research studies during these unscheduled times as well as before and after camp times. Going further, with some imagination, planning, and work it may even be possible to create summer "communication camps" where children of all ages could come to work on public speaking skills, group communication leadership skills, interpersonal communication skills, conflict management skills, media production skills, media literacy and, more. Such a camp would not only add important value to children's lives but with proper parental permissions would offer an ongoing lab in which to conduct communication research studies of children.

Finally, gaining access to a diverse population of children is challenging. Depending on their geographic locations, the populations of the aforementioned aftercare and summer camp programs may overrepresent children of middle and upper socioeconomic standings as well as possibly oversample white children (limiting generalizability). Here are some suggestions to manage this important problem. First, choose to partner with Head Start programs, inner-city youth programs, rural 4-H clubs, the YMCA, and other similar programs that include a wide variety of children. Second, partner with a variety of churches, synagogues, temples, and mosques that sponsor youth programs. Children from only one religious denomination will, of course, skew the sample. And, coming from religious organizations may also skew a sample depending on what is being studied. Organizations like the Boys/Girls Clubs and Scouting might also be helpful. Finally, researchers might also want to elicit the help of college students to recruit their brothers, sisters, cousins, and friends. Although still non-random, this kind of approach might be useful in generating a sample of children.

Human Subjects Protections and Children

Children are unable to give legal consent and therefore written permission of a parent/guardian is required before researchers can seek the assent of a person under age18 to participate in a research study. Further, children are a specially protected class of human subjects and as such researchers must take extra care when working with children to make especially certain that no harms arise in the course of a given study. Because of this, it is also not possible for college-level Human Subjects Review Committees to consider studies involving children for an exempt review. Studies with children must be reviewed by a university's full IRB. This, of course, requires detailed paperwork and extra time. In the experience of the first author, researchers should allow 30–60 days to complete the IRB review process for a study involving children. It is often quicker but how long will depend in part on the agenda of the IRB (some months are busier than others).

To increase the chances of success with the IRB, here are some tips. First, include a written statement from the program administrator that the researcher has permission to conduct the study with his/her cooperation. Second, in creating the informed consent document for parents be very clear about what exactly the child will be asked to do in the study, step by step. Paint a very clear picture. Third, offer the children a meaningful incentive. In the experience of the first author, university swag (e.g., pencils, etc.) is preferred over empty-calorie snacks. Fourth, once parental permissions are secured, at a minimum, verbal assent is required from the children to participate in the study. Gathering written children's assent is typically waived by the IRB to afford children anonymity, but this is a matter to negotiate with the IRB. Children who say "no" to a study are thanked, reassured, and returned to free play. Tell the IRB this in the proposal. Fifth, seek the assistance of the program's administrator in gathering parents' signatures on informed consent documents. Program officials usually have systems in place for distributing and managing parental permission slips and lots of documents. As a part of this process, an administrator might ask a researcher to attend scheduled parent meetings to talk about a study and gather signatures there. Flexibility is needed for success. Finally, as a part of the process researchers should be clear about what he/she/they is(are) willing to do for a program in exchange for help. In the experience of the first author, lectures (about the study or another topic of interest) at PTA or similar parent meetings are often most welcomed. And in order to develop long-term partnerships for his graduate students and him, the first author has also participated in faculty in-service days by giving workshops and guest lectures about children's communication and more. Programs and schools are more likely to provide assistance if they are partners in research.

The process of getting any study through IRB review is an important and necessary part of conducting good research. The extra steps necessary in order to conduct research with children in terms of human subject protections are really not all that much onerous than conducting any study that involves risk. And just like any study success involves planning, review, and proper execution.

Conclusion

Research involving children may take a bit more time, planning, and paperwork. But it is not all that much more effort than planning and executing any good research study. And, once good community partnerships are formed, the process of conducting research studies with children is made far easier for researchers and graduate students. Further, these kinds of partnerships may also result in creating new research studies about topics that scholars might not have considered. Going forward, teaching graduate and undergraduate students how to conduct communication research with children should be a standard part of all communication research methods courses so that children can be fully included in communication. Children are communicators too.

References

Bajgrowicz, B. (2018). *30 ridiculous guidelines Disney parks employees have to obey*. Retrieved from https://www.thegamer.com/disney-parks-guidelines-employees-trivia/

Gunning, R. (1952). *The technique of clear writing*. McGraw-Hill.

Harwood, J. (2007). *Understanding communication and aging: Developing knowledge and awareness*. Thousand Oaks, CA: Sage.

Haslett, B. B., & Samter, W. (1997). *Children communicating: The first five years*. Mahwah, NJ: Lawrence Erlbaum.

Heywood, C. M. (2001). *A history of childhood*. Cambridge, UK: Polity.

Moore, K. A. (2014). The use of Likert scales with children. *Journal of Pediatric Psychology*, *39*(3), 369–379.

Meyer, J. C. (2003). *Kid's talking: Learning relationships and culture with children*. Lanham, MD: Rowan & Littlefield.

Miller, S. A. (2007). *Developmental research methods* (3rd ed.). Thousand Oaks, CA: Sage.

Miller-Day, M., Pezalla, A., & Chesnut, R. (2013). Children are in families too!: The presence of children in communication research. *Journal of Family Communication*, *13*(2), 150–165.

Myers, S. A., & Goodboy, A. K. (2005). A study of grouphate in a course in small group communication. *Psychological Reports*, *97*, 381–386.

National Institutes of Health (NIH). (2018). *Inclusion across the lifespan – Policy implementation*. Retrieved from https://grants.nih.gov/grants/funding/lifespan/lifespan.htm

Nelson, S., & Fredricksm B. (2020, February 6). Trump calls Russian probe 'bullshit' in post-impeachment remarks. *New York Post*, retrieved from https://nypost.com/2020/02/06/trump-calls-russia-probe-bullshit-in-post-impeachment-remarks/

Nussbaum. J. F. (Ed.). (2014). *The handbook of lifespan communication*. New York: Peter Lang.

Olsson, C. (2004). Dyadic interaction with a child with multiple disabilities: A system theory perspective on communication. *Augmentative and Alternative Communication, 20,* 228–242.

Pellegrini. A. D. (2009). *The role of play in human development.* Oxford, UK: Oxford University Press.

Pitts, M. J., & Hummert, M. L. (2014). Lifespan communication methodology. In J. F. Nussbaum (Ed.). *The handbook of lifespan communication* (pp. 29–52). New York: Peter Lang.

Schroeder, S. (2014, November). Exploring infant cognition. *Association for Psychological Science Observer,* retrieved from https://www.psychologicalscience.org/observer/exploring-infant-cognition

Socha, T. J., & Kelly, B. (1994). Children making fun: Humorous communication, impression management, and moral development. *Child Study Journal, 24,* 237–252.

Socha, T. J., & Socha, D. M. (1994). Children's task group communication: Did we learn it all in kindergarten? In L. Frey (Ed.), *Group communication in context: Studies of natural groups* (pp. 227–246). Hillsdale, NJ: Lawrence Erlbaum.

Socha, T. J., & Yingling, J, A. (2010). *Families communicating with children.* Cambridge, UK: Polity.

Wood, B. S. (1976). *Children and communication: Verbal and nonverbal language development.* New York: Prentice Hall.

Wright, T. (2015, August 7). *Kids are learning curse words earlier than they used to: And it's all because they hear you using them.* Retrieved from https://www.washingtonpost.com/posteverything/wp/2015/08/07/kids-are-learning-curse-words-earlier-than-they-used-to/

Section Two: Relational Communication Development

4. Children, Parents, and Resilience

Exploring Challenges and Potential of Communication's Contributions to Developmental Thriving

GARY A. BECK
Old Dominion University

KRISTEN CARR
Texas Christian University

For decades, scholars across a variety of disciplines have attempted to explicate the often-detrimental consequences of adverse childhood experiences. As a result of this extensive focus, we know that children who endure stressful, non-normative, and adverse events early in childhood are often more likely to face a variety of social and emotional issues later in life (Benson, 1997; Richardson, 2002). Yet despite these potentially negative consequences of childhood adversity, a small but significant subset of children emerge from adverse childhood circumstances as happy, healthy, and well-functioning adults (Werner & Smith, 1992). When children are able to anticipate, respond, and recover from significant early-life circumstances, we call them resilient.

Resilience is defined as the "successful adaption to adversity" and is often investigated as an individual response to stressful experiences (Zautra, Hall, & Murray, 2010, p. 4). Understanding and promoting resilience in children is particularly important because it provides an opportunity to shape and benefit their later-life functioning as adults. If children develop the early ability to respond resiliently to adverse childhood experiences, it likely becomes a pattern that is built upon and carried into adulthood. Yet increasingly, childhood experiences present numerous and varied sets of challenges across multiple domains with the opportunity to evoke a resilient response to each as they develop.

It is an understatement that in today's society, children are faced with complex challenges. A landmark study examining adverse childhood experiences (ACEs, a cross-section of middle-class adults of varied racial backgrounds and education levels reported that nearly two-thirds of children experienced some type of abuse, neglect or other traumatic experience prior to the age of 18 (Felitti et al., 1998). More than half reported two or more types of childhood adversity, with nearly 60% reporting some form of abuse, 25% reported emotional or physical neglect, and 80% reported one or more household challenges such as parental divorce, parental substance abuse, and/ or domestic violence (Felitti et al., 1998). Even in the absence of these more severe forms of adversity, children face other issues originating from a variety of sources. For example, over 60% of children indicate that they witnessed two or more incidents of bullying in the last month (Gulemetova, Drury, & Bradshaw, 2011), 38% of 12th graders reported using alcohol in the past month (Johnston, O'Malley, Miech, Bachman, & Schulenberg, 2016), and 47% are eligible for free or reduced lunch as a result of their family's socioeconomic status (Glander, 2015).

Some people argue that in an ideal world, childhood would be an easy, idyllic experience, markedly absent of these or any types of adversity. However, given that these stressors cover a wide variety of social and economic issues that continue into adulthood, it seems nearly impossible (and potentially detrimental) to completely shelter children in this way. Additionally, there is some evidence to suggest that early exposure to manageable levels of adversity provides tools to more effectively respond to stress later in life (Lyons & Parker, 2007). The question then becomes, how can we best promote resilience in children, and more specifically, what communication practices contribute to this process?

For children and adults alike, Luthar (2006) summarizes nearly four decades of resilience inquiry by concluding, "resilience rests, fundamentally, on relationships" (p. 780). Because most adverse events have a social component in that we tend to discuss them with others, communication in close relationships plays a significant role in developing a resilient response to stressful events across the lifespan (Carr & Koenig Kellas, 2018; Montpetit, Bergeman, Deboeck, Tiberio, & Boker, 2010). Yet, understanding how communication might promote resilience in children requires an acknowledgment that innovations to our social connections, shifts in modern family structures, and corresponding social, political, and economic uncertainty present contemporary challenges to child development. A common theme across these challenges is that they concurrently create opportunities to clarify the role of communication in the development of children's resilience to stress, adversity, and difficult situations.

When children are faced with adversity, communication often functions as a reflective process associated with incremental learning and experience in a variety of ways. For example, perspective can be offered as a sense-making mechanism from older to younger generations (Lucas & Buzzanell, 2012), and allows for a more mindful approach with more complex schemas and procedural knowledge through advice-giving (MacGeorge et al. 2004), mentorship (Walker, 2007), and a variety of memorable messages (Kranstuber, Carr, & Hosek, 2012; Waldron et al., 2014). Drawing from resilience theory, communication scholars have started to identify the collaborative and fundamental roles of both communication and resilience in successfully responding to challenging life circumstances (Afifi & Keith, 2004, Afifi, Merrill, & Davis, 2015; Buzzanell, 2010; Beck & Socha, 2015; Carr, 2015; Frisby et al. 2012; Wilson et al., 2014). Most recently, Brian Houston and Patrice Buzzanell have served as guest editors on two different issues of the Journal of Applied Communication focused on communication contributions to resilience (Buzzanell & Houston, 2018; Houston & Buzzanell, 2020).

Collectively, this body of developing literature illustrates that resilience can be effectively viewed as a process that emerges *between* people, rather than simply within them. Shifting our focus from a primarily psychological perspective focused on resiliency (i.e., a personality trait) to resilience (i.e., the outcome of a communicative process) highlights the unique contributions of communication to the interdisciplinary concept. Thus, in this chapter, we examine how various communication phenomena promote or compromise the resilient development of capacity for children to deal with stress, adversity, change, uncertainty, hurt, and failure.

Potential for Resilience and Communication

In an effort to identify a more specific framework for the roles that communication plays in the lives of children and their families, four fundamental (but overlapping) areas of inquiry emerge as salient. First, how does communication *function* in promoting resilience in children's lives (e.g., development, well-being, health, and happiness)? Second, in what ways do those with *connections* to children (i.e., the proverbial "village") communicate in ways that contribute (both positively and negatively) to child development? Third, how does communication *manifest* itself? What messages or forms of communication are commonly used to promote and support resilience, and what needs to be used more? Finally, how might we communicatively undermine the resilience in our children, or provide *impediments* towards the opportunity to develop resilience on their own (e.g., counter-productive communicative acts & habits)? The following subsections address these questions with answers supported by theory and research representing both interdisciplinary and communication perspectives.

Functions

Much of the early child development research in resilience focused on *competence*, or effective functioning in the world. At that time, the goal of resilience research was to identify relevant areas of aptitude, often using relative developmental benchmarks or standards of behavior (see Masten & O'Dougherty Wright, 2010). Age-related communication competencies for children include uttering first words, labeling objects, participating in early interaction sequences, displaying empathy and perspective taking, making friends, initiating complex requests, and developing complex models of the other (Miller & DeThorne, 2014; Socha & Yingling, 2010). These general competencies, as well as additional others across various life stages, have been conceptualized as *developmental tasks* (e.g., Bruner, 1966; Elder, 1998), and their achievement signifies comparison points relative to those in one's cohort (e.g., "She's advanced for her age" or "He's behind his classmates"). As children mature, the standard for evaluating competence similarly evolves, reflecting the more complex social structures embedded in relationships and workplace effectiveness (Haslett & Samter, 1997; Masten & O'Dougherty Wright, 2010).

Indeed, the lifespan progression in competence standards reflects the integral role of communication in support of lifelong success and the promotion of social and emotional well-being. Success in one developmental period often leads to success in others. For example, the social skills developed at age 4 in forging early friendships help children identify what qualifies as a "best friend" at age 8, and perhaps what characteristics are desirable in a potential romantic partner in the teenage years (e.g., Haslett & Samter, chapter 7, 1997; Meyer, 2003). It follows that a *lack* of these opportunities to learn, enjoy successes, and even fail has the potential to create a "knowledge gap" or deficiency, which could be compounded in later years (i.e., "developmental cascades," Masten et al., 2005). Therefore, these deficiencies can have a cumulative effect, creating sizeable differences between a child and others in their developmental cohort.

Accepting these communication competency milestones as related to fostering resilience suggests the need for attention to how we address these well in advance of the challenges that typify late adolescence, teenage years, and young adulthood. Some communication behaviors serve as effective in both times of heightened distress and less challenging routine, "day to day" functioning. For example, modeling general social practices and efficacious interaction patterns (Bandura, 1979), positive communication and habits (Socha & Pitts, 2012; Socha & Yingling, 2010), practicing mindfulness (Manusov & Harvey-Knowles, 2015), and engaging in effective conflict management (Wilmot & Hocker, 2013) typify fundamental characteristics of strength-promoting communication regardless of context.

To this point, ongoing communication has an iterative function in helping family members (children included) coordinate meaning, make sense of the routine and the unexpected moments in life, and actively create a sense of balance and predictability in each other's lives. Such communication practices function in a manner that generally benefit all members in a system (Bowen, 1974), operating in interdependent and corresponding ways to preserve the system as it reacts to both internal and external disruptions.

Connections

A central premise to interpersonal, relational, and family communication research is the role of interdependence. In close relationships, the communication choices we make are not conducted in a vacuum; rather, they are impacted by and have an impact on those closest to us. As noted above, family systems theory (e.g., Bowen, 1974) invokes a web of influence and interdependence among family members and extended network members in the sense making and relevant interaction before, throughout, and following significant life events (Galvin & Young, 2010; Theiss, 2018). As such, the individual potential for resilience is inherently tied to the meaning we create and continue to co-construct with close others including children.

Uri Bronfenbrenner's socio-ecological model is a useful framework for considering the child (or parent-child relationship) at the center different levels of influence that shape developmental outcomes and wellbeing (Bronfenbrenner, 1979; Ungar, Gazinour, & Richer, 2013). Rather than simply focus on the individual, more inclusive and sophisticated theorizing can account for the complexity of the social ecology in which individuals are imbedded. After mapping current resilience work across Bronfenbrenner's model, Ungar et al. (2013) derived three patterns important to a socio-ecological view on resilience: *Equifinality* (i.e., multiple different factors can have an effect on outcomes given the circumstances), *differential impact* (i.e., resources function in different ways: compensating, buffering, mediating, and so on), and *cultural moderation* (i.e., access and utilization of particular resources is filtered through cultural expectations and value-systems). Thus, interrelationships between the micro, macro, and social and historical context emerge as a byproduct of the extended system in which the resilience process and those it affects are imbedded (Bogenschneider, 1996). Importantly, this also implies that depending on context and culture, communication's effectiveness or purpose may vary across families and children.

Consistent with this recognition of multiple contributors across a social ecology, communal coping is a conceptual model that accounts for the variety of factors in response to a serious stressor. Those that are coping with a stressor or challenge communally often use shared interpretations and resources to coordinate their responses (Krouse & Afifi, 2007; Lyons et al., 1998). Through this process, stressors are not solely experienced as isolated individual level phenomena (e.g., "my issues" or "your challenge") but instead, as something to be faced together ("our struggle"). With open communication within and across families, children and their parents are not struggling alone, but instead share the challenges and uncertainty with a larger community. Indeed, when families communicate to maintain a balance of both family cohesion (i.e., emotional bonding) and adaptability (i.e., flexibility in family roles), they are better able to promote resilience, regardless of the amount of adversity they experienced (Carr & Koenig Kellas, 2018).

Scholars have attempted to characterize how communication in both close relationships (e.g., communication characterized by tact, respect, civility, partnership, tension release, and discretion; see Beck, 2016) and families (e.g., family communication patterns, e.g., Ledbetter & Beck, 2014; maintenance and coping strategies, see Afifi et al., 2015) has the potential to promote resilience. Family communication patterns, in particular the conversation dimension (i.e., encouraging openness, dialogue), was found to contribute to family strengths (Thompson & Schrodt, 2014). Those families found to have been assessed with higher levels of family strengths can be characterized by (a) regular expressions of affection and appreciation, (b) a commitment to the wellbeing of each family member, (c) positive communication and the ability to resolve conflict constructively, (d) a tendency to enjoy quality time together, (e) a sense of spiritual well-being, and (f) an ability to effectively manage stress and unexpected crisis (DeFrain & Stinett, 2003).

While such a list may seem in some ways like an idealized (utopian) family checklist, it does suggest that most of these characteristics are proactively established patterns of interaction during "normal" or typical day-to-day experiences. Promoting positive communication, finding moments to enjoy life and each other, and appreciating children, parents, and extended members of the family are all things that can be developed and established as part of typical family functioning. Perhaps only two, (c) "... resolving conflict effectively" and (f) "... managing stress and unexpected crisis," are more deliberately about handling stressors or negative experiences, or more standard "reactive" conceptions of resilience. Across all of the above representations of family and relational communication, an emphasis on engaging in positive and respectful communication plays a particularly relevant role in children's communication development. Looking more specifically as particular communication practices and messages that manifest within these contexts highlights the benefits of specific, targeted investigations.

Manifestations

From birth, children receive a variety of messages that promote developmental competencies and support the development of resilience. Perhaps the most significant sources of resilience-supporting messages come from both regular and meaningful family interaction (Socha & Yingling, 2010). Indeed, families provide the first lens through which children see the world, and communicative behaviors that emerge in family interaction–whether good or bad–often have long-ranging effects for children (Socha & Yingling, 2010). Thus, to account for how resilience-promoting messages enter our children's lives from the sources that influence them, the sections below summarize theories and perspectives that examine the incremental modeling and scaffolding (e.g., Bruner, 1966) of fundamental social skills: Social cognitive theory, media effect theories, storytelling and family narratives, redemption and contamination sequences, coping and support, memorable messages, and advice.

Social cognitive theory. As one of the central theories of development, social cognitive theory (SCT) provides an explanation for how children learn by watching the actions of others, and then modeling those behaviors (Bandura, 1979). The theory remains one of the most popular theoretical frameworks for investigations of children's communication (Miller-Day, Pezalla, & Chesnutt, 2013). Within a resilience framework, children consistently observe how their family members interact, cope with life's challenges, and recover with varying degrees of effectiveness, all while innately internalizing schemas and procedural knowledge. SCT is commonly used to investigate the degree of impact of negative media messages, such as the internalization of the "thin ideal" (Te'eni-Harai, & Eyal, 2015) and sexual content (Bond & Drogos, 2014).

Media effects theories. Aside from more routine, daily forms of parent-child interaction, the average day for a modern child is beset with a preponderance of media messages. Data from the Kaiser foundation (Rideout, Foehr, & Roberts, 2010) suggests that children ages 8–18 spent approximately seven and a half hours per day viewing media. After accounting for sleep and school, this doesn't leave much time for regular meaningful or substantive family interaction. However, media consumption has the potential to promote prosocial behavior (Mares & Woodard, 2007), school readiness (Fisch, 2004), and general thriving and flourishing (de Leeuw & Buijzen (2016; and see Webb, 201, for an overview of digital and social media in families).

Storytelling and narratives. According to narrative theory, humans are "homo-narrans," or inherently storytelling creatures (Fisher, 1984). We talk about past events, experiences, or significant times to others in the form of narrative stories as a way to make sense of difficult experiences (Bochner, Ellis, & Tillmann-Healy, 1997). Narratives can be particularly beneficial in coping with adversity and promoting resilience in children because as we tell stories, we think about ourselves and enact certain behaviors according to what we believe to be true about ourselves, based on the narratives we tell. One example of narrative sense-making that may be salient in understanding the development of resilience in children is the process of joint family story-telling.

Families can be enormously influential in helping children make sense of difficulty through the way they frame and jointly tell stories about their collective challenging experiences. For example, Koenig-Kellas and Trees (2006) reported that in family triads (which included at least one child and one parent), families were able to reach a shared conclusion regarding the meaning of a shared difficult experience when the telling of these stories reflects family members' higher level of engagement, perspective taking, turn-taking, and expressed interpretations.

Yet another way that a narrative perspective can inform the development of resilience in children is through the creation of redemption sequences in our life stories. McAdams (1990) argues that during the creation of our life stories, we are both "history and historians–storytellers who create the self in the process" (p. 151). Yet, beginning at a very early age, individuals can, and do, communicatively alter the tone of their life stories. For example, young adults who were able to "re-story" negative life experiences as redemptive enjoyed increased life satisfaction and well-being, regardless of the degree of negative affect present in their original story (McAdams, Reynold, Lewis, Patten, & Bowman, 2001). In addition, narratives often include both factual details and personal interpretation of events, affected by those who listen to them (Pasupathi, 2001) Thus, it seems that the way children frame themselves in their life stories is ultimately more influential in the development of their resilience than the events that actually occur.

Coping and support. In the context of managing adversity, social support is defined as "the process of interaction which improves coping, esteem, belonging, and competence through actual or perceived exchanges of physical or psychosocial resources" (Gottlieb, 2000, p. 28). Theoretically, there are two ways of conceptualizing the impact of social support in developing children's resilience. First, the main effects model suggests that social support is beneficial to the physical and psychological wellbeing of an individual, irrespective of whether that children are experiencing stress. According to this model, a sense of integration within a larger social network such as a family or community may provide children with regular positive interactions and the feeling that they have a safety net to fall back on should adversity occur. In contrast, the buffering effect model posits that social support, though generally helpful, is particularly critical in times of acute stress as it serves as a protective buffer from its negative effects. In this model, social support alters children's appraisal of stressful events, such that even significant adverse occurrences seem less negative in the presence of supportive interaction. Although there is empirical support for both models, the distinction between them (and, indeed, the importance of communication) is highlighted by examining variations in the nature of the supportive message.

All supportive messages are not created equal and, consequently, all support is not equally beneficial to children. The concept of person-centeredness assesses the degree to which a support provider communicates to validate a person's feelings and encourages him or her to talk about the adverse or stressful event (Burleson, 1994). Highly person-centered messages invite distressed individuals to explicitly verbalize their feelings surrounding the stressful event, and to examine why they are experiencing those emotions. In contrast, low person-centered messages often avoid the discussion of emotions surrounding the stressful event, and instead offer dismissive "quick fix" solutions that minimize the presence of the problem. As one might expect, highly person-centered messages often have a direct beneficial effect on emotional improvement, but also encourage individuals to verbalize their thoughts and emotions, which allows them to reappraise stressful situations in ways that are beneficial in facilitating emotional improvement (Jones & Wirtz, 2006) and resilience in children.

Memorable messages. Memorable messages (Knapp et al., 1981; Lucas & Buzzanell, 2010) often function as intergenerational transmissions of prescriptive insight that people hold onto across time. Numerous communication scholars have expanded upon Knapp and colleagues' (1981) initial conceptualization, adding forms and functions such messages can take: Moral messages (Waldron, 2014), cultural indoctrination (Stohl, 1986), revelations, universal truths, and aphorisms (Merolla, Beck, & Jones, 2016), and guidelines for behavior (Smith & Ellis, 2001). Regardless, these messages are often reported as received by those younger (e.g., children) and deemed addition-ally memorable the more they are seen as credible and positive. Indeed while a receiver's hindsight bias may prefer to report messages that match positive views of the past, these messages and their retention at all seems to suggest an overall preference at the time of reception for messages that promote positive views of the world.

Memorable messages play a particular relevant role in providing guid-ance to children in experiences relevant to them, including school suc-cess (Kranstuber, Carr, & Hosek, 2012). Although their study focused on college-aged offspring, they reported that parents provided guidance across their lifespan in a number of ways that linked message interpreta-tion (i.e., valance) and sender characteristics (e.g., relationship satisfaction) with outcomes like empowerment, motivation, and satisfaction with the college experience. Of importance here was not necessarily *what was said* (content-wise), but more how it was said and the nature of the connection between the parent and the offspring. Thus, children's potential for pro-ducing resilience in the face of school-related challenges was established well ahead of the experience in the form of a quality, open, and trusting parent-child connection.

Advice. Similar in some ways to memorable messages, advice often also has a lasting effect on those who retain it. This instrumental behavior has a wide variety of outcomes depending on its delivery and its perceived ability to address problem solving (MacGeorge et al., 2004). In a child's life, parents, siblings, extended family members, mentors, and teachers, among others, are in positions to provide advice for a variety of developmental circumstances (e.g., see Socha & Stamp, 2009). But when can advice be most effective, and potentially contribute to the child's resilience? In an inventory of "advice about giving advice" MacGeorge, Feng, & Thompson (2008), list five con-siderations: (1) situational appropriateness, (2) the credibility and relationship between advice-giver and receiver, (3) delivered in a style that isn't threaten-ing or demeaning, (4) quality advice (e.g., useful, effective, feasible, ideally free from drawbacks), and (5) hesitations on the side of the receiver. Those looking to contribute to a child's resilience must weight their words carefully, even realizing that not everyone is looking for advice.

Impediments. Factors that impact resilience and the (in)ability to respond effectively to challenges in life are primarily in line with risk factors to development. These include meeting physical and emotional developmen-tal needs such as receiving proper nutrition, securing connections with pri-mary caregivers (Bowlby, 1979), and ongoing engagement and stimulation across childhood. Additionally, and as unique contributions, children need opportunities to challenge themselves, both with and without the guidance and structure provided by more competent "teachers" (Vygotsky, 1978).

Thus, an important question emerges: How might we communicatively (albeit, unintentionally) undermine the resilience in our children, or prevent them from the opportunity to develop resilience on their own? There are at least three related but distinct patterns of interaction with potential to impede or diminish children's resilience. First, and perhaps most obviously, children's resilience is frequently affected by dysfunctional practices that are communicatively reinforced over time and become part of the larger fabric of a family's coping practices. Second, children's ability to respond resiliently might be impeded by parents' and caregivers' seemingly helpful but counter-productive communicative practices while earning victories. Finally, it is also likely that children's resilience might be minimized through actions that limit opportunities for self-expansion.

Dysfunctional communication practices. Less than ideal responses to challenging and adverse circumstances are bound to happen within families. Taken independently, these less beneficial responses are not inherently detrimental. However, when these dysfunctional responses emerge as patterns and habits that become a part of their collective identity, they have the potential to negatively affect children's resilience. Examples of dysfunctional communication practices that impact a child's potential for producing resilience include: Conflict riddled households, domestic violence, verbal aggression, neglect, lack of supervision (including regarding media), sibling bullying, and various forms of abuse (for a review, Olsen, Baiocchi-Wagner, Kratzer, Symonds, 2012). Additionally compromising communication practices may include the lack of fundamental uplifting communication, including laughter, encouragement, joy, love, and overall senses of feeling valued and heard. If a family resolves "things need to change," it may be salient to remember that developing new and improved communication habits usually involves dropping bad ones. This is a corresponding change, as the old practices must make way for new ones in regular and consistent ways. Given that practices taken as new communication habits typically take time, families need to allow themselves the time and patience to see a change through. More serious dysfunction, related to any of the more extreme practices listed above will require family therapy and possibly additional levels of intervention.

Denying victories. Developmental growth depends on not only nurturing environments but also on challenging ones. Such fertile contexts provide safe environments that allow children to try novel activities, make new friendships, and develop skills previously unknown. The role of the teacher (or parent) in this is crucial: Too much oversight and the child won't actually acquire the competences for themselves (e.g., the proverbial providing fish versus teaching how to catch them), but not enough guidance and the child may not be able to perform (and potentially become discouraged). Contemporary examples across this spectrum of involvement include *helicopter parenting* (Odenweller, Booth-Butterfield, & Weber, 2004) and general over-involvement (Givertz & Segrin, 2014). Parents that are vested in the success of their children may find self-assessment in this regard challenging, as well as balancing healthy amounts of involvement. Generally, maintaining open dialogue, positive encouragement, and perspective on the developmental level of the child can generate circumstances where children feel personally responsible for achieving important developmental victories.

Limiting opportunities: Self-expansion theory. An intriguing process of social growth has been explored through self-expansion theory (Aron & Aron, 1997; Schindler, Paech, & Löwenbrück, 2015). Hand in hand with resilience theory, children need to be put into situations to learn from others that provide additional perspectives, experiences, and worldviews. In this way, the theory suggests that people can expand their sense of self by building meaningful connections and developing communication skills allow for more fortuitous interaction. Parents are no stranger to finding such opportunities for their children; they often include activities such as sending the child to summer camp, joining a team sport or club, attending church and generally becoming connected to that larger community. Historically, these have been hallmark developmental experiences, with reflecting both joyous and "traumatic" experiences in challenging social situations (Masten & O'Dougherty Wright, 2010).

Where the challenges for the modern child present themselves are in modern online interactions. Online interactions over the last decade have increased the anonymity, social isolation, body image issues, and lead to a rise in online bullying. These interactions, often through social media, chat applications, and gaming communities are clearly a part of the modern socialization, and yet so few are prepared or resistant enough to "turn the other cheek." Evidence suggests that bystander's reactions to bullying attempts are an important deterrent (Davis & Davis, 2007), and even parental involvement with a child's media consumption can play an important mediator (Livingstone & Helsper, 2008). Children may not welcome adult intrusion in a world they feel they populate free from adult supervision, but being proactively accessible and interested likely serves as a resource managing new experiences with resilience.

Praxis: Application and Intervention

Resilience interventions fit within a larger conversation about the role of social science in addressing concerns related to human functioning. More traditional interdisciplinary models, many establishing prominence in the 1940s and 1950s, emphasized treating the dysfunction (i.e., illness model, deficit model), with a focus on mental illness. As noted by Shatte, Seligman, Gillham, and Reivich (2003), "societies under conditions of threat or deficit, as was the case in the immediate postwar years, trend naturally toward a focus on the negative aspects of life" (p. 66). Importantly, recent experiences with the worldwide economic recession, enduring challenges with global terrorism, and the uncertainties related to the technological changes to education, healthcare, and socialization once again pushed not only prevalent thinking but research to dark places (Cupach & Spitzberg, 2010; Olsen, Baiocchi-Wagner, Kratzer, Symonds, 2012). In these times, people seek to understand and then respond to the experiences that caused them discomfort, pain, and loss.

The corresponding piece to the illness model is the prevention model. Prevention models are more in line with positive psychology, and have alternatively been labeled "capacity building" or "strength building" models. For practitioners, this means either developing positive therapeutic outcomes within traditional psychotherapy or counseling, building a pre-emptive response to anticipate developmental challenges, or minimizing the impact of challenges already present (see Gillham et al., 2000). Indeed, prevention programs often set themselves apart by the notion that they are "equal opportunity": Illness models tend to only treat or focus on the sick, whereas prevention programs see benefits in building strengths in everyone. An important component of prevention is knowing what you are preventing: Often times, lived experiences and shared stories of challenges become warnings and a part of a culture that wants to preserve its way of life. In this way, proactive awareness and readiness become hallmarks of effective demonstrations of resilience. A recent example of this as it relates to our present topic are Youth Mentoring prevention-style programs that emerged as a result of increased awareness of risks in a community's youth and in those surrounding (Wilson & Gettings, 2012).

Given the broad scope of interdisciplinary research that has embraced resilience theory and applied developmental scholarship (e.g., interventions, case studies), there is a plethora of viable examples that may serve as buildings blocks for future applied resilience work. Importantly, youth intervention often represents bookends of the resilience spectrum: Either promoting strengths (proactive) or dealing with problems when they occur (or are identified as significant, see deficit-based approaches or reactive, Zimmerman & Brenner, 2010). A comprehensive intervention plan (i.e., proactive, active, reactive), while embracing the nature of this cyclical maturation process would likely need broader and more programmatic support (see Chapter 1, this volume).

Within schools, programs seek to bolster educational outcomes through character building, social skill development, and reinforcing study habits (Wilson, Chernichky, Wilkum, & Owlett, 2014); positive school environments buffer adolescents from risks (Garmezy, 1991; Werner & Smith, 1992), whether the focus of the intervention is developing strengths (i.e., assets, identifying and building resources) or addressing problem areas. The home and community are also important sites for resilience intervention. These include programs for families struggling with alcoholism (Spoth, Redmond, & Shin, 1998), Father & Sons Programs (e.g., Caldwell et al., 2004), and Youth Empowerment Solutions for Peaceful Communities (Franzen, Morrel-Samuels, Reichl, & Zimmerman, 2009).

Child interventions run in parallel to framing resilience as a process; the function of interventions is often to compensate, modify, or eliminate negative or challenging circumstances. To further inform readers regarding how such interventions fit within resilience theory, the following subsections highlight several representative examples of effective interventions in contexts relevant to children. Although both have the potential to be equally effective, these programs can be broadly categorized as focusing on either resilience-promoting messages, or resilience-promoting relationships. The first two examples, the *Penn Resiliency Program* and *Transforming Lives*, have message-specific components that center on a prescriptive, structured approach to using communication to support the development of resilience in children. The second two examples, the *Urban Warriors* program and CASA, both focus instead on establishing and developing interpersonal relationships between at-risk children and adults as a means to provide social support and resilience.

Penn Resiliency Program

Originating in the 1980s as the Penn Optimism Program for children, this 20-hour program was renamed the Penn Resiliency Program (PRP) after a serendipitous few years of accepting children that were less "at risk" than the program typically worked with. (Shatte et al., 2003). The eureka moment that occurred from expanding their work to a broader group of children were that their interventions worked more effectively as general problem solving and resilience development. In addition to teaching children to adopt alternative explanatory styles (e.g., generate multiple reasons why they did poorly on a test), there were eleven specific skill sets developed over the course of the intervention. Although all have relevance toward a larger sense of agency in school and problem solving, of particular active communicative and message-based relevance include putting things in perspective (Skill 5), assertiveness and negotiating (Skill 7), and social problem solving (including perspective taking, Skill 1; Shatte el al., 2003).

Transforming Lives

At the University of Texas at Austin, Dr. Mary A. Steinhardt has developed a web-based program called "Transforming Lives through Resilience Education." In each of the four online modules, participants are guided through lectures, assignments, activities, and quizzes designed to promote message-based competence as well as cognitive flexibility and strength in the face of life's challenges. Perhaps more importantly, a 2008 study found that college students in the experimental group reported significant increases in coping strategies and protective factors, and significant decreases in stress-related symptomology after completing the programs in 4 two-hour weekly sessions (Steinhardt & Dolbier, 2008).

Urban Warriors

Children growing up in dangerous urban environments such as East Garfield Park in Chicago are often considered at risk because of the amount of violence they experience at an early age. Bearing witness to beatings, shootings, and other gang-related deaths is difficult to endure and make sense of. Many children lack an outlet to discuss these experiences with others, and perhaps as a result, become accustomed to them as a part of life among truly challenging developmental circumstances (Cicchetti & Lynch, 1993).

The YMCA of Metro Chicago's *Urban Warriors* program centers on the idea that children in urban neighborhoods such as this one need to talk about these difficult experiences with other people who can relate as a means to help them cope and respond in a more resilient way. Because many of the children frame their experiences as war-like, the program connects kids who live in high-violence neighborhood with veterans who have served in Iraq or Afghanistan. Together, they can "process their experiences with violence, develop and share coping skills, and identify the strengths they have developed and how they can channel them to benefit their communities," (http://www.ymcachicago.org/programs/youth-safety-and-violence-prevention-urban-warriors). In a way, these veterans become valuable mentors to children about surviving violence and then finding a way out.

Court Appointed Special Advocates (CASA) for Children

Many people mistakenly believe that simply removing children from their harmful environment can ameliorate some types of childhood adversity such as abuse or neglect. What many don't realize is that the process of removing a child from their home is, in itself, traumatic, regardless of how negative the circumstances, and children are often thrust into an overburdened foster care system that makes it easy for them to get lost (Ward, 2012).

With this in mind, CASA volunteers are appointed by judges to build relationships with and advocate for abused and neglected children in the foster care system. Volunteers develop and maintain an interpersonal relationship with the child as a means to provide both perceived and enacted social support until the case is closed and the child is placed in a safe, permanent home. Unlike other aspects of the foster care system, CASA volunteers are solely invested in the well-being of the child. For many abused children, their CASA volunteer is the one consistent adult presence in their lives. Research confirms that children who have CASA volunteers do better in school, display more positive attitudes, value their own achievements, and demonstrate an ability to work out conflicts. In this way, CASA involvement helps to foster resilience in the lives of these children, despite the immense challenges of their home environment towards positive functioning.

Future Directions

As demonstrated by this review, there is a clear need and opportunity for communication scholarship to inform the functions, connections, manifestations, and applications that messages and interaction plays in developing resilience. Given that process perspectives attempt to account for not only the responses to adverse circumstances (reactive), but also factors that contribute to the anticipation (proactive) and ongoing experiences (active), investigations of family communication patterns, climates, conflict management strategies, positive communication habits, and even celebrations of life's best moments all have a role to play in this emerging paradigm (Reich, Zautra, & Hall, 2010).

Many would argue that such communication phenomena are already being investigated, some with richer traditions than others (e.g., coping, relationship maintenance, social support). Indeed, there are examples of scholarship that resemble resilience theorizing, at least in the sense that it isn't primarily operating from "deficit" or disease models. This work has often operated from the starting place of alternative communication theories, with different assumptions and (in some cases long-standing) expectations for how to test those theories' assumptions. There is a fallacy in conflating similar concepts to resilience if the goal of that scholarship is to inform resilience in a way that communication research can converse with the work from related disciplines.

As this pertains to the study of children's communication, the reality is that there are limited organized investigations as a field. Among family communication scholarship (in which the parent is often reporting about the family and children), only 14% focused on the children themselves (Miller-Day, Pezalla, & Chesnutt, 2013, and see Socha & Yingling, 2010, as well as Chapter 1, this volume). Further, there are no children's communication divisions at any national or regional communication associations. Standout scholars and "lifespan" theorists aside, much of the work relating to "communication and age" has been focused on the aging or older adult populations. This is a critical growth area for not only communication scholars, but also for investigations into resilience, which has often been framed as a developmental and lifespanning topic (Masten et al., 2005).

Thankfully, the answer to this situation is within reach: Communication scholars within instructional, interpersonal, family, and health communication divisions, as well as media scholars all have the potential to coordinate investigations towards communication's contribution to children's communication development and towards understanding the development of resilience. Further, our field has a wide-range of theories that can be extended into childhood, especially as we examine logical overlaps with the development of resilience across life experiences and in meaningful relationships. Resilience theory, as cast more deliberately with attention to contributing communication phenomena, may help lead to way toward more concentrated research and faculty collaboration in years to come.

Conclusions

For scholars, parents, and the proverbial "village" attempting to raise healthy children capable of achievement and confident responses to life challenges, fostering resilience has never been a more appropriate life competency worthy of our attention. Historically, we have been interested in developing children with self-esteem, a sense of discipline, and who are capable of love and deserving of happiness. All of these have been worthy goals, but most have been positioned with the assumption that their achievement is largely possible when we determine what dysfunction needs to be addressed that is holding them back. For those with serious mental or emotional deficiencies, this approach is clearly warranted. For many others, the promotion of positive communication practices and competencies towards growth, fostering opportunities, and healthy responses to adversity seems like a viable counterpart to existing methods. Our contention is communication theory and practice (both extant and future scholarship) has a valuable and important role to play in charting a course forward for our children and their resilience.

References

Afifi, T., & Keith, S. (2004). A risk and resiliency model of ambiguous loss in postdivorce stepfamlies. *Journal of Family Communication, 4,* 65–98.

Afifi, T. D., Merrill, A., Davis. S. (2015). *The theory of resilience and relational load.* Paper presented at the annual meeting of the International Communication Association, San Juan, Puerto, Rico.

Aron, A., & Aron, E. N. (1997). Self-expansion motivation and including other in the self. In S. Duck (Ed.), *Handbook of personal relationships: Theory, research and interventions* (2nd ed., pp. 251–270). Hoboken, NJ: John Wiley & Sons.

Bandura, A. (1979). *Social learning theory.* Englewood Cliffs, NJ: Prentice Hall.

Beck, G. A. (2016). Surviving involuntary unemployment together: The role of resilience-promoting communication. *Journal of Family Communication, 16*(4), 369–385. doi:10.1080/15267431.2016.1215315.

Beck, G. A., & Socha, T. J. (Eds.). (2015). *Communicating hope & resilience across the lifespan.* New York: Peter Lang.

Benson, P. I. (1997). *All kids are our kids.* Minneapolis, MN: Search Institute.

Bochner, A. P., Ellis, C., & Tillmann-Healy, L. M. (1997). Relationships as stories. In S. W. Duck (Ed.), *Handbook of personal relationships: Theory, research, and interventions* (2nd ed., pp. 107–124). Chichester, England: Wiley.

Bogenschneider, K. (1996). An ecological risk protective theory for building prevention programs, policies, and community capacity to support youth. *Family Relations, 45,* 127–138.

Bond, B. J., & Drogos, K. L. (2014). Sex on the shore: Wishful identification and parasocial relationships as mediators in the relationship between jersey shore exposure and emerging adults' sexual attitudes and behaviors. *Media Psychology, 17*(1), 102–126. doi:10.1080/15213269.2013.872039.

Bowen, M. (1974). Alcoholism as viewed through family systems theory and psychotheraphy. *Annals of the New York Academy of Sciences, 233,* 115–122. doi:10.1111/j.1749-6632.1974.tb40288.x.

Bowlby, J. (1979). *The making and breaking of affectional bonds.* London: Tavistock.

Bronfenbrenner, E. (1979). *Theecology of human development: Experiments by nature and design.* Cambridge, MA: Harvard University Press.

Bruner, J. S. (1966). *Toward a theory of instruction.* Cambridge, MA: Belkapp Press.

Burleson, B. R. (1994). Comforting messages: Significance, approaches, and effects. In B. R. Burleson, T. L. Albrecht, & I. G. Sarason (Eds.), *Communication of social support: Messages, interactions, relationships, and community* (pp. 3–29). Thousand Oaks, CA: Sage.

Buzzanell, P. M. (2010). Presidential address – resilience: Talking, resisting, and imagining, new normalcies into being. *Journal of Communication, 60*, 1–14.

Buzzanell, P. M., & Houston, J. B. (2018). Communication and resilience: Multilevel applications and insights – A Journal of Applied Communication Research forum. *Journal of Applied Communication Research, 46*(1), 1–4. doi:10.1080/00909882.2017.1412086.

Caldwell C. H., Sellers, R. M., Bernat, D. H., & Zimmerman, M. A. (2004). Racial identity, parental support, and alcohol use in a sample of academically atrisk African American high school students. *American Journal of Community Psychology. 34*, 71–81.

Carr, K. (2015). Communication and family resilience. In C. R. Berger & M. E. Roloff (Eds.), *International encyclopedia of interpersonal communication*. Hoboken, NJ: Wiley Blackwell.

Carr, K., & Koenig Kellas, J. (2018). Examining the role of family and marital communication in understanding resilience to family-of-origin adversity. *Journal of Family Communication, 18*, 68–84. doi:10.1080/15267431.2017.1369415.

Cicchetti, D., & Lynch, M. (1993). An ecological-transactional analysis of children and contexts: The longitudinal interplay among child maltreatment, community violence, and children's symptomatology. *Development and Psychopathology, 10*, 235–257.

and adjustment of early adolescent boys. *Child Development, 63*, 526–541.

Cupach, W. R., & Spitzberg, B. H. (2010). *The dark side of close relationships II*. New York: Routledge.

Davis, S., & Davis, J. (2007). Empowering bystanders in bullying prevention. City: Research Press.

DeFrain, J., & Stinnett, N. (2003). Family strengths. In J. J. Ponzetti (Ed.), *International encyclopedia of marriage and family* (2nd ed., pp. 637–642). New York, NY: Macmillan Reference Group.

de Leeuw, R. N. H., & Buijzen, M. (2016). Introducing positive media psychology to the field of children, adolescents, and media. *Journal of Children & Media, 10*(1), 39–46.

Elder, G. H. (1998). The life course as developmental theory. *Child Development, 69*, 1–12.

Felitti, V. J., Anda, R. F., Nordenberg, D., Williamson, D. F., Spitz, A. M., Edwards, V., ... Marks, J. S. (1998). Relationship of childhood abuse and household dysfunction to many of the leading causes of death in adults. *American Journal of Preventative Medicine, 14*, 245–258. doi:10.1016/S0749–3797(98)00017–8.

Fisch, S. M. (2004). *Children's learning from educational television*. Mahwah, NJ: Erlbaum.

Fisher, Walter R. (1984). Narration as human communication paradigm: The case of public moral argument. *Communication Monographs, 51*, 1–22.

Franzen, S., Morrel-Samuels, S., Reischl, T., & Zimmerman, M. (2009). Using process evaluation to strengthen intergenerational partnerships in the Youth Empowerment Solutions program. *Journal of Intervention and Prevention in the Community, 37*(4), 289–301.

Frisby, B. N., Booth-Butterfield, M., Dillow, M. R., Martin, M., & Weber, K. (2012). Face and resilience in divorce: The impact on emotions, stress, and post-divorce relationships. *Journal of Social and Personal Relationships, 29*(6), 715–735. doi:10.1177/0265407512443452.

Galvin, K. M. & Young, M. A. (2010). Family systems theory and genetics: Synergistic interconnections. In C. Gaff & C. L. Bylund (Eds.). *Family communication about genetics* (pp. 102–119). New York, NY: Oxford University Press.

Garmezy, N. (1991). Resiliency and vulnerability to adverse developmental outcomes associated with poverty. *American Behavioral Scientist, 34*, 416–430.

Gillham, J. E. (Ed). (2000). *The science of optimism and hope: Research essays in honor of Martin E. P. Seligman.* Philadelphia: Templeton Foundation Press.

Givertz, M., & Segrin, C. (2014). The association between overinvolved parenting and young adults' self-efficacy, psychological entitlement, and family communication. *Communication Research, 41*(8), 1111–1136. doi:10.1177/0093650212456392.

Glander, M. (2015). Selected statistics from the public elementary and secondary education universe: School year 2013–14. Retrieved from http://nces.ed.gov/pubs2015/2015151.pdf

Gottlieb, B. H. (2000). Selecting and planning support interventions. In S. Cohen, L. G. Underwood, & B. H. Gottlieb (Eds.), *Social support measurement and intervention: A guide for health and social scientists* (pp. 195–220). New York: Oxford University Press.

Gulemetova, M., Drury, D., & Bradshaw, C. (2011) National Education Association bullying study. *Colleagues, 6*, 13–15.

Haslett, B., & Samter, W. (1997). *Children communicating: The first five years.* Mahwah, NJ: Lawrence Erlbaum.

Houston, J. B., & Buzzanell, P. M. (2020). Communication and resilience: Introduction to the journal of applied communication research special issue. *Journal of Applied Communication Research, 48*(1), 1–4. doi:10.1080/00909882.2020.1711956.

Johnston, L. D., O'Malley, P. M., Miech, R. A., Bachman, J. G., & Schulenberg, J. E. (2016). *Monitoring the future national survey results on drug use, 1975–2015: Overview, key findings on adolescent drug use.* Ann Arbor: Institute for Social Research, The University of Michigan.

Jones, S. M., & Wirtz, J. G. (2006). How does the comforting process work? An empirical test of an appraisal-based model of comforting. *Human Communication Research, 32*, 217–243.

Koenig Kellas, J., & Trees, A. R. (2006). Finding meaning in difficult family experiences: Sense-making and interaction processes during joint family storytelling. *Journal of Family Communication, 6*, 49–76. doi:10.1207/s15327698jfc0601_4.

Knapp, M. L., Stohl, C., & Reardon, K. K. (1981). "Memorable" messages. *Journal of Communication 31*, 27–41. doi:10.1111/j.1460-2466.1981.tb00448.x.

Kranstuber, H., Carr, K., & Hosek, A. M. (2012). "If you can dream it, you can achieve it." Parental messages as indicators of college success. *Communication Education, 61*, 41–66. doi:10.1080/03634523.2011.620617.

Krouse, S. S., & Afifi, T. D. (2007). Family-to-work spillover stress: Coping communicatively in the workplace. *Journal of Family Communication, 7*(2), 85–122. doi:10.1080/15267430701221537.

Ledbetter, A. M., & Beck, S. J. (2014). A theoretical comparison of relational maintenance and closeness as mediators of family communication patterns in parent-child relationships. *Journal of Family Communication, 14*(3), 230–252. doi:10.1080/15267431.2014.908196.

Livingstone, S., & Helsper, E. (2008). Parental mediation and children's Internet use. *Journal of Broadcasting & Electronic Media*, 52(4), 581–599. doi: 10.1080/08838150802437396.

Lucas, K., & Buzzanell, P. M. (2010, April). *Communicating during economic downturns: Construction of family resilience through intergenerational processes.* Paper presented at the annual meeting of the Central States Communication Association, Cincinnati, OH.

Lucas, K., & Buzzanell, P. M. (2012). Memorable messages of hard times: Constructing short and long-term resiliencies through family communication. *Journal of Family Communication, 12*, 189–208.

Luthar, S. (2006). Resilience in development: A synthesis of research across five decades. In D. Cicchetti & D. J. Cohen (Eds.), *Developmental psychopathology: Risk, disorder, and adaptation* (2nd ed., pp. 739–795). New York: Wiley.

Lyons, R., Mickelson, K., Sullivan, M., & Coyne, J. (1998). Coping as communal process. *Journal of Social and Personal Relationships, 15*(5), 579–605.

Lyons, D. M., & Parker, K. J. (2007). Stress inoculation-induced indications of resilience in monkeys. *Journal of Traumatic Stress, 20*, 423–433. doi:10.1002/jts.20265.

MacGeorge, E. L., Feng, B., Butler, G. L., & Budarz, S. K. (2004). Understanding advice in supportive interactions: Beyond the facework and message evaluation paradigm. *Human Communication Research*, 30, 42–70. doi:10.1111/j.1468-2958.2004.tb00724.x.

MacGeorge, E. L., Feng, B., & Thompson, E. R. (2008). "Good" and "bad" advice: How to advise more effectively. In M. T. Motley (Ed.), *Studies in applied interpersonal communication* (pp. 145–164). Thousand Oaks, CA: Sage.

Manusov, V., & Harvey-Knowles, J. (2015). On being (and becoming) mindful: One pathway to greater resilience. In G. A. Beck & T. J. Socha (Eds.), *Communicating hope and resilience across the lifespan* (pp. 15–33). New York, NY: Peter Lang.

Mares, M., & Woodard, E. (2007). Positive effects of television on children's social interaction: A meta-analysis. In R. W. Preiss, B. M. Gayle, N. Burrell, M. Allen, & J. Bryant (Eds.), *Mass media effects research: Advances through meta-analysis* (pp. 281–300). Mahwah, NJ: Erlbaum. doi:10.1207/S1532785XMEP0703_4.

Masten, A. S., & O'Dougherty Wright, M. (2010). Resilience over the lifespan: Developmental perspectives on resistance, recovery, and transformation. In Reich J., Zautra A. J., Hall J. S. (Eds.), *Handbook of adult resilience* (pp. 213–237). New York, NY: Guilford Press.

Masten, A. S., Roisman, G. I., Long, J. D., Burt, K. B., Obradovic, J., Riley, J. R., et al. (2005). Developmental cascades: Linking academic achievement, externalizing and internalizing symptoms over 20 years. *Developmental Psychology, 41*, 733–746.

McAdams, D. P. (1990). Unity and purpose in human lives: The emergence of identity as a life story. In A. I. Rabin, R. A. Zucker, R. A. Emmons, & S. Frank (Eds.), *Studying persons and lives* (pp. 148–200). New York: Springer.

McAdams, D. P., Reynolds, J., Lewis, M., Patten, A., & Bowman, P. J. (2001). When bad things turn good and good things turn bad: Sequences of redemption and contamination in life narrative, and their relation to psychosocial adaptation in midlife adults and in students. *Personality and Social Psychology Bulletin, 27*, 472–483. doi:10.1177/0146167201274008.

Merolla, A., Beck, G. A., & Jones, A (2016). Memorable messages as sources of hope in relationships, academics, and finance. Manuscript submitted for publication.

Meyer, J. C. (2003). *Kid's talking: Learning relationships and culture with children.* New York: Rowan & Littlefield.

Miller, C. A., & DeThorne, L. S. (2014). Communication development: Distributed across people, resources, and time. In J. Nussbaum (Ed.), *The handbook of lifespan communication* (pp. 53–70). New York: Peter Lang.

Miller-Day, M., Pezalla, A., & Chesnut, R. (2013). Children are in families too! The presence of children in communication research. *Journal of Family Communication Research, 13*(2), 150–165. doi:10.1080/15267431.2013.768251.

Montpetit, M. A., Bergeman, C. S., Deboeck, P. R., Tiberio, S. S., & Boker, S. M. (2010). Resilience-as-process: Negative affect, stress, and coupled dynamical systems. *Psychology and Aging, 25*, 631–640. doi:10.1037/a0019268.

Odenweller, K. G., Booth-Butterfield, M., & Weber, K. (2004). Investigating helicopter parenting, family environments, and relational outcomes for millenials, *Communication Studies, 65*(4), 407–425. doi: 10.1080/10510974.2013.811434.

Olson, L. N., Baiocchi-Wagner, E. A., Kratzer, J. M., & Symonds, S. E. (2012). *The dark side of family communication.* UK: Polity Press.

Pasupathi, M. (2001). The social construction of the personal past and its implications for adult development. *Psychological Bulletin, 127*, 1–11. doi:10.1037/0033-2909.127.5.000.

Richardson, G. E. (2002). The metatheory of resilience and resiliency. *Journal of Clinical Psychology, 58*, 307–321. doi:10.1002/jclp.10020.

Rideout, V. J., Foher, U. G., Roberts, D. F. (2010). *Generation M2: Media in the lives of 8–18-year-olds: A Kaiser Family Foundation Study.* Menlo Park, CA. Retrieved from https://kaiserfamilyfoundation.files.wordpress.com/2013/01/8010.pdf (PDF, 2.73MB).

Schindler, I., Paech, J., & Löwenbrück, F. (2015). Linking admiration and adoration to self-expansion: Different ways to enhance one's potential. *Cognition & Emotion, 29*(2), 292–310. doi:10.1080/02699931.2014.903230.

Shatté, A. J., Seligman, M. E. P., Gillham, J. E., & Reivich, K. (2003). The role of Positive Psychology in child, adolescent, and family development. In Lerner, R. E., Jacobs, F., & Wertlieb, D. (Eds.). *Handbook of applied developmental science: Promoting positive child, adolescent, and family development through research, policies, and programs.* Thousand Oaks, CA: Sage Publications.

Smith, S. W., & Ellis, J. B. (2001). Memorable messages as guides to self-assessment of behavior: An initial investigation. *Communication Monographs, 68,* 154–168. doi:10.1080/03637750128058.

Socha, T., & Pitts, M. J. (Eds.) (2012). *The positive side of interpersonal communication.* New York, NY: Peter Lang.

Socha, T. J., & Stamp, G. H. (Eds.). (2009). *Parents and children communicating with society: Managing relationships outside of home.* New York: Routledge.

Socha, T. J., & Yingling, J. A. (2010). *Families communicating with children. Building positive developmental foundations.* Cambridge, UK: Polity.

Spoth, R., Redmond, C., & Shin, C. (1998). Direct and indirect latent-variable parenting outcomes of two universal family-focused preventive interventions: Extending a public health-oriented research base. *Journal of Consulting and Clinical Psychology, 66,* 385–399.

Steinhardt, M., & Dolbier, C. (2008). Evaluation of a resilience intervention to enhance coping strategies and protective factors and decrease symptomatology. *Journal of American College Health, 56,* 445–453.

Stohl, C. (1986). The role of memorable messages in the process of organizational socialization. *Communication Quarterly, 34*(3), 231–249. doi:10.1080/01463378609369638.

Te'eni-Harari, T., & Eyal, K. (2015). Liking them thin: Adolescents' favorite television characters and body image. *Journal of Health Communication, 20*(5), 607–615. doi: 10.1080/10810730.2015.1012241.

Theiss, J. A. (2018). Family communication and resilience. *Journal of Applied Communication Research, 46*(1), 10–13. doi:10.1080/00909882.2018.1426706.

Thompson, P. A., & Schrodt, P. (2014). Perceptions of joint family storytelling as mediators of family communication patterns and family strengths. *Communication Quarterly, 63*(4), 405–426. doi:10.1080/01463373.2015.1058286.

Ungar, M., Gazinour, M., & Richer, J. (2013). Annual research review: What is resilience within the social ecology of human development? *Journal of Child Psychology and Psychiatry, 54*(4), 348–366.

University of Michigan. (2014). Monitoring the future study. https://www.drugabuse.gov/publications/drugfacts/high-school-youth-trends

Vygotsky, L. S. (1978). *Mind in Society: Development of higher psychological processes.* Cambridge, MA: Harvard University Press.

Waldeck, J. H. (2014). Communication and learning. In J. F. Nussbaum (Ed.), *The handbook of lifespan communication* (pp. 135–158). New York: Peter Lang.

Waldron, V. R., Kloeber, D., Goman, C., Piemonte, N., & Danaher, J. (2014). How parents communicate right and wrong: A study of memorable moral messages recalled by emerging adults. *Journal of Family Communication, 14,* 374–397. doi:10.1080/15267431.2014.946032.

Walker, B. (2007). No more heroes anymore: The 'older brother' as role model. *Cambridge Journal of Education,* 37(4), 503–518. doi:10.1080/03057640701706169.

Ward, J. (2012). *A question of balance. [Kindle edition].* Retrieved from https://www.amazon.com/Question-Balance-Janet-Ward-ebook/dp/B007NMQF20?ie=UTF8&*Version*=1&*entries*=0

Webb, L. M. (2015). Research on technology and the family: From misconceptions to more accurate understandings. In C. Bruess (Ed.), *Family communication in the age of digital and social media* (pp. 3–31). New York: Peter Lang.

Werner, E., & Smith, R. (1992). *Overcoming the odds: High risk children from birth to adulthood.* Ithaca, NY: Cornell University. doi:10.1097/00004703-199404000-00012.

Wilmot W. W., & Hocker, J. L. (2013). *Interpersonal conflict* (9th ed.). New York: McGraw-Hill Education.

Wilson, S. R., Chernichky, S. M., Wilkum, K., & Owlett, J. S. (2014). Do family communication patterns buffer children from difficulties associated with a military parent's deployment? Examining deployed and at-home parents' perspectives. *Journal of Family Communication, 14,* 32–52. doi:10.1080/15267431.2013.857325.

Wilson, S. R., & Gettings, P. E. (2012). Nurturing children as assets: A positive approach to preventing child maltreatment and promoting healthy youth development. In T. J. Socha & M. Pitts (Eds.), *The positive side of interpersonal communication.* New York, NY: Peter Lang.

Zautra, A. J., Hall, J. S., & Murray, K. E. (2010) Resilience: A new definition of health for people and communities. In J. Reich, A. Zautra, & J. Hall (Eds.), *Handbook of adult resilience* (pp. 3–29). New York: Guilford.

Zimmerman, M. A., & Brenner, A. B. (2010). Resilience in adolescence: Overcoming neighborhood disadvantage. In J. Reich, A. J. Zautra, & J. S. Hall (Eds.), *Handbook of adult resilience* (pp. 283–308). New York, NY: Guilford Press.

5. Socio-emotional Development in Childhood and Adolescence

Through Communication: An Overview

MALINDA J. COLWELL
Texas Tech University

ELIZABETH TREJOS-CASTILLO
Texas Tech University

This chapter critically examines context and relationships for developmentally appropriate communication from early childhood through adolescence. The main focus of the chapter is how communication and relationships are linked from a developmental perspective. Primacy is given to the complex issue of whether relationship quality, messages communicated, or a combination of both are most influential for positive development from early childhood through adolescence. Communication is considered as a platform for expression of emotional and social needs and relationship building by discussing theoretical underpinnings from relevant developmental theories (e.g., Attachment, Self-Regulation, Socio-Cultural). We also explore communication skills and needs (verbal/non-verbal) developmentally from childhood to adolescence. A critical review of the quality and depth of communication from childhood to adolescence and recommendations for improving communication as a positive coping/life skill for supporting children and adolescent positive development also are discussed.

Theoretical Underpinnings

In this section, three theoretical frameworks that have been used to study children are examined. We then review the strengths and limitations of each as ways to study children's communication development. The theoretical frameworks examined in this section emphasize critical aspects of development: relationship with caregiver, ability to self-regulate, and influence of culture. The theories are presented to highlight developmental influences throughout childhood.

Attachment Theory. Beginning in infancy, a child's first communications are to indicate and express instrumental as well as socio-emotional needs. For example, from an attachment perspective, infants' first communication signals (e.g., crying, gazing, grasping) are attachment behaviors, which indicate needs that ensure survival (e.g., food, comfort, closeness). These early signals lay a foundation for an infant's relationship with his/her caregivers (e.g., Ainsworth & Bell, 1969; Bowlby, 1958).

Ainsworth (1973) defined attachment as an enduring affectional tie that unites two people. According to attachment theory, infants proceed through four stages of attachment. Indiscriminate response to others is the first stage (birth to 3 months). In the first three months of an infant's life, he or she responds similarly to any caregiver and does not show specific preferences for certain people. Between 4 and 7 months, infants show a preference for certain people. Between 7 and 9 months, infants show preference for a single attachment figure. During this period infants show separation anxiety and a fear of strangers, both of which reinforce that a particular caregiver is the main source of comfort and need fulfillment for the infant. A primary caregiver serves as a secure base from which the infant can explore. Imagine a caregiver and infant attending a new play group. The caregiver may put the infant on the floor and sit down. An infant may crawl away from the caregiver a couple of feet, sit down, and look back at the caregiver. During this brief separation, an infant may utilize the caregiver as a secure base and "check in" with the caregiver to seek affirmation that exploration is safe (Ainsworth, 1963). These exchanges between infant and caregiver/secure base are powerful in affecting (and reflecting) an infant's social and emotional needs.

The final stage of attachment is after 9 months when infants are capable of having multiple attachment figures. Throughout each of these stages, the responses of caregivers influence the quality of relationship (i.e., attachment style) that will be formed between infant and caregiver. The responses of primary caregivers in response to an infant's signals lay the foundation of the infant's mental characterization of relationships, or internal working model (Bowlby, 1969, 1973, 1980). If an infant's experiences consist of responsiveness and has his or her needs met by the caregiver, an internal working model is formed that represents the infant's security in the relationship with the caregiver and is thus referred to as a secure attachment style. For example, if a primary caregiver consistently and warmly comforts an infant when the infant cries for attention, the infant will develop a sense of worthiness to have needs met, as well as an expectation that others will respond when a need arises. However, an infant who experiences a non-responsive caregiver is likely to develop an insecure attachment relationship with that caregiver.

The internal working model of an infant with an insecure attachment style (i.e., insecure avoidant or insecure ambivalent) is one that signifies inconsistency and unreliability in others. The internal working model is the basis for a person's understanding of and expectations of relationships not only in children, but also through adulthood. Communication between infant and caregiver is a "dance" that signals and affects the infant's socio-emotional development. Infants who have a secure attachment relationship with their caregivers are more well-adjusted, more likely to have high quality adult relationships, and have secure attachment relationships with their offspring (Pinquart, FeuBner, & Ahnert, 2013). The attachment perspective is important for understanding young children's communication of their needs, as well as the quality of relationships they form with caregivers during early childhood.

Later, during adolescence, the attachments established during childhood with parents and family members remain central to youth's psychosocial development. Though the frequency of the communication along with the amount of time spent with parents decreases—as teenagers start to rely more on their peers and romantic partners for intimacy and support—the quality of the communication with the parents continues to play a significant role in the lives of teenagers as they would turn to their attachment figures for guidance and comfort (Moretti & Peled, 2004).

Attachment theory lends itself well to understanding children's communication because of its emphasis on the child-caregiver relationship as the context for communication. The relationship context and internal working model of relationships help define the quality and type of communication learned and exchanged. However, attachment theory does not provide insight into specifically how communication skills develop or how children learn to use their burgeoning communication skills. The second theory presented, Self-Regulation Theory, addresses some of these limitations.

Self-Regulation Theory. As active agents in their development, human beings have the innate capacity to exercise control over their thoughts, emotions, behaviors, and impulses and to adapt those to inner processes, responses to external factors, as well as short and long-term goals and expectations (Baumeister, 1999; Baumeister, 2005; Vohs & Baumeister, 2004). Through the interactions with their environment and individuals surrounding them, infants first learn to transform their experiences into informational clues they will use to regulate their emotions and behaviors during their first years of life. For instance, infants learn self-soothing skills supported by constant routines (e.g., bedtime, bathing, eating), being in a calming environment (e.g., soft sounds, having comforting items such as a blanket), and listening to positive feedback from their caregivers (e.g., "that's ok", "you will be fine"). Individual differences can be accounted for self-regulatory skills in infants and small children based on their temperament and innate capacities to auto-control. In addition, the role of positive parenting and caregiving is not only key for mastering self-regulatory skills but for developing internal sources of control during infancy that will develop into positive coping skills, stress management, and emotional control (Koop, 1989; Raffaelli, Crockett, & Shen, 2005).

Parent-child communications and interactions allow children to better understand how to process and organize their emotions, use appropriate behaviors to respond to the context and life experiences, and build more effective self-regulatory skills (Williamson & Anzalone, 2001). During childhood, the regulation process continues to be supported by the interactions with others but also becomes an individual practice of exercising internal control over their emotions and their urgencies to act on impulses (e.g., biting someone, grabbing a toy from someone else, crying constantly, throwing a tantrum). As they grow, children further learn through the interactions and communications with their parents or caring adults, to self-regulate their emotions and behaviors which in turn will also affect their thoughts and decision-making processes later in life during adolescence and adulthood (Demetriou, 2000; Lerner & Dombro, 2000; Zimmerman, 2000). Self-regulatory skills in children and adolescents support the advance of internal mechanism of control that permeate to other areas of development including cognition, motivation, short-long term planning, learning, and interpersonal relationships (Blair & Diamond 2008; Bronson, 2000).

One salient area of self-regulatory skills is related to interpersonal skills and communication. During the transitioning into early adolescence, approximately 9–10 years old, youth experience significant physical, cognitive, emotional and psychosocial changes that prepare them to become independent adults. Substantial brain changes that further the development of higher executive functions (e.g., auto-control/regulation, working memory, reasoning, problem solving, etc.) are also occurring at this time and impact communication functions in youth. Prefrontal cortex activity and the increase of brain white matter during adolescence influences the speed of processing of information such as making inferences, maintaining steady conversations shifting across different topics, and responding to feedback provided by other speakers (Conklin, Luciana, Hooper, & Yarger, 2007).

The refinement of executive functions influences self-regulatory skills including goal-oriented behaviors, working memory, cognitive plasticity and exercising of control over behaviors, emotions, and overall communications. Indeed, thinking and communication processes evolve into more mature levels as youth transition from middle to late adolescents and into young adults exhibiting greater capacities to process abstract information, use language in more complex ways in verbal and written forms (e.g., persuasion, assertion, empathy), and use critical thinking skills to plan, evaluate, think, reflect, and negotiate their personal perspectives and communicate appropriately with others (Crone, 2009).

One of the strengths of Self-Regulation Theory for our understanding of children's communication is the focus on a child's cognitive developmental process and how changes in cognitive development facilitate (or hinder) the development of more complex communication. The ability to self-regulate is necessary to learn the "mechanics" of communication (e.g., turn-taking, waiting, clarity of messages). Therefore, Self-Regulation Theory addresses one of the theoretical gaps from the Attachment perspective. However, Self-Regulation Theory somewhat "decontextualizes" the development of children's communication skills. Emphasis is placed primarily within the child, with less attention to the role of relationships or interactions. Sociocultural Theory, discussed in the next section, provides a perspective to focus on both individual development and relationships and larger contexts in understanding children's communication.

Sociocultural Theory. Vygotsky's sociocultural theory examines the role of psychological tools (e.g., speech, numerical systems, mental maps) in developing a person's understanding of the environment as well as how to communicate with one another. Similar to Self-Regulation Theory, Sociocultural Theory posits that through interactions with adults, children learn to construct knowledge by acquiring language and developing new communication skills. Those skills would support inner and outer thinking processes, reasoning, reading-writing skills, and the internalization of meaning of words and ideas that are central for the acquisition of values, beliefs, expectations, and other socio-cultural symbols. From Vygotsky's perspective, as we internalize speech that we have experienced with others, we are better able to self-regulate our own behavior (Vygotsky, 1978). In addition, the cultural context, as well as the more immediate interactional context, influences how we understand the world in which we live (Vygotsky, 1978; Wertsch, 1985).

Three main types of language as communication tools are identified in the Sociocultural Theory. *Egocentric Thought* involves internal mental representations based on symbols that have a particular meaning for oneself but not necessarily for others. The dynamic structure of word compositions and vocabulary changes as words acquire new and diverse meanings supporting the construction of knowledge and reality used by the child to try to internally interpret and explain the external world (Fisher, 1976). Internal Speech represents the internal processing of experiences, meanings, and symbols to construct one's views and analytical reasoning about the world; the internal speech is indeed expressed as a private language according to Vygotsky (Hess, 2009; Vygotsky, 1978). That is, as children grow they are able to transform experiences into abstract symbolic constructs that are used to classify and label those experiences in their minds; over time, those constructs acquire deeper meanings that are used to communicate and interact with others.

That process is what Vygotsky (1981) describes as mental maps that comprise sets of ideas/constructs that are grouped together in the child's mind as a way to capture reality into an internal representation. *External Speech* allows children to reproduce messages acquired from others and use their own personal thoughts to interact with others. In a way, the external speech bridges internal and external worlds and helps children negotiate their own world views with others. Over time, youth master new communication skills that allow them to use the external speech in a more effective way to sensor and evaluate emotions, perceptions, and actions from others. Thus, internal representations resulting from interpersonal interactions over time are organized in more elaborate ways in the youth's mind supporting logical mental connections across representations and meanings from the external world and allowing for more reflective dialogues, debating and negotiation abstract ideas, and making deeper inferences.

According to Vygotsky (1981) it is through our communication systems (i.e., egocentric though, external and internal speech) that we come to master our interaction with the environment, think with others in a context, and elaborate on past, present, and future experiences and thoughts (Fisher, 197; Hess, 2009). Two main sources shape the growing individual's psychosocial and behavioral development. The child relies heavily on his/her caregivers for learning opportunities and on his/her own personal experiences. Through interpersonal interactions, children become active participants in the construction of their own knowledge, learn new skills, as well as they get exposed to different world views and participate in other's activities which impact their socio-cultural experiences.

The process of constructing knowledge and mastering new skills through the interactions with others who have more advanced knowledge and life experiences is described by Vygotsky (1978) as the Zone of Proximal Development (ZPD). The ZPD marks the distance between independent problem solving and problem solving with the help of others including adults and peers. As part of the ZPD, Vygotsky discusses the concept of scaffolding as a way to building on a person's existing knowledge to advance it to a higher level of understanding. Scaffolding occurs by pairing a more skilled person with a less skilled person (Bodrova & Leong, 2007; Vygotsky, 1978). Scaffolding also serves the purpose of developing and mastering self-regulatory skills that are acquired from adults and caregivers and allow youth to learn how to manage their emotions and behaviors in more socio-culturally accepted ways (John-Steiner & Mann, 1996).

Sociocultural Theory offers a perspective that includes the larger context of children's development, as well as the individuality of the developmental process. By acknowledging not only the importance of culture, but also the interactions a child has within the culture, this perspective provides a contextual backdrop of the many factors that influence children's communication. Additionally, the concept of the zone of proximal development provides a framework for teaching children new skills by building on information they already possess, including their self-regulatory skills. Although Sociocultural Theory does not specifically offer a roadmap to the development of communication skills, it contextualizes communication. The next section will build on the contextual perspective by providing an overview of specific communication skills needed during various developmental periods from infancy to adolescence.

Communication Skills and Needs during Childhood/Adolescence

Verbal Skills. During early childhood, a child's communication becomes more complex and organized than in infancy. For example, toddlers and preschoolers can use their words to express their feelings, needs, desires, and dislikes. As children's communication blossoms to include language and more intentional communicative actions, children's relationships become more representative of partnering behaviors, rather than early infant relationships that rely more strongly on the expertise of the adult to guide the child (Thompson, 1998).

Communication is an important tool to guide and direct children's behavior throughout development, particularly as the foundations for behavior are formed during early childhood. Many researchers have examined associations between specific messages children receive within the context of the parent-child and children's social and emotional development (e.g., Mize & Pettit, 1997; Raikes & Thompson, 2005; Thompson, 2006). For example, Thompson (2006) asserts that one predictor of children's social competence is their attachment security with a caregiver. Within the context of a secure attachment, caregivers who openly discuss emotions with their children have children who are better able to understand and respond to the emotions of others. In other words, relationship quality provides the foundation for clear communication about emotions and social responsiveness. Similarly, Mize and Pettit (1997) found that both mother-child relationship quality and mothers' direct coaching about peer relationships were predictive of children's social competence. These findings suggest that the content of parental messages about peers and prosocial behavior (e.g., sharing, helping), as well as the shared relationship between parent and child are helpful for young children to learn about relationships and behavior. Therefore, the way in which information is shared is as important, if not more important, than the particular message conveyed. Thinking about messages in the context of delivery is important in developing relationships and in engaging in "teaching moments."

During adolescence, deeper reasoning capacities are developed through relationships and interactions supported by communication skills that allow for engaging in discussions and receiving feedback as a way to construct knowledge and elaborate on individual and contextual experiences (Wertsch,1985). It is normative at this stage that the frequency of communication with parents or caregivers might decrease, since communication becomes a fundamental tool for negotiating interpersonal relationships as adolescents are seeking for developing new relationships beyond their parents, siblings, and extended family members. Scholarship on communication transitions from childhood to adolescence provides evidence of increase in personal communication (self-disclosure) and closer communication with friends until approximately age 15 whereas less communication (frequency) is reported with parents (Valkenburg & Peter, 2007).

Communication strategies learned during the course of childhood and adolescence might support either a defensive (e.g., neutral communication, superiority) or a supportive (e.g., empathic communication, equality) climate for relationships during adolescence and adulthood (Devito 2008 citing Gibb's Model 1961 of communication climate). Indeed, studies have found a strong connection between effective communication skills and positive interpersonal solving skills providing evidence of the impact of communication on individual functioning, interpersonal negotiation and social interactions (Erozkan, 2013; Purcell, 2011; Subrahmanyam & Greenfield, 2008).

Non-Verbal Skills. The communication interactions among children and teenagers and their parents, peers, and others around them are not only limited to spoken language or verbal /written communications. For example, the use of gestures by infants is often a child's first indication of intentionality and they are among the first ways a child communicates with others (e.g., Crais, Watson, & Baranek, 2009). As children transition into adolescence and spend less time with their parents and more time alone, non-verbal communication becomes an important part of family interactions. Gestures, eye contact, body posture, and other forms of non-verbal communication are ways to express emotions when the verbal communication might be a source of conflict among teens and their parents (Robin & Foster, 2003).

Nonverbal gestures are a powerful way that infants and caregivers engage in social interaction. Joint attention emerges when an infant is 6 months of age and becomes more intentional by 12 months of age (Paparella, Good, Freeman, & Kasari, 2011). By 20 months of age, infants use a variety of gestures to engage others including responding to another's focus of attention and initiating a shared focus of attention by pointing or showing (Paparella et al., 2011). Importantly, the gestures used by infants to request or elicit joint attention continue to be used when children's verbal skills improve (Paparella et al., 2011). Mother-infant gestures also are associated with infants' action sequencing and imitation (Tamis-LaMonda et al., 2012). Gestures continue to be a part of children's communication skills as they learn to engage others in new and complex ways. Parents and caregivers also use gestures to communicate with nonverbal infants (e.g., Goodwyn, Acredolo, & Brown, 2000). In fact, the number of gestures mothers use with 14-month-old infants is associated with the child's vocabulary at 54-months (Dickinson, 2011). Gestures invite mutual attention to facilitate social interactions between nonverbal infants and their caregivers.

From an attachment perspective, nonverbal behaviors between caregiver and infant form the foundation of children's social and emotional development. Meins (1997) describes five behaviors based on Ainsworth, Blehar, Waters, and Wall (1978) sensitivity behaviors that promote children's socio-emotional development: responding promptly to a cry signaling distress, comforting an upset infant, being available to the infant for interaction, interpreting the infant's behavior as meaningful, and interacting with the infant as an intentional agent. In addition to these behaviors, maternal responsive and contingent behaviors provide a model for children's emotion regulation and social development (McElwain & Booth-LaForce, 2006). Sensitive and responsive interactions from caregivers provide children with a sense of their ability to be an active participant in social interactions. As children gain verbal skills and progress from responding primarily to nonverbal gestures, interaction patterns learned with caregivers continue to be influential. Early caregiver-child interactions provide a model for rules of socialization with others (Landry, Smith, & Swank, 2006).

Children throughout the toddler and preschool years also start developing "rules" of communication and boundaries with others. Corson, Colwell, Bell, and Trejos-Castillo (2014) found that 3- to 5-year-old children use their physical space and placement within spaces (i.e., hiding places) to create boundaries from others, set aside time for reflection, to play, and to have self-imposed time out. This shows that young children communicate their social and emotional needs not only verbally, but also through how they interact with their environments. Children's communication through the environment send important cues to their peers, parents, siblings, and teachers about who is welcome and when. For children who are developing language skills and learning the nuisance of their language, these physical manifestations of communication are important to consider.

During the transition from late childhood into adolescence, non-verbal communications seems to gain a particularly important place in the negotiating skills and social interactions of youth. For example, Kahlbaugh and Haviland (1994) found evidence that compared to preadolescent children (7–9 years old), early adolescents (10–14 years old) and middle adolescents (15–17 years old) displayed more avoidance behaviors towards their parents while receiving disapproval behaviors from them as a way for navigating the adolescents' needs for autonomy development and individual decision-making.

The dynamics of non-verbal communication between parents and youth during adolescence seem to be concentrated into two extreme poles: avoiding (e.g., physical distance, posture, lack of eye contact, unhappy facial expressions and gestures) and approaching (e.g., smiling, hugging, physical proximity). Non-verbal communication during adolescence represents a key way to communicate since adolescents might perceived certain types of verbal communications as criticisms or those might become a source of misunderstandings and conflict. Body language, facial expressions, and gestures represent the most salient non-verbal communication outlets for youth during adolescence as documented by a robust body of research (Kahlbaugh & Haviland, 1994; Ozmete & Bayoglu, 2009; Shearman & Dumlao, 2008).

Quality and Depth of Communication during Childhood and Adolescence

The impact of communication across multiple domains in child and adolescent development also has been broadly documented. From language acquisition to emotion processing, cognitive development, decision making, social interactions and other domains, communication is a key component of the child's socio-emotional development in the family and in the broader context (Bartolotta & Shulman, 2014). Understanding developmental differences in communication from childhood to adolescence can help families learn to more clearly communicate with each other.

Infant-directed speech has a higher pitch than adult-directed speech, includes a limited vocabulary and shorter statements (e.g., Fernald et al. 1989; Golinkoff, Can, Soderstrom, & Hirsch-Pasek, 2015). Infant-directed speech is associated with children's processing ability, as well as efficiency of learning and language development (e.g., Golinkoff et al., 2015; Weisleder & Fernald, 2013). Emotion coaching (i.e., recognizing emotional events as times of teaching and intimacy, being aware of emotions in self and others, encouraging emotional labeling and self-soothing) is one approach to effectively communicating with young children about emotions in a prosocial manner. Gottman, Katz, and Hooven (1996, 1997) found that for preschoolers, parents who engage in emotion coaching have better academic performance, emotional knowledge, and peer relationships. Emotion coaching helps children to recognize their own emotions and guides them to express and regulate themselves in socially acceptable ways. For instance, a young boy who expresses anger at being told "no" may throw a temper tantrum or scream. A parent may label for that child that he is angry and disappointed at not getting to do what he wants and suggest that the child draw a picture of how he is feeling. This strategy acknowledges the child's emotional experience and provides an acceptable outlet for him to express himself. "Connecting the dots" about emotions and behaviors during early childhood communicates to the child that a parent understands what the child is feeling, that is ok, and that there is a way to show how they feel that is constructive. All of these messages help children not only with their emotional competence, but also with their social competence.

As children transition into adolescence, the depth of communication with family members, peers and adults increases. In fact, as adolescents become more self-sufficient and claim more autonomy, the parent-child conflict increases making it more difficult for maintaining a balance between parental authority and negotiating communication skills. Relationships with adults outside the family circle such as teachers and mentors (e.g., couches, counselors) might provide teens with opportunities for social development, learning about acceptable vs. non-acceptable ways to communicate with adults, and proper ways to interact in communications with adults (verbal, written forms). Multiple studies have described the importance of parent-child communication as a protective factor supporting positive developmental outcomes in youth in areas including sexual development, decision-making skills, and risk-taking behaviors (Bersamin, Todd, Fisher, Hill, Grube, & Walker, 2008). Supportive communication in youth also has been found to be associated with academic achievement, goal-orientation (Shute, Hansen, Underwood, & Razzouk, 2011), self-esteem, self-regulation, self-concept, well-being (Tronick, 1989; Tronick & Beeghly, 2011), problem-solving and coping strategies (Offrey & Rinaldi, 2014).

Communication has also acquired a new meaning for children and adolescents living in a digital era where interactions are getting increasingly dominated by virtual spaces and digital networking social experiences. Adolescents today engage in numerous forms of electronic communication including but not limited to emails, text messaging, instant messaging blogs, chat rooms, social networks, video and photo sharing applications, online gaming, and the list of new communication applications continues to grow exponentially as new technology develops. Studies on the effects of electronic communications and social media on adolescents' outcomes is a robust area of research that highlights the benefits (e.g., opportunities for socialization and communication with friends and family, access to worldwide information, enhance learning activities, etc) as well as the risks of online communications (e.g., cyberbullying, sexting, online harassment, mental health consequences, etc; Liu, Yin, & Huang, 2013; Tartari, 2011; Wolak, Mitchell, & Finkelhor, 2003).

Cultural influences, ethnic background, geographic location and other manifestations of cultural heritage have been associated with different communication strategies across groups in society ranging from open and liberal communication practices to more conservative and traditional ones. Cultural influences might determine the ways in which adolescents are expected to communicate with adults, peers, and family members as well as how their opinions and communication skills are viewed in socio-cultural contexts (Shearman & Dumlao, 2008; Smetana & Gaines, 2003). Other factors influencing the depth and quality of adolescents' communications strategies have been related to generational gaps with parents, other adults (e.g., teachers), and older relatives in the family (e.g., grandparents, uncles, aunts) as well as gender differences (Renk, Liljequist, Simpson, & Phares, 2005; Riesch, Gray, Hoeffs, Keenan, Ertl,& Mathison, 2003).

Recommendations for Improving Communication as a Positive Life Skill

Although the role of effective and positive communication across parents/ caregivers and youth comprises a robust area of research, the application of empirical evidence to communication practices with children and youth is an area that has gained more attention during the last 2 decades. Worldwide, scholars across different fields (e.g., child development, medicine, psychology, social work, media and communications, education, etc.) have started to generate new knowledge on the impact of effective communication skills as an integral part of child development and for supporting youth's socio-emotional well-being and the transmission of positive life skills (Kolucki & Lemish, 2011).

For young children, interventions focused on increasing communication in the play context can benefit children's social behavior (Craig-Unkefer & Kaiser, 2002). Play allows children to learn about themselves, as well as their caregivers and peers. Milteer, Ginsburg, Mulligan, and The Council on Communications and Media and Committee on Psychosocial Aspects of Child and Family Health (2012, p. e205) states "Play allows for a different quality of interaction between parent and child, one that allows parents to 'listen' in a very different, but productive, way." Indeed, when caregivers can view the world from their child's perspective, they can learn about how to communicate more clearly and effectively with their child. Communication between young children and their parents/caregivers also lays a relationship foundation (Ainsworth & Bell, 1969). Peer play (both pretend and physical play) allows children to learn many important skills, including how to negotiate, share, resolve conflicts, and advocate from themselves (e.g., Hartup, Laursen, Stewart, & Eastenson, 1988; Lindsey & Colwell, 2003; McElwain & Volling, 2005).

The quality of communication has a direct impact on the quality of the interpersonal relationships that adolescents develop and that carry into their adult lives. Theories of human development, as well as sound scholarship, provide evidence of the importance of communication skills developed during childhood and adolescence that are the base of developing positive coping and life skills, decision-making abilities, effective interpersonal skills, and the capacity to reason and negotiate with others (Riesch, Gray, Hoeffs, Keenan, Ertl, & Mathison, 2003). For example, a growing area of interest on communication with children and teenagers is related to family dinners and/or shared meal times. Fulkerson and colleagues (Fulkerson, Pasch, Stigler, Farbakhsh, Perry, & Komro, 2010) found evidence that the protective effects of family dinner in 6th graders may be protective through 8th grade by supporting youth's positive development and well-being. Other empirical evidence also provides evidence that targeted communications with youth about particular topics (e.g., substance use, sexual behaviors), expectations, and rules might act as a buffer against negative behavioral outcomes (Miller-Day

& Dodd, 2004; Rangarajan & Kelly, 2006). The buffering effects of effective communication skills also have been documented for interpersonal conflict across different cultures (Shearman & Dumlao; 2008).

Knowing that developing effective communication skills is key to support positive short and long-term outcomes in children and adolescents, scholars have provided suggestions for improving communication with youth using active listening, engaging in face-to-face communications, making eye contact, using a positive voice tone, reading body language during the conversation, avoiding negative statements, and using problem-solving and negotiating phrases are among the recommendations provided for improving communication skills (Burleson, 1982; Erozkan, 2013; Fergus & Zimmerman, 2005; Hess, 2009; Kolucki & Lemish, 2011). Furthermore, nurturing communication skills in the family supports positive development from childhood to adolescence and into adulthood as individuals acquire life skills necessary to negotiate, handle conflicts, make important decisions, and adjust and adapt to different contexts and social interactions throughout their lives (Socha & Yingling, 2010).

Final Remarks

Communication is a complex process that changes tremendously from infancy to adolescence. At every developmental stage, communication acquires new functions and new meanings allowing us to construct and de-construct our internal world while we learn to negotiate our emotions and thoughts through the interactions with others. Understanding the mechanisms through which communication influences socio-emotional development in children and adolescents is key for advancing age and culturally appropriate efforts to support positive outcomes that would have lasting effects into adulthood.

References

Ainsworth, M. D. S. (1963). The development of infant-mother interaction among the Ganda. In B. M. Foss (Ed.), *Determinants of infant behavior* (Vol. 2, pp. 67–104). New York: Wiley.

Ainsworth, M. D. S. (1973). The development of infant-mother attachment. In B. Caldwell & H. Ricciuti (Eds.), *Review of child development research* (Vol. 3, pp. 1–94). Chicago: University of Chicago Press.

Ainsworth, M. D. S., & Bell, S. M. (1969). Some contemporary patterns of mother-infant interaction in the feeding situation. In A. Ambrose (Ed.), *Stimulation in early infancy* (pp. 133–170). San Diego, CA: Academic Press.

Ainsworth, M. D. S., Blehar, M. C., Waters, E., & Wall, S. (1978). *Patterns of attachment: Assessed in the Strange Situation and at home*. Hillsdale, NJ: Erlbaum.

Bartolotta, T., & Shulman, B. (2014). Child development. In Brian B. Shulman & Nina Capone (Eds.), *Language development: Foundations, processes, and clinical applications* (pp. 35–53). Burlington, MA: Jones & Barlett Publishers.

Baumeister, R. F. (1999). The nature and structure of the self: An overview. In R. F. Baumeister (Ed.), *The self in social psychology* (pp. 1–24). Philadelphia, PA: Psychology Press.

Baumeister, R. F. (2005). *The cultural animal: Human nature, meaning, and social life*. New York: Oxford University Press.

Bersamin, M. M., Todd, M., Fisher, D. A., Hill, D. L., Grube, J. W., & Walker, S. (2008). Parenting practices and adolescent sexual behavior: A longitudinal study. *Journal of Marriage and Family, 70*(1), 97–112.

Blair, C., & Diamond, A. (2008). Biological processes in prevention and intervention: The promotion of self-regulation as a means of preventing school failure. *Development and Psychopathology, 20*, 899–911.

Bodrova, E., & Leong, D. L. (2007). *Tools of the mind: The Vygotskian approach to early childhood education*. Upper Saddle River, NJ: Merrill/Prentice Hall.

Bowlby, J. (1958). The nature of a child's tie to his mother. *International Journal of Psycho-Analysis, 39*, 350–373.

Bowlby, J. (1969/1982). *Attachment and loss: Vol. 1. Attachment* (2nd ed.). New York: Basic.

Bowlby, J. (1973). *Attachment and loss: Vol. 2. Separation: Anxiety and anger*. New York: Basic.

Bowlby, J. (1980). *Attachment and loss: Vol. 3. Loss: Sadness and depression*. New York: Basic.

Bronson, M. B. (2000). *Self-regulation in early childhood: Nature and nurture*. New York: Guilford.

Burleson, B. R. (1982). The development of comforting communication skills in childhood and adolescence. *Child Development, 53*, 1578–1588.

Conklin, H. M., Luciana, M., Hooper, C. J., & Yarger, R. S. (2007). Working memory performance in typically developing children and adolescents: Behavioral evidence of protracted frontal lobe development. *Developmental Neuropsychology, 31*(1), 103–128.

Corson, K., Colwell, M. J., Bell, N. J., & Trejos-Castillo, E. (2014). Wrapped up in covers:Preschoolers' secrets and secret hiding places. *Early Child Development and Care, 184*, 1769–1786.

Craig-Unkefer, L. A., & Kaiser, A. P. (2002). Improving the social communication skills of at-risk preschool children in a play context. *Topics in Early Childhood Special Education, 22*, 3–13.

Crais, E. R., Watson, L. R., & Baranek, G. T. (2009). Use of gesture development in profiling children's prelinguistic communication skills. *American Journal of Speech-Language Pathology, 18*, 95–108.

Crone, E. A. (2009). Executive functions in adolescence: Inferences from brain and behavior. *Developmental Science, 12*(6), 825–830.

Demetriou, A. (2000). Organization and development of self-understanding and self-regulation: Toward a general theory. In M. Boekaerts, P. R. Pintrich, & M. Zeidner (Eds.), *Handbook of self-regulation* (pp. 209–251). San Diego, CA: Academic.

Devito, J. (2008). *Interpersonal messages: Communication and relationship skills.* Boston: Allyn & Bacon.

Dickinson, D. K. (2011). Teachers' language practices and academic outcomes of preschool children. *Science, 333,* 964–967. doi:10.1126/science.1204526.

Erozkan, A. (2013). The effect of communication skills and interpersonal problem solving skills on social self-efficacy. *Educational Sciences: Theory & Practice, 13,* 739–745.

Fergus, S., & Zimmerman, M. A. (2005). Adolescent resilience: A framework for understanding healthy development in the face of risk. *Annual Review of Public Health, 26,* 399–419.

Fernald, A., Taeschner, T., Dunn, J., Papousek, M., de Boysson-Bardies, B., & Fukui, I. (1989). A cross-language study of prosodic modifications in mothers' and fathers' speech to preverbal infants. *Journal of Child Language 16,* 477–501.

Fisher, H. (1976). The language and logic of forming an idea. *Journal for the Theory of Social Behaviour, 6,* 177–209.

Fulkerson, J. A., Pasch, K. E., Stigler, M. H., Farbakhsh, K., Perry, C. L., & Komro, K. A. (2010). Longitudinal associations between family dinner and adolescent perceptions of parent-child communication among racially-diverse urban youth. *Journal of Family Psychology 42*(3), 261–270.

Gibb, J. R. (1961). Defensive communication. *Journal of Communication, 11,* 141–148.

Golinkoff, R. M., Can, D. D., Soderstrom, M., & Hirsh-Pasek, K. (2015). (Baby) talk to me: The social context of infant-directed speech and its effects on early language acquisition. *Current Directions in Psychological Science, 24,* 339–344.

Goodwyn, S., Acredolo, L., & Brown, C. (2000). Impact of symbolic gesturing on early language development. *Journal of Nonverbal Behavior, 24,* 81–103.

Gottman, J. M., Katz, L. F., & Hooven, C. (1996). Parental meta-emotion philosophy and the emotional life of families: Theoretical models and preliminary data. *Journal of Family Psychology, 10,* 243–268. doi:10.1037/0893-3200.10.3.243.

Gottman, J. M., Katz, L. F., & Hooven, D. (1997). *Meta-emotion: How families communicate emotionally.* Mahwah, NJ: Lawrence Erlbaum.

Hartup, W. W., Laursen, B., Stewart, M. I., & Eastenson, A. (1988). Conflict and the friendship relations of young children. *Child Development, 59,* 1590–1600. doi: 10.2307/1130673.

Hess, A. K. (2009). Sense-of-the-other: At the core of interpersonal theory and practice. *Journal of Contemporary Psychotherapy, 39,* 25–32.

John-Steiner, V., & Mahn, H. (1996). Sociocultural approaches to learning and development: A Vygotskian framework. *Educational Psychologist, 31*(3/4), 191–206.

Kahlbaugh, P. E., & Haviland, J. M. (1994). Nonverbal communication between parents and adolescents: A study of approach and avoidance behaviors. *Journal of Nonverbal Behavior, 18, 91*(23). ISSN: 0191-5886.

Kolucki, B., & Lemish, D. (2011). *Communicating with children: Principles and practices to nurture, inspire, excite, educate and heal.* NY: UNICEF. Retrieve April 30, 2016, from http://www.unicef.org/cwc/

Kopp, C. B. (1989). Regulation of distress and negative emotions: A developmental view. *Developmental Psychology, 2,* 343–354.

Landry, S. H., Smith, K. E., & Swank, P. R. (2006). Responsive parenting: Establishing early foundations for social, communication, and independent problem-solving skills. *Developmental Psychology, 42,* 627–642. doi:10.1037/0012-1649.42.4.627.

Lerner, C., & Dombro, A. L. (2000). *Learning and growing together: Understanding and supporting your child's development.* Washington, DC: ZERO TO THREE Press.

Lindsey, E.W., & Colwell, M. J. (2003). Preschoolers' emotional competence: Links to pretend and physical play. *Child Study Journal, 33,* 39–52.

Liu, S. H., Yin, M. C., & Huang, T. H. (2013). Adolescents' interpersonal relationships with friends, parents and teacher when using Facebook for interaction. *Creative Education, 4,* 335–339.

McElwain, N. L., & Booth-LaForce, C. (2006). Maternal sensitivity to infant distress and nondistress as predictors of mother-infant attachment security. *Journal of Family Psychology, 20,* 247–255. doi:10.1037/0893-3200.20.2.247.

McElwain, N. L., & Volling, B. L. (2005). Preschool children's interactions with friends and older siblings: Relationship specificity and joint contributions to problem behavior. *Journal of Family Psychology, 19,* 486–496.

Meins, E. (1997). Security of attachment and maternal tutoring strategies: Interaction within the zone of proximal development. *British Journal of Developmental Psychology, 15,*129–144. doi:10.1111/j.2044-835X.1997.tb00730.x.

Mikami, A. Y., Szwedo, D. E., Allen, J. P., Evans, M. A., & Hare, A. L. (2010). Adolescent peer relationships and behavior problems predict young adults' communication on social networking websites. *Developmental Psychology, 46,* 46–56.

Miller-Day, M., & Dodd, A. (2004) Toward a descriptive model of parent-offspring communication about alcohol and other drugs. *Journal of Social and Personal Relationships, 21*(1), 73–95.

Milteer, R. M., Ginsburg, K. R., Mulligan, D. A., Council on Communications and Media, & Committee on Psychosocial Aspects of Child and Family Health (2012). The importance of play in promoting healthy child development and maintaining strong parent-child bond: Focus on children in poverty. *Pediatrics, 129,* e204–e213.

Mize, J., & Pettit, G. S. (1997). Mothers' social coaching, mother-child relationship style, and children's peer competence: Is the medium the message? *Child Development, 68,* 312–332.

Moretti, M. M. (2004). Adolescent-parent attachment: Bonds that support healthy development. *Paediatrics & Child Health, 9*(8), 551–555.

Offrey, L. D., & Rinaldi, C. M. (2014). Parent–child communication and adolescents' problem-solving strategies in hypothetical bullying situations. *International Journal of Adolescence and Youth.* doi:10.1080/02673843.2014.884006.

Ozmete, E., & Bayoglu, A. S. (2009). Parent-youth conflict: A measurement on frequency and intensity of conflict issues. *Journal of International Social Research, 8,* 313–322.

Paparella, T., Good, K. S., Freeman, S., & Kasari, C. (2011). The emergence of nonverbal joint attention and requesting skills in young children with autism. *Journal of Communication Disorders, 46,* 569–583.

Pinquart, M., FeuBner, C., & Ahnert, L. (2013). Meta-analytic evidence for stability in attachments from infancy to early adulthood. *Attachment and Human Development, 15,* 189–218. doi:10.1080/14616734.2013.746257.

Purcell, K. (2011). *Trends in teen communication and social media use.* Retrieved April 12, 2016, from Pew Internet & American Life Project website: http://www.pewinternet.org/Presentations/2011/Feb/PIP-Girl-Scout-Webinar.aspx

Raffaelli, M., Crockett, L. J., & Shen, Y. L. (2005). Developmental stability and change in self-regulation from childhood to adolescence. *Journal of Genetic Psychology, 166,* 54–75.

Raikes, H. A., & Thompson, R. A. (2005). Links between risk and attachment security: Models of influence. *Applied Developmental Psychology, 26,* 440–455.

Rangarajan, S., & Kelly, L. (2006). Family communication patterns, family environment, and the impact of parental alcoholism on offspring self-esteem. *Journal of Social and Personal Relationships, 23,* 655–671.

Renk, K., Liljequist, L., Simpson, J. E., & Phares, V. (2005). Gender and age differences in the topics of parent-adolescent conflict. *The Family Journal, 13,* 139–149.

Riesch, S. K., Gray, J., Hoeffs, M., Keenan, T., Ertl, T., & Mathison, K. (2003). Conflict and conflict resolution: Parent and young teen perceptions. *Journal of Pediatric Health Care, 17,* 22–31.

Robin, A. L., & Foster, S. L. (2003). Negotiating parent-adolescent conflict: A behavioral-family systems approach. New York: Guilford.

Shearman, S. M., & Dumlao, R. (2008). A cross-cultural comparison of family communication patterns and conflict between young adults and parents. *Journal of Family Communication, 8,* 186–211.

Shute, V. J., Hansen, E. G., Underwood, J. S., & Razzouk, R. (2011). A review of the relationship between parental involvement and secondary school students' academic achievement. *Education Research International,* 915326. doi:10.1155/2011/915326.

Smetana, J., & Gaines, C. (2003). Family, school, and community adolescent-parent conflict in middle-class African American families. *Child Development, 70,* 1447–1463.

Socha, T. J., & Yingling, J. A. (2010). *Families communicating with children: Building positive developmental foundations.* Cambridge, UK: Polity.

Subrahmanyam, K., & Greenfield, P. (2008). Online communication and adolescent relationships. *The Future of Children, 18,* 119–146. Princeton University.

Tamis-LeMonda, C. S., Song, L., Leavell, A. S., Kahana-Kalman, R., & Yoshikawa, H. (2012). Ethnic differences in mother-infant language and gestural communications are associated with specific skills in infants. *Developmental Science, 15,* 384–397, doi:10.1111/j.1467-7687.2012.01136.x.

Tartari, E. (2011). Benefits and risks of children and adolescents using social media. *European Scientific Journal, 11,* 321–332.

Thompson, R. A. (1998). Early sociopersonality development. In W. Damon & N. Eisenberg (Eds.), *Handbook of child psychology* (Vol. 3, pp. 25–104). New York: Wiley and Sons.

Thompson, R. (2006). The development of the person: Social understanding, relationships, conscience, self. In W. Damon & R. Lerner (Series Eds.) & N. Eisenberg (Vol. Ed.), *Handbook of child psychology: Vol. 3. Social, emotional, and personality development* (6th ed., pp. 24–98). New York: Wiley.

Tronick, E. Z. (1989). Emotions and emotional communication in infants. *American Psychologist, 44* (2), 112–119.

Tronick, E. Z., & Beeghly, M. (2011). Infants' meaning-making and the development of mental health problems. *American Psychologist 66*(2), 107–119.

Valkenburg, P. M., & Peter, J. (2007). Preadolescents' and adolescents' online communication and their closeness to friends. *Developmental Psychology, 43,* 276–277.

Vohs, K. D., & Baumeister, R. F. (2004). Understanding self-regulation: An introduction. In R. F. Baumeister & K. D. Vohs (Eds.), *Handbook of self-regulation. Research, theory, and applications* (pp. 1–9). New York: Guilford.

Vygotsky, L. S. (1978). *Mind in society: The development of higher psychological processes.* Cambridge, MA: Harvard University Press.

Vygotsky, L. S. (1981). The instrumental method in psychology. In J. V. Wertsch (Ed.), *The concept of activity in Soviet psychology.* Armonk, NY: M.E. Sharpe.

Weisleder, A., & Fernald, A. (2013). Talking to children matters: Early language experience strengthens processing and builds vocabulary. *Psychological Science, 24,* 2143–2152.

Wertsch, J. V. (1985). *Cultural, communication, and cognition: Vygotskian perspectives.* Cambridge, UK: Cambridge University Press.

Williamson, G. G., & Anzalone, M. E. (2001). *Sensory integration and self-regulation in infants and toddlers: Helping very young children interact with their environment.* Washington, D.C.: ZERO TO THREE Press.

Wolak, J., Mitchell, K., & Finkelhor, D. (2003). Escaping of connecting? Characteristics of youth who form close online relationships. *Journal of Adolescence, 26,* 105–119.

Zimmerman, B. J. (2000). Attaining self-regulation: A social cognitive perspective. In M. Boekaerts, P. R. Pintrich, & M. Zeidner (Eds.), *Handbook of self-regulation* (pp. 13–39). San Diego, CA: Academic Press.

6. Communication and Children's Moral Development

PAULA S. TOMPKINS
St. Cloud State University

This chapter outlines an intersection between philosophical theories of ethics and communication ethics in examining the moral development of children.[1] Study of ethics in human communication focuses primarily on adults (e.g., Cheney, May & Munshi, 2011). Similarly, communication is understudied in child development in its focus on biological and cognitive development, language acquisition, and social development, often through research of deficiencies (e.g., Kagan, 2013). How infants, children and adolescents develop as communicators—how they grow as speakers, listeners, turn takers or collaborators—has not been a significant focus of study (e.g., Miller-Day, Pezalla & Chesnut, 2013; Socha & Yingling, 2010). Scholarly interest in communication across the lifespan, such as Socha and Eller's ecological model of lifespan communication (2015), brings into focus the importance of studying the communication of children and adolescents for understanding human communication (e.g., Soliz & Rittenour, 2015; Waldron et al., 2015). This chapter offers an initial exploration of how infants and children develop as ethically responsive communicators. Communication ethics is conceptualized here as a practice or practical philosophy (Toulmin, 1988, 2001), rather than an application of philosophical theories of ethics in human communication (Ballard et al., 2014). As a practice, communication ethics asks how do you ethically discern or judge, as well as whether, what, or how you act as an ethically responsive communicator.

Beginning with a new developmental stage called "extended adolescence" or "emerging adulthood" (Arnett, 2006), this chapter will examine current research in moral psychology of infants, toddlers, and children especially relevant to developing ethical sensitivity, a foundational process for ethically responsive action. It will then examine the communication act of acknowledgment (Hyde, 2006) as a starting point for exploring how adults can construct communicative scaffolding that promotes development of ethically responsive communication practices in infants, toddlers, and children.

A Profile of Emerging Adulthood (Ages 18–23)

To examine the development of ethical practice, it is useful to first consider distinguishing qualities of ethical action that occur within ethical communication's developmental arc, to identify kinds of outcomes that occur later in moral development. Ethical action requires four processes—ethical sensitivity, judgment, motivation, and character (Rest, Navarez, Bebeau & Thomas, 1999). Sensitivity to existence of ethical issues is foundational to the other three. Lacking ethical sensitivity, capacities for judgment, motivation to act, or relevant qualities of character are not engaged. Sensitivity to ethical issues, the capacity to recognize and begin to think about them, is the starting point for any practice of ethics.

Sociologist Christian Smith and his research team (Smith, Christoffersen, Davidson & Herzog, 2011) presented a profile of ethical practices of emerging adults (ages 18–23)[2] in how they conceptualized what is good in life (not moral philosophy), how they thought about moral beliefs and problems, and how they explained what they believe. In short, can emerging adults articulate their ethical sensitivity and explain their discernment and judgments to others? Smith and his team found that many emerging adults lacked some combination of the abilities to discern ethically relevant issues, think coherently about those issues, or articulate a thoughtful and cogent explanation for their choices. Using a metaphor of light, they identified shadows where emerging adults live, a sense of being in limbo or transition, confusion, anxiety, self-obsession, melodrama, conflict, disappointments, and sometimes emotional devastation. A significant portion of emerging adults ignored ethical issues, lacking sensitivity to their existence. Many focused on materialistic consumption, their personal financial security, or seeking intoxication. Although many said relationships were important to them, this was not necessarily evident to the researchers. These findings are comparable to scholarship on the dark side of interpersonal communication (Spitzberg & Cupach, 2007).

While Smith et al. (2011) presented findings on consumerism, intoxication, sexual activity, and civic and political disengagement, ethics conceptually organizes this research. Key to ethical practice is discerning what proportionate weight to place on legitimate interests of one's Self to survive and thrive, relative to the legitimate interests of Others to survive and thrive, a weight that is good according to an ethical standard derived from some combination of cultural or social values, religious or spiritual traditions, or philosophical theories of ethics (Tompkins, 2009). Smith's team found that how most emerging adults understood what is good or bad often made the ethical features of their lives invisible. This is due, in part, to lack of preparation in thinking and communicating about difficult issues, combined with a desire to avoid what is seen as coercive absolutism. While the greatest proportion of emerging adults (60%) articulated a form of moral individualism and another 30% were moral relativists who saw ethics as a social construction or as subjective, 34% of respondents stated that that "they simply did not know what makes anything morally right or wrong" (p. 64). About half of those who disagreed with moral relativism could not explain why they thought it was wrong. About 40% defined what is ethically right or wrong by "what other people would think about someone" (pp. 37–38). Another 17% defined ethics as Karma, but could not explain what Karma is—"Mostly just Karma. I really do believe in Karma. What you give and what you do really does come back to you, whether you realize it or not. It's just, I don't know" (p. 46).[3]

The invisibility of ethics identified in Smith's et al.'s research (2011) is similar to Brummett's (1981) image of the communicative impotence of traditional ethical relativism, in contrast to a rhetorical grounding of ethical relativism, an impotence that I have called almost perpetual listening (Tompkins, 2019, pp. 110–111). Almost perpetual listening occurs when someone recognizes the existence of an ethical issue and perhaps discerns what is ethically good but says nothing because communicating her discernment is considered judgmental. This makes a combination of self-censorship and minimally responsive listening "the ethically best" communication practice, a practice that obscures the existence of ethics in the listener's social world. The emerging adult profile offers another possible explanation for the invisibility of ethics, that there may be no internal dialogue about what is right or wrong because (1) many emerging adults do not think about ethical issues or (2) do not recognize possible ethical issues with their behavior because they are not "terrible" people (Smith et al., 2011, pp. 66–67). If they do think about ethical issues, it is likely they cannot explain their thoughts with sufficient clarity so that Others understand, a practice of communication ethics that co-constructs ethics in their relationships. Smith and his team conclude that for the social worlds of many emerging adults the presence of ethics is "thin and spotty" (p. 65).

The social worlds of emerging adults were co-constructed with adults, particularly those responsible for socializing youth. Many interviewees attended public schools where teachers sidestepped difficult issues or controversies in a manner more typical of dysfunctional families (Smith et al., 2011). While avoidance or repression of potential conflict is an understandable, but problematic strategy for managing pressures to teach academically, socially and racially diverse student populations to perform well on standardized tests, it does not provide good models for thinking or communicating. It does not teach skills needed to recognize and think critically about difficult or divisive issues, articulate thoughts and have them examined by others in order to identify strengths and weaknesses in reasoning or develop the ability to distinguish between rationalizations and ethical justifications. Moreover, Smith and his team suggest that emerging adults' facile and fragmented understanding of postmodernism discouraged them from communicating with Others in their social relationships, in contrast to personal relationships. In social Others they saw differences and few or no commonalities to justify communicating with them. Emerging adults appeared to lack a willingness to take the time and effort to listen and understand those who are different, including those with whom they disagreed. Such thinking and the accompanying communication practices promoted withdrawal from social relationships and the public sphere to focus on Self, family, and enclaves of like-minded individuals.

Smith and et al.'s (2011) profile of emerging adulthood stands in contrast to popular conceptions of the millennial generation, which include the current generation of emerging adults. Millennials, the most educated generation ever, are seen as sophisticated and adept users of digital technology and social media who are deeply disillusioned with societal institutions such as marriage, religion, and government (See Pew Research Center, 2011 and 2014). The Case Foundation, for example, focuses on millennials who want to make social change and consults with businesses, government, and non-profits on how they must change to attract and motivate these millennials, e.g., becoming more like a social movement.[4] Broader examination of what some consider the next greatest generation, paints a more complex picture, especially from a perspective of moral development and communication ethics. Longitudinal and large sample studies of generational differences by social psychologist Jean Twenge, herself a millennial, finds a decline of trust in institutions and a decline of trust in other persons, which has implications for trust in general, social capital, and civic engagement (Twenge, Campbell, & Carter, 2014). More controversial are her findings of a rise in cultural narcissism (in contrast to individual narcissism) over time, the highest point in the millennial generation. Cultural narcissism is created by communication processes that promote over-inflated views of Self and de-emphasize deep and caring relationships with Others (Twenge & Campbell, 2009; Twenge et al.,

2008). These studies point to socialization of children and adolescents as contributing to trends of diminished ethical practices in society.

While the communication theory and research examine how communication co-constructs social worlds (e.g., Stewart, 1995), the adult focus of the discipline does not encourage examination of how children and adolescents develop as communicators. Both communication theory and the social trends described above point to the importance of examining how children and adolescents develop as ethically responsive communicators. If children and adolescents have not developed their capacities for ethical sensitivity and ethically responsive communication practices, it is less likely that ethically responsive communication will be a significant part of the relationships and social worlds they co-create as they grow into adulthood. Unasked questions about communication's role in how children develop as ethically responsive communicators merit examination. Research of the moral development of children is helpful in thinking about such questions.

Moral Development in Infants and Children

Theories of child and moral development have expanded beyond the sequential stages of Piaget and Kohlberg's stages of moral reasoning to offer richer explanations of human development that include a child's individual biological growth and maturation, family, friendships, social relationships, and culture (see Killen & Smetana, 2006; Socha & Eller, 2015; Vozzola, 2014). One group of theories explores the role of emotion in moral development, especially empathy. Moral psychologists developed methods for studying moral emotions in infants, toddlers and young children that, despite their non-existent or limited vocabulary, provide insights into their ethical and communication potential. Using duration of attention or eye contact as an indicator of interest, research indicates the infants as young as six months have an appreciation of the difference between what adults call good and bad behavior. Toddlers able to express or represent their thoughts in comparable situations identify who was good or bad, nice or mean (Bloom, 2013). Research identifies three moral emotions—empathy, an equality bias, and disgust—that influence how humans understand what is good or bad. Of the three, empathy is key for moral development and ethical sensitivity.[5]

Moral psychology studies empathy as a biologically innate, value neutral response to emotional distress that stimulates prosocial behavior needed for human survival (Hasting, Zahn Waxler & McShane, 2006). Newborns exhibit a global and reactive empathic capacity when they confuse the distress of other infants as their own distress (Hoffman, 2001), making it difficult to identify the actual source of distress—is it your experience of pain or sadness or is it my empathetic response to your distress? Distinguishing between Self and Other is critical to human development, helping a child empathize with the distress of Others and offer appropriate responses to relieve that distress in acts of compassion and care (Bloom, 2013). Empathy and compassion or care are not the same (Nussbaum 2001; Tronto, 1993). Care and compassion are responsive acts that involve a choice, as when a person recognizes someone's distress and feels some empathy but faces a decision whether to turn away or toward that person to relieve her distress. Other emotions, including the equality bias or disgust, may interrupt an experience of empathy, precluding acts of care or compassion.

A well-developed empathic capacity aids in understanding Others' emotions, creating an entry-point for perspective-taking. Socio-neurobiology identifies mirror neurons as a biological foundation for empathy (Walter, 2012). Still in its early stages, research using f(unctional)MRI raises interesting questions about human development and empathy. In brief, by facilitating imitation of behavior, such as facial expressions of emotion, mirror neurons create an automatic biological basis for emotionally understanding Others (automatic empathy), also referred to as "mind reading" (Molnar-Szakacs, 2010; Shoemaker, 2012). Secondary, non-automatic empathy is cognitive, engaging other parts of the brain in the cortex. Cognitive empathy involves perspective-taking and pro-social sympathetic actions found in ethical judgment, ethical reasoning, ethical action, or communication. While fMRI and other socio-neurobiological research methods cannot explain ethical judgment, ethical reasoning or altruism, for example (See Baird, Schefer, & Wilson, 2011), one study found differences in brain architecture, specifically increased regional grey matter, in the brains of persons who were at the post-conventional level of moral reasoning when compared with persons at the conventional level of moral reasoning (Prehn et al., 2015). Brain plasticity is a link between these socio-neurobiological findings and moral development of children (even adults). Over time, repeated action changes the brain by growing neurons and synaptic connections, while also pruning connections to less or unresponsive neurons.[6]

While socio-neurobiological research offers insights into brain development and automatic and cognitive empathy, moral and social psychology offers a more extensive research literature on children and moral emotions. Hoffman (2001) identifies 4 levels of empathy. First, is the global and reactive empathy of infants mentioned above, which can be explained by mirror neurons. Second, is ego-centric empathy which occurs when a child comforts an Other, but in a way that simultaneously reduces the child's own reactive empathic distress. An example would be when a child comforts someone crying by patting his arm, while also patting her arm to ease her own distress. While the Self-comforting behaviors arguably point to mirror neurons, the Other-comforting behavior point to the child's developing capacity to recognize Others and distinguish them from Herself. The third level of empathy is when a child is cognitively capable of empathizing with a wide array of emotions and offers comfort to Others in an increasing array of behaviors. This more cognitive empathy involves a child's more complex understanding of her Self in relation to Others, employing perspective-taking and drawing inferences about feelings and motivations of Others. Hoffman's proposed fourth level of empathy does not depend upon direct experience of an Other's distress to experience empathy, relying even more on cognitive skills of perspective taking, reasoning, and imagination.

The moral development literature recognizes that experiencing empathy does not necessarily lead to ethical action. As Hoffman notes—"Empathic morality should promote prosocial behavior and discourage aggression in cultures guided by caring and justice principles. But it does not operate in a vacuum, and in multicultural societies with intergroup rivalry, it might, calling to empathy's familiarity bias, contribute to violence between groups" (2001, p. 22). While creating a capacity for ethical sensitivity, empathy alone can be insufficient to promote ethical action. Yet, the necessity of empathy for ethical action is evident in brain research that found when empathic centers of the brain are damaged, the human capacity for ethical response is diminished, perhaps non-existent (See Baron-Cohen, 2011; Lough et al., 2005).

Moral psychology considers sympathy an emotion related to cognitive empathy. Sympathy does not depend on sharing or fully understanding an Other's feelings of distress, while empathy does (Eisenberg, 2000; Eisenberg, Spinrad & Sadovsky, 2006). Sympathy involves an actor's concern, sadness or sorrow for an Other's experience even when an actor's understanding of the feelings of an other is limited, partial, or differs from the feelings of an Other: "there is more to you than I can understand." Sympathy may be more important than empathy in promoting ethical sensitivity toward Others who are different or not physically present (Vetlesen, 1994). Like empathy, the experience of sympathy also does not guarantee ethical action, as when people allocate resources based upon their sympathy for an individual in violation of principles of justice (Eisenberg, 2000). Unexamined sympathy may create unintended harms, as in the inundation of Newtown, Connecticut with teddy bears after the Sandy Hook Elementary School mass shooting. The quantity of gifts from sympathetic outsiders required the town to set aside resources for storage of the gifts, instead of focusing those resources on healing the community (Riveria, 2013). Actions motivated by unexamined empathy or sympathy, however well intended, may hurt or harm Others.

A bias toward equality focusing on equality of outcome is a second moral emotion that develops alongside empathy. By age 16 months, infants prefer equal or fair dividers of objects such as candy, stickers or toys. At 19 months toddlers appear to recognize social loafers (Bloom, 2013). Fairness based on equality of outcome, however, does not necessarily include the observing toddler. When allowed to keep a piece of candy for themselves, 80% of 7- and 8-year-olds gave away a candy to a stranger, but about half of the younger children did not. When other children would get more candy than the research subjects, a different study showed that child subjects frequently chose the option where no child received any candy to assure that they would not receive a lesser amount (Blake & McAuliffe, 2011). If it is not equal for me, then no one will get anything. Another study points to a less extreme solution—if it assures that no one gets more than I do, everyone should get an equal but lesser amount of candy or stickers, including myself. Relative disadvantage that involves my disadvantage is unfair (Sheskin, Bloom & Wynn, 2014). These findings indicate that an emotional bias for equality could interrupt experience of empathy, precluding acts of care and compassion for Others. As toddlers develop the capacity to distinguish between themselves and Others, they also confront issues of ethical practice faced by adults, discerning how to balance my self-interest with the self-interests of Others in ways that can be both fair and caring.

Disgust is the third moral emotion evident in children. It differs from empathy and the emotional bias for equality, in that disgust is learned. It is the opposite of empathy, leading to repulsion instead of compassion, making us indifferent to the suffering of Others, even promoting cruelty and dehumanization (Bloom, 2013). Disgust may be an evolutionary adaptation to avoiding bad food or sources of disease, as well as human waste that potentially harbors germs. Studies show persons who experienced even subtle reminders of cleanliness, such as standing next to a hand-sanitizer dispenser or seeing a sign asking to keep an area clean, rated themselves as more politically conservative and were disapproving of actions than persons who were not exposed to these reminders of cleanliness. Add disgust for a person or group to psychological preferences for the similarity of kinship groups with whom we are more likely to empathize, strangers are to be feared, perhaps as a possible source of contamination. Just because we initially experience empathy toward a person's misfortune, does not mean that we will act toward him with compassion or kindness. The emotions of disgust or fairness based on the equality bias can interrupt automatic or cognitive empathy for an

Other, dampening ethical sensitivity and diminishing the likelihood of acts of care or compassion. If empathy is critical for ethical sensitivity and action as the research indicates, we must explore how to support development of the empathic capacity in infants and children to lay a groundwork for ethical sensitivity and ethically responsive communication in adolescence and adulthood.

Acknowledgment and Moral Development

Although biology provides a fairly standardized starting point, how adults interact with children influences their development in significant ways (Shumaker & Heckel, 2007). Adult interaction influences development of a child's empathic capacity which, in turn, influences her communication and moral development. Elsewhere I have argued that practices of ethics and communication are entwined, that ethical values such as justice develop out of responsiveness of communicators to one another, beginning in the communication act of acknowledgment (Tompkins, 2015). Michael Hyde (2006) argued that life-giving or ethically responsive acknowledgment is a gift that begins the co-construction of social worlds that become dwelling places for people in their relationships. Human experience of acknowledgment begins at birth, in a care-giver's acknowledging response "Here I am" to the crying infant's call—"Where art thou?" This life-giving communication response begins creating scaffolding that can support the infant's development, including her communication and moral development. At the most basic level, acknowledgment activates mirror neurons of the infant, encouraging growth of neurons and synaptic connections that facilitate all domains of her development. An infant's call—"Where art Thou?"—and the care-giver's response—"Here I am."—is the foundational interaction that scientists have called "serve and return." This tennis metaphor describes how actions of a care-giver sync in response to the infant—to return the infant's initiating action or serve. "If adult response is not in sync, engaging the child in responsive, complementary behaviors, the child's learning process is disrupted with negative implications for later development" (National Scientific Council on the Developing child, cited in Schonkoff & Bales, 2011, p. 26).

The life-giving significance of positive acknowledgment, its relational syncing with an Other, extends beyond infancy throughout the human life span (Hyde, 2006). Beginning with the call—"Where art Thou?" and acknowledging response—"Here I am."—positive acknowledgment co-creates practices of care within relationships, as well as practices of truth, freedom, and justice (Tompkins, 2015). As an ontological communication act, acknowledgment co-creates relationships, preventing social death (isolation) by creating relational connection. Positive acknowledgment finds its parallel in child development theories of attachment, where a child's sense of relational attachment to an adult as secure or insecure influences her development across multiple domains (Brownell & Kopp, 2010; Davies, 2004; Shumaker & Heckel, 2007; Vozzola, 2014). Ethically responsive acknowledgment by adults to the call of infants and children creates a foundation for their survival and thriving, supporting their capacity to become ethically responsive communicators in adolescence and adulthood.

Disagreements in child development about: (1) the nature and characterization of competence and skill at a given age and (2) theoretical frameworks and stages (Brownell & Kopp, 2010) preclude definitive explanation of how children develop as ethically responsive communicators. Despite the many factors involved, including biological and cultural variation, there are patterns to be studied. Human development comes in packages across multiple domains (e.g. motor skills and language acquisition) so that a child appears to be a different person when she crosses a developmental threshold (Davies, 2004). While biology of brain plasticity allows for variation in the progressive biological foundation of human development, with the greatest period of plasticity occurring from infancy through adolescence (de Haan & Martinos, 2008; Spear, 2011), socio-neurobiology researches patterns in development of brain architecture. Communication is another source of pattern and variation, specifically the communicative environment created by adults in which a child grows and develops. A pattern of ethically responsive adult communication acts constructs communicative scaffolding that supports a child's development across multiple domains, including communication and moral development. Ethically responsive communication initially engages a child's mirror neurons, prompting over time attempts to imitate a care-giver's communication behavior. If caregiver communication is significantly inconsistent or relies on negative rather than positive acknowledgment, a child's mirror neurons will be similarly engaged. The adult-generated communicative scaffolding contributes to the social world of the child and influences her cognitive development, which includes her moral emotions, language acquisition, perspective-taking, reasoning, and executive brain functions.

Clarifying key qualities of acknowledgment is important in understanding its role in creating communicative scaffolding that supports a child's development. One quality of acknowledgment is how an acknowledger focuses attention on the Other who nonverbally or verbally calls—"Where art Thou?" Positive acknowledgment involves attunement of the acknowledger's consciousness towards the Other, attunement that does not presume that the acknowledger knows or understands the Other. Listening, for example, as a practice of acknowledgment is characterized by openness to the Other's difference from the acknowledger, of the Other's alterity (Levinas, 1981, 1996, 1997; Lipari, 2009). If the acknowledger's responds as if she already understands the Other, then the acknowledger is treating the Other as the Same as her understanding, denying any difference from the acknowledger. Levinas argues that imposing our understanding of the Other on the Other is a form of communicative violence (1997, 1981; Arnett, 2017), a violence that undermines rather than promotes survival and thriving. An ethically responsive communicator recognizes that her understanding of the Other is partial and limited, so she must attune her consciousness to the Other to understand as best she is able. This relies on the moral emotion of sympathy more than empathy. Sympathetic understanding characteristic of positive acknowledgment is more apparent when communicating with infants and toddlers than with adults. Responsive communication with infants and toddlers, who lack language and knowledge of social cues, requires caregivers to accept the limitation of their understanding and attune their consciousness to the child. How else can symbol-dependent adults begin to comprehend the nonverbal behaviors of a newborn or the limited vocabulary of a toddler? When a caregiver is not open to the possibility that he does not understand or that his understanding is limited and partial, the caregiver is not attuned to the child and is not ethically responsive, even when listening.

Distinguishing between recognition and acknowledgment of an Other clarifies a second quality of acknowledgment (Hyde, 2006; Tompkins, 2009, 2015). This distinction also helps conceptualize how humans develop from a stance of being acknowledged in infancy to possessing capacities and skills for acknowledging Others. According to Ricoeur (2005), recognition is a perceptual act that distinguishes something from what surrounds it, moving a stimulus into the foreground of the recognizer's perceptual field. Until the point of recognition, personal knowledge and understanding of the stimulus are impossible. Recognition produces knowledge of existence, identifying a pathway to further knowledge and potential understanding. Recognition cognitively differs from acknowledgment in that recognition lacks personal understanding, attunement, and simultaneous openness to the limitations of one's personal understanding. Beginning in infancy, children must recognize objects in their environment to explore them. Communication skills such as asking questions, listening, turn taking and symbolization play critical roles in how a child understands people and objects in her environment. Introduction and support of these communication skills by caregivers occurs alongside a child's growing understanding of differences between her Self and Others, aiding her exploration of how she differs from people and objects around her. Practice of these communication skills also promote development of her cognitive skills, empathy/sympathy, perspective-taking, making inferences, and reasoning needed for ethical sensitivity. Practices of communication and ethics are developmentally entwined.

Communicative scaffolding, created by adult acknowledgment of a child, works in tandem with a child's growing brain. A challenge for adults is how to build this scaffolding so that it responsively supports a child's developing capacities for recognition, empathy/sympathy, and cognition. When adults acknowledge an infant at birth and thereafter, they engage the child's mirror neurons, laying a foundation for a child's imitation of adult acknowledgment. The attunement of consciousness and openness to alterity of the child by caregivers is ethically responsive to her development as she moves through different developmental thresholds. Adults help build this scaffolding when their communication acts model and recognize a child's recognition of the existence of objects and people in the child's environment and encourage developmentally appropriate communication practices (such as touch, asking questions, verbalization of ideas and feelings, listening, turn taking (sharing), etc.) that promote a child's recognition of things that are different from her. Listening and asking questions are important for practices of recognition and acknowledgment. How adults encourage these communication practices is critical to prompting or facilitating whether or how a child may communicate, even when adults are not present (See appendix). When adults recognize, support and encourage recognition in developmentally appropriate ways, they encourage a child's curiosity and openness to the world around her. Curiosity and openness promote attunement of consciousness that characterizes positive acknowledgment. Adult modeling, recognition, and support of a child asking questions and listening also promote her recognizing the partial nature of her understanding of Others and the world. Arguably, she becomes less likely to engage in the communicative violence of treating Others as the Same as her Self.

Fundamental to developing a child's capacity for acknowledgment is her capacity to recognize and understand that an Other is both similar and different from her Self. While the empathic capacity is present from birth, distinguishing between Self and Other is a milestone in a child's development. Both are important to developing communication skills and ethical practices as a child balances her self-interest with the self-interests of Others. How a child develops her capacity to ethically respond—"Here I am"—to the Other's call—"Where art Thou?"—depends on her capacity to recognize and understand how she is similar to yet different from an Other, as she attunes her consciousness to the Other.

This discussion of the both/and of empathy and difference in the attunement of positive acknowledgment could lead to a conclusion that toddlers are not cognitively capable of positive acknowledgment. A child should not be expected to practice ethically responsive acknowledgment as would an adult. The challenge for care-givers in their attunement to a child is to discern what is developmentally possible, while also being open to the possibility that a child is capable of more than adults suspect. For example, a two-year old who looks up at his great-grandmother (who has dementia and walks with an unsteady gait) and then offers his hand to walk down a hallway, is practicing developmentally appropriate positive acknowledgment. The great-grandmother's nonverbal call "Where art Thou?" prompted the two-year old's attunement and acknowledging nonverbal response of care, despite their physical and age differences. If appropriately recognized and supported by observant adults, the child's empathetic attunement and offering of his hand can be a building block for more complex empathetic/sympathetic attunement in future developmentally appropriate acts of life-giving acknowledgment.

Conclusion

This exploration of communication and moral development began with discussion of a current lack of ethical sensitivity in many emerging adults identified in social scientific research. A product of moral development, ethical sensitivity is a foundational process for individual ethical action. For communication ethics, diminished ethical sensitivity decreases the presence of ethics in the communication acts that construct the social worlds of communicators, offering an explanation for research findings of the thinness of ethics in the social worlds of many emerging adults. While research points to adult socialization of adolescents for this state of affairs, moral psychology and child development point to earlier beginnings of ethical sensitivity in a moral emotion present at birth, the capacity for empathy. While theory and research in child development and moral psychology make clear that linear stages of child development do not exist, socio-neurobiological research is studying patterns in the human brain that influence human development. Using this research as a starting point, this chapter has presented a claim that communication, specifically ethically responsive acknowledgment of a child by adult caregivers, begins construction of communicative scaffolding that supports development of a child's innate and automatic empathic capacity which, in turn, supports development of a child's ethical sensitivity and ethical responsiveness as a communicator. A caregiver's ethically responsive acknowledgment—"Here I am."—is attuned to the child and her call—"Where art Thou?"—assuring the child's survival and thriving. Over time, ethically responsive acknowledgment by caregivers co-construct communicative scaffolding that supports a child's development as she explores her world and achieves the developmental milestone of recognizing that she is different from objects and persons in the world around her. Understanding the myriad ways she is different from Others is critical to a child's moral and communicative development, influencing her capacity to discern the proper weight to place on her self-interest and the self-interest of Others in her daily interactions. This discernment of difference, of alterity is critical to practice of both communication and ethics.

A developmental function of the communicative scaffolding created by acknowledgment is to facilitate a child's development from a receiver of acknowledgment to an acknowledger. Caregiver modeling, recognition, and encouragement of a child's developmentally appropriate communication skills of recognition and acknowledgment, such as listening, asking questions, and turn taking, support development of a child's empathic capacity and ethical sensitivity as she becomes capable of developmentally appropriate acknowledgment. Beginning in caregivers' acknowledgment of the newborn, practices of communication and ethics are developmentally entwined. Development of an ethically responsive communicator begins at her birth. It begins in the life-giving gift of acknowledgment.

Notes

1. For simplicity, I use "ethics" to refer to both ethics and morals, unless "morals" is in a direct quotation, title or the name of a concept, such as "moral" philosophy.

2. Building upon two previous studies of 3,290 adolescents aged 13–17 in 45 states, a third study is the initial basis for this profile. The profile is based upon 230 in-depth personal interviews from this pool (Smith et al., 2011).

3. These numbers add up to more than 100%, because many respondents included more than one ethical perspective in their answer (Smith et al., 2011).

4. The Case Foundation's mission is to research millennials to "revolutionize philanthropy, unleash entrepreneurship and ignite civic engagement" through annual reports from its *Millennial Impact Project* and consulting workshops (Case Foundation, 2016).

5. Moral psychologist Jonathan Haidt (2008) argues for the importance of disgust in moral development and personal ethics. This chapter focuses on the biological-evolutionary bases of ethics in empathy and its role in development of ethically responsive communication.

6. Significance of developmental neural plasticity is evident in growth of the human brain. The human brain grows from 25% of adult size at birth to 90% at age 5 (de Haan & Martinos, 2008), with significant synaptic pruning in adolescence (Spear, 2011).

Appendix 6.1: Suggested Adult Communication Practices for Developing Acknowledgment—Birth to Age 11 Developed from Davies, 2004.

Developmental Periods	Recognition & Understanding of Others	Caregiver/Adult Scaffolding of Acknowledgment
Infancy: Birth–12 months (approx.) Developmental Goals Include: Develop attachments with care givers & maintain them	Recognize primary caregiver(s) exist. Recognize that points of view (gaze) exist (9–12 mos.)	Positive acknowledgment of infant co-creates secure attachment, grounding future development & capacities for empathy, recognition, & acknowledgment.
Toddler: 1–3 years (approx.) Developmental Goals Include: Balance secure attachment with exploration to promote individuality & autonomy. Increased symbolization Internalize parental values & standards	Recognize Others in terms of Self—"I", "me," & "mine." Late toddlers recognize Others have thoughts, feelings or intentions that differ from their own. Some recognition of aggressive impulses in Others and Self (e.g. hair pulling or taking toys.) Recognize discomfort of Others (empathy) as evident in comforting of peers. Recognize differences in distribution of toys or goodies as evident in demands for reciprocity (emotional bias for equality).	Model acknowledgment, listening & perspective-taking in communication with toddler. Recognize and explain how child's behaviors help or hurt others (e.g., put away toys or pull hair). Encourage recognition of existence of Others. Encourage verbalization of feelings & thoughts, e.g. "Calm means your voice matches mine. Then I can understand you." Encourage toddler making requests & asking questions & recognize when she does so. Encourage listening by reading aloud & answering "why" questions. Encourage sharing by guiding turn-taking to show what sharing looks like.

Continued

Appendix 6.1: Continued

Developmental Periods	Recognition & Understanding of Others	Caregiver/Adult Scaffolding of Acknowledgment
Preschooler: 3–6 yrs. (approx.) Developmental Goals Include: Play to explore; transitioning from egocentric/magical view of world to more causal logic & evidence based.	Improved cognition (e.g., increased memory, causal thinking, drawing inferences, etc.) increases capacity for recognizing how Others are different. Increased exposure to peers decreases egocentrism and increases capacity to recognize Others' perspectives, while remaining egocentric. Play is important in recognizing Others' perspectives and learning how to navigate their own wants and needs. Such recognition can appear during play in negotiation and conflict with peers.	Model acknowledgment by acknowledging the child & Others, as appropriate. Model active listening, perception checking & empathic listening by summarizing & paraphrasing ideas & feelings of the toddler. Model acknowledgment in ways that does not undermine secure attachment. Encourage asking questions, even if preschooler thinks she knows & understands everything. Recognize when she understands. Answer her questions. Explain "why." Encourage listening by reading aloud & answering the preschooler's questions. Encourage listening & asking questions to foster empathy & perspective-taking in problem-solving. Recognize when the preschooler has done so. Monitor play behavior with peers for exclusion or over-competitiveness, but do not intervene unless needed. When intervening, encourage listening & developmentally appropriate perspective-taking.

Appendix 6.1: Continued

Developmental Periods	Recognition & Understanding of Others	Caregiver/Adult Scaffolding of Acknowledgment
Middle Childhood: 6–11 Years (approx.) Developmental Goals Include: Develop sense of calm, capability for learning, & self-control. Develop executive skills & competence—task initiation, working memory, & organization. Establish self in world of peers.	Increasing cognitive skills of perspective-taking increases capacity to recognize & initially understand Others' viewpoints. This decreases egocentrism & increases de-centered thought, promoting empathy and empathic behaviors. Reality testing to test expectations, a recognition that personal understanding may be incomplete. Recognize conflicting views exist & some capacity to tolerate ambivalence (10+ yrs.)	Model acknowledgment by acknowledging the child & Others, as appropriate. Model active listening & perception-checking by summarizing & paraphrasing the child's feelings & thoughts, as appropriate. Encourage listening by reading aloud & answering questions. Encourage the child to verbalize her understanding of Others' views & feelings. Recognize when she does so. Encourage the child to ask questions to check her perceptions. Recognize appropriately when she does so. When intervening in conflict, encourage children to take turns, summarize/ or paraphrase each Other before offering solutions. Recognize appropriately when they do so. Recognize the child's empathetic & sympathetic responses, as appropriate. Affirm, as appropriate (both developmentally & contextually) that these responses do not require complete & accurate knowledge of an Other's thoughts & feelings.

References

Arnett, J. (2006). *Emerging adulthood: The winding road from late teens through the twenties.* New York: Oxford UP.

Arnett, R. C. (2017). *Levinas's rhetorical demand: The unending obligation of communication ethics.* Carbondale, IL: Southern Illinois University Press.

Baird, A. D., Scheffer, I. E. & Wilson, S. J. (2011). Mirror neuron system involvement in empathy: A critical look at the evidence. *Social Neuroscience, 6,* 327–335. doi:10.10 80/17470919.2010.547085

Ballard, R. L., Bell McManus, L., Holba, A. M., Jovanovic, S., Tompkins, P. S., Charron, L. J. N., Hoffer, M. L., Leavitt, M. A., & Swenson-Lepper, T. (2014). Teaching communication ethics as central to the discipline. *Journal of the Association for Communication Administration, 33,* 2–20.

Baron-Cohen, S. (2011). *The science of evil: On empathy and the origins of cruelty.* New York: Basic Books.

Blake, P. R., & McAuliffe, K. (2011). "I had so much it didn't seem fair": Eight-year-olds reject two forms of inequity. *Cognition, 120,* 215–24.

Bloom, P. (2013). *Just babies: The origins of good and evil.* NY: Crown Publishers.

Brownell, C. A., & Kopp, C. B. (Eds.). (2010). *Socioemotional development in the toddler years: Transitions and transformations.* New York: Guilford.

Brummett, B. (1981). Ethical relativism as rhetorically grounded. *The Western Journal of Speech Communication, 45,* 286–298.

The Case Foundation. "The millennial impact." The Case Foundation. http://themillennialimpact.com

Cheney, G., May, S., & Munshi, D. (2011). *The handbook of communication ethics.* NY: Routledge.

Davies, D. (2004). *Child development: A practitioner's guide.* New York: Guilford Press.

De Haan, M., & Martinos, M. (2008). Brain function. *Encyclopedia of Infant and Early Childhood Development,* 225–239. doi:10.1016/B978-01237077-9.00028-1.

Eisenberg, N. (2000). Empathy and sympathy. In M. Lewis & J. M. Haviland-Jones (Eds.), *Handbook of emotions* (2nd ed., pp. 677–691). New York: Guilford Press.

Eisenberg, N., Spinrad, T., & Sadovsky, A. (2006). Empathy-related responding in children. In M. Killen & J. G. Smetana (Eds.), *Handbook of moral development* (pp. 517–50). Mahwah, NJ: Lawrence Earlbaum Associates.

Haidt, J. (2008). Morality. *Perspectives on Psychological Science 3,* 65–72.

Hastings, P. D., Zahn-Waxler, C., & McShane, K. (2006). We are by nature moral creatures: Biological bases of concern for others. In M. Killen & J. G. Smetana (Eds.), *Handbook of moral development* (pp. 482–516). Mahwah, NJ: Lawrence Erlbaum Associates.

Hoffman, M. L. (2001). *Empathy and moral development: Implications for caring and justice.* New York: Cambridge University Press.

Hyde, M. J. (2006). *The life-giving gift of acknowledgment.* West Lafayette, IN: Purdue UP.

Kagan, J. (2013). *The human spark: The science of human development.* NY: Basic Books.

Levinas, E. (1996). Meaning and sense. In A. T. Peperzak, S. Critchley, & R. Bernasconi (Eds.), *Emmanuel Levinas: Basic philosophical writings* (pp. 33–64). Bloomington, IN: U of Indiana Press.

Levinas, E. (1997; 1981). *Otherwise than being or beyond essence*. A. Lingus (Trans.). Pittsburg, PA: Duquesne UP.

Lipari, L. (2009). Listening otherwise: The voice of ethics. *International Journal of Listening (the)*, *23*, 44–59.

Lough, S., Kipps, C. M., Treise, C., Watson, P., Blair J. R., & Hodges, J. R. (2005). Social reasoning, emotions and empathy in frontotempral dementia. *Neuropsychologica*, *44*(6), 950–958.

Miller-Day, M., Pezalla, A., & Chesnut, R. (2013). Children are in families too! The prescence of children in communication research. *Journal of Family Communication, 13*, 150–165. doi:10.1080/15267431.2013.768251.

Nussbaum, M. C. (2001). *Upheavals of thought: The intelligence of emotions*. New York, Cambridge UP.

Pew Research Center. (March 2011). "For millennials, parenthood trumps marriage." Pew social and demographic trends. Available: http://pewresearchcenter.org

Pew Research Center. (March 2014). "Millennials in adulthood: Detached from institutions, networked with friends." Available: http://pewresearchcenter.org

Prehn, K., Korczykowski, M., Rao, H., Fang, Z., Detre, J. A., & Robertson, D. C. (2015). Natural correlates of post-conventional moral reasoning: A voxel-based morphometry study. *PloS ONE, 10*(6), e0122914. doi:10.1371/journal.pone.0122914.

Rest, J., Navarez, D., Bebeau, M. J., & Thomas, S. J. (1999). *Postconventional moral thinking: A neo-Kohlbergian approach*. Mahwah, NJ: Lawrence Erlbaum Associates.

Ricoeur, P. (2005). *The course of recognition*. D. Pellauer, trans. Cambridge, MA: Harvard University Press.

Riveria, R. (5 January 2013). "Asking what to do with symbols of grief as memorials pile up." *New York Times*. http://www.nytimes.com/2013/01/06/nyregion/as-memorials-pile-up-newtown-struggles-to-move-on.html?_r=0

Schonkoff, J. P., & Bailes, S. N. (2011). Science does not speak for itself: Translating child development research for the public and its policymakers. *Child Development, 82*, 17–32. doi:10.1111/j.1467–8624.2010.01538.x.

Sheskin, M., Bloom, P., & Wynn, K. (2014). Anti-equality: Social comparison in young children. *Cognition, 130*, 152–156. doi:10.1016/j.cognition.2013.10.008.

Shoemaker, W. (2012). The social brain network and human moral behavior. *Journal of Religion and Science, 47*, 806–820.

Shumaker, D. M., & Heckel, R. V. (2007). *Kids of character*. Westport, CT: Praeger.

Smith, C., Christoffersen, K., Davidson, H., & Herzog, P. A. (2011). *Lost in transition: The dark side of emerging adulthood*. New York: Oxford UP.

Socha, T. J., & Eller, A. (2015). Parent/caregiver-child communication and moral development: Toward a conceptual foundation of an ecological model of lifespan communication and good relationships. In V. Waldron & D. Kelley (Eds.), *Moral talk across the lifespan: Creating good relationships*. (pp. 15–35). New York: Peter Lang.

Socha, T. J., & Yingling, J. (2010). *Families communicating with children*. Cambridge, UK: Polity.

Soliz, J., & Rittenour, C. E. (2015). Generativity in the family: Grandparent-grandchild relationships and the intergenerational transmission of values and worldviews. In V. Waldron & D. Kelley (Eds.), *Moral talk across the lifespan: Creating good relationships*. (pp. 55–74). New York: Peter Lang.

Spear, L. P. (2011). Brain development. *Encyclopedia of Adolescence, 1,* 87–9. Waltham, MA: Elsevier. doi:10.1016/8979-0-12-373915-500006-1.

Spitzberg, B. H., & Cupach, W. (Eds.). (2007) *The dark side of interpersonal communication* (2nd ed.). New York: Routledge.

Stewart, J. (1995). *Language as articulate contact: Toward a post-semiotic philosophy of communication.* Albany, NY: SUNY University Press.

Tompkins, P. S. (2009). Rhetorical listening and moral sensitivity. *International Journal of Listening 23,* 60–79.

Tompkins, P. S. (2015). Acknowledgment, justice, and communication ethics. *Review of Communication, 15,* 240–257. doi:10.1080/15358593.2015.1078490.

Tompkins, P. S. (2019). *Practicing communication ethics: Development, discernment and decision making* (2nd ed.). New York: Routledge.

Toulmin, S. E. (1988). The recovery of practical reason. *The American Scholar, 57,* 337–352.

Toulmin, S. E. (2001). *Return to reason.* Cambridge, MA: Harvard University Press.

Tronto, J. C. (1993). *Moral boundaries: A political argument for an ethic of care.* New York: Routledge.

Twenge, J. M., & Campbell, W. K. (2009). *The narcissism epidemic: Living in the age of entitlement.* NY: Free Press.

Twenge, J. M., Campbell, W. K., & Carter, N. T. (2014). Declines in trust in others and confidence in institutions among American adults and late adolescents, 1972–2012. *Psychological Science, 25,* 1914–1923. doi:10.1177/0956797614545133.

Twenge, J. M., Konrath, S., Foster, J. D., Campbell, W. K., & Bushman, B. J. (2008). Egos inflating over time: A cross-temporal meta-analysis of the Narcissistic Personality Inventory. *Journal of Personality, 76,* 875–901.

Vetlesen, A. J. (1994). *Perception, empathy and judgment: An inquiry into the preconditions of moral performance.* University Park, PA: Penn State University Press.

Vozzola, E. C. (2014). *Moral development: Theory and applications.* Routledge: Taylor & Francis.

Waldron, V., Danaher, J., Goman, C., Piemonte, N., & Kloeber, D. (2015). Which parental messages about morality are accepted by emerging adults? In V. Waldron & D. Kelley (Eds.), *Moral talk across the lifespan: Creating good relationships* (pp. 35–54). New York: Peter Lang.

Walter, H. (2012). Social cognitive neuroscience of empathy: Concepts, circuits and genes. *Emotion Review, 4,* 9–77. doi:10.1177/1754073911421379.

Section Three: Digital Communication Development

7. An Historical Look at Children and Media Research

Lessons Learned and Questions Revisited

ALEXIS R. LAURICELLA
Northwestern University

FASHINA ALADE
Northwestern University

ELLEN WARTELLA
Northwestern University

Children's use of electronic media technology has been a topic of recurring concern, study, and public policy since at least the early 20th century (Wartella & Robb, 2007). With each new generation of media to occupy public interest and, most importantly, children's leisure time, concerns about media's impact on children's social and cognitive development have recurred with each new technological innovation. Rooted in the fact that children have been early adopters and, by and large, heavy users of media, concerned parents, teachers, and caregivers have consistently worried about the impact of such media use on children's knowledge, attitudes, and behaviors. So it has been, and so it is today. Drawing on both popular and political discourse around children and media as well as empirical research, we present an overview of children's media use today, along with a historical framework for looking at these issues, and, finally, a modern perspective for considering the effects of media on children.

The Ubiquity of Media as the Root of Concern

Recent national studies have demonstrated that children are using media at very early ages. According to Rideout (2013), children age zero to eight use screen media (including television, DVDs, computers, video games, and mobile devices) almost every day, and, on average, for nearly two hours each day. While use of traditional media like television and DVDs has decreased slightly in recent years, time spent with mobile devices has increased substantially. Rideout (2013) found that nearly three-quarters of children under eight have used a mobile device for playing games, watching videos, or using apps. Children now spend an average of 15 minutes per day with mobile devices (Rideout, 2013).

The most recent survey of older children's media use by Common Sense Media (Rideout, 2015), which was completed by 2,600 8- to 18-year-olds, shows that today's youth are entrenched in media: 13- to 18-year-olds average nine hours (8:56) of entertainment media use each day. This excludes time youth spend doing homework or at school where they also may be using media such as computers, iPads, or using mobile phones. Eight- to 12-year-olds, or *tweens*, spent slightly less time with media, averaging about 6 hours (5:55) of media use per day. Despite the increase in use of mobile, interactive media like smartphones and tablets, watching TV and listening to music still rein in the lives of American youth with 62% of tweens and 58% of teens reporting watching TV everyday and 54% of tweens and 73% of tweens listening to music daily. Most surprisingly, this 2015 study of tweens and teens found that social media use lagged behind traditional media use with only 45% of teens reporting using social media every day. These data illustrate the undeniable ubiquity and diversity of technology in children and adolescents' lives.

With so many entertainment media options, today it is important to acknowledge that not all youth use media in the same ways. Common Sense Media found several different profiles of young media users. For tweens, a little over one-quarter of the sample (27%) were light media users averaging only two hours and 16 minutes of screen time per day. The next largest subgroup was "video gamers," comprising 23% of the sample of tweens and averaging seven hours and 41 minutes per day. "Social networkers" who spend their time on Facebook, Twitter, and Instagram, represent 15% of the sample and average about 10 hours with media each day, followed by mobile gamers (14%), readers (11%), and heavy television viewers (10%).

A different typology of media users emerged for teens aged 13–18 (Rideout, 2015). About a third (32%) of the teens were considered light media users, spending a little over two hours a day with media. About a quarter (26%) reported being heavy viewers of television and spending 16.5 hours a day with media. One in five were labeled gamers/computer users, and they spend nine hours and seventeen minutes a day with media followed by readers (who spend about 6 hours a day with media) and social networkers (10% of the sample who spend about 9.5 hours a day with media). Beyond media use types, Rideout (2015) found gender differences in older youth's media preferences. Specifically, girls were more like to report listening to music, reading, and using social media as their favorite activity whereas boys were more likely to report playing videogames as their favorite activity.

The ubiquity of media in the lives of children demonstrated in these studies has been the supported the questioning regarding media's impact on youth. Over the last century, each new medium, including film, radio, television, computers and now social media and mobile media, has been thought to hold promise for the educational and social benefits for children but also led to concern for children's exposure to inappropriate or harmful content, and especially violent or sexualized content, as well as commercialized content (Wartella & Robb, 2007). To a large extent, these questions about potential positive effect coupled with public concerns about negative consequences helped establish a research agenda for scholars concerned about the role of media and technology in children's development (Wartella & Reeves, 1985).

An Historical Overview of Public Concerns Regarding Children's Media Use

Over the past 30 or so years, there have been multiple recounting of the history of recurring controversies that surround the introduction of new media technology into American society (Paik, 2001; Singhal, Cody, Rogers, & Sabido, 2003; Wartella & Reeves, 1985; Wartella & Robb, 2007) which influenced the social science research agenda for studying the impact of media technology on children's development.

When films were first introduced into American society in the early 1900s, they were accompanied with great expectations for how they might afford a means of mass education outside of classrooms and a great social force for business, religion, and entertainment (Wartella & Jennings, 2000). It did not take long, however, for concerns about the potential corrupting influences of movies on youth to emerge. By 1931, some 40 national religious and educational groups had adopted resolutions asking for federal regulation of film and especially mechanisms to prohibit youth from gaining access to inappropriate content (Wartella & Jennings, 2000). What emerged was a series of studies, first detailing how much time youth spent with film, then studying the impact of film-going on youth. Indeed, the history of studies of film and youth set the stage for many subsequent analyses of radio and television as well (Wartella & Reeves, 1985).

According to Wartella and Reeves' (1985) historical analysis, the earliest social science studies of film, the Payne Fund studies, were conducted between 1933 and 1934. These 12 volumes of research, conducted by the most prominent psychologists, sociologists, and educators of the time, examined the effects of film and movies on such diverse topics as sleep patterns, leisure time use, attitudes toward violence, and delinquent behavior.

The conclusions of the Payne Fund studies presaged later work of the Surgeon General's multivolume investigation of Television and Social Behavior (1972). The Payne Fund studies found that film's effects on youth depended on the child's age, sex, predispositions, perceptions, social experiences, and so on. Similar research on children's radio listening behaviors demonstrated that child age influenced child's preference for radio programming (see Herzog, 1941). That is, there is no magic bullet in which a media presentation impacts all children in the same manner.

Nonetheless, film content does influence children's knowledge about the world, their attitudes, and their social behaviors. Youth do learn from and model that which they see in film and other media (e.g., see Wartella & Jennings, 2000). Moreover, effects of radio on children were also being demonstrated including influences on school performance (Herzog, 1941) and children's responses to advertising and product requests (for an historical review see Wartella & Reeves, 1985).

The emergence of television as a mass medium in 1948 and its prominent adoption by America as to be almost universal in American homes by the late 1950s brought about another round of public concerns and social science research on media and youth. While proponents of television liked to describe it as "the biggest classroom the world has ever seen" (Wartella & Jennings, 2000, p. 34) opponents noted how this new "Pied Piper" could disrupt family life and hold inordinate influences on children (Wartella & Robb, 2011) by exposing them to violence and crime, to a debased and low brow culture, and to the world of adults brought into their living rooms (Wartella & Jennings, 2000).

By 1960, 90% of US households had a television set (Mitroff & Stephenson, 2007), but with growing popularity came growing criticism. It was now implicated as a cause for children's deleterious behaviors. In the 1960s Senate hearings about the televised images and child behavior were aired on television raising the level of public awareness and concern about violence and television (Murray, 2007) and subsequently fueled decades of research on the associations between violent television content and children's aggressive behaviors (Paik & Comstock, 1994). The increased governmental concern about media violence urged broadcasters to self-regulate content. Standards and Practices departments were enlarged, and increased regulation of violence was seen in both general and children's programming (Hendershot, 1998). In 1968, Action for Children's Television (ACT) was established to advocate for better quality, less commercial television. The work of ACT led the FCC to establish a permanent children's unit and issue a Children's Policy Statement in 1974 (Hendershot, 1998).

As regulation efforts were increasing, advertisers began to shift their focus to adult viewers, resulting in increased value of advertising slots during primetime thus relegating children's shows to Saturday morning because of their inability to attract advertisers willing to pay prime time rates. Despite a temporary drop in the educational quality of children's programs, the establishment of Saturday morning programs was a significant step in segmenting the television viewing audience. This segmentation not only enabled advertisers to target adult viewers in primetime, but also ultimately encouraged programmers to create age-targeted programming for young viewers (Mitroff & Stephenson, 2007).

Various government investigations of television's impact on youth were held from the 1950s to 1970s, including the 1955 Congressional hearings on televised crime and juvenile delinquency, and the Congressional hearings following the 1972 release of the Surgeon General's study of television and social behavior (1972). Through these hearings an enormous literature on television's impact on youth emerged. Much like the Payne Fund Studies of the 1930s, the 1972 Surgeon General's multi-volume report and the 1982 update reviewed both new studies and the vast and growing literature on television's impact on youth and adults to assess the power of television to influence viewers. Although the major focus of these studies was the impact of violent content, to a lesser extent, they also examined advertising content and educational programming. As with other reviews (for instance a 1980 Boys Town review of nearly 3000 studies of children and television), a consensus was emerging that television could have a powerful impact on child viewers, and that what determined that impact was both the content of the television programming and the particular nature of the child watching the screen. The famous adage from the 1972 Surgeon General's study was that "For some children, under some circumstances, some media content can have powerful effect" (p. 520).

During the 1980s, a strong push for governmental deregulation of television emerged. The FCC voted in 1984 to allow unrestricted commercial airtime, which left the number of commercials shown in any given program up to the discretion of the broadcaster. Since children's shows did not bring in the same amount of advertising revenue as popular shows for adult audiences, networks began to discontinue shows created specifically for young viewers

(Mitroff & Stephenson, 2007). This opened up a place for inexpensive animated shows based on licensed characters, and thus, the program-length commercial was created. By 1985, at least 40 licensed character-based programs were on the air. Their educational and aesthetic quality was questionable, but they were inexpensive to produce and an effective means for advertising (Mitroff & Stephenson, 2007).

In an attempt to rein in children's television after the deregulatory period of the 1980s, the Children's Television Act was passed in 1990 (Jordan & Woodard, 1998). This act stipulated that any station wishing to renew its broadcast license had to provide proof that children's educational and informational programming was part of its program schedule. However, this attempt at industry self-regulation was unsuccessful in changing the landscape of children's television because it lacked clear parameters. Educational and information programming was broadly defined as content that would "further the positive development of the child in any respect, including the child's cognitive/intellectual, or emotional/social needs" (Children's Television Act 1990). Issues such as how much programming was sufficient, how age-specific the programming needed to be, when the programming needed to air, and how the programming should be identified were largely undefined (Strasburger, Wilson, & Jordan, 2009).

In 1996, the Children's Television Act was amended with stricter guidelines that required three hours of educational/informational (E/I) programming per week be aired between 7 am and 10 pm and more defined what could be considered E/I programming. The Children's Television Act made two important statements about children's television. First, this Act made it clear that children can and do learn from television. Second, this Act made the important statement that broadcast television should be used to serve the public interest (Jordan, 2004). By the time the new regulations were in place, however, many viewers had switched over to cable networks. Further, American television continued on its path towards increased audience segmentation with its vast adoption of Cable television and multiple channels. Children could now watch "children television" channels like Disney and Nickelodeon that were outside of the jurisdiction of the Act. Thus, much of the young television audience was unaffected (Mitroff & Stephenson, 2007).

Digital Technology's Unfolding History

While the vast majority of the history on children and media centers on television, recent decades have introduced new digital technologies, and a reprise of old concerns. The rise of computers and the Internet presented a very similar paradox to what was seen with earlier technologies. A report released right at the turn of the century found that, on the one hand, 70% of parents said the Internet was a place for children to discover "fascinating, useful things," while on the other hand, more than 75% were concerned that their children might give out personal information or view sexually explicit images on the Internet (Turow, 1999 as cited in Wartella & Jennings, 2000). Similarly, early public discussions around the rise of social media noted that using social networking sites might be important in tweens' and teens' development of a social identity and to connect adolescents with likeminded others outside of their physically organized social groups (Foot, 2014). At the same time though, a pushback of negative discourse began to be voiced, including such concerns as insuring that social media users find downtime where media might not be used; concerns that if we only connect with others online, the powerful role of face to face communication will be lost (e.g., Turkle, 2015); that children's abilities to engage in outdoor play and more traditional childhood play will be lost; and that all of us, including our youth, loose a sense of privacy from online sharing (Foot, 2014).

Most recently, the sharp rise in ownership of mobile media has simply added to these concerns by providing children 24/7 access to screen time anywhere and everywhere (Rideout, 2013, 2015). While parent's report that mobile technologies can be useful parenting tools (Wartella, Rideout, Lauricella, & Connell, 2014) enabling them to keep their children occupied while parents are occupied in or out of the home, the overall study of mobile media access at young ages, and over the course of childhood is not very well understood or studied. Because new media involves greater potential for interactivity compared with earlier media, some contend that it also holds more promise for enriched learning experiences (Wartella & Jennings, 2000).

A Modern Approach to Studying the Effects of Media on Children

It is only in the relatively recent past that we have begun to truly incorporate what we know about child development into our interpretation and understanding of the effects of media on children. In an attempt to refocus the conversation, there has been increased discussion about factors related to the individual *child* using the media, the specific *content* presented via the media device, and the *context* in which the media technology is being used. Lisa Guernsey (Guernsey, 2007) coined the term the "3 C's" to reflect the need to examine these three factors in order to more accurately understand the effects of media on children.

Child

Characteristics of the individual child affect the way the child will process the content and be influenced by the context of the media experience. Although many media scholars have acknowledged the importance of individual differences, very few empirical studies have taken them into account in a meaningful way. Instead, empirical studies tend to control for individual differences in pursuit of universal effects (Valkenburg & Peter, 2013). But in order to gain a full understanding of the media experience, researchers must consider the users as individuals. Media users do not just respond to the screen; they also bring their own perceptions and attributions to the viewing/playing experience, which affects their individual experiences with the medium (Salomon, 1983). For example, individual differences in child age, cognitive abilities, and personality traits may largely impact how the child is affected by each media experience.

Age

Age is an important variable that can powerfully influence the experience the child has with media. What may be educational and informative to an elementary school-age student may not be educational for an infant or toddler. Recent research has examined the impact of media specifically on infants and toddlers, both positive and negative. Anderson and Pempek (2005) coined the term *video deficit effect* to describe the phenomenon that infants and toddlers appear to learn better and more easily from a live demonstration than from an identical on-screen presentation. This was based on research of infant imitation (e.g., Barr & Hayne, 1999; Hayne, Herbert, & Simcock, 2003), language learning (e.g., Grela, Lin, & Krcmar, 2003), and object search tasks (e.g., Evans, Crawley, & Anderson, 2004; Schmitt & Anderson, 2002) that largely demonstrated that learning suffered when material was presented on a screen until the child was about 2.5 years old. In the last decade, new research has suggested that it may not be a video deficit but rather a transfer deficit in which young children struggle to transfer information across contexts or platforms (Barr, 2010).

Cognitive Abilities

Recently, Aladé and Nathanson (2016) looked specifically at how individual differences impact preschoolers' learning from educational television. In accordance with the Capacity Model (Fisch, 2000)—a theoretical framework for understanding how children process the narrative and educational content that they encounter on TV—the authors found that verbal ability, short-term memory, and prior knowledge related to the content were highly significant factors that impacted how much a child was able to learn from an educational television program. Children who were high in verbal ability, for example, spent less mental effort on processing the narrative content, and were thus able to comprehend more of the educational content presented in the show.

Personality Traits

While research has shown that media can have significant negative effects on children, it is important to note that not all children who are exposed to violent or sexual content, for example, will experience the associated negative effects. Rather, research has demonstrated that there are differential susceptibility factors that should be taken into account. Research on the impact of "the thin ideal" has demonstrated that risk factors such as prior body image disturbance moderate how the media directly affects the child. For example, one study found that those who were more satisfied with their physical appearance were less affected by exposure to thin-ideal images in the media than those who had lower body satisfaction (Posavac, Posavac, & Posavac, 1998). Another study by Anschutz and colleagues (2011) found that highly restrained students exposed to commercials with slim models and diet-related products ate less snack food while watching television, whereas less restrained eaters ate slightly more after seeing those same commercials. Furthermore, the authors found that girls in sixth grade specifically seemed to be most susceptible to exposure to thin-ideal characters, indicating that gender and age were also important contributing factors.

While certainly not exhaustive, this list demonstrates that many types of individual differences can affect children's experiences with media. Future research should continue to consider media users as individuals in order to advance our understanding of the effects that have been studied for decades.

Content

After years of researcher demonstrating both positive and negative effects of technologies, many began to accept Marshall McLuhan's famous quote,[1] *the medium isn't the message; the message is the message.* In other words, the same technology that can be used for good can also be used for evil; the important

---

1 "The medium is the message" is a phrase coined by communication theorist Marshall McLuhan, first introduced in his most widely known book, *Understanding Media: The Extensions of Man*, published in 1964.

factor that determines what effect the technology will have is the actual content being presented on that device. As Fisch (2004, p.) writes, "The same medium that influences children to act aggressively after exposure to violent programming should also be able to influence them toward cooperative behavior after watching prosocial programming." Thus, in recent years we've seen a shift in focus from the impact of the media platforms themselves to the impact of exposure to the content being displayed.

Educational

Despite concerns voiced by naysayers of educational television, it has been well documented over the last several decades that high-quality, curriculum-based, educational television can in fact support child learning. This has been shown across a host of educational outcomes including school readiness (Anderson, Huston, Schmitt, Linebarger, & Wright, 2001), literacy skills (Linebarger, Kosanic, Greenwood, & Doku, 2004), mathematical skills (Fisch & McCann, 1993), science skills (Dingwall & Aldridge, 2006), and prosocial skills (Mares & Woodard, 2005). For the past 40 years, Sesame Workshop and independent academic researchers have repeatedly documented that *Sesame Street* positively impacts children in a range of outcomes (Fisch, Truglio, & Cole, 1999). More broadly, research with preschool-aged children has found that watching educational media at home is positively associated with preschoolers' development of literacy, mathematics, science, and prosocial behavior (e.g., Comstock & Scharrer, 2007; Fisch, 2004; Friedrich & Stein, 1973; Kirkorian, Wartella, & Anderson, 2008).

Violence

While quality educational content can have positive effects on children, other types of content can have adverse or mixed effects on children depending on the type of content they are exposed to. For example, viewing violent media content continues to be associated with aggressive and violent behavior, and this has been shown across several large-scale reviews of research (see C. A. Anderson et al., 2003; Brown & Hamilton-Giachritsis, 2005; Bushman & Huesmann, 2006; Huesmann, 1986). Similarly, it has been documented that violent videogames specifically are associated with increased aggressive behavior and decreased prosocial behavior (see Anderson & Bushman, 2001). For example, in one early study, children who played violent martial arts videogames were more physically and verbally aggressive in their play compared to children who played a non-violent game (Irwin & Gross, 1995).

Violent content is not the only type of content that has been associated with negative effects. Exposure to unhealthy food marketing has been consistently associated with unhealthy eating behaviors and obesity in young children (Borzekowski & Robinson, 2001; Gorn & Goldberg, 1982). Specifically, research demonstrates that exposure to advertising for junk food increases children's choice and preference for the advertised unhealthy foods (Halford, Gillespie, Brown, Pontin, & Dovey, 2004; Harris, Speers, Schwartz, & Brownell, 2012). In contrast, when healthier foods are marketing to children, the effect of this content can positively influence their rates of healthy food selection (Dias & Agante, 2011). Similarly, Pempek and Calvert (2009) found that low-income, African-American children who played a computer game that promoted healthy foods were more likely to select and eat a healthier food at the end of exposure compared to children who played a game with less healthy foods.

Context

Finally, in addition to considering child factors and the specific content portrayed, understanding the context of media exposure is crucial for understanding the collective impact or effect of children's experiences with media.

Co-use. Although empirical research often treats media use as a solo activity, in reality, children often consume media alongside siblings, friends, and parents (Connell, Lauricella, & Wartella, 2015). When media is used as a social opportunity in which parents and children co-use or co-watch the media together there is increased opportunity for parent-child interaction and mediation of the material. Research demonstrates that parents are more likely to co-use television and books and least likely to co-use video games with their young children (Connell et al., 2015). The way in which parents interact or mediate children's media experiences has been shown to relate to how the children are influenced by the exposure (e.g., Austin, 1993; Buijzen & Valkenburg, 2005).

Physical space. Additionally, the physical place and use of media in the home has shown to influence media effects on young children. Research has demonstrated that television on in the background results in decreased parent-child interaction (Kirkorian, Pempek, Murphy, Schmidt, & Anderson, 2009) and interrupted toy play behavior in young children (Schmidt, Pempek, Kirkorian, Lund, & Anderson, 2008). Furthermore, consistent background TV in the household has been associated with detrimental effects on cognitive development (Lapierre, Piotrowski, & Linebarger, 2012; Nathanson, Alade, Sharp, Rasmussen, & Christy, 2014).

Technological features. The context of a media use experience is also affected by the affordances of the specific technology platform. For example, television content on a TV screen is minimally interactive, whereas tablet apps and games are increasingly interactive and often require child response for the activity to continue. These affordances can either provide opportunities for the child to benefit from the interaction or possibly result in experiences that are less positive. Recent research testing the effectiveness of interactivity has demonstrated mixed results with regard to learning. For example, an object search task with toddlers found that a contingent computer game supported learning and transfer of knowledge (Lauricella, Pempek, Barr, & Calvert, 2010). However, another study found that for some toddlers, contingent touchscreen was less effective for word learning than non-contingent video (Kirkorian, Choi, & Pempek, 2016). Yet another study found that the influence of interactivity was highly dependent on the nature of the assessment task (Aladé, Lauricella, Beaudoin-Ryan, & Wartella, 2016). Preschoolers who played a measuring game on an interactive/contingent touchscreen tablet performed better on a measuring task that was highly similar to the game, but their peers who watched a non-contingent video of the same content were better able to apply the skills to a task that required higher levels of transfer.

Generally speaking, it requires a great deal of cognitive effort for very young children to successfully learn from screen media (Wartella, Richert, & Robb, 2010), but there are certain technological features than can support or improve their learning. For example, research has demonstrated that factors related to the depictions of the show may influence the way in which infants and toddlers learn from screen presentations. There is evidence that young children may benefit from video experiences that have higher levels of social relevancy to the child. For example, the video or transfer deficit effect was ameliorated when infants and toddlers viewed videos that featured characters that they were familiar with (Gola, Richards, Lauricella, & Calvert, 2013; Krcmar, 2010; Lauricella, Gola, & Calvert, 2011) or when the character directly interacted with the child through the screen (Troseth, Saylor, & Archer, 2006). This evidence reinforces the importance of looking at a wide array of factors that may influence the effects of media on children, rather than making broad claims across different media types and/or media users.

The Future of Children and Media Research

An historical look at children and media discourse helps bring to light important areas for current and future children's communication research. Some parts of the picture are now clear; every new technology is accompanied by a wave of both panic and excitement about potential effects that is reflected in both popular press and empirical research. To a large extent, both the panic and the optimism are warranted. Media undoubtedly can have both direct and indirect influences on the youth. But the valence of that influence varies greatly and is highly dependent on the content, the context, and the child.

As new technologies bring about new affordances, our research questions must continue to change and evolve. For example, in our current booming age of mobile media, there is still much to discover about the effects of constant connectedness on children's development. Virtual and augmented reality platforms are new sources children and media buzz that have barely begun to be tapped. But even as technology changes at increasingly rapid rates, it is important to stay grounded in the history of the children and media field so that future research can capitalize on what we have come to know and understand so far.

References

Aladé, F., Lauricella, A. R., Beaudoin-Ryan, L., & Wartella, E. (2016). Measuring with Murray: Touchscreen technology and preschoolers' STEM learning. *Computers in Human Behavior, 62*, 433–441. doi:10.1016/j.chb.2016.03.080.

Aladé, F., & Nathanson, A. I. (2016). What preschoolers bring to the show: The relation between viewer characteristics and children's learning from educational TV. *Media Psychology.* doi:10.1080/15213269.2015.1054945.

Anderson, C. A., Berkowitz, L., Donnerstein, E., Huesmann, L. R., Johnson, J. D., Linz, D., ... Wartella, E. (2003). The influence of media violence on youth. *Psychological Science in the Public Interest, 4*, 81–110.

Anderson, C. A., & Bushman, B. J. (2001). Effects of violent video games on aggressive behavior, aggressive cognition, aggressive affect, physiological arousal, and prosocial behavior: A meta-analytic review of the scientific literature. *Psychological Science, 12*, 353–359.

Anderson, D. R., Huston, A. C., Schmitt, K. L., Linebarger, D. L., & Wright, J. C. (2001). Early childhood television viewing and adolescent behavior: The recontact study. *Monographs of the Society for Research in Child Development, 66*, 1–143. doi:10.1111/1540-5834.00121.

Anderson, D. R., & Pempek, T. A. (2005). Television and very young children. *The American Behavioral Scientist, 48*, 505–522.

Anschutz, D. J., Van Strien, T., & Engels, R. C. (2011). Exposure to slim images in mass media: Television commercials as reminders of restriction in restrained eaters. *Psychology of Popular Media Culture, 1*, 48–59.

Austin, E. W. (1993). Exploring the effects of active parental mediation of television content. *Journal of Broadcasting & Electronic Media, 37*, 147–158.

Barr, R. (2010). Transfer of learning between 2D and 3D sources during infancy: Informing theory and practice. *Developmental Review, 30,* 128–154.

Barr, R., & Hayne, H. (1999). Developmental changes in imitation from television during infancy. *Child Development, 70,* 1067–1081.

Borzekowski, D. L., & Robinson, T. N. (2001). The 30-second effect: An experiment revealing the impact of television commercials on food preferences of preschoolers. *Journal of the American Dietetic Association, 101,* 42–46.

Brown, K. D., & Hamilton-Giachritsis, C. (2005). The influence of violent media on children and adolescents: A public health approach. *Lancet, 365,* 702–710.

Buijzen, M., & Valkenburg, P. M. (2005). Parental mediation of undesired advertising effects. *Journal of Broadcasting & Electronic Media, 49,* 153–165.

Bushman, B. J., & Huesmann, L. R. (2006). Short-term and long-term effects of violent media on aggression in children and adults. *Archives of Pediatrics & Adolescent Medicine, 160,* 348–352.

Comstock, G., & Scharrer, E. (2007). *Media and the American child.* Burlington, MA: Elsevier.

Connell, S. L., Lauricella, A. R., & Wartella, E. (2015). Parental co-use of media technology with their young children in the USA. *Journal of Children and Media, 9,* 5–21. doi:10.1080/17482798.2015.997440.

Dias, M., & Agante, L. (2011). Can advergames boost children's healthier eating habits? A comparison between healthy and non-healthy food. *Journal of Consumer Behaviour, 10,* 152–160.

Dingwall, R., & Aldridge, M. (2006). Television wildlife programming as a source of popular scientific information: A case study of evolution. *Public Understanding of Science, 15,* 131–152.

Eisenberg, A. L. (1936). *Children and radio Programs.* New York: Columbia University Press

Evans, M., Crawley, A., & Anderson, D. (2004). Two-year-olds' object retrieval based on television: Testing a perceptual account. *Unpublished manuscript, University of Massachusetts-Amherst.*

Fisch, S. M. (2000). A capacity model of children's comprehension of educational content on television. *Media Psychology, 2,* 63–91. doi:10.1207/S1532785XMEP0201_4.

Fisch, S. M. (2004). *Children's learning from educational television.* Mahwah, New Jersey: Lawrence Erlbaum.

Fisch, S. M., & McCann, S. K. (1993). Making broadcast television participative: Eliciting mathematical behavior through "Square One TV". *Educational Technology Research and Development, 41*(3), 103–109.

Fisch, S. M., Truglio, R. T., & Cole, C. F. (1999). The impact of sesame street on preschool children: A review and synthesis of 30 years' research. *Media Psychology, 1,* 165–190.

Foot, K. (2014). The online emergence of pushback on social media in the United States: A historical discourse analysis. *International Journal of Communication, 8,* 30.

Friedrich, L. K., & Stein, A. H. (1973). Aggressive and prosocial television programs and the natural behavior of preschool children. *Monographs of the Society for Research in Child Development, 38*, 1–64.

Gola, A. A. H., Richards, M. N., Lauricella, A. R., & Calvert, S. L. (2013). Building meaningful parasocial relationships between toddlers and media characters to teach early mathematical skills. *Media Psychology, 16*, 390–411.

Gorn, G. J., & Goldberg, M. E. (1982). Behavioral evidence of the effects of televised food messages on children. *Journal of Consumer Research, 9*, 200–205.

Grela, B., Lin, Y., & Krcmar, M. (2003). *Can television be used to teach vocabulary to toddlers.* Paper presented at the annual meeting of the American Speech Language Hearing Association, Chicago.

Guernsey, L. (2007). *Into the minds of babes: How screen time affects children from birth to age five.* Arlington, VA: Basic Books.

Halford, J. C., Gillespie, J., Brown, V., Pontin, E. E., & Dovey, T. M. (2004). Effect of television advertisements for foods on food consumption in children. *appetite, 42*, 221–225.

Harris, J. L., Speers, S. E., Schwartz, M. B., & Brownell, K. D. (2012). US food company branded advergames on the internet: Children's exposure and effects on snack consumption. *Journal of Children and Media, 6*, 51–68.

Hayne, H., Herbert, J., & Simcock, G. (2003). Imitation from television by 24-and 30-month-olds. *Developmental Science, 6*, 254–261.

Hendershot, H. (1998). *Saturday morning censors.* Durham, NC: Duke University Press.

Herzog, H. (1941). On borrowed experience. In S. Bengtsson (Ed.), *Medievetenskapens idétraditioner* (pp. 37–51). Lund: Studentlitteratur.

Huesmann, L. R. (1986). Psychological processes promoting the relation between exposure to media violence and aggressive behavior by the viewer. *Journal of Social Issues, 42*, 125–139.

Irwin, A. R., & Gross, A. M. (1995). Cognitive tempo, violent video games, and aggressive behavior in young boys. *Journal of Family Violence, 10*, 337–350.

Jordan, A. B. (2004). The three-hour rule and educational television for children. *Popular Communication: The International Journal of Media and Culture, 2*(2), 103–118.

Jordan, A. B., & Woodard, E. H. (1998). Growing pains: Children's television in the new regulatory environment. *Annals of the American Academy of Political and Social Science, 557* (ArticleType: research-article / Issue Title: Children and Television / Full publication date: May, 1998 / Copyright ¬© 1998 American Academy of Political and Social Science), 83–95.

Kirkorian, H. L., Choi, K., & Pempek, T. A. (2016). Toddlers' word learning from contingent and noncontingent video on touch screens. *Child Development, 87*, 405–413.

Kirkorian, H. L., Pempek, T. A., Murphy, L. A., Schmidt, M. E., & Anderson, D. R. (2009). The impact of background television on parent–child interaction. *Child Development, 80*, 1350–1359.

Kirkorian, H. L., Wartella, E. A., & Anderson, D. R. (2008). Media and young children's learning. *The Future of Children, 18*(1), 39–61. doi:10.1353/foc.0.0002.

Krcmar, M. (2010). Can social meaningfulness and repeat exposure help infants and toddlers overcome the video deficit? *Media Psychology, 13,* 31–53.

Lapierre, M. A., Piotrowski, J. T., & Linebarger, D. L. (2012). Background television in the homes of US children. *Pediatrics, 130,* 839846. doi:10.1542/peds.2011-2581.

Lauricella, A. R., Gola, A. A. H., & Calvert, S. L. (2011). Toddlers' learning from socially meaningful video characters. *Media Psychology, 14,* 216–232.

Lauricella, A. R., Pempek, T. A., Barr, R., & Calvert, S. L. (2010). Contingent computer interactions for young children's object retrieval success. *Journal of Applied – Developmental Psychology, 31*(5), 362–369.

Linebarger, D. L., Kosanic, A. Z., Greenwood, C. R., & Doku, N. S. (2004). Effects of viewing the television program between the Lions on the emergent literacy skills of young children. *Journal of Educational Psychology, 96,* 297–308. doi:10.1037/0022-0663.96.2.297.

Mares, M.-L., & Woodard, E. (2005). Positive effects of television on children's social interactions: A meta-analysis. *Media Psychology, 7,* 301–322.

Mitroff, D., & Stephenson, R. H. (2007). The television Tug-of-war: A brief history of children's television programming in the United States. In J. A. Bryant (Ed.), *The children's television community* (pp. 3–34). Mahwah, NJ: Lawrence Erlbaum Associates.

Murray, J. P. (2007). TV violence: Research and controversy. In N. Pecora, J. P. Murray, & E. A. Wartella (Eds.), *Children and television: Fifty years of research* (pp. 183–204). Mahwah, New Jersey: Lawrence Erlbaum.

Nathanson, A. I., Alade, F., Sharp, M. L., Rasmussen, E. E., & Christy, K. (2014). The relation between television exposure and executive function among preschoolers. *Developmental Psychology, 50,* 1497–1506.

Paik, H. (2001). The history of children's use of electronic media. In D. G. Singer & J. L. Singer (Eds.), *Handbook of children and the media* (pp. 7–27). Thousand Oaks, CA: Sage Publications.

Paik, H., & Comstock, G. (1994). The effects of television violence on antisocial behavior: A meta-analysis. *Communication Research, 21,* 516–546. doi:10.1177/009365094021004004.

Pempek, T. A., & Calvert, S. L. (2009). Tipping the balance: Use of advergames to promote consumption of nutritious foods and beverages by low-income African American children. *Archives of Pediatrics & Adolescent Medicine, 163,* 633–637.

Posavac, H. D., Posavac, S. S., & Posavac, E. J. (1998). Exposure to media images of female attractiveness and concern with body weight among young women. *Sex Roles, 38,* 187–201.

(2013). *Zero to eight: Children's media use in America 2013.* San Francisco, CA: Common Sense Media.

Rideout, V. (2015). *The common sense census: Media use by tweens and teens.* San Francisco, CA: Common Sense Media.

Salomon, G. (1983). Television watching and mental effort: A social psychological view. In J. Bryant & D. R. Anderson (Eds.), *Children's understanding of television: Research on attention and comprehension* (pp. 181–198). New York: Academic Press.

Schmidt, M. E., Pempek, T. A., Kirkorian, H. L., Lund, A. F., & Anderson, D. R. (2008). The effects of background television on the toy play behavior of very young children. *Child Development, 79,* 1137–1151.

Schmitt, K. L., & Anderson, D. R. (2002). Television and reality: Toddlers' use of visual information from video to guide behavior. *Media Psychology, 4,* 51–76.

Singhal, A., Cody, M. J., Rogers, E. M., & Sabido, M. (2003). *Entertainment-education and social change: History, research, and practice*: New York: Routledge.

Strasburger, V. C., Wilson, B. J., & Jordan, A. B. (2014). *Children, adolescents, and the media.* Los Angelos: SAGE.

Troseth, G. L., Saylor, M. M., & Archer, A. H. (2006). Young children's use of video as a source of socially relevant information. *Child Development, 77,* 786–799.

Turow, J. (1999). *The Internet and the family: The view from parents, the view from the press.* Philadelphia: Annenberg Public Policy Center, University of Pennsylvania, May 1999.

Valkenburg, P. M., & Peter, J. (2013). Five challenges for the future of media-effects research. *International Journal of Communication, 7,* 197–215.

Wartella, E., & Jennings, N. (2000). Children and computers: New technology. Old concerns. *The Future of Children, 10,* 31–43.

Wartella, E., & Reeves, B. (1985). Historical trends in research on children and the media: 1900–1960. *Journal of Communication, 35,* 118–133.

Wartella, E., Richert, R. A., & Robb, M. B. (2010). Babies, television and videos: How did we get here? *Developmental Review, 30,* 116–127.

Wartella, E., Rideout, V., Lauricella, A. R., & Connell, S. (2014). *Revised parenting in the age of digital technology: A national survey.* Retrieved from Evanston, IL.

Wartella, E., & Robb, M. (2007). Young children, new media. *Journal of Children and Media, 1,* 35–44. doi:10.1080/17482790601005207.

8. *Parasocial Relationships and Children*

ROBIN DUFFEE
The Pennsylvania State University

SYDNEY COX
Texas Tech University

NARISSRA MARIA PUNYANUNT-CARTER
Texas Tech University

In 1956, Horton and Wohl coined the term parasocial interaction (PSI) to describe the illusionary "face-to-face" interaction between a television persona and a television viewer. These interactions give the viewer an illusion of conversational give-and-take in which there is a "faux sense of mutual awareness" (Dibble, Hartmann, & Rosaen, 2016, p. 25). Continued parasocial interactions may cause a television viewer to develop a deeper sense of connection with a television persona that extends beyond a single viewing session. These long-term bonds are then considered parasocial relationships (PSR). The purpose of this chapter is to offer a broad overview of key concepts in parasocial communication research, highlighting in particular the different types of parasocial communication behaviors that children engage in. To this end, this chapter unfolds in four parts. First, this chapter will define parasocial interactions and parasocial relationships. Second, this chapter will review relevant research on the formation and maintenance of children's parasocial relationships. Third, this chapter will investigate the various potential effects of these relationships. Fourth and finally, this chapter identifies current limitations and potential opportunities in research about children's parasocial relationships.

Defining Parasocial Interactions and Parasocial Relationships

Since Horton and Wohl's original conceptualization of parasocial interaction was published in the 1950s, our technological landscape has continued to evolve, prompting communication scholars to expand the concept of para-social interaction and apply it to new contexts.[2] In the early 1990s, PSI/PSR research saw a sharp increase in popularity and with this proliferation, scholars began to base their research upon varying definitions of PSI/PSR. By the mid-2000s, consistent confusion, conflation, and contradiction made the PSI/PSR literature difficult to navigate.[3] In response to this issue, many parasocial researchers have called for a conceptual clarification and reassess-ment of measures used to study PSI/PSR.[4] Thus, we begin this chapter by clearly defining what exactly parasocial relationships and parasocial interac-tions are, and distinguishing them from one another.

It was in Horton and Wohl's 1956 article "Mass Communication and Para-Social Interaction: Observation on Intimacy at a Distance" that the concept of parasocial interaction was first introduced. Horton and Wohl suggested that television viewers sometimes perceive their interactions with television persona as "an intimate reciprocal social interaction, despite know-ing that it is an illusion" (Dibble, Hartmann, & Rosaen, 2016, p. 23), and described this type of interaction as "parasocial." The original definition of parasocial interaction also stressed that parasocial interactions are *initiated by the media performer* and are *only* possible when "media performers acknowl-edge the presence of the audience in their performance, adapt the conver-sational style of informal face-to-face gatherings, and bodily and verbally address their users" (Dibble, Hartmann, & Rosaen, 2016, p. 23).

Contemporary research allows the definition of parasocial interaction more flexibility to fit our modern media context. Three extensions are par-ticularly relevant to this chapter. First, researchers have established that PSI can be facilitated through media other than television, such as books, radio, social media platforms, YouTube, and more. Second, scholars accept that

---

2 For two comprehensive accounts of the rise of PSR research, see Giles, 2002; Liebers & Schramm, 2019.

3 While there has been considerable improvement in the clarity of PSI/PSR research since the mid-2000s, many scholars still operate under varying conceptions and mea-sures of PSI/PSR. In this chapter, we offer a simplified overview of key findings in the research, but we strongly encourage invested parties to fully review the original sources in order to understand the nuances and potential implications of each study.

4 In addition to the above, see Brown, 2015; Dibble, Hartmann, & Rosaen, 2016; Hartmann, 2008; Hartmann & Goldhoorn, 2011; Rosaen & Dibble, 2016; Schramm & Hartmann, 2008; Schramm & Wirth, 2010.

children can engage in PSI even if they are not yet able to distinguish television from reality and, therefore, are not aware that the connection they feel with a character is an illusion. Third, the literature agrees that direct verbal and nonverbal address is not required for a media figure to evoke a parasocial interaction with a viewer.

Scholars have also developed a fuller picture of what types of actions constitute a parasocial interaction on the viewer's side. PSI can manifest as behavioral, cognitive, or affective responses to a media figure. Behavioral responses may include talking directly to the television (Rubin & Perse, 1987, p. 248), responding to a character on television with paraverbal reactions such as groans (Schramm & Hartmann, 2008, p. 389), mimicking a character's gestures (Ramasubramanian & Kornfield, 2012, p. 194), or other similar behaviors. Cognitive responses may be more subtle. For example, a viewer devoting focused attention to a character, thinking about how they are similar or dissimilar to a character (Schramm & Hartmann, 2008, p. 389), or making inferences about a character's motivations and behaviors (Giles, 2002, p. 289) all fall under the category of cognitive engagement in a parasocial interaction. A variety of affective responses to parasocial interactions are also possible, such as feeling happy when the character on screen is happy (Ramasubramanian & Kornfield, 2012, p. 194) or feeling empathy for a character (Schramm & Hartmann, 2008, p. 389).

Parasocial *interactions* are limited to the timeframe in which a media user is exposed to a media figure. However, as a user continues to have parasocial interactions with a media figure, the user may or may not develop a parasocial *relationship* with the media figure, or a "long-term, enduring intimacy at a distance that can extend beyond the viewing episode" (Rosaen & Dibble, 2016, pp. 149–150). It is important to remember that, though parasocial interactions and parasocial relationships are related, they are distinct communication phenomena. Unfortunately, these two terms are often conflated in PSI/PSR literature. Additionally, PSI/PSR are often correlated with other similar types of interactions and relationships between media users and media figures[5] and studied in tandem and, without careful delineation and measurement, results can become blurred. As we move forward in the chapter, we take care to note whether the findings we summarize are based upon research focused on parasocial *interactions* or *relationships* wherever possible, but we

5 Jonathan Cohen (1999) offers a useful explanation of four such user-figure relationships and their similarities and differences: PSI, identification, wishful identification, and affinity. William Brown's 2015 *Communication Theory* article offers another notable comprehensive examination of four processes of audience involvement: transportation, PSI, identification, and worship.

encourage interested readers to refer back to the original sources to under-stand how each researcher operationalizes these terms. With that disclaimer offered and with a foundational understanding of PSI/PSR laid, we now move into a discussion of children's parasocial relationships, their formation and maintenance, and their potential effects.

Understanding Children's Parasocial Relationships

Considering the widespread popularity of PSI/PSR research across disci-plines, there is a relative lack of research on *children's* parasocial interactions and relationships,[6] though publications in this area have been increasing since about 2010. Adult participants are able to more easily and effectively understand and articulate their complex experiences with media figures than children are, so this skewed pool makes sense. However, as more PSI/PSR research focused on children has been published, it has become clear that some of the conclusions drawn from studies looking at adults' PSI/PSR may not apply to populations of children, adolescents, or teenagers. Parasocial interactions and relationships function differently and serve different pur-poses at different stages in an individual's development. Thus, in this section, we cover key findings in the research on the formation and maintenance of children's parasocial relationships, as well as their potential effects, and take care to note differences across age groups.

Formation and Maintenance of Children's Parasocial Relationships

The formation of parasocial relationships and interactions has been a popu-lar topic of study since PSI/PSR research began. Early studies of PSI/PSR formation grew out of uses and gratifications research and, since then, many scholars have also used attachment theory as a lens to explore this phenom-enon (Rosaen & Dibble, 2016, pp. 150–151). The influences of these two theoretical perspectives can be traced throughout the research.

Jinshi Tsao's *Communication Studies* article, "Compensatory Media Use: An Exploration of Two Paradigms," provides an excellent summary of the two primary schools of thought about why individuals seek out PSI/PSR. Tsao defines these two paradigms as the deficiency paradigm and the global-use paradigm. The deficiency paradigm assumes that people turn to parasocial interactions as "a *functional alternative* to unattainable face-to-face interactions" (p. 90, emphasis in original). An individual may find

6 Richards and Calvert 2015 p. 462; Rosaen, Sherry, and Smith 2011; Theran, Newberg, and Gleason, 2012, p. 270.

face-to-face interactions unattainable due to a combination of environmental factors (availability of potential interaction partners, social status, material resources, etc.) and psychological or personality factors (introversion, neuroticism, etc.). The global-use paradigm, by contrast, views parasocial interaction as a normal extension of everyday social interaction (p. 91). Rather than replacing face-to-face interactions, the global-use paradigm views PSI and F2F interactions as complimentary. Though Tsao's article was published in 1996, the results of contemporary research about PSI/PSR formation still generally fall into one of these two paradigms. Tsao's own study concluded that the global-use paradigm received more support when it came to parasocial interaction, and most scholars side with the global-use explanation as well.[7] While these broad paradigms offer two potential explanations as to how, why, and whether children will form PSI/PSR, specific characteristics of the child, the persona, and the interaction also come into play.

Characteristics of the Child

Anxiety. Specific characteristics of a child will affect how and whether they form PSI/PSR. Scholars have found that children who are anxious in social relationships or exhibit an anxious attachment style are more likely to develop PSI/PSR. Researchers Tracy Gleason, Sally Theran, and Emily Newberg have found a connection between anxious attachment style and PSI in adolescents in multiple studies (Gleason, Theran, & Newberg, 2020, p. 253; Theran, Newberg, & Gleason, 2010, p. 275). In their 2010 article, titled "Adolescent Girls' Parasocial Interactions with Media Figures," Theran, Newberg, and Gleason found that adolescent girls with a preoccupied attachment style were more likely to engage in parasocial interactions, and that the emotional intensity of their parasocial relationships was higher (p. 275). In their 2020 article, "Connections Between Adolescents' Parasocial Interactions and Recollections of Childhood Imaginative Activities," they concluded that adolescents with an anxious attachment style, regardless of gender, all are more likely to exhibit PSI. Rosaen and Dibble (2017) identified the same trend in a slightly older population when they found that undergraduate students who were more anxious in their social relationships exhibited the strongest parasocial relationships (pp. 17).

Gender. Many researchers have also tried to discover how a child's gender may affect their PSI/PSR, but these findings have been inconsistent and definite patterns are difficult to distinguish. Still, here we highlight some

---

7 Rosaen & Dibble, 2016; Rubin & McHugh, 1987.

potentially relevant findings from individual studies. In 1996, Hoffman studied parasocial interactions between children (ages 7–12) and their favorite TV character and found that nearly all boys selected same-sex characters as their favorite, while only about half of girls did so (p. 397). This finding is consistent with Jennings and Alper's (2016) later conclusion that, of children in the 5- to 7-year-old age group, boys were significantly more likely to report a same-sex character as a friend (97.7%) than girls (55.6%) (p. 99). In their study of tween's parasocial relationships with YouTubers, Tolbert and Drogos (2019) found that 97.2% of boys chose a same-sex YouTuber as their favorite, which remains consistent with past findings, but reported that a significantly higher portion of girls (65.3%) chose a same-sex YouTuber as their favorite (pp. 6–7). Bond and Calvert (2014b) found that gender differences in children's parasocial relationships may also depend upon the age of the children. Their study of 2- to 8-year-old children revealed that boys were significantly more inclined to have favored female media characters when they were younger, but, as they aged, shifted to favoring male characters (p. 482). It is difficult to assess why girls tend to choose more opposite-sex characters as their favorites than boys, but Bond and Calvert (2014b, p. 485) and Hoffner (1996, p. 398) both point to the nature of media's portrayals of gender stereotypes as one possible explanation. This explanation may offer insight into why Tolbert and Drogos' study alone found a higher rate of girls selecting same-sex characters or personas as their favorites, as YouTube offers a wider variety of female personas to potentially identify with.

Periods of Transition and Identity Development. Scholars also agree that children, adolescents, and teenagers turn to parasocial interactions and relationships in times of transition and periods of identity development. Giles and Maltby (2004) found that adolescents may lean on PSI/PSR as they age and experience increasing autonomy from their parents (p. 813). Gleason, Theran, and Newberg (2017) concluded that participation in PSI/PSR can be a part of the identity development process for young adolescents. Unlike younger children, some adolescents begin to explicitly view media figures that they maintain PSI/PSR with as role models to potentially emulate (p. 9). In this capacity, adolescents may try on parasocial relationships with various media figures as they explore options for modeling their ideal selves (Gleason, Theran, & Newberg, 2020, p. 254).

Characteristics of the Media Persona

Specific characteristics of the media persona may also affect whether a child will develop a PSI/PSR with them. For younger children, three characteristics of the media persona are particularly important and are repeatedly proven to promote PSI/PSR formation across the literature. These three characteristics are character personification, attachment, and social realism. Character personification is the process by which children ascribe personhood to a character and view the character as having thoughts and emotions (Richards & Calvert, 2016, p. 464) and is often considered the necessary first step toward establishing PSI/PSR (Bond & Calvert, 2014; Richards & Calvert, 2016). Attachment is when a character makes a child feel soothed, comfortable, and safe (Richards & Calvert, 2016, p. 464), and also correlates with PSI/PSR (Bond & Calvert, 2014; Richards & Calvert, 2016). Social realism, or the belief that a media persona exists in the real world (Richards & Calvert, 2016, p. 464), is consistently noted as an important factor for young children's PSI/PSR formation (Bond & Calvert, 2014; Richards & Calvert, 2016; Rosaen & Dibble, 2008).

In research on PSI/PSR in older children, other characteristics of the media persona are mentioned as positively related to the formation of PSI/PSR. In her study of children ages 7–12, Hoffner (1996) found that children are more likely to have parasocial interactions with characters who exhibit intelligence, kindness, helpfulness, and attractiveness. In their study of adolescents' parasocial relationships with social media influencers, Lou and Kim (2019) found that the perceived similarity, trustworthiness, and attractiveness of an influencer were all important to adolescents. In a similar study, Tolbert and Drogos (2019) found that tweens were more likely to develop parasocial relationships with YouTubers who were humorous (p. 10). It is important to pause here and note that, while the characteristics listed above are positive in nature, it is also possible for an individual to develop a PSR with a media persona that they assess as having negative traits or that they dislike (Dibble & Rosaen, 2011; Jennings & Alper, 2016).

Characteristics of the Interaction

Beyond the characteristics of the child and the media persona, other elements of the interaction can influence children's PSI/PSR formation and maintenance. There is a consensus in the scholarship that increased media exposure in general leads to increased rates of PSI (Bond & Calvert, 2014a; Tolbert & Drogos, 2019). Jennings and Alper (2016) added an additional element to this common assumption when they found that children who engage with media personas on multiple platforms as opposed to a single platform experience stronger positive parasocial relationships with those figures (p. 100). Related to this line of logic, toy engagement and play is another factor in the formation and maintenance of PSI/PSR. Gola, Richards, Lauricella, and Calvert (2013) found that toddlers who played with a toy version of a media character developed a stronger parasocial relationship with that character overall (p. 404). Bond and Calvert (2014a) surveyed parents of children 8-years-old or younger about their children's parasocial interactions and also found that PSI and toy use were connected. Bond and Calvert (2014a) also concluded that parent encouragement had the strongest positive relationship with PSR formation (p. 299).

Potential Effects of Children's Parasocial Relationships

Moving beyond the initial formation of PSI/PSI, continued participation in PSI/PSR can lead to many potential effects for children, adolescents, and teenagers. While most of the potential effects recorded in the literature are positive, fear about the potential negative effects of PSI/PSR persists in both scholarly and colloquial conversations. In this section, we review key findings in the research about the potential effects of children's PSI/PSR by theme: social effects, educational effects, and health effects.

Social. Much of the research on children's PSI/PSR points out the potential social benefits of these parasocial forms of engagement, in addition to the benefits related to identity development processes as discussed earlier in the chapter. As Gleason, Theran, and Newberg (2020) note, parasocial relationships can act as a supplement to face-to-face relationships. PSRs may provide adolescents with a positive sense of affiliation, with some security from rejection, and can help individuals compensate for problems in social functioning. In an earlier study by the same three authors, Theran, Newberg, and Gleason (2010) discussed how parasocial interactions can provide adolescents with opportunities for risk-free interactions with admired figures without the fear of rejection or typical social anxiety. Parasocial relationships can also be a source of entertainment, fun, and a positive distraction (Rihl & Wegener, 2019, p. 563; Tolbert & Drogos, 2019).

Education. One of the most exciting areas of research in this area looks into the potential effects that PSI/PSR can have on children's learning and retention. In their 2013 study published in *Media Psychology*, titled "Building Meaningful Parasocial Relationships Between Toddlers and Media Characters to Teach Early Mathematical Skills," Alice Ann Howard Gola, Melissa Richards, Alexis Lauricella, and Sandra Calvert conducted an experiment in which they prompted three groups of 21-month-old toddlers to order a set of five plastic cups from smallest to largest. Ordering the cups in this way is a type of a seriation task, which is a foundational early mathematical skill. Toddlers from the control group were given cups to play with and their seriation ability was tested without any instruction or video. The other two groups of toddlers were shown a video in which a popular Taiwanese cartoon character, DoDo, demonstrated the seriation task to them. Of these two groups, one group of toddlers was unfamiliar with the DoDo character. However, the other group of toddlers had been intentionally familiarized with the DoDo character for three months leading up to the seriation task. To familiarize these toddlers with DoDo, two research assistants visited them in their homes three months prior to their seriation test, introduced them to DoDo, and provided the toddlers and their parents with a DVD containing several animated clips of DoDo, "a DoDo puppet . . ., a child-sized red backpack identical to the one DoDo carried in the DVD, and a miniature DoDo doll that could be attached to the backpack" (p. 398). On a second visit, toddlers were additionally given a DoDo coloring book and DoDo stickers. Over the three-month period before the seriation test, parents were asked to view the DoDo DVD with their toddlers at least twice a week and encourage play with the DoDo toys. Ultimately, the toddlers who were familiarized with DoDo before they were shown the DoDo instruction video performed the best on the seriation task compared with the other two toddler groups (p. 402). Of the toddlers who were familiarized with DoDo, those who exhibited stronger parasocial relationships with DoDo were also able to learn better from the character (p. 404).

Building off of this study, Sandra Calvert, Melissa Richards, and Courtney Kent (2014) performed a similar experiment testing toddler's ability to complete seriation tasks after being presented with a video of a character demonstrating it. In this experiment, as before, one control group of toddlers was not shown a video at all. Two groups of toddlers were familiarized with the character in the video demonstration, an interactive toy dog, for three months prior to the seriation test. For one group of toddlers, the interactive toy dog was programmed to be personalized to each individual toddler (i.e. the dog would say the toddler's name, play the toddler's favorite song, say that their favorite food was the same as the toddler's, etc.), and the other group was given the same toy dog but without individual personalization. In this experiment, the group who was familiarized with the personalized character performed the best on the seriation test (p. 152). Both of these studies indicate that children learn better from characters that they have parasocial relationships with.

Health. PSI/PSR may also influence children and adolescents' health decisions. Castonguay, Kunkel, Wright, and Duff (2013) analyzed 577 food advertisements that aired during popular children's programming on broadcast and cable television channels. They found that 73% of the advertisements that were targeted to children employed the use of a familiar media character, but, of those ads, 72% promoted foods of low nutritional value (p. 573). While this study did not specifically measure PSI/PSR, the researchers pointed out the potential for PSI/PSR with the characters used in these advertisements to affect children's food decisions.

Though they did not directly test any PSI/PSR variables, research conducted by Kotler, Schiffman, and Hanson (2012) may add to the concerns raised above. They found that, when offered two foods of the same type (i.e., 2 fruits, 2 grains, etc.), character branding strongly influenced children's food choice. However, when offered the choice between a healthy snack that was branded with a familiar character and a sugary or salty snack that was branded with an unknown character or no character, Kotler, Schiffman, and Hanson found that the branding of the healthy snack with the favored character did not significantly change the appeal of the healthy snack (p. 886). Though the researchers point to a potential connection to PSI/PSR in their literature review, though, because they did explicitly measure the children's PSI/PSR levels with the characters involved in the experiments, we cannot be certain whether PSI/PSR affected the children's decisions, or another factor. Additionally, research from Richards and Calvert (2015) and Williams and Danovitch (2019) demonstrates that many children are able to accurately judge the credibility of correct information presented by experts about food, even if it means going against a familiar, favored character.

Limitations and Future Research

Though existing research on children's PSI/PSR has yielded many valuable insights, the current body of research does have a few limitations and opportunities for expansion. First, as Richards and Calvert (2016) report, collecting data on children's PSI/PSR can be difficult. Especially when studying young children, researchers must often rely upon parents' accounts of their children's PSI/PSR, which may or may not accurately reflect the experience of the child. Richards and Calvert advocate for researchers to collect data from both children and their parents to get the best view of the situation but recognize that this is not always feasible (p. 477).

Cultural differences in children's PSI/PSR are not widely studied in the current literature. The vast majority of PSI/PSR research is conducted in the United States, and little cross-cultural comparative analyses are performed.[8]

8 For notable exceptions, see Auteur, Ashton, & Soliman, 2008; Ramasubramanian & Kornfield, 2012; and Schmid & Klimmt, 2011, not mentioned at-length in this chapter because they primarily study adult populations.

Even in the PSI/PSR research conducted within the United States, factors such as race, socioeconomic status, or disability are seldom mentioned, much less focused on as a central element of studies. How might a child's race, or the race of a media persona, affect the development of PSI/PSR? How might a blind child experience PSI/PSR differently from their sighted peers?

We also believe that, as children's social media use continues to increase, two emerging considerations in PSI/PSR research become more relevant to the study of children's PSI/PSR: a focus on transmedia, and PSR with disliked characters. Children now have increased access to media personas they are interested in via multiple social media platforms and Internet sources.[9] The transmedia experience of interacting with a media persona in a variety of ways across multiple platforms is fundamentally different than the type of PSI Horton and Wohl originally envisioned and must be considered as a unique form of engagement. Along with this unique form of engagement, children, adolescents, and teenagers may also encounter consistent parasocial interactions with figures that they dislike, mediated via social media and new media platforms. Therefore, further understanding how PSI/PSR function outside of with liked characters would be a useful endeavor.

References

Boerman, S. C., & van Reijmersdal, E. A. (2020). Disclosing influencer marketing on YouTube to children: The moderating role of para-social relationship. *Frontiers in Psychology, 10*, 1–15.

Bond, B. J., & Calvert, S. L. (2014a). A model and measure of US parents' perceptions of young children's parasocial relationships. *Journal of Children and Media, 8*(3), 286–304.

Bond, B. J., & Calvert, S. L. (2014b). Parasocial breakup among young children in the United States. *Journal of Children and Media, 8*(4), 474–490.

Brown, W. J. (2015). Examining four processes of audience involvement with media personae: Transportation, parasocial interaction, identification, and worship. *Communication Theory, 25*(3), 259–283.

Calvert, S. L., & Richards, M. N. (2014). Children's parasocial relationships. In A. B. Jordan, D. Romer, A. B. Jordan, D. Romer (Eds.), *Media and the well-being of children and adolescents* (pp. 187–200). New York, NY, US: Oxford University Press.

9 Boerman & van Reijmersdal, 2020; Hu, Zhang, & Wang, 2017; Kassing & Sanderson, 2009; Lou & Kim, 2019; Rihl & Wegener, 2019; Tolbert & Drogos, 2019

Calvert, S. L., Richards, M. N., & Kent, C. C. (2014). Personalized interactive characters for toddlers' learning of seriation from a video presentation. *Journal of Applied Developmental Psychology, 35*(3), 148–155.

Castonguay, J., Kunkel, D., Wright, P., & Duff, C. (2013). Healthy characters? An investigation of marketing practices in children's food advertising. *Journal of Nutrition Education and Behavior, 45*(6), 571–577.

Cohen, J. (1999). Favorite characters of teenage viewers of Israeli serials. *Journal of Broadcasting and Electronic Media, 43*, 327–345.

Dibble, J. L., Hartmann, T., & Rosaen, S. F. (2016). Parasocial interaction and parasocial relationship: Conceptual clarification and a critical assessment of measures. *Human Communication Research, 42*, 21–44.

Dibble, J. L., & Rosaen, S. F. (2011). Parasocial interaction as more than friendship. *Journal of Media Psychology, 23*(3), 122–132.

Giles, D. C. (2002). Parasocial interaction: A review of the literature and a model for future research. *Media Psychology, 4*(3), 279–305.

Giles, D. C., & Maltby, J. (2004). The role of media figures in adolescent development: Relations between autonomy, attachment, and interest in celebrities. *Personality and Individual Differences, 36*(4), 813–822.

Gleason, T. R., Theran, S. A., & Newberg, E. M. (2017). Parasocial interactions and relationships in early adolescence. *Frontiers in Psychology, 8*, 1–11.

Gleason, T. R., Theran, S. A., & Newberg, E. M. (2020). Connections between adolescents' parasocial interactions and recollections of childhood imaginative activities. *Imagination, Cognition and Personality, 39*(3), 241–260.

Gola, A. A. H., Richards, M. N., Lauricella, A. R., & Calvert, S. L. (2013). Building meaningful parasocial relationships between toddlers and media characters to teach early mathematical skills. *Media Psychology, 16*(4), 390–411.

Hartmann, T. (2008). Parasocial interaction and paracommunication with new media characters. In E. A. Konijn, S. Utz, M. Tanis & S. B. Barnes (Eds.), *Mediated interpersonal communication* (pp. 177–199). New York and London: Routledge.

Hartmann, T., & Goldhoorn, C. (2011). Horton and Wohl revisited: Exploring viewers' experience of parasocial interaction. *Journal of Communication, 61*(6), 1104–1121.

Hoffner, C. (1996). Children's wishful identification and parasocial interaction with favorite television characters. *Journal of Broadcasting, 40*, 389–402.

Horton, D., & Wohl, R. R. (1956). Mass communication and para-social interaction: Observation on intimacy at a distance. *Psychiatry, 193*, 215–229.

Hu, M., Zhang, M., & Wang, Y. (2017). Why do audiences choose to keep watching on live video streaming platforms? An explanation of dual identification framework. *Computers in Human Behavior, 75*, 594–606.

Jennings, N., & Alper, M. (2016). Young children's positive and negative parasocial relationships with media characters. *Communication Research Reports, 33*(2), 96–102.

Kassing, J., & Sanderson, J. (2009). "You're the kind of guy that we all want for a drinking buddy": Expressions of parasocial interaction on Floydlandis.com. *Western Journal of Communication, 73*(2), 182–203.

Kotler, J. A., Schiffman, J. M., & Hanson, K. G. (2012, September). The influence of media characters on children's food choices. *Journal of Health Communication, 17*(8), 886–98.

Liebers, N., & Schramm, H. (2019). Parasocial interactions and relationships with media characters – An inventory of 60 years of research. *Communication Research Trends, 38*(2), 4–31.

Lou, C., & Kim, H. K. (2019). Fancying the new rich and famous? Explicating the roles of influencer content, credibility, and parental mediation in adolescents' parasocial relationship, materialism, and purchase intentions. *Frontiers in Psychology, 10*, 1–17.

Ramasubramanian, S., & Kornfield, S. (2012). Japanese anime heroines as role models for U.S. youth: Wishful identification, parasocial interaction, and intercultural entertainment effects. *Journal of International and Intercultural Communication, 5*(3), 189–207.

Richards, M. N., & Calvert, S. L. (2015). Toddlers' judgments of media character source credibility on touchscreens. *American Behavioral Scientist, 59*(14), 1755–1775.

Richards, M. N., & Calvert, S. L. (2016). Parent versus child report of young children's parasocial relationships in the United States. *Journal of Children and Media, 10*(4), 462–480.

Rihl, A., & Wegener, C. (2019). YouTube celebrities and parasocial interaction: Using feedback channels in mediatized relationships. *Convergence, 25*(3), 554–566.

Rosaen, S. F., & Dibble, J. L. (2008). Investigating the relationship among child's age, parasocial interactions, and the social realism of favorite television characters. *Communication Research Reports, 25*(2), 145–154.

Rosaen, S. F., & Dibble, J. L. (2016). Clarifying the role of attachment and social compensation on parasocial relationships with television characters. *Communication Studies, 67*(2), 147–162.

Rosaen, S., & Dibble, J. L. (2017). The impact of viewer perceptions of media personae and viewer characteristics on the strength, enjoyment, and satisfaction of parasocial relationships. *Communication Studies, 25*, 1–21.

Rosaen, S. F., Sherry, J. L., & Smith, S. L. (2011). Maltreatment and parasocial relationships in US children. *Journal of Children and Media, 5*(4), 379–394.

Rubin, R. B., & McHugh, M. P. (1987). Development of parasocial interaction relationships. *Journal of Broadcasting and Electronic Media, 31*, 279–292.

Rubin, A. M., & Perse, E. M. (1987). Audience activity and soap opera involvement: A uses and effects investigation. *Human Communication Research, 14*, 246–268.

Schmid, H., & Klimmt, C. (2011). A magically nice guy: Parasocial relationships with Harry Potter across different cultures. *International Communication Gazette, 73*(3), 252–269.

Schramm, H., & Hartmann, T. (2008). The PSI-process scales. A new measure to assess the intensity and breadth of parasocial processes. *Communications, 33,* 385–401.

Schramm, H., & Wirth, W. (2010). Testing a universal tool for measuring parasocial interactions across different situations and media. *Journal of Media Psychology, 22*(1), 26–36.

Theran, S., Newberg, E., & Gleason, T. (2010). Adolescent girls' parasocial interactions with media figures. *The Journal of Genetic Psychology, 171*(3), 270–277.

Tolbert, A. N., & Drogos, K. L. (2019). Tweens' wishful identification and parasocial relationships with YouTubers. *Frontiers in Psychology, 10,* 1–15.

Tsao, J. (1996). Compensatory media use: An exploration of two paradigms. *Communication Studies, 47*(1–2), 89–109.

Williams, A. J., & Danovitch, J. H. (2019). What does Mickey Mouse know about food? Children's trust in favorite characters versus experts. *Journal of Experimental Child Psychology, 187,* 104647.

9. Family Communication, Media Consumption, Children's and Teens' Body Image and Problematic Eating Behaviors

A Review

ANDREA MCCOURT
South Plains College

JILLIAN YARBROUGH
West Texas A&M University

Concerns related to children's and teens' weight, eating behaviors, and body image are commonly expressed by the medical community, community health agencies and by parents (Arteaga et al., 2018). The Center for Disease Control and Prevention has also expressed concern over both negative body image and problematic eating-related behaviors (Centers for Disease Control and Prevention [CDC], 2020). Body image can be defined as a subjective mental image of one's body and physical appearance (Tiwari & Kumar, 2015). Because body image is based at least partially on personal observation and opinion, it is important to note that individuals' body image is not always accurate. This mismatch between perception and reality can cause anxiety and dissatisfaction with one's body (Latiff et al., 2018). This anxiety and dissatisfaction can be challenging for children and adolescents. Body image dissatisfaction can be linked to problematic eating behaviors (Amissah et al., 2015). Problematic eating-related behaviors include things such as anxiety about food or body size, anxiety, overeating, loss of control when eating, and concerns about body shape (Yoon et al., 2018).

Research indicates that children (typically defined as those twelve years old or younger) and adolescents struggle their body image and problematic eating behaviors. Voelker et al. (2015) argued that due to body changes, both male and female adolescents are particularly susceptible to messages that minimize their self-esteem, impact how one thinks and feels about oneself, and influence thoughts and feelings about one's body. This can lead to unhealthy body image and problematic eating behaviors. Since the mid-1900s, the rate of development of new cases of eating disorders has been steadily increasing (Hudson et al., 2007; Streigel-Moore &Franko, 2003; Wade et al., 2011). This trend appears to be somewhat ubiquitous, impacting both males and females as well as individuals from different racial or ethnic groups. Evidence suggests that children and adolescents in different racial/ethnic groups struggle equally with body image and eating disorder-related behaviors (Hudson et al., 2007; Wade et al., 2011). Parents as well as academic, community, and medical experts seeking answers regarding the steady global increase in problematic eating behaviors in young children and adolescents.

According to Tiwari and Kumar (2015), body image is influenced by external messages. Family communication and the media are particularly salient influences on both body image and problematic eating behaviors. Family communication plays a strong role in children's and teens' body images and problematic eating behaviors (Arroyo et al., 2018; Taniguchi & Aune, 2013). Research also indicates that consumption of media sources such as television, movies, magazines, and social media impact children's body image and eating behaviors (Bissell & Hays, 2010; Ferguson, Munoz, Garza, & Galindo, 2014). While the media alone have a significant impact on children (see Laucicella et al., this volume), it seems likely that family media use might also play an important role in children's body image. For example, the family environment can impact children's susceptibility to the media and thus influence problematic body images (Patton et al., 2014). Familial attitudes and behaviors related to that media consumption likely also matter. Due to the significant influence that both the family and popular media have on children, it seems likely that both family communication patterns and media consumption in the family environment will influence children. This chapter will explore specific ways that both family communication and media consumption impact children' and teens body image and problematic eating behaviors. Practices that promote healthy body image and eating behaviors will also be discussed.

The Influence of Family Communication on Body Image and Problematic Eating Behaviors

Family communication patterns and processes have been shown to impact the development of children's and teens' body image (Carter et al., 2014).

Comments that parents make to their children, media images that parents emphasize, and even family attitudes towards a healthy lifestyle can all impact young people's perceptions about body image and healthy eating patterns. This position is supported by a substantial body of research that indicates that the parent-child relationship is a singularly significant contributor to the development of body image (Botta & Dumlao, 2002). Indeed, research has consistently shown that appearance-related parental communication is particularly impactful (Keery, Boutelle, van den Berg, & Thompson, 2005). Evidence suggests that parents should carefully consider what kinds of messages regarding body size, healthy eating, and exercise their children are exposed to.

One aspect of family communication that is worthy of further examination is communication between parents and children. Parent-child communication can impact individuals' attitude towards body image in a variety of ways. It appears that both low quality communication and critical comments between children and parents can negatively impact children's body images (Lantzouni et al., 2015). Criticizing children and adolescents' body shape or size can damage body image. These kinds of messages from parents can be particularly impactful. Indeed, Sheldon (2013) suggested that communication between parents and adolescents has the greatest impact on the child's body image. Similarly, Francisco et al. (2014) found that parental statements that criticize adolescents' body size predicted higher levels of body image dissatisfaction. This is just one example of how parental-child communication impacts body image.

Parental communication also impacts children's and teens' problematic eating behaviors. Haleama et al. (2009) found that parental communication has a significant influence on adolescents' behavior and perceptions surrounding eating, body image and weight. It is harmful for parents criticize children and teens for being overweight or not muscular enough. Indeed, Franciso et al. (2014) found that parental statements that criticize adolescents' body size predicted both body-image dissatisfaction and disordered eating. One specific type of parent-child communication involves direct conversations between the parent and child. Examples of direct comments might include statements such as 'you should lose weight to get a boyfriend/girlfriend' or 'you shouldn't eat so much—you'll get fat'. Research supports the idea that parental communication can contribute to body image satisfaction or dissatisfaction in children and adolescents. For example, Abraczinskas et al. (2012) found that parent's direct comments to their daughters regarding their weight and eating behaviors predicted problematic behaviors such as the drive to be thin and the development of eating disorder-related behaviors.

Not surprisingly, negative or teasing parental comments about weight cause potential damage to body image (Loth, MacLehose, Fulkerson, Crow, & Neumark-Sztainer, 2013). It is important to note that general communication patterns that include higher levels of critical or negative comments likely have a larger impact than single, isolated comments. Taniguchi and Aune (2013) argued that "examining the general quality of children's communication with parents is important because it is through communication in everyday life that individuals develop their self-image, including their own body image," (p. 388). Findings such as these exemplify the importance of examining the role of parent-child communication in both body image and problematic eating behaviors.

It appears that the gender of the parent and the child can play a role in how communication impacts body image and problematic eating behaviors (Taniguchi & Aune, 2013). Communication from mothers can have different outcomes on body satisfaction than communications from fathers. Nickelson et al. (2012) found that perceived maternal weight comments were associated with adolescents' weight concerns. This indicates that mother's negative comments about weight, size, and shape play a larger role in problematic body image and eating behaviors than comments made by another. While communication with the mother is important, children's and teens' personal relationship with their father may play an important role. For both boys and girls, a difficulty in communicating with their father was associated with weight dissatisfaction (Haleama et al., 2009). These findings highlight how parents can influence problematic body image and eating behaviors. Problematic communication is not limited to communication that is directly between parents and children. Research indicates that parent-to-parent dialogue can also impact children and teens' concepts of body image, even if that communication is not directed to children and teens. When children and teens overhear their parents discussing weight, the need to diet, and so on, they can internalize those messages. Taniguchi and Aune (2013) found that dialogue among the parents impacts body satisfaction in daughters and sons.

In addition to parent-child communication, there are other family influences including parental support for parental dieting, parental encouragement for children or adolescents to diet, and weight talk at home (Neumark-Sztainer & Eisenberg, 2005). The more time families spend talking about diet and weight-related topics, the more likely it is that children and teens will identify these topics as important. Sheldon (2013) found that when families discuss things such as how much someone ate or someone's lack of exercise, it can lead to unhealthy attitudes towards diet and exercise. These unhealthy attitudes might lead to behaviors such as extreme dieting or unnecessary dieting. One example of a problematic eating behavior is unnecessary dieting. Girls who diet, despite being under-weight and those who have gone beyond experimentation to extreme dieting on a regular basis report greater psychological distress and reduced emotional bonding in the family (Wertheim et al., 1992).

It is important to examine family communication beyond the parent-child dyad. The overall impact of family communication style on children's body image and problematic eating behaviors has also been evaluated. According to Family Communication Patterns Theory (Koerner & Fitzpatrick, 2002b, 2002c, 2006), families communicate using two different cognitive orientations, conversation or conformity. Conversation-oriented families tend toward a climate in which all family members are encouraged to participate in unrestrained interaction concerning a wide variety of topics. Families high in this area are free to interact with one another as they share ideas, express concerns and participate in decision making. Families who are low in this area interact less frequently with each other on a variety of topics, including private thoughts, feelings and activities. Conformity-oriented dynamics tend toward more uniform codes of beliefs and values with a hierarchical family structure. Koerner and Fitzpatrick (2002c, 2006), found individuals with any number of eating problems or disorders came from families that have less open communication or are conformity-oriented. Similarly, Riebel and Kaplan (1989) found that children from conformity-oriented families have a hard time expressing their wants and complaints, often hear and remember criticism but ignore praise. Strober and Humphrey (1987) found some evidence that the families of adolescents with eating disorders are characterized by enmeshment, poor conflict resolution, emotional over involvement or detachment and lack of affection and empathy.

Marital conflict might also be problematic for children's and teens' development of healthy body image and eating behaviors. Blodgett et al. (2014) argued that conflict within the marriage relationship is associated with adolescents' disordered eating. Higher levels of conflict between parents can led to higher levels of body image dissatisfaction and problematic eating behaviors. Blodgett-Salafia et al.'s (2014) study of adolescent girls found a direct association was found between marital conflict and disordered eating. A similar study of children between the ages of 5 and 12 found that marital conflict was related to higher levels of problematic eating behaviors such as emotional eating (Bi et al., 2017). These research findings support the idea that low or critical communication between children and parents can negatively impact the child's body image. It appears that family conflict does indeed play a role in children's and teens' body image and problematic eating behaviors.

Negative communication is not the only type of communication to influence children and teens. It is important to note that positive parental messages about body size or eating habits also impact children and adolescents. Research indicates that supportive communication from parents can also have positive impacts on children's and teens' body image. Arroyo et al. (2018) found that positive maternal communication regarding body image increased the likelihood of positive body image for daughters. Clearly, parental communication can impact children and teens in both positive and negative ways. This topic will be revisited at the end of the chapter.

Media Impact on Body Image and Problematic Eating Behaviors

Children and teens of today are exposed to a variety of media sources including the internet, magazines, movies, and television as well as social media sites such as Facebook, Instagram, and Twitter. Along with family communication, these media sources are considered some of the strongest and most important sociocultural influences on body image (Mulgrew et al., 2013; Tiggemann & Slater, 2004). This influence may be especially strong given the almost ubiquitous presence of media in children's and teens' lives. This is concerning as media messages frequently send unhealthy messages about body size and appearance. For example, media sources consistently indicate that physical beauty is of extreme importance (Aubrey, 2006). Additionally, the media often present ideal body sizes and shapes for males and females. The media depict the ideal man to be muscular and physically fit (Lien et al., 2001) while the ideal woman that is portrayed is getting increasingly leaner and slimmer (Katzmarzyk & Davis, 2001). These portrayals indicate to children and adolescents that these body types are ideal. Unfortunately, these body ideals are extreme and difficult to attain in a healthy manner.

While the content of media messages is concerning, the level of access that children and adolescents have the media is also alarming. Today's children and teens have greater exposure to all forms of media than previous generations (Lien et al., 2001). Cellular phone access has provided unprecedented access to a variety of media sources, and many children and teens have access to cell phones. Madden et al. (2013) estimate cell phone usage at 4.55 billion people in the world with 78% of US teens reporting they have cell phones. Through cell phones and other media channels, adolescents throughout the world are experiencing media-idealized images and gendered beauty ideals that negatively influence self-esteem and correlate with eating disorders in North America (Mulgrew et al., 2013), Europe (Dakanalis, et al., 2015), Fiji,

Tonga, Tongans, New Zealand and Australia (McCabe et al., 2011). The following passages will explore different ways that media messages impact body image and problematic eating behaviors.

The relationship between children/teens and the media has been studied for decades. Horton and Wohl (1956) found that adolescents normally get to know celebrities through media consumption. In the 1980s, television was arguably the most available and influential form of mass media for adolescents (Tiggeman & Pickering, 1996). Early on, it was apparent that popular media was having a significant impact on children and teen. Because they use so much media and because they are more susceptible to suggestion, it is likely that media impacts young people differently than adults. This impact may be stronger because adolescence is a time when problematic eating behaviors develop (Beumont & Touyz, 1985). Disordered eating, increased susceptibility to the opinion of others, and low self-esteem all occur disproportionately in adolescents and thus increase the media's potential impact as well as the influence of media celebrities. In fact, Singh et al. (2016) found that both males (47%) and females (53%) who self-reported being influenced by celebrities were at greater (31.09%) risk of for developing an eating disorder.

It has been established that media sources such as movies, television, magazines and social media impact children and adolescent's body image and problematic eating behaviors (Uchôa et al., 2019). For decades, television shows and movies that target children as their primary audience have portrayed overly thin heroines and muscular heroes. It is likely that these media messages can have negative influences on children and adolescents. Indeed, Uchôa et al. (2019) found that idealized body images and messages in the media play a significant role in both body dissatisfaction and problematic eating behaviors. It is likely that media sources impact children's understandings of concepts of such as healthy diet and exercise.

While the media can affect anyone, it has been argued that children are particularly susceptible to media messages and likely to perceive the presented imagery such as character thinness and fatness as real and not part of a story (Van Evra, 1990). Researchers are concerned that negative media messages will increase the probability of children becoming discontent with their body if their body type differs from the "norm" (Stice et al., 1994). Likewise, adolescents also receive a variety of media messages relating to body image. Adolescents receive frequent messages regarding body image through television, movies, magazines, and social media that impact their body image and eating behaviors (Bissell & Hays, 2010; Ferguson et al., 2014). During this process, feedback from others is particularly significant. According to Tiggemann (2006) a constant portrayal of extremely thin females provides feedback to teens this is the ideal female body. During adolescence, individuals experience body changes, growth, and a struggle to create their identity. Problematic eating behaviors, poor self-esteem and low body image are also prevalent among adolescents (Loth et al., 2015) and may be particularly influential during this time of adolescent identity-seeking. Popular media is one of the sources adolescents view as they are seeking feedback about their identities. It seems plausible that these factors impact children's and teens' development of body image and eating behaviors.

Gender and Media Influences

While the media affects both females and males, it does not necessarily impact them in the same manner. Media sources such as children' movies frequently portray female characters as overly thin. In a content analysis of children's movies, Herbozo et al. (2004) found that 60% of the videos portrayed female thinness and 64% equated obesity as a negative trait. These portrayals are damaging in two ways. Not only is the thin body seen as ideal, but that being overweight is "bad" or unappealing. Together, this sends a strong message to children. This repeated portrayal of thin characters as heroes and obese characters as supporting characters or villains, suggests cultural expectations of beauty (Herbozo et al., 2004). These messages go beyond teaching children about beauty expectations, impacting children's perceptions of themselves and others through a distorted view (Gilbert, 1998; Martin & Kennedy, 1993).

When viewing media, adolescents report understanding that media are presenting an idealized body and many of them desire that same body type (Spurr, 2013). However, these media portrayals of the ideal body vary by gender. While young females are often pressured to emulate beauty and thinness, males are exposed to muscular and physically fit ideals (Mulgrew et al., 2013). Although the messages are different, both males and females are susceptible to these unrealistic and unhealthy depictions of people (Spurr, 2013). In fact, the presentation of the desired ideal body shape is considered one of the key sociocultural risk factors in the development of body dissatisfaction (Labre, 2002). The overwhelming presentation of these ideal body types leaves adolescents feeling inadequate and that they must begin to experiment with weight control behaviors.

These idealized images may be particularly harmful for adolescents. Johnson and Schlundt (1985) suggested that pressures to be thin are particularly influential during adolescence. The media have a significant impact on female adolescents, particularly in relation to the constant bombardment of the thin ideal. This constant view of thinness in magazines, movies, television, and the internet leads to increased body dissatisfaction and disordered eating particularly in females (Andrist, 2003). Women are constantly being subjected to messages of body ideals that are both likely unattainable and unhealthy. The inability of women to attain the expected body, supports damaged self-esteem, damaged body image and finally disordered eating as the individual attempts to change their eating to obtain the ideal body. There is a link between the media's promotion of unrealistic female body image and the increasingly high levels of body dissatisfaction in females (Agliata & Tantleff-Dunn, 2004). For example, Martin 2010 found that among American elementary school girls who read magazines, 69% say that the pictures influence their concept of the ideal body shape while 47% say the pictures make them want to lose weight. Wertheim et al. (1997) found that 15-year-old young women are under the strongest pressure to be thin. These findings indicate that young girls see overly thin images in media and incorporate them into their concept of how women should look. Internalization of the thin ideal is a key component in the development of body dissatisfaction (Cusumano & Thomson, 2001). These studies are part of the growing body of empirical evidence suggesting various media outlets are a significant factor causing negative body image, leading to low self-esteem, unhealthy body image, problematic eating behaviors, and perhaps even eating disorders. This leads to an inverse relationship between media use and self-esteem in adolescent girls. (Racine, 2011). The more time young girls spend viewing media, the lower their self-esteem. McLean et al.'s (2015) study of 7th grade females found that girls who regularly shared self-images on social media, compared to ones that did not, reported higher over-valuation of shape, weight, dietary restraint and body dissatisfaction.

Males also report dissatisfaction with their body during pre-adolescence and adolescence (Cohane & Pope, 2001; McCabe & Ricciardelli, 2004; Smolak, 2004). However, males are affected differently by the media than females. Media often depicts a level of muscularity that is impossible for most men and boys to achieve by natural or healthy means (Leit et al., 2002). Young males' body images are also impacted negatively through the media (Agliata & Tantleff, 2004). Possible due to the media portrayal of muscular and physically fit heroes, boys have concerns about both weight and muscularity (Jones and Crawford, 2005). Norman (2011) found that male adolescents are motivated to work on and transform their bodies into culturally recognizable ideals, while at the same time remaining less conscious of the actual size, shape, and appearance of their bodies. Agliata and Tantleff (2004) found that males' exposure to television advertisements depicting ideal image correlated positively with depression and higher levels of muscle dissatisfaction. Mulgrew et al. (2013) examined the effects of idealized male representation in music television on adolescent boys and their body satisfaction or dissatisfaction. The boys exposed to the clips portraying overly muscular men felt significantly less happy and significantly higher levels of post-test depressive feelings that the boys that watched the average clips.

Through the years, other researchers have found that adolescents exposed to ideal body images as portrayed by the media had increased body dissatisfaction, negative mood states and decreased self-esteem (Andrist, 2003; Bell et al., 2007; Knauss et al., 2007; Paxton et al., 2006; Stice, 2002; Strahan et al., 2008). These idealized images can be found on a variety of forms of media (magazines, television programs, the internet, social media, etc. Do different types of media, impact children's and teens' self-esteem and body image differently? The following will review research answering this question.

Television

For many decades, television was the primary source of media for adolescents. Research on television's impact on adolescents began as early as the 1970s. This early research indicated that for males, exposure to entertainment television predicted dissatisfaction with height and physical appearance and for females tended to be more dissatisfied with their weight (Anderson, 2001). More recently, Kapidzic (2015) found that the more television an individual watches the more likely they are to wear revealing clothing in their profile pictures of Facebook. It seems clear that television viewing has been certainly shown to contribute to body dissatisfaction in males and females (Harrison & Cantor, 1997; Tiggeman, 2003). Television has a wide impact on young children and adolescents. Anschutz et al. (2012) studied the direct effect of watching the thin ideal portrayed on children's television on body satisfaction in preadolescent (6–8 years old) girls. They found that girls with higher levels of thin ideal internalization showed higher body dissatisfaction after exposure to characters portraying the thin ideal than after exposure to animated or real characters who did not feature thin ideal. Clearly, television plays a role in impacting body image of children and teens.

Finally, there is evidence to suggest that the type of television show viewed may play a role in the internalization of media messages. Tiggeman and Pickering (1996) studied the specific effects of media exposure on body dissatisfaction and how this relates to women in their drive to be thin. They concluded that the type of television the girls watched, not just that they watched television that affected body image. Time spent watching soaps, movies and programs with women in stereotypical roles was positively correlated with body dissatisfaction. One particularly disturbing finding is that music videos are a primary predictor for anorexia nervosa (Tiggeman & Pickering, 1996).

Magazines

Evidence suggests that magazines also impact children and teens in terms of body image and problematic eating behaviors. Tiggeman and Miller (2010) found both internet exposure and magazine reading correlated with greater internalization of thin ideas. In a 2004 study, Morrison et al. studied how exposure to magazines and television programs impact adolescents' body image and ideas about the idea body size/shape. Results indicated that both males and females engaged in universalistic social comparisons that predicted issues with self-esteem, and increased number of diets, and the use of pathogenic weight controls practices. Similarly, Project EAT found that girls who read articles on dieting or weight loss were 6 times more likely to engage in unhealthy weight control behaviors, while boys were 4 times more likely (Gallivan, 2012). Specialized magazines might have unique impact on children and adolescents. For example, Outram (2015) found that men's health magazines offer a wide spectrum of "self-care" information and advice. As they read these articles, young boys perceive messages regarding socially acceptable and desirable levels of health, well-being and portrayal of optimization (Outram, 2015). These results all indicate that magazines can influence children and adolescents.

The Internet and Social Media

Television and magazines have long been viewed as impacting adolescents' views of the ideal self. In recent years, researchers have explored newer types of media such as the internet and social media. These new forms of media are rapidly evolving, and research is focused on identifying whether media outlets like the internet and social networking sites have a similar or even greater impact on body image than magazines and television. We can see a whole new way of interacting and communicating with children and teens via the Internet. It should not be a surprise that Meliolos et al. (2015) found that internet use impacted body image. Study participants reported engaging in body image avoidance (e.g., not looking in mirrors, avoiding scales) to minimize the significant negative impact of weekly internet usage. Some of these new forms of media are especially concerning. For example, pro-anorexic websites like Pro-ana and Thinspiration are receiving millions of hits

(Gallivan, 2012). It is easy to see the potential harm of website such as these that promote eating disordered behaviors. It is concerning that some children and teens are visiting such sites to learn more about disordered eating practices. Indeed, a recent Stanford University study titled "Surfing for Thinness" found that 96% of girls with eating disorders were visiting pro-anorexic sites to learn how to further support the illness (Wilson et al., 2007). Clearly, the internet has the potential to impact children's and teens' body images and eating behaviors.

Social media has increased in popularity over the last decade. According to Duggan and Brenner (2013) 86% of online young people report using Facebook. Other social media sites such as Instagram, Twitter, Snapchat and TikTok are extremely popular with children and adolescents. Researchers are still seeking answers as to the impact that social media has on children and adolescents. Dina Borzekowski, professor at Johns Hopkins school of public health, noted that "social media may have a stronger impact on children's body image than traditional media. Messages and images are more targeted: if the message comes from a friend it is perceived as more meaningful and credible" (as cited in Gallavan, 2012, p. 22). It appears that children and teens model the behaviors they observe on social media. For example, children and adolescents imitate the candy intake of their social media peers (Bevelander et al., 2013). Social networking sites allow users to communicate to many others, in real time. Social networking has changed the way adolescents communicate. One unique aspect of social media is that people can post pictures to large groups (Kapidzic & Martins, 2015). The fact that these images are frequently altered by technology means that they are increasingly unrealistic and difficult to attain in the real world. These altered images may promote unhealthy body ideals, which in turn distresses the audience. Racine et al. (2011) found that the more time girls spent on Facebook, the more they suffered conditions of anorexia, bulimia, poor body image, negative approach to eating and more urges to be on a weight loss diet. This indicates how powerful social media can be.

It is clear that social media have similar impacts when compared with traditional media. Stronge et al. (2015) found that for both men and women body dissatisfaction is equally related to peer-based media in the same way as it is related to traditional media sources. Flynn (2016) further studied Facebook exposure as it relates to self-esteem and body dissatisfaction and found those that were predisposed to body satisfaction issues had a significant relationship between body ideal pictures and the reduction of their own body satisfaction. Finally, Facebook is not only opening opportunities for harsh self-evaluations, Facebook is creating environments that perpetuate bullying, specifically cyberbullying. Anderson et al. (2015) have studied weight-based cyberbullying. Theses researchers have found that cyberbullying can be more damaging than traditional bullying as the bullies can remain anonymous and comments are permanent and can be viewed by all seeking peers. Weight-based cyberbullying is particularly pervasive in adolescents and it is the most common form, with 61% of all adolescents reporting having received mean or embarrassing posts online.

There are many media outlets and ways to measure media impact. Research shows that all media outlets can potentially impact self-esteem and body image for both adolescent boys and girls. Further, issues that exist in one media outlet can create or support issues that develop in other media outlets. For example, Kapidzic and Martin (2015) showed that frequent users of mainstream media attempt to model mainstream media stereotypes of sexual attractiveness in their visual self-presentation on Facebook. The internet is far-reaching and this dialogue should continue as more internet-based communication tools (such as Snapchap and TikTok) become available. What can parents do to support health body image and eating behavior? The next part of this chapter will explore strategies to support healthy attitudes and behavior in children and teens.

Supporting Healthy Body Image and Eating Behaviors in Children and Adolescents

Research and everyday experience alike support the idea that children and teens are at particular risk for developing unhealthy body image and eating habits. Without question, family communication and the media are influencing children and adolescents' perceptions of their bodies (Pop, 2013). These influences play a strong role in the development of health attitudes towards body image, eating, and exercise. They also influence some children and adolescents to develop unhealthy eating behaviors and even eating disorders. What can be done to support a healthy body image and eating habits? It seems that early action is an important part of preventing problems with body image and eating-related behaviors. Hart et al. (2015) argued that it is important to take steps early in a child's life to create healthy body image and eating behaviors. These measures help prevent damage later in life from diagnoses such as eating disorders. Parents can take several steps early in life to help their children develop positive, healthy attitudes towards their bodies, eating, and exercise. There are a variety of steps that can be part of this process. Research indicates that a multi-component intervention is needed to support children and teens (Booth et al., 2008). Parents and family communication are a key component of the solution. Two key strategies include (1) creating family communication patterns and behaviors that support health body image and eating behaviors and (2) developing pathways for healthy media consumption for children and teens.

The first recommendation is very simple—parents should focus on positive messages and communication about body size, shape, eating habits, and exercise regimens. These positive messages support healthy habits and are less likely to damage children's and teens' self-esteem. Parental communication that focuses on positive attributes and behaviors helps promote healthy self-images in children and adolescents. It is also important to discuss internal qualities such as courage, honesty, dedication, and work-ethic rather than simply talking about how one looks. This is consistent with advice from Brown University (2015) to compliment children's and teens' physical and inner qualities rather than focusing on external, physical characteristics. While focusing on increasing positive communication, parents should also work on decreasing or eliminating negative or critical comments about body size, weight, or eating behaviors. For example, parents should eliminate hurtful and critical language such as calling people "fat" (Weaver, 2020). This goes for language directed at family members as well as other members of society. Avoiding this type of critical language can prevent children and adolescents from seeing size or weight as a way to measure people's value as a human being. Parents should focus on positive messages that compliment, rather than criticize their children and adolescents' bodies.

It is important for families to openly discuss topics related to body image and eating behaviors. When staring these conversations, parents should be careful to discuss positive behaviors related to eating, exercise, etc. Indeed Neumark-Sztainer and Eisenberg (2005) suggest that parents promote an open conversation that focusing on overall health rather than focusing on negative topics such weight loss. Discussing nutrition and healthy exercise regimes is an important part of this dialogue. For example, it is much more beneficial to discuss healthy snack options than to scold a child for eating candy. It is also helpful if parent model these healthy behaviors in their own lives. Weaver (2020) recommends discussing positive topics such as how bodies work. For example, instead of talking how large legs can be, parents could say 'your legs are strong and can help you do things like walk, run, and jump'. Together, these messages promote healthy attitudes towards one's body and food. It is also important for families to have discussions regarding eating disorders and the damage they can impart on an individual. According to Thompson and Heinberg (1999), it is important for parents to provide information about the negative correlates of extreme weight loss behaviors.

Parents should tell their children how eating disorders can damage them physically and mentally. Helping children see that potential harm can help them make healthier decisions.

Clearly, it is important for families to employ positive language and communication regarding body image and eating habits. Part of this conversation should include helping children and adolescents make good choices about media consumption. This likely involves limiting their access to certain media outlets. Gallivan (2012) stressed the importance of keeping media sources (such as television sets, cellular phones, and computers) out of kids' rooms so that parents can actively screen children's and teens' internet, magazine, social media, and television choices. This is an important part of protecting children and teens from unhealthy messages about body image and eating-related behaviors. It is also important for parents to talk to children and adolescents about the media and how it works. Neumark-Sztainer and Eisenberg (2005) argues that families need to be proactive to counteract negative societal messages about body image and unhealthy eating habits. It is important for parents to dissect negative messages and discuss the impact of media on self-image (Brown University, 2015). For example, parents should talk about the ways that characters and people are physically portrayed in the media. It can be helpful for children and teens to learn how those images are created and how much preparation is involved in getting models and actors "camera ready". These conversations can help children and adolescents see what is real and what is illusion. These conversations can help prevent the internalization of negative media messages such as idealized body sizes and shapes. Neumark-Sztainer and Eisenberg (2005) argued that adolescents should be informed that images in the media are both unhealthy and unattainable. One important part of this conversation is showing children and teens how the media can manipulate physical images. It is important to show showing children and teens how programs such as Photoshop or filters can be used to alter images (Gallivan, 2012; Weaver, 2020). It is essential for children and teens to understand that media images are not always what they appear to be.

It is also important to show children and adolescents examples of healthy sized males and females in the media. Parents should talk to their children about what healthy bodies might look like so that they can learn to recognize what that looks like. Thompson and Heinberg (1999) recommended purposely exposing kids/adolescents to images of healthy-sized people in the media to make sure that they can see the different from idealized images. This process can help support healthy body image and eating habits. It is also helpful for parents to highlight body-positive media messages (Weaver, 2020). Thankfully, body-positive messages are becoming more prevalent in the media (Murphy and Jackson, 2011). Dove's Campaign for Real Beauty is one example of a body-positive media campaign. This campaign launched in September 2004 and featured real women who do not exemplify the typical "ideal" appearances. Dove's Real Beauty campaign helped define a wider definition of beauty (Gallivan, 2012). Social media can be another source of body-positive messages. Howard (2020) argues that social media campaigns such as Fatkini, that asks women to share (without shame) their real bikini pictures, help promote a variety of body sizes and shapes.

Certainly, family communication about body image, healthy eating behaviors, and the media play an important role in helping children and teens. Parents may do well to include other professionals in the conversation regarding healthy body image and eating habits. Community experts can be recruited as allies in this process. According to Singh et al. (2016) an effective intervention could involve parents, teachers and healthcare providers who work together to help children develop healthy body image and eating behaviors. Educators might help children and teens develop healthy body images and eating behaviors. There is increasing support for the inclusion of media literacy into school-based educational programs for adolescents. Formal, school-based training specific to weight, healthy eating, understanding the media, and self-care many be helpful. Golan et al. (2014) found that school-based interactive wellness programs can reducing self-worth being contingent upon others and both genders exhibited improvement in self-esteem, while girls exhibited greater gains in self-esteem. Finally, Kater et al. (2002) found that elementary aged- boys and girls completing the body-positive curriculum showed notable to significant improvement in their body image. Together these research studies suggest it is possible to provide children adolescents with a knowledge base to use as they face increasing pressures about appearance, weight, and eating in the critical middle school years. In addition to media literacy programs in schools, McIlhaney (2005) advocated for the inclusion of media literacy training in health professional education. Similarly, Spurr et al. (2013) support the inclusion of nurses in combating the influence of media on adolescents and their body image. This training could help medical professionals to educate families about the potential negative impact of media on body image (Strasburger et al., 2010). Working together, we can help children and teens to develop more positive body image and eating behaviors.

Conclusions

There are many factors that contribute to children's and teens' body images and eating behaviors. Two of these factors include family communication and the media. Although the rates of problematic body image and eating behaviors have been increasing over time, there are significant steps that can be taken to help their children and adolescents. It is clear that family communication can have a significant positive impact on the development of body image and problematic eating behaviors in children and adolescents. It is essential for parents to understand the ways that family communication can negatively impact their children. Parents should be educated regarding methods for discussing and modeling healthy habits that contribute to a positive body image. These communication strategies help children develop positive body images and healthy eating habits. The media can have a strong influence, but that influence can be moderated through careful communication. Parents should help their offspring understand media messages and teach them to process them in a healthy manner. Additionally, parent can educate children on thoughtful use of technology and provide them with strategies to minimize media impact on self-perception. Communication is a powerful tool that can be used to help the children and teens develop and maintain healthy body images and eating behaviors.

References

Abraczinskas, M., Fisak, B., Barnew, & R. D. (2012). The relations between parental influence, body image, and eating behaviors in a nonclinical female sample. *Body Image, 9*, 93–100.

Aubrey, J. S. (2006). Effects of sexual objectifying media on self-objectification and body surveillance in undergraduates: Results of a 2-year panel study. *Journal of Communication, 56*, 366–386.

Agliata, D., & Tantleff-Dunn, S. (2004). The impact of media exposure on males body image. *Journal of Social & Clinical Psychology, 23*(1), 7–22.

Amissah, C. M., Nyarko, K., Gyasi-Gyamerah, A. A., & Anto-Winne, M. N. (2015). Relationships among body image, eating behavior, and psychological health of university of Ghana students. *International Journal of Humanities and Social Science, 6*, 192–203.

Anderson, D. R., Huston, A. C., Schmitt, K. L., Linebarger, D. L., & Wright, J. C. (2001). Self-image: Role model preference and body image. *Monographs of the Society for Research in Child Development, 66*(1), 108–118.

Andrist, L. C. (2003). Media images, body dissatisfaction, and disordered eating in adolescent women. *MCN American Journal Maternal Child Nursing, 28*, 119–123.

Anschutz, D. J., Engels, R. C., & Van Strien, T. (2012). Increased body satisfaction after exposure to thin ideal children's television in young girls showing thin ideal internalization. *Psychology & Health, 27*(5), 603–617.

Arroyo, A., Stillion-Southard, B. A., Cohen, H., & Caban, S. (2018). Maternal communication strategies that promote body image in daughters. *Communication Research, 47*(3), 402–427.

Arteaga, S. S., Esposito, L., Osganian, S. K., Pratt, C. A., Reedy, J., & Young-Hyman, D. (2018). Childhood obesity research at the NIH: Efforts, gaps, and opportunities. *Translational Behavioral Medicine,* 8(6), 962–967.

Bi, S., Haak, E., Gilbert, L., & Keller, P. (2017). Children exposed to marital conflict exhibit more disordered eating behaviors: Child emotional insecurity and anxiety as mechanisms of risk. *Journal of Child and Family Studies, 26*(1), 1–11.

Bell, B. T., Lawton, R., & Dittmar, H. (2007). The impact of thin models in music videos on adolescent girls' body dissatisfaction. *Body Image, 4,* 137–145.

Bevelander, K. E., Anschutz, D. J., Creemers, D. M., Kleinjan, M., & Engels, R. E. (2013). The role of explicit and implicit self-esteem in peer modeling of palatable food intake: A study on social media interaction among youngsters. *Plos One, 8*(8), 1–11.

Blodgett, S. E., Schaefer, M., & Haugem, E. (2014). Connections between marital conflict and adolescent girls' disordered eating: Parent-adolescent relationship quality as a mediator. *Journal of Child & Family Studies, 26*(6), 1128–1138.

Bissell, K. & Hays, H. (2010) Understanding anti-fat bias in children: The role of media and appearance anxiety in third to sixth graders' implicit and explicit attitudes yoward obesity. *Mass Communication and Society, 14,* 113–140, DOI: 10.1080/15205430903464592.

Booth, M. L., Wilkenfeld, R. L., Pagnini, D. L., Booth, S. L., & King, L. A. (2008). Perceptions of adolescents on overweight and obesity: The weight of opinion study. *Journal of Pediatrics & Child Health, 44*(5), 248–252.

Borzekowski, D. L., & Bayer, A. M. (2005). Body image and media use among adolescents. *Adolescent Medicine, 16,* 289–313.

Botta, R. A, & Dumlao R. (2002). How do conflict and communication patterns between fathers and daughters contribute to or offset eating disorders? *Health Communication, 14*(2), 199–219. doi: 10.1207/S15327027HC1402_3. PMID: 12046798.

Brown University. (2015). *Body image concerns.* Retrieved from: https://www.brown.edu/campus-life/health/services/promotion/nutrition-eating-concerns-eating-concerns-and-body-image/body-image-concerns

Carter, J. S., Smith, S., Bostick S., & Grant, K. E. (2014). Mediating effects of parent–child relationships and body image in the prediction of internalizing symptoms in urban youth. *Journal of Youth and Adolescence, 43,* 554–567.

Centers for Disease Control and Prevention. (2020, June 11). *Child obesity causes and concerns.* CDC.gov. https://www.cdc.gov/obesity/childhood/causes.html

Cohane, G. H., & Pope, H. G., Jr. (2001). Body image in boys: A review of the literature. *International Journal of Eating Disorders, 29,* 373–379.

Cusumano, D. L., & Thomson, J. K. (2001). Media influence and body image in 8–11 year old boys and girls: A preliminary report on the Multidimensional Media Influence Scale. *International Journal of Eating Disorders, 29,* 37–44.

Dakanalis, A., Carra, G., Calogero, R., Fida, R., Clerici, M., Zanetti, M., & Riva, G. (2015). The developmental effects of media-ideal internationalization and self-objectification processes on adolescents' negative body-feelings, dietary restrain, and binge eating. *EuropeanChild & Adolescent Psychiatry, 24*(8), 997–1010.

Duggan, M., & Brenner, J. (2013). The demographic of social media users-2012. Per Internet and American Life Project. Retrieved from http://www.pwerinternet. org/`/media//Files/Reports/20130PIP_SocialMediaUsers.pdf

Encouraging healthy body image in teens and adolescents: A guide for parents. (2014). *Brown University Child & Adolescent Behavior Letter,* 301–302.

Ferguson, C., Munoz, M., Garza, A., & Galindo, M. (2014). Concurrent and prospective analyses of peer, television and social media influences on body dissatisfaction, eating disorder symptoms and life satisfaction in adolescents girls. *Journal of Youth & Adolescence, 43*(1), 1–14.

Flynn, M. A. (2016). The effects of profile pictures and friends' comments on social network site users' body image and adherence to the norm. *Cyberpyschology, Behavior & Social Networking, 18*(4), 239–245.

Gallivan, H. R. (2012). *Teens, social media and body image.* Park Nicollet Melrose Center.

Gilbert, K. (1998). The body, young children and popular culture. In N. Yelland (Ed.), *Gender in early childhood* (pp. 55–71). New York: Routledge.

Golan, M., Hagay, N., & Tamir, S. (2014). Gender related differences in response to "in favor of myself" wellness program to enhance positive self & body image among adolescents. *Plos One, 9*(3), 1–9.

Harrison, K., & Cantor, J. (1997). The relationship between media consumption and eating disorders. *Journal of Communication, 47*(1), 40–67. https://doi.org/10.1111/j.1460-2466.1997.tb02692.x

Hart, L. M., Cornell, C., Damiano, S. R., & Paxton, S. J. (2015). Parents and prevention: A systematic review of interventions involving parents that aim to prevent body dissatisfaction or eating disorders. *The International Journal of Eating Disorders, 48*(2), 157–169. doi:10.1002/eat.22284.

Herbozo, S., Tantleff-Dunn, S., Gokee-Laroso, J., & Thompson, J. K. (2004). Beauty and thinness messages in children's media: A content analysis. *Eating Disorders, 12*(1), 21–34.

Horton, D., & Wohl, R. R. (1956). Mass communication and para-social interaction: Observation on intimacy at a distance. *Psychiatry, 193,* 215–229.

Howard, C. (2020). *Positive uses of body image in social media. Eating Disorder Hope.* Accessed at: https://www.eatingdisorderhope.com/blog/positive-social-media-body-image

Hudson, J. I., Hiripi, E., Pope, H. G., Jr., & Kessler, R. C. (2007). The prevalence and correlates of eating disorders in the National Comorbidity Survey Replication. *Biological Psychiatry, 61,* 348–358.

Johnson, W. G., & Schlundt, D. G. (1985). Eating disorders: Assessment and treatment. *Clinical Obstetrics and Gynaecology, 28,* 598–613.

Jones, D. C., & Crawford, J. K. (2005). Adolescent boys and body image: Weight and muscularity concerns as dual pathways to body dissatisfaction. *Journal of Youth and Adolescence, 34*, 629–636.

Kapidzic, S., & Martins, N. (2015). Mirroring the media: The relationship between media consumption, media internalization, and profile picture characteristics on Facebook. *Journal of Broadcasting & Electronic Media, 59*(2), 278–297.

Kater, K. J., Rohwer, J., & Londre, K. (2002). Evaluation of an upper elementary school program to prevent body image, eating, and weight concerns. *Journal of School Health, 72*(5), 199.

Katzmarzyk, P.T., & Davis, C. (2001). Thinness and body shape of Playboy centerfolds from 1978 to 1998. *International Journal of Obesity and Related Metabolic Disorders, 25*, 590–592.

Keery, H., Boutelle, K., van den Berg, P., & Thompson, J. K. (2005). The impact of appearance-related teasing by family members. *Journal of Adolescent Health, 37*, 120–127. doi: 10.1016/j.jadohealth.2004.08.015. PMID: 16026721.

Knauss, C., Paxton, S. J., & Alsaker, F. D. (2007). Relationships amongst body dissatisfaction, internalisation of the media body ideal and perceived pressure from media in adolescent girls and boys. *Body Image, 4*(4), 353–360.

Labre, M. P. (2002). Adolescent boys and the muscular male body ideal. *Journal of Adolescent Health, 30*, 233–242.

Lantzouni, E., Cox, M. H., Salvator, A., & Crosby, R. D. (2015). Mother-daughter coping and disordered eating. *European Eating Disorders Review, 23*(2), 126–132.

Latiff, A. A., Muhamad, J., & Rahman, R. A. (2018). Body image dissatisfaction and its determinants among young primary-school adolescents. *Journal of Taibah University Medical Services, 13*(1), 34–41.

Leit, R. A., Gray, J. J., & Pope, H. G. (2002). The media's representation of the ideal male body: A cause for muscle dysmorphia? *International Journal of Eating Disorders, 31*, 334–338.

Lien, A., Pope, H. G., & Gray, J. J. (2001). Cultural expectations of muscularity in men: The evaluation of Playgirl centerfolds. *International Journal of Eating Disorders, 29*, 90–93.

Loth, K. A., MacLohose, R. F., Fulkerson, J. A., Crow, S. & Neumark-Sztainer, D. (2013). Food-related parenting practices and adolescent weight Status: A population-based study. *Pediatrics, 131*, 1443–1450, DOI: 10.1542/peds.2012-3073

Loth, K., Wall, M., Larson, N., & Neumark-Sctainer, D. (2015). Disordered eating and psychological well-being in overweight and nonoverweight adolescents: Secular trends from 1999 to 2010. *International Journal of Eating Disorders, 48*(3), 323–327.

Madden, M., Lenhart, A., Duggan, M., Cortesi, S., & Gasser, U. (March, 2013). *Teens and technology 2013*. Retrieved from: http://www.pewinternet.org/2013/03/13/teens-and-technology-2013/

Martin, J. B. (2010). The development of ideal body image perceptions in the united states. *Nutrition Today,45*(3), 98–100. Retrieved from nursingcenter.com/pdf.asp?AID=1023485

Martin, M. C., & Kennedy, P. F. (1993). Advertising and social comparison: Consequences for female preadolescents and adolescents. *Psychology and Marketing, 10,* 513–530.

McCabe, M. P., Mavoa, H., Ricciardelli, L. A., Schultz, J. T., Waqa, G., & Fotu, K. F. (2011). Socio-cultural agents and their impact on body image and body change strategies among adolescents in Fili, Tonga, Tongans in New Swaland and Australia. *Obesity Reviews, 12,* 61–67.

McCabe, M. P., & Ricciardelli, L. A. (2004). Body image dissatisfaction among males across the lifespan: A review of past literature. *Journal of Psychosomatic Research, 56,* 675–685.

McIlhaney, Jr., J. S. (2005). Problems and solutions associated with media consumption: The role of the practitioner. *Pediatrics, 116*(1), 327–328.

McLean, S. A., Paxton, S. J., Wertheim, E. H., & Masters, J. (2015). Photoshopping the selfie: Self photo editing and photo investment are associated with body dissatisfaction in adolescent girls. *International Journal of Eating Disorders, 48*(8), 1132–1140.

Morrison, T. G., Kalin, R., & Morrison, M. A. (2004). Body image evaluation and body image among adolescents: A test of sociocultural and social comparison theories. *Adolscence, 39*(155), 571–592.

Mulgrew, K., Volcevski-Kostas, D., & Rendell, P. (2013). The effect of music video clips on adolescent boys' body image, mood, and schema activation. *Journal of Youth & Adolescence, 43*(1).

Murphy, R., & Jackson, S. (2011). Bodies-as-image? The body made visible in magazine love your body content. *Women's Studies Journal, 25*(1), 17–30.

Nickelson, J., Bryant, C. A., McDermott, R. J., Buhi, E. R., & Debate, R. D. (2012). A modified obesity proneness model predicts adolescent weight concerns and inability to self-regulate eating. *Journal of School Health, 82*(12), 560–571.

Neumark-Sztainer, D., & Eisenberg, M. (2005). *Weight bias in a teen's world.* In K. D. Brownell, R. M. Puhl, M. B. Schwartz, & L. Rudd (Eds.), *Weight bias: Nature, consequences, and remedies* (pp. 68–79). New York: Guilford.

Norman, M. E. (2011). Embodying the double–bind of masculinity: Young men and discourses of normalcy, health, heterosexuality, and individualism. *Men and Masculinities, 14*(4), 430–449.

Outram, S. (2015). Why do young men take nutritional supplements? An analysis of the advice provided in men's health magazine. *International Journal of Men's Health, 14*(1), 71–85.

Patton, S. C., Beaujean, A. A., & Benedict, H. E. (2014). Parental bonds, attachment anxiety, media susceptibility, and body dissatisfaction: A mediation model. *Developmental Psychology, 50*(8), 2124–2133.

Paxton, S. J., Neumark-Sztainer, D., Hannan, P. J., & Eisenberg, M. E. (2006). Body dis-satisfaction prospectively predicts depressive mood and low self-esteem in adolescent girls and boys. *Journal of Clinical Child and Adolescent Psychology, 35*(4), 539–549.

Pop, C. (2013). Overweight – Cultural and educational aspects. *Romanian Journal for Multidimensional Education, 5*(2), 57–65.

Racine, E. F., Debate, R. D., Gabriel, K. P., & High, R. R. (2011). The relationship between media use and psychological and physical assets among third- to fifth-grade girls. *Journal of School Health, 81*(12), 749–755.

Sheldon, P. (2013). Testing parental and peer communication influence on young adults' body satisfaction. *Southern Communication Journal, 78*(3), 215–232.

Smolak, L. (2004). Body image in children and adolescents: Where do we go from here? *Body Image, 1*, 15–28.

Spurr, S., Berry, L., & Walker, K. (2013). Exploring adolescent views of body image: The influence of media. *Pediatric Nursing, 36*(1/2), 17–36.

Stanford, J. N., & McCabe, M. P. (2005). Sociocultural influences on adolescent boys' body image and body change strategies. *Body Image, 2*(2), 105–113.

Stice, E. (2002). Risk and maintenance factors for eating pathology: A meta-analytic review. *Psychological Bulletin, 128*(5), 825–848.

Stice, E., & Shaw, H. (1994). Adverse effects of the media portrayed thin-idea on women and linkages to bulimic symptomatology. *Journal of Social and Clinical Psychology, 13*, 288–308.

Stice, E. M., Schipak-Neuberg, E., Shar, H. E., & Stein, R. I. (1994). Relation of media exposure to eating disorder symptomatology: An examination of mediating mecha-nisms. *Journal of Abnormal Psychology, 103*, 836–844.

Strahan, E. J., Lafrance, A., Wilson, A. E., Ethier, N., Spencer, S. J., & Zanna, M. P. (2008). Victoria's dirty secret: How sociocultural norms influence adolescent girls and women. *Personality and Social Psychology Bulletin, 34*(2), 288–301.

Strasburger, V. C., Jordan, A. B., & Donnerstein, E. (2010). Health effects of media on children and adolescents. *Pediatrics, 125*(4), 756–767.

Stronge, S., Greaves, L., Milojey, P., West-Newman, T., Barlow, F., & Sibley, C. (2015). Facebook is linked to body dissatisfaction: Comparing users and non-users. *Sex Roles, 73*(5/6), 200–213.

Taniguchi, E., & Aune, R. K. (2013). Communication with parents and body satisfaction in college students. *Journal of American College Health, 61*(7), 387–396. https://doi.org/10.1080/07448481.2013.820189

Thompson, J. K., & Heinberg, L. J. (1999). The media's influence on body image dis-turbance and eating disorders: We've reviled them, now can we rehabilitate them? *Journal of Social Issues, 55*(2), 339–353.

Thompson, J. K., Heinberg, L. J., Altabe, M., & Tantleff-Dunn, S. (1999). *Eating beauty: Theory, assessment and treatment of body image disturbance.* Washington, DC: American Psychological Association.

Tiggemann, M. (2006). The role of media exposure in adolescent girls' body dissatisfaction and drive for thinness: Prospective results. *Journal of Social and Clinical Psychology, 25*, 523–541.

Tiggemann, M., & Slater, A. (2004). Thin ideals in music television: A source of social comparison and body dissatisfaction. *International Journal of Eating Disorders, 35*(1), 48–58. https://doi.org/10.1002/eat.10214

Tiwari, G., & Kumar, S. (2015). Psychology and body image: A review. *Shodh Perak, 5*(1), 1–9.

Uchôa, F., Uchôa, N. M., Daniele, T., Lustosa, R. P., Garrido, N. D., Deana, N. F., Aranha, Á., & Alves, N. (2019). Influence of the mass media and body dissatisfaction on the risk in adolescents of developing eating disorders. *International Journal of Environmental Research and Public Health, 16*(9), 1508.

Van Evra, J. (1990). *Television and child development.* Hillsdale, NJ: Erlbaum.

Voelker, D. K., Reel, J. J., & Greenleaf, C. (2015). Weight status and body image perceptions in adolescents: Current perspectives. *Adolescent Health, Medicine and Therapeutics, 6*, 149–158.

Wade, T. D., Keski-Rahkonen, A., & Hudson, J. (2011). Epidemiology of eating disorders. In M. Tsuang & M. Tohen (Eds.), *Textbook in psychiatric epidemiology* (3rd ed., pp. 343–360). New York: Wiley.

Weaver, L. (2020). Tips to promote a healthy body image. Children's Hospital of Philadelphia. Accessed at: https://www.chop.edu/news/health-tip/tips-promote-healthy-body-image.

Wertheim, E. H., Paxton, S. J., Maude, D., Szmukler, G. I., Gibbons, K., & Hiller, L. (1992). Psychosocial predictors of weight loss behaviors and binge eating in adolescent girls and boys. *International Journal of Eating Disorders, 12*(2), 151–160.

Wertheim, E. H., Paxton, S. J., Schultz, H. K., & Muir, S. L. (1997). Why do adolescent girls watch their weight? An interview study examining sociocultural pressures to be thin. *Journal of Psychosomatic Research, 42*, 345–355.

Wilson, J., Peebles, R., Hardy, K., & Litt, I. (2007). Surfing for thinness: A pilot study of pro-eating disorder web site usage in adolescents with eating disorders. *Pediatrics, 118*(6), 1635–1643. doi:10.1542/peds.2006-1133.

Yoon, C., Duprez, D. A., Dutton, G., Lewis, C. E., Neumark-Sztainer, D., Steffen, L. M., West, D. S., Mason, S. M. (2018). Questionnaire-based problematic relationship to eating and food is associated with 25-year body mass index trajectories during midlife: The Coronary Artery Risk Development In Young Adults (CARDIA) Study. *International Journal of Eating Disorders, 51*(1), 10–17.

10. Arthur, Gay Marriage, and Contesting the Boundaries of Childhood

Socially Constructing Sexuality in Children's Educational Television

DANYELLA B. JONES
Old Dominion University

Watching broadcast news today, one may wonder whether the acceptance and tolerance of others has at least somewhat improved. *Obergefell v. Hodges* (2015), for example, was a landmark case in civil rights for the LGBTQ community where the Supreme Court ruled in favor of same-sex marriages across all the U.S. Yet, five years later, the ideologies of traditional marriage and family structures continue to be perceived by some as "challenged" simply by the increased representation of diverse relationships, cultures, and sexual practices in the media, and in particular representations of family life of LGBTQ individuals. Among media portrayals of LGBTQ family life, an episode of a recent children's television show sparked a new contestation about the boundaries that socially construct and frame "childhood" and LGBTQ family life. In May 2019 the PBS Kids' animated TV series *Arthur* (1996) opened its 22nd season with one of the show's main characters, Mr. Ratburn—Arthur's 3rd grade teacher—getting married and revealing at the end of the episode that it was to another male character. The episode raised polarized responses: acts of support that praised the portrayal of a same-sex couple in a kids' show, protests of the episode opposing the presentation as airing inappropriate content for children, and even astonishment that the long-running show was *still* creating episodes. Although the legal debate about same-sex marriage and family has ended, via the episode, the debate however is continued on the fronts of morality, modernity, and childhood.

The purpose of this chapter is to take a closer look at how PBS Kids and the creators of *Arthur* decided to structure the episode to portray same-sex marriage as well as inform its audiences of children that are often perceived by adults as needing "protection." I argue that although educational television's intended purposes are entertainment and information, it has the power to influence social constructions of foundational concepts such as "family" and "childhood." Further, I will show that some adults' perceptions of "children" may not be developing at the same pace as the information that children are receiving. Ultimately, I argue for the full inclusion of LGBTQ individuals into the topic of childhood communication research.

In order to understand how meanings about childhood are being influenced by television, I first seek to understand how messages about human sexuality targeting children are being structured and broadcasted through television. This will include research about children's culture and children's educational television relying on Barthes' (1972) semiology theory in order to understand how meaning is presented through messages and aided by Moscovici's (2001) theory of social representation. This chapter then analyzes the aforementioned *Arthur* episode and evaluates its narrative structure, representation of characters, and what messages are being structured through this format in the episode.

Review

In theory, most everyone believes that everyone deserves a chance to pursue and live happy lives as "family." Yet, in practice, segments of society struggle to accept and include same-sex family relationships within this framing. Days after the airing of the *Arthur* episode in question, Alabama Public Television (APT) programming director, Mike McKenzie, banned the episode from further broadcasting, reasoning that, "parents trust that their children can be left unsupervised to watch APT without having to worry about them being exposed to inappropriate content" (Griffith, 2019; Hayes, 2019; Quinn, 2019). It is an understatement to say that the episode sparked controversy, stemming from a simple, yet core question: What is appropriate and acceptable information for children to view as "educational" television? On the one hand, creators of *Arthur* are seeking to widen the definition of childhood to include LGBTQ individuals, while on the other hand broadcasters, out of stated concern for preserving an essence of "child innocence" (Benson & Elder, 2011) and optimal childhood development, sought to preserve the status quo and leave the social construction of LGBTQ family life as a matter for the "adult" viewing community. However, neither side seems to be fully considering children's perceptions or needs, nor how children are processing this information.

Constructing Children and Childhood

Studies of children and children's culture discuss the concept of "childhood" as not only defined in biological terms, but also as structured by social and historical situations (Aries, 1962; Buckingham, 2000) that affect children's experiential, behavioral, and cognitive development. Among these latter areas, television adds to as well as shapes children's cognitive development (Bandura, 1969), how children perceive themselves, as well as perceive others in their environment (Kirkpatrick & Epstein, 1992). These various communication efforts are part of what forms a culture of children that is also open to the shifting vagaries of popular culture. Studies have shown a varied approach to the portrayal of childhood from portraying young children as free-spirits, innocent humans whose only role is to play and learn, to showing no regard for their well-being by exposing them to extreme working conditions. Children are often referred to as "moldable" to be shaped into who society, as well as their parents want them to be and what they want them to be able to do (DeMause, 1974). Cultural values of childhood development have also been constructed for modern children. James, Jenks, and Prout (1998) state characteristics of childhood to include a biological state of asexuality of ambiguous preferences to other individuals. Social dependency is also placed on their adult caregivers to protect them from what may affect or debase this "fragile" state of mind (Wyness, 2019).

Children are often perceived as young, small, and simple individuals and therefore considered unable to process complex concepts and ideas (Wyness, 2019) no matter what the age throughout childhood development. An eight year old child's intellect is combined and collected with the understandings of children as young as three years old, which is often used for television broadcasters giving a target audience age range for their programming, yet adults don't take in what the older children may have experienced based on their level of education, physical ability (Hardwood, 2014) to communication and behavioral roles in the family household (Socha & Yingling, 2010). Progression in a child's communication also affects their maturity to various topics some adults may not be able to comprehend solely based on the age constraints of the child (Hardwood, 2014).

Children's Television

Cartoon Animation Representation and Storytelling. Representation can be stand-ins captured by a collective viewpoint determined as "real";

however, they can be interpretations for how the world is being presented with subjective signs towards "societal selective truths" (Barthes, 1972). Moscovici (2001) explored a model of social representation, a collection of ethics, philosophies, beliefs and practices that are shared among individuals within groups and communities. According to this approach, society interprets the quick succession of illustrated images as a kind of animated cartoon, a style typically used to indicate media aimed at children. Cartooning seems to be linked to childhood in part because of child's attentiveness and curiosity to understand what is happening while constantly assessing animated characters through their distinct yet exaggerated characteristics and features to one's own disposition (Vossen et al., 2014). When thinking about the concept of cartoon animation media, one often associates its style with children's entertainment.

There was a point in time when consideration for quality children's programming was next to nothing. Since near the advent of television, children's programming has come a long away to become the structured model used today that ensures the educational and informational needs of young viewers. Strasburger, Wison, and Jordan (2014) discuss how the market for children's media was often part of a multi-corporation. These mega-conglomerates did not always have the best interest of the child's development at the center of their products (Strasburger, Wilson, & Jordan, 2014). Child-awareness advocacy groups, like Action for Children's Television (1968), looked out for the well-being of young viewers by pressuring the FCC to communicate to television broadcasters to make more of an effort to produce age-appropriate educational content. Legislation came along later—the Children's Television Act of 1990—to further solidify the guidelines to keep the interests of children's educational and informational needs at the core of programming. This is often captured through elements of production, based on distinctive and bold design choices for characters, settings, and behaviors portrayed within a narrative, often exaggerated to capture the attention of younger audiences. The narrative and the underlying educational content can be seen to intertwine and uphold their messages separately within a television episode and children learn how to process and comprehend them both (Fisch, 2000). This model of thinking also process the social and emotional understandings of characters within context of the narrative that can be related to everyday life (Bandura, 1969).

LGBTQ Representation in Children's Television

The portrayal of LGBTQ individuals in media continues to expand, however their presence in a family role is limited, particularly in children's programming. Children's programming continues to address the various types of families within the heteronormative framework: married couple, blended families (step-mother / step-father), single-parent, and even extended family or adopted families (Socha & Yingling, 2010), however there is little addressing same-sex families. Though there have been attempts in the past to portray LGBTQ representation in children's programming, specifically looking at public television, the backlash brought up economic concerns and censorship.

In 2005, an episode from the series *Postcards from Buster* (2004)—a spinoff animated series from *Arthur*—has Buster visit real-life children in Vermont, and the children have lesbian parents. The episode was targeted by Christian groups for portraying homosexuality in a children's programming and [then] Education Secretary, Margaret Spellings, stated that exposing children to an "lesbian lifestyle" was something that America's tax dollars should not have to pay for (Salamon, 2005) and warned the network not to air it (de Moraes, 2005). The episode was pulled off the air when it showed a family with two mothers (Salamon, 2005; Moore, 2005) until the WGBH series producer offered the episode to any PBS station that wanted to air it (Moore, 2005). When the episode released, an article reported that one of the children mentioned one parent as a stepmom and that was all that was seen of the family (de Moraes, 2005). Where Spellings and those on the opposition of the episode focused on the sexuality of the parents, WGBH's vice president of children's programming, Brigid Sullivan, spoke on the diversity aspect children would learn about from other children who live in different types of family households (de Moraes, 2005).

The Episode

The Brand of Arthur and PBS Kids

Public broadcasting is a readily available channel of television media that allows free access to content for anyone in the U.S. to view. Under the Children's Television Act (1990) overseen by the Federal Communications Commission (FCC), television production companies are obligated to provide special core programming content designed specifically to serve the intellectual/cognitive or emotional/social educational and informational needs of a child. The affiliates of PBS (such as WHRO for the Hampton-Norfolk areas of Virginia) publicly commit to improving the lives of its viewers by producing and distributing programs considered by a variety of community, broadcasting, and professional groups important, impactful, and educational. They create and air content that revolves around practically anything excluding advocacy, commercial and promotional, or religious programming.

[PBS Kids] is committed to making a positive impact on the lives of children through curriculum-based entertainment. With a 360-degree approach towards learning and reaching children, PBS Kids leverages the full spectrum of media and technology to build knowledge, critical thinking, imagination and curiosity. By involving parents, teachers, caregivers, and communities as learning partners, PBS Kids helps to empower children for success in school and life. (About PBS Kids, 2020)

Arthur's first episode debuted in 1996 (Web Archive, 1996). The plot of the show *Arthur* (1996) revolves around everyday life of an eight-year-old aardvark looking boy, in an anthropomorphic world, and his interactions with family and friends in his hometown of Elwood City. The show, alongside promoting the joys and importance of reading, also seeks to portray how to deal with childhood challenges and traumas from the first day of school to the loss of a loved one.

According to Commonsense Media (2003) and other online television review webpages, the show's target audience is aimed at children ages 4–8, though many parents and journalist note that younger children are also watching. Today in 2020, the show is one of most the highly rated and longest running weekday children's series on PBS and continues to engage children with educational content revolving around the joys of books and read as well as relationships with friends, family and the community (Frank, 2019). The series has won seven Daytime Emmy Awards with twenty-five nominations, the George Foster Peabody Award for excellence in broadcasting, and the Humanitas Prize in 2016 (Internet Movie Database, 2020). Through its 232+ episodes, the development of this series has passed through several production companies and animation studios, all while attempting to preserve the traditional 2D visual style and narrative of the storybooks.

Official Arthur merchandise is available through the online PBS Kids shop, where some of the proceeds go to help support public television and PBS Kids programs. There is an interestingly limited offering of branded "official" toys, dolls or plushies created of the iconic characters. Playskool (1996) released one of the first Arthur plush dolls. Followed by Microsoft Corp that released an Arthur Read interactive plush toy in 1998. Purchase of most Arthur toys are rarely found in popular stores and are most likely sold through online shopping sites such as eBay, Amazon, or Etsy.

Mr. Ratburn and the "Special Someone" Episode

Mr. Ratburn and the Special Someone (2019) episode tells the story of Arthur and his friends—Buster, Francine, and Muffy—investigating who their 3rd grade teacher, Mr. Ratburn, is marrying. Class is interrupted by a mysterious phone call, communicated by a *Bridal Chorus* ringtone going off in Mr. Ratburn's pocket as he swiftly moves to answer it. He mentions by name someone named "Patty" as he turns to inform the caller he is in the middle of class and can't talk, gesturing his hands over his mouth to give the appears of hesitancy. Arthur and his classmates stare at each other in puzzlement as Mr. Ratburn continues to briefly discuss floral arrangements. Mr. Ratburn ends the call and apologizes to the class, stating it was rude to have answered his phone during class, though this time it was warranted by an exceptional reason. When asked about the flowers, he tells them they are for an unspecified wedding. When he is asked whose wedding, he looks to the camera, smiles, and states, "Me," before the students gasp in disbelief and the title credit rolls.

The story picks up with Arthur and his friends at the local eat-in diner, the Sugar Bowl, where they discuss how they cannot believe someone would marry their teacher, and their disbelief that teachers have personal lives outside of school. This is followed by an imaginative scenario of how teachers are expected to be when the school day is over, yet their role of an educator continues in a creative and humorous manner (e.g. Buster claiming that [teachers] "sharpen pencils, eat kale, and dream up homework assignments"). While Francine questions who would want to marry Mr. Ratburn, music cues a cut to Mr. Ratburn and another unknown female character, later revealed as the caller, Patty, entering the diner. The students hide as they listen-in on Mr. Ratburn and Patty discussing wedding plans. Patty's character comes off as very abrasive and very meticulous; Mr. Ratburn, notably known for his character being a tough 3rd grade teacher, is considered being 'too soft' by Patty in how he wants his wedding designed, leading her to state that she'll need to toughen him up more; the students are audibly shocked.

Arthur and his friends, afraid of how tough Mr. Ratburn will become if he stays with Patty, assuming (mistakenly) that she is the person he'll be marrying, devise schemes to attempt to get Mr. Ratburn to leave Patty and marry someone else. The first scheme uses Muffy's cellphone in and an app called Hippie Morph, where they take an image of Mr. Ratburn and transform his appearance to a style, they think Patty would not appreciate: a hippie. When they show Patty the image of Mr. Ratburn as a hippie, she laughs. The next plan is for the gang to set Mr. Ratburn up with the librarian, Miss Turner. Arthur and Francine enter a chocolate shop where a new character, Patrick, is introduced. They purchase a box of chocolates to give to Miss Turner, while Muffy and Buster write a love poem to give to her, signing their teacher's name. But Miss Turner doesn't fall for it. Their final plan is for all of them to object at the wedding ceremony.

At the ceremony, they see Patty opening the wedding ceremony, confused as to why the bride would already be waiting and seen by everyone. Arthur and his friends become too nervous to object when everyone looks at them and don't go through with the plan, which then Patty reveals to the viewers that she is Mr. Ratburn's sister and not the bride. Approximately fifteen seconds later, there is a wide shot of Mr. Ratburn walking down the aisle arm in arm with Patrick from the chocolate shop. Another ten seconds of screen time show Mr. Ratburn and Patrick walking down the aisle before it cuts to the reception. In the remaining thirty seconds of the episode, Arthur and his friends stand around praising how delicious the wedding cake was. Arthur makes the comment, 'I can't believe Mr. Ratburn is married,' to which Francine responses, "Yup, it's a brand-new world." But then the camera locks on a close up of Francine as she makes the statement, "But there's one thing that teachers should never ever do," then points to Mr. Ratburn and Patrick dancing.

Apparent and Latent Messages of Love and Marriage through Representation

When news of the episode spread across the internet, the image most articles used to sell their story was of Mr. Ratburn and Patrick at the wedding (Fetters & Escobar, 2019; Frank, 2019; Garcia, 2019; Rao, 2019; Martin, 2019; Griffith, 2019; Hayes, 2019; Quinn, 2019; Leary, 2019; Wong, 2019; Krotoszynski, 2019). This image was used in all news articles reporting on the story as well as radical groups and communities wanting to ban the episode, such as groups affiliated with the American Family Association organization, such as One Million Moms (2012). Seeing this image and the title of the episode to some signifies a great change in how children's television is becoming more inclusive and accepting of diverse family into a more normative structure. Though through the single image most adults come across when scrolling through the internet, children viewers are also viewing the image within the context of the entire narrative, which only appears within the last sixty seconds of the episode.

Children at young ages can attempt to understand the simple attributes of a wedding as representing two people who love each other getting married. However, there is a lot of passive word play and vague imaging used in this episode that vaguely resembles an idea of the Mr. Ratburn and Patrick getting married. Yet the audience is expected to gather enough information from the context of them walking down the aisle together to understand this is a wedding ceremony. The production decision to not set the location of the wedding scene in a church could represent more contemporary styles and/or be seen as not wanting to clash morals of some religious communities and their views on homosexual marriage. During legislation on same-sex marriage in 2015, notable groups that prohibited same-sex marriage in their organizations included the American Baptist Churches, Assemblies of God, Church of Jesus Christ of Latter-day Saints (Mormons), Islam, the National Baptist Convention, the Orthodox Jewish Movement, the Roman Catholic Church, Southern Baptist Convention, and the United Methodist Church, for the prohibition of same-sex marriage (Masci & Lipka, 2015). The decision to allow same-sex marriage created concern around most religious organizations as to whether their opposition would result in legal persecution for discrimination of LGBTQ people (Masci, 2015). As of now, according to the Family Research Council (1983), only the state must issue and recognize licenses for same-sex marriages in the U.S.; churches and pastors are not under any legal obligation to solemnize same-sex marriages within their facilities (Weber, 2020).

The musical choice they used instead of the traditional organ performance of *Bridal Chorus* (though briefly used as an 8-bit ringtone in the beginning of the episode) was YoYo Ma's *Unaccompanied Cello Suite No. 1*, something still classical that children could perceive as 'adult formal music.' Over the entire fifteen-minute episode, the amount of screen time Mr. Ratburn and Patrick shared together totaled approximately one minute. However, when they are walking down the aisle, the scene ends before they actually arrive at the "altar" or even get a chance to look at each other. They are looking at each other during their "first dance", but it's not the traditional slow dance together, they are standing away from each other and not touching.

The creators and writers of this episode chose to leave this detail until the very end of the episode. They made no mention of *who* he was marrying but left the assumption to the relational screen time Mr. Ratburn had with the first characters he mentions. The lack of detail in keeping this 'twist ending' never refers to either character as a *bride* or *groom*, only by their proper names, leaving the audience to associate hearing about weddings, flowers, and chocolates to the only names said in relation to Mr. Ratburn (e.g. Patty and Miss Turner) to heteronormativity. Even when the reveal of who Mr. Ratburn is walking down the aisle with, the character's name is not mentioned in the episode. The audience learned indirectly of it as Patrick from the chocolate shop scene, so the viewer knows it but is not proclaimed in the episode that Mr. Ratburn and Patrick are getting married.

Conclusion

A wedding celebrates a commitment and faithful love between two people becoming one whole; it is a custom shared through many cultures, ethnicities, countries, and social classes. The acceptance and tolerance of others, in terms of lifestyle, has increased tremendously within the last five years. *Obergefell v. Hodges* (2015) was a significant case in civil rights for the LGBTQ community in which the Supreme Court ruled in favor to allow same-sex marriage across all the U.S. The ideologies of traditional marriage and family structures are transforming in the light of the screen, allowing children to perceive various types of households, and for some, see a more accurate understanding of their homes with same-sex parents. Recent years will show that the US Census Bureau (2019) released estimations of same-sex couples, both married and unmarried, showing the transformation of the concept of the family household. Over 190,000 children currently live with same-sex parents, yet media for children's programming is not reflecting these changes as quickly as most would expect.

The issue of boundaries when these portrayals through media are directed towards communities who oppose these messages continue to collide in a debate of controversies when determining the exposure of certain content to young audiences, however, the acceptance of same-sex marriages and parents is on the rise to encourage one day children's programming will show a wider selection of families to young audiences. Since the *Arthur* episode's release, more recent developments report most of the aforementioned religious organizations have since announced official statements welcoming LGBTQ individuals as members of their organizations. As of recent, the Human Rights Campaign (1980) recognizes church groups and organizations that have since taken a supportive stand on fighting for freedom from discrimination, solemnizing of same-sex marriage and the ordination of openly LGBTQ clergy to include American Baptist Churches, Church of Jesus Christ of Latter-day Saints, the National Baptist Convention, the Roman Catholic Church, Southern Baptist Convention and the United Methodist Church.

Children today are developing rapidly as they are immersed in the digital and technological era more than ever before. Their minds are capable of processing a lot more information from multiple channels at a single time, yet that raw data has to be structured in a way for them to comprehend it. How adult individuals perceive the concept of childhood aids in the way they choose to shape how the child will take in information. Television is also used to aid in how adults communicate ideas to children about how they should behave, think and learn. This is important to examine how messages are being structured to children in a way that they are likely to comprehend.

References

Aries, P. (1962). *Centuries of childhood: A social history of family life.* New York: Random House.

Bandura, A. (1969). Social-learning theory of identificatory processes. *Handbook of Socialization Theory and Research, 3,* 213–255.

Barthes, R. (1972). *Mythologies.* New York: Hill and Yang.

Benson, J. E., & Elder, G. H. (2011). Young adult identities and their pathways: A developmental and life course model. *Developmental Psychology, 47*(6) 1646–1657.

Buckingham, D. (2000). *After the death of childhood—Growing up in the age of electronic media.* Cambridge: Polity Press.

DeMause, L. (1974). *The history of childhood.* New York: Psychohistory Press.

De Moraes, L. (2005, January 27). PBS's 'Buster' gets an education. *Washington Post.* Retrieved from https://www.washingtonpost.com/wp-dyn/articles/A40188-2005Jan26.html

Fetters, A., & Escobar, N. (2019, May 14). How a gay character on *Arthur* reflects changing norms in the U.S. *The Atlantic.* Retrieved from https://www.theatlantic.com/family/archive/2019/05/mr-ratburns-gay-wedding-on-arthur-was-quietly-profound/589462/

Fisch, S. M. (2000). A capacity model of children's comprehension of educational content on television. *Media Psychology, 2,* 63–91. doi:10.1207/S1532785XMEP0201_4.

Frank, A. (2019, May 14, 2019). Kids' tv rarely shows same-sex marriage. PBS's Arthur just did—and it was, wonderfully, no big deal. *Vox.* Retrieved from https://www.vox.com/culture/2019/5/14/18623162/arthur-mr-ratburn-gay-marriage-pbs

Frank, T. (2019, July 12). Longest running animated series. *Ranker.* Retrieved from https://www.ranker.com/list/longest-running-animated-series/tvs-frank

Garcia, S. E. (2019, May 14). 'Arthur' opens season with a same-sex wedding and a cake. *The New York Times.* Retrieved from https://www.nytimes.com/2019/05/14/arts/television/ratburn-arthur.html

Griffith, J. (2019, May 21). Alabama Public Television refuses to air 'Arthur' episode with gay wedding. *CNBC News.* Retrieved from https://cnbc.com 2019/05/21/alabama-public-television-refuses-to-air-arthur-gay-wedding-episode.html

Hardwood, J. (2014). Lifespan communication theory. *The Handbook of Lifespan Communication, 1,* 9–28.

Hayes, K. T. (2019, May 21). Alabama Public Television refuses to air 'Arthur' episode with gay wedding. *Fox 5 Atlanta.* Retrieved from https://www.fox5atlanta.com/news/alabama-public-television-refuses-to-air-arthur-episode-with-gay-wedding

Human Rights Campaign. (2020). *Faith positions.* Retrieved from https://www.hrc.org/resources/faith-positions

Internet Movie Database. (2020). Arthur awards. *IMDb.* Retrieved from https://www.imdb.com/title/tt0169414/awards

James, A., Jenks, C., & Prout, A. (1998). *Theorising childhood,* Cambridge: Polity Press.

Kirkpatrick, L. A., & Epstein, S. (1992). Cognitive-experiential self-theory and subjective probability: Further evidence for two conceptual systems. *Journal of Personal Social Psychology, 63*(4), 534–544.

Krotoszynski, R. (2019, May 23). "By censoring *Arthur's* same-sex wedding, Alabama Public Television betrayed Mr. Roger's legacy." *Slate Magazine*. Retrieved from https://slate.com/human-interest/2019/05/arthur-gay-wedding-alabama-mister-rogers.html

Leary, D. (2019, May 22). Gay marriage in *Arthur* pushes the limits of social realism in children's tv. *National Review*. Retrieved from https://www.nationalreview.com/2019/05/arthur-gay-marriage-pushes-limits-social-realism-childrens-television/

Martin, R. (2019, May 15). PBS shoe 'Arthur' introduces children to same-sex marriage. *NPR*. Retrieved from https://www.nytimes.com/2019/05/14/arts/television/ratburn-arthur.html

Masci, D. (2015, June 26). How the supreme court's decision for gay marriage could affect religious institutions. *Pew Research Center*. Retrieved from https://www.pewresearch.org/fact-tank/2015/06/26/how-a-supreme-court-decision-for-gay-marriage-would-affect-religious-institutions/

Masci, D., & Lipka, M. (2015, December 21). Where are Christian churches, other religions stand on gay marriage. *Pew Research Center*. Retrieved from https://www.pewresearch.org/fact-tank/2015/12/21/where-christian-churches-stand-on-gay-marriage/

Moore, F. (2005, February 9). What's the big deal about 'Buster'? *Today*. Retrieved from https://www.today.com/popculture/what-s-big-deal-about-buster-wbna6941861

Moscovici, S. (2001). *Social representations exploration in social psychology*. New York: University Press.

Obergefell v. Hodges, 14-556, 576 U.S. ___ (06/26/2015).

PBS Kids. (1996, December 25). Arthur on TV. *Web Archive*. Retrieved from http://www.pbs.org/wgbh/pages/arthur/tv.html

Quinn, D. (2019, May 21). *Arthur* creator 'disappointed' after Alabama public television refuses to air gay wedding episode. *People*. Retrieved from https://people.com/tv/alabama-pulls-arthur-gay-wedding-episode-marc-brown-responds/

Rao, S. (2019, May 14). Mr. Ratburn came out as gay and got married in the 'Arthur' season premiere. *The Washington Post*. Retrieved from https://www.washingtonpost.com/arts-entertainment/2019/05/14/mr-ratburn-came-out-gay-got-married-arthur-season-premiere/

Salamon, J. (2005, January 27). Culture wars pull Buster into the fray. *The New York Times*. Retrieved from https://www.nytimes.com/2005/01/27/arts/culture-wars-pull-buster-into-the-fray.html

Socha, T. J., & Yingling, J. (2010). *Families communicating with children*. Cambridge, UK: Polity.

Strasburger, V. C., Wilson, B. J., & Jordan, A. B. (2014). *Children, adolescents, and the media* (3rd ed.). Thousand, Oaks, CA: Sage.

United States Census Bureau. (2019, November 19). U.S. Census Bureau releases CPS estimates of same-sex households. Retrieved from https://www.census.gov/newsroom/press-releases/2019/same-sex-households.html

Vossen, H., Piotrowski, J., & Valkenburg, P. (2014). Media use and effects in childhood. *The Handbook of Lifespan Communication, 5*, 93–108.

Wong, C. M. (2019, May 22). 'Arthur' creator defends gay marriage episode following backlash. *HuffPost Entertainment.* Retrieved from https://www.huffpost.com/entry/arthur-creator-gay-wedding-backlash_n_5ce583a2e4b0547bd1311a34

Wyness, M. (2019). *Childhood and society* (3rd ed.). London, UK: Red Globe Press.

11. Media Literacy Education as a Context for Children's Communication

RONDA M. SCANTLIN
University of Dayton

Introduction

We now live in complex, media-saturated environments filled with televisions, Blu-ray players, personal computers, tablets and laptops, the Internet, video gaming systems, smart phones, and other portable devices. They offer constant exposure to media messages and abundant opportunities to interact within social contexts—from connecting with friends on Facebook to posting a photo on Instagram. Media and digital technologies have transformed the ways in which we communicate, educate, work, entertain, consume, and create. Furthermore, we continue to develop dependencies on our technological devices without fully understanding the consequences for social relationships, academic achievement, digital security and privacy, or personal health and well-being to name a few. It is within this context that media literacy—competencies that enable us to access, analyze, evaluate, create, and act—must play a critical role. Teaching media literacy translates into user awareness and control over media experiences; such skills also develop or cultivate empowerment. This is particularly important for young media users, as they are just beginning to interpret media messages in more sophisticated ways and create content with lasting impact.

The purpose of this chapter is to explore critical issues surrounding the acquisition of media literacy skills from childhood through late adolescence as well as examine the influence of these types of experiences on well-being. Specific goals include examining media literacy in all its forms, reviewing effects of media literacy education initiatives on developmental outcomes, exploring media socialization and opportunities for mentorship, and reflecting on the perspectives of children and adolescents. It is within this framework that we can learn about the perceptions of young people in a complex media environment. Such experiences also provide opportunities for them to communicate understandings, values, and concerns about life in the digital age.

Exploring the "Ecology" of Media Literacy

Multiple definitions of media literacy have been proposed and debated, yet most scholars and educators agree that the core competencies include accessing, analyzing, evaluating, creating and communicating messages (e.g., Aufderheide, 1993; Hobbs, 2010; National Association for Media Literacy Education, 2007). The term "media literacy" is often considered an umbrella concept including elements of the following: mass media literacy (i.e., understanding how messages are constructed as well as examining how individuals interpret those messages differently), digital literacy (i.e., using digital technology, communication tools, and/or networks to access, manage, evaluate and create), and information literacy (i.e., accessing information efficiently, evaluating it critically, and using it accurately) (e.g., "Partnership for 21st Century Learning", n.d.). What follows is further delineation of these various constructs.

Working from a cognitive information-processing perspective, Potter (2019, p. 23) defines media literacy as "a set of perspectives that we actively use to expose ourselves to the mass media to process and interpret the meaning of the messages we encounter". He suggests there are three building blocks of media literacy: (1) *skills* that include analysis, evaluation, grouping, induction, deduction, synthesis, and abstracting, (2) *knowledge structures*, or organized information housed in our memory that has meaning, and (3) *personal locus*, or one's personal goals and drives. The latter is akin to Uses and Gratifications Theory (e.g., Rubin, 2002), which emphasizes user motivations (e.g., What motivates viewers to choose particular genres of programming?) and needs met by engaging with particular media messages (e.g., using media to meet cognitive, diversion or social utility needs.). Acquiring media literacy, then, theoretically results in control over exposure to and time spent with media messages as well as control over the influence on self and others.

Of particular importance for this chapter is Potter's description of media literacy as a *continuum*, rather than a category (2019, p. 25). This perspective suggests that developing media literacy is a life-long process with infants acquiring fundamentals (e.g., recognizing colors, shapes, movement), toddlers learning language, and preschoolers understanding increasingly complex narratives. Numerous PBS programs—*Sesame Street, Peg + Cat, Daniel*

Tiger's Neighborhood, Wild Kratts, Super Why!—provide a scaffold for acquiring and refining these essential skills. Elementary-age children are developing skepticism and now understand why Play-Doh's "Doctor Drill-N-Fill" does not work exactly as promised in the television advertisement. They compare their hands-on product experiences with persuasive tactics that make product advertising so appealing. Adolescents and young adults will potentially acquire higher level skills such as critical appreciation of messages (e.g., making simultaneous comparisons or constructing judgments) and social responsibility (e.g., recognizing one's personal decisions and actions can influence others). Interestingly, Potter (2019) suggests that these latter categories may not be acquired by some; for instance, social responsibility eludes too many social media users, as online posts lacking in civility or accuracy are all too common.

Other authors and organizations discuss domain, genre or platform specific literacies including news, cinema, gaming, and advertising literacy (e.g., Wilson, Grizzle, Tuazon, Akyempong, & Cheung, 2011). Within each category, literacy entails understanding the economic context of the media industry, recognizing the production values that guide attention and impact comprehension, and considering the multitude of effects on development. In their work exploring the impact of image retouching on adolescent body image, Harrison and Hefner (2014) utilize visual literacy or an ability to interpret information presented in pictorial or graphic images. Moreover, Livingstone (2014, p. 299) introduces the concept of social media literacy and characterizes it as, "the perceptions and understanding that account for how children engage with social media." She emphasizes the evolving nature of social media literacy, which is based on children's age and social context. As children develop from early childhood through adolescence, they experience changes in their relationships with parents and peers, changes in sense of self or identity formation, and changes in how social media will (or will not) meet their needs. A primary challenge is to balance acquiring skills for purposes of safety and avoiding risk versus acquiring competencies that facilitate exploration and opportunity. And, in the 21st century, the notion of "communication competency" requires expansion as individuals, children and adults alike, incorporate portable media into their everyday communication lives (e.g., see Socha et al., 2017).

Acquiring the above-mentioned skills affords tremendous opportunities and is an essential component of participating in our media-saturated culture. "Today full participation in contemporary culture requires not only consuming messages, but also creating and sharing them ... Americans must acquire multimedia communication skills that include the ability to compose messages using language, graphic design, images and sound ..." (Hobbs, 2010, p. vii). Similarly, Jenkins et al. (2009) recommend expanding competencies (i.e., digital literacy skills) while retaining important foundational skills (i.e., reading and writing, research skills, and technical skills). Consistent with multiple definitions of media literacy, Jenkins and colleagues identify 11 "new media literacies" in their work with the MacArthur Foundation: play, performance, simulation, appropriation, multitasking, distributed cognition, collective intelligence, judgment, transmedia navigation, networking, and negotiation. These skills emphasize interacting with one's environment (e.g., play), constructing new meaning (e.g., appropriation) and transforming one's perspective (e.g., negotiation). For instance, transmedia navigation (or following narrative/storytelling across platforms) is particularly relevant for young audiences. The term *transmedia* was coined by Kinder (1991) and refers to narrative and non-narrative media components occurring across platforms. Correspondingly, children's media properties offer multiple points of entry, enable many different forms of participation, and engage the interests of multiple consumers (Jenkins et al., 2009). This is evident within the *Star Wars* franchise. Not only does *Star Wars* have multi-generational appeal, but revenue (and knowledge) is generated across platforms: theatrical releases, televised or streamed animated series, DVD/Blu-ray sales, video game content, mobile apps, adult collectibles, a myriad of toys, book series, licensed food items, and the list continues. Children and adolescents acquire knowledge while engaging in one activity (e.g., watching *Star Wars: The Rise of Skywalker*) and then use that knowledge when participating in another activity (e.g., playing *Star Wars: The Skywalker Saga* on their Xbox One.) *Star Wars* is of course an iconic brand experience with the Disney corporation now reaping the benefits, but this also has consequences for the consumer. A significant amount of work has focused on the concept of "brand personality"—defined as a set of human characteristics associated with a brand. In this early work, Aaker (1997) described how the personality of a brand enables a consumer to express his or her own self or specific dimensions of self—one's identity. These connections with brands drive consumer preferences and use, evoke emotions, and increase trust and loyalty. Transmedia navigation facilitates such outcomes.

In contrast to the commercial underpinnings of media-based products, consider the creative element of transmedia literacy—focusing on narrative expansion. Young media users create or produce new content, mashups, or re-conceptualizations of existing material. Scolari describes the development of these skills in informal learning spaces outside of school (e.g., uploading to YouTube, posting on social media, journaling on blog sites) (Elea & Mikos,

2017). Moreover, he reminds us that most of adolescents' knowledge about interactive media or technology often comes from informal environments.

> When a child or a teen has a problem to solve (How to move to next level in this videogame? How to manipulate an Instagram filter?), they do not ask their parents or the teachers: they check their favorite YouTube channels, ask their friends, or consult an online community (Elea & Mikos, 2017, p. 127).

Transmedia skills clearly enhance participation, collaboration, and creativity. Interesting questions remain, however, surrounding transmedia navigation or play. Ethical and legal issues potentially arise when children share content online; moreover, there may be uncertainty about which producers and audience members may integrate part or all material into transmedia storyworlds (Alper & Herr-Stephenson, 2013).

Within these diverse conceptualizations of media literacy, what does it mean to be "media literate" in our technological age? What skills should we be teaching children, adolescents, young adults, and parents? Are there consequences of not acquiring such skills? The challenge, then, is to rethink the concept of media literacy and the process of participation in this complex media environment as such competencies go hand in hand with equally vital interpersonal communication competencies. One promising path forward is the work focused on digital intelligence.

Evolving Competencies: Digital Intelligence

In 2018, Dr. Yuhyun Park and collaborating organizations (i.e., DQ Institute, Coalition for Digital Intelligence, World Economic Forum, Organization for Economic Co-operation and Development, and the Institute of Electronics and Electrical Engineers Standards Association) officially introduced the concept of *Digital Intelligence*[10] with the objective of creating a common framework and global standards for digital literacy, skills, and readiness.

> Digital intelligence (DQ) is a comprehensive set of technical, cognitive, meta-cognitive, and socio-emotional competencies that are grounded in universal moral values and that enable individuals to face the challenges and harness the opportunities of digital life. DQ has three levels, eight areas, and 24 competencies composed of knowledge, skills, attitudes, and values (Park, 2019, p. 6).

Details of this framework are illustrated in Figure 11.1.

---

10 The term *Digital Intelligence* is copyrighted by the DQ Institute, an international think tank committed to setting global standards for digital intelligence education, outreach and policies.

	Digital Identity	Digital Use	Digital Safety	Digital Security	Digital Emotional Intelligence	Digital Communication	Digital Literacy	Digital Rights
Digital Citizenship	1 Digital Citizen Identity	2 Balanced Use of Technology	3 Behavioural Cyber-Risk Management	4 Personal Cyber Security Management	5 Digital Empathy	6 Digital Footprint Management	7 Media and Information Literacy	8 Privacy Management
Digital Creativity	9 Digital Co-Creator Identity	10 Healthy Use of Technology	11 Content Cyber-Risk Management	12 Network Security Management	13 Self-Awareness and Management	14 Online Communication and Collaboration	15 Content Creation and Computational Literacy	16 Intellectual Property Rights Management
Digital Competitiveness	17 Digital Changemaker Identity	18 Civic Use of Technology	19 Commercial and Community Cyber-Risk Management	20 Organisational Cyber Security Management	21 Relationship Management	22 Public and Mass Communication	23 Data and AI Literacy	24 Participatory Rights Management

Figure 11.1. DQ Levels, Areas, and Competencies. Source: DQ Competencies (2020). Reprinted with permission from the DQ Institute https://www.dqinstitute.org/dq-framework/.

While a comprehensive description of the *Digital Intelligence* framework can be explored on the DQ Institute website (see embedded materials in Figure 11.1 online), a brief discussion of its foundational principles and selected competencies is beneficial. Park (2019) and collaborators recognized the urgent need for shared understanding and a common structure among those working and educating in the digital environment. Hence while creating the DQ framework, they reviewed existing frameworks from multiple organizations and nations (e.g., Common Sense Media's *K-12 Digital Citizenship Curriculum*/United States, UNICEF's *Global Kids Online*/UK, Ministry of Education's *Cyber Wellness 101*/Singapore, *Battelle for Kids Partnership for 21st Century Learning*/United States, UNESCO's *Global Media and Information Literacy Assessment Framework*/France.) The result is a comprehensive set of competencies guided by ethical principles, as presented in Table 11.1.

Table 11.1. DQ Competencies and Guiding Ethical Principles. Source: Adapted from Park (2019). Reprinted with permission from the DQ Institute. https://www.dqinstitute.org/wpcontent/uploads/2019/11/DQGlobalStandardsReport2019.pdf

8 Areas of DQ Competencies	Definitions	Guiding Ethical Principles
Digital Identity	Ability to build a wholesome online and offline identity.	Respect for oneself
Digital Use	Ability to use technology in a balanced, healthy, and civic way.	Respect for time and the environment
Digital Safety	Ability to understand, mitigate and manage cyber-risks through safe, responsible and ethical use of technology.	Respect for life
Digital Security	Ability to detect, avoid and manage different levels of cyber threats to protect data, devices, networks, systems.	Respect for property
Digital Emotional Intelligence	Ability to recognize, navigate and express emotions in one's digital intra- and inter-personal interactions.	Respect for others
Digital Communication	Ability to communicate and collaborate with others using technology.	Respect for reputation and relationships
Digital Literacy	Ability to find, read, evaluate, synthesize, create, adapt, and share information, media and technology.	Respect for knowledge
Digital Rights	Ability to understand and uphold human rights and legal rights when using technology.	Respect for rights

The *Digital Intelligence* framework addresses several concerns and recommendations of Bulger and Davison (2018) in their review of the current state of media literacy including developing a coherent understanding of the media environment, improving cross-disciplinary collaborations, and creating a national media literacy evidence base. *DQ* provides opportunities for individuals and organizations to adopt standards, align their own educational and assessment efforts with standards, and engage with other members of this global community.

Effects of Media Literacy Education on Development

Children and adolescents encounter a myriad of messages and images daily as they interact with their devices. Favorite Netflix dramas regularly contain portrayals of aggressive exchanges, sexual innuendo and/or risky behaviors, alcohol consumption, stereotyped characters, and coarse language. The most popular video games feature battle-style game play and use of weapons. Perusing Instagram offers filtered images and self-comparisons to unrealistic ideals. Twitter and Facebook news feeds are littered with misinformation. These examples can have behavioral, physiological, emotional, attitudinal, cognitive, and societal effects. Consequently, critical analysis and deconstruction of messages and/or images—components of media literacy frameworks—are precursors to moderating negative effects on children's and adolescents' development (i.e., protection perspective). In contrast, media in all its forms can provide benefits to the user, whether that be facilitating educational achievement via multiple media platforms, using digital tools for communication, producing innovative content, or connecting with communities of interest (i.e., empowerment perspective). Hobbs (2010, p. ix) approaches the complexities in this way:

> Rather than viewing empowerment and protection as an either-or proposition, they must be seen as two sides of the same coin. Because mass media, popular culture and digital technologies contribute to shaping people's attitudes, behaviors and values, not only in childhood but across a lifetime, there is a public interest in addressing potential harms. For healthy development, children and youth need privacy, physical and psychological safety, and freedom from exposure to objectionable, disturbing, or inappropriate material. At the same time, media and technology can empower individuals and groups. People gain many personal, social and cultural benefits from making wise choices about information and entertainment, using digital tools for self-expression and communication, and participating in online communities with people around the neighborhood and around the world who share their interests and concerns.

Both protection and empowerment can be accomplished through all forms of media literacy education: ongoing integration into school curricula, stand-alone lessons, teachable moments, and personal exploration.

Integration into School Curricula
In her review of the foundations of media literacy, Hobbs (2019, pp. 1–2) states that "media literacy has entered the education and cultural system in four distinct ways: as an expanded form of literacy; as an intervention to address potential harms of media exposure; as an approach to integrate digital technology into education; and as a dimension of global citizenship." Integrating media literacy into school curricula, however, is not without challenges. Teachers face significant pressures to prepare their students to meet state standards, to achieve goals with limited resources, to balance diverse learning needs, and to engage in self-care to manage stress (to name a few). In fact, Culver and Redmond's (2019) report on *The State of Media Literacy Education in the U.S.* indicates that significant obstacles to teaching media literacy in the classroom include competing curricular requirements and lack of time. Numerous educational institutions have also struggled with inequity across social groups, which hinders delivering opportunities to all youth (e.g., Ito et al., 2013). Moreover, media literacy education across school systems tends to vary by pedagogical approaches, delivery methods, and assessment strategies (Bulger & Davison, 2018). Finding ways to effectively bridge media literacy and existing curricular requirements, therefore, is beneficial for both teachers and students. While a comprehensive review of school-based programs is beyond the scope of this chapter, what follows is an illustration of lessons that are taught by teachers trained in media literacy, content that flows across disciplines, and opportunities for students to demonstrate their understanding through media production projects. Programs that connect analysis and media production activities tend to be more effective than those using analysis alone (Banerjee & Greene, 2007). Similarly, Ito and colleagues (2013) emphasize the importance of production-centered learning (i.e., using digital tools to create and produce varied media, knowledge and cultural content); it is a core element of *Connected Learning*[11] which suggests interest-driven learning promotes life-long learning.

Scholars agree that robust and comprehensive learning occur with repeated exposure to information in various contexts. Bickham and Slaby's

---

11 *Connected Learning* originated from the work of the Connected Learning Research Network and is an educational approach focused on bridging the in-school and out-of-school environments; it is interest-driven, supported by peers and caregivers, and aligned with academic achievement, career success, or civic engagement (Ito et al., 2013).

(2012) evaluation of the *Media Power Youth* (MPY) program (i.e., a set of health-focused media literacy programs serving students in early elementary through high school) attests to the effectiveness of this strategy. In this study, fifth-grade students participated in 40-minute media literacy lessons delivered twice a week for six weeks. The MPY program employs susceptibility-reduction strategies, which are designed to teach critical evaluation skills needed to counter unhealthy messages or challenge misinformation. Of particular interest is integration across academic disciplines, "allowing for both the analysis of the messages (in the health class) and the translation of the program lesson into art and media production (in the art class)" (Bickham & Slaby, 2012, p. 257). The authors found that the MPY approach was effective in meeting its goals. The fifth-grade students who participated in the program increased understanding that (1) media violence is often glorified, unrealistic and can impact children's behaviors and (2) advertising can make smoking and fast foods look healthy and increase desire for these products (Bickham & Slaby, 2012). Furthermore, these fifth-graders were able to successfully apply those skills to novel media stimuli. Programs such this one provide children with essential cognitive tools needed to counter potentially harmful media messages and limit problematic effects of those messages. These skills can be employed as children grow and encounter both similar and more complex media narratives.

The bridge between media literacy efforts and existing school curricula becomes even more important when public policy dictates elements of that curricula; the Common Core State Standards[12] (CCSS) initiative is one such example. It is important to note that since the CCSS roll out in 2010, more than 20 states eventually repealed, revised, or rolled back parts of the program so its success or failure is yet to be determined (Goldstein, 2019). Within this environment, however, Redmond (2015) explored expanding the conception of *texts* and integrating media literacy into the Common Core. In this case study of a class called *Media Literacy Workshop*, seventh-grade students participated in 10 analysis and evaluation classes (September through December) and 15 media production classes (January through March). Students not only *analyzed* texts (e.g., persuasive argumentation) but also *produced* texts (e.g., scriptwriting for an advertising video project). Students felt valued and commented that materials used in class resonated with them personally. "While part of the students' engagement and interest in the class was a result of the

---

12 Complete descriptions of the Common Core State Standards and resources for teachers and parents can be found at http://www.corestandards.org/about-the-standards/.

types of media texts that they read, namely media from the popular culture, the practice of co-learning suggested that students felt ownership over the curriculum, contributing a legacy in text suggestions for future Media Literacy Workshop students" (Redmond, 2015, p. 15).

Redmond (2015, pp. 16–17) describes how these curricular activities connect to CCSS in ELA (e.g., access how point of view or purpose shapes the content and style of text), in mathematics (e.g., integrate and evaluate content presented in diverse media and formats, including visually and quantitatively) and in science (e.g., cite the textual evidence that most strongly supports an analysis of what the text says explicitly as well as inference drawn from the text). Following a successful experience in the *Media Literacy Workshop* classes, the teachers of record applied for a grant to offer professional development opportunities in media literacy for their colleagues outside of the classroom. This work strengthens the case for integrating media literacy lessons within existing curricular requirements, across disciplines, and among a community of learners.

Numerous resources have been developed to incorporate media literacy concepts in venues within and outside the school environment. Organizations like *Common Sense Media* have increased awareness and provided comprehensive, credible resources for educators, parents, and youth. Their *Digital Citizenship Curriculum* includes lessons addressing media balance/well-being, privacy/security, digital footprint/identity, relationships/communication, cyberbullying/digital drama/hate speech, and news media literacy. The *National Association for Media Literacy Education* has created a community of support and collaboration, as well as guidelines for parents and discussion of common core standards. *Parenting for a Digital Future* was originally part of the Connected Learning Research Network funded by the MacArthur Foundation and now explores wide-ranging topics (e.g., parenting and learning during a global pandemic, navigating online spaces, fake news and critical literacy) associated with children and teens growing up in digital environments. Finally as noted earlier in this chapter, the *Digital Intelligence* initiative strives to create a common framework and global standards for digital literacy, skills, and readiness in the domains of digital identity, use, safety, security, emotional intelligence, communication, literacy, and rights. While these more programmatic efforts are essential and provide a foundation for media literacy education, exploring teachable moments within the context of family or other mentoring relationships highlights the importance of beginning the teaching and learning process early in life.

Opportunities for Socialization & Mentorship

Childhood is characterized by early and frequent media use, preparing youth for life-long relationships with communication technologies. As discussed throughout this chapter, implications of this life-long relationship include potential risks as well as enhanced opportunities. Decisions made surrounding media and digital technologies have implications for personal well-being, social relationships, individual privacy and security, work environments, and academic outcomes, to name a few. Developing the abilities needed to access, analyze, evaluate, create, and act within this environment is now considered an essential set of life skills. These media literacy skills, however, do not develop in a vacuum. Jenkins et al. (2009) remind us that **adult intervention and supervision are necessary despite the knowledge structures and skills of young people.** There has, in fact, been some debate about skill acquisition by "digital natives", a term coined by Prensky (2001) describing young people who have grown up with technology. A decade ago, Pierce (2010) discussed how high school students were unaware of how Google sorts and ranks its search results, accepting the validity of information on the first few lines. Moreover, many instructors of college courses suggest the narrative about tech-savvy young people is false; for instance, knowledge about corporate data collection practices, personal privacy, and online reputation management is lacking (O'Neil, 2014).

Socialization of children and adolescents surrounding media-related issues requires an "all hands on deck" approach. Hobbs (2010) offered a plan of action necessitating sustained support by educational leaders at local, state, and federal levels; members of Congress and the Department of Education; libraries; charitable organizations; news organizations; technology companies and many others. Parents, of course, are perhaps the most important contributors to this process. Media use has an impact on concurrent social interactions and is itself conditioned by the social context in which it is used. The **home environment** is clearly an important context as parents make technology available and play a role in socializing children to use media in specific ways. It is within this environment that parents have the opportunity to establish boundaries that influence their children's media use—how much time they spend in front of screens, the specific content they watch or use, and what messages they take away from those media choices. They can engage in enabling communication behaviors (active talking or active mediation) or restrictive communication behaviors (establishing rules or using online filters) (e.g., Livingstone et al., 2018; Potter, 2019). Parents are also in a crucial position to advocate for their children's interests and passions. Livingstone and Blum-Ross (2019) emphasize that parents play a key role in enabling and sustaining these interest-driven activities across contexts and over time.

Parenting is filled with contradictions—restricting in the name of safety and encouraging to promote opportunities. To manage these complexities effectively, parents must become media literate themselves and serve as role models. "Future advice to parents should encourage them to develop their digital skills and those of their child, and reflect on how these can enhance online opportunities and build resilience through coping with adversity as it arises" (Livingstone et al., 2017, p. 100). In doing so, parents can encourage responsible digital citizenship. This includes acquiring the technical and social competencies to interact in ethical ways in our digital culture.

Ethical Use of Technology & Digital Citizenship
James (2014, p. 107) argues that mentors (including parents, educators and other adults) are poised to influence the moral and ethical dispositions of young people in significant ways; yet, such mentors must seize these opportunities. Jenkins et al. (2009) discuss an "ethics challenge" while James (2014) highlights an "ethics gap", both of which refer to concerns about whether young media users engage in careful thought and contemplate the ethical dilemmas present in the online environment. The same concerns, of course, could be directed toward adults. The creators of media-literacy initiatives incorporate some element of ethics into their resources. For instance, an underlying premise of the *Digital Intelligence* framework is *respect*. This fundamental moral principle is integrated within each of the eight DQ competencies (refer to Table 11.1). In sum, scholars, educators, and professionals working in multiple disciplines and approaching media literacy from varied perspectives encourage ethical use of technology.

Much can be learned from conversations with young people pertaining to these matters. A mindset characterized by "It's just the Internet" (James, 2014, p. 90) has become more frequent, suggesting that what happens online has little significance and users should not take it so seriously. Contrast this with the notion that language has power. The ethical choices that users make influence members of their culture. Too often, we see insufficient recognition that individual decisions can have detrimental consequences for others—from cyberbullying to perpetuating misinformation on social media sites. Jenkins et al. (2009, p. 32) fittingly suggest that "the new media literacies should be conceptualized as social skills, as ways of interacting within a larger community, and not simply as individualized skills to be used for personal expression." Over a decade later, serious concerns have been voiced about how social media users interact within the larger community—being less about connectivity and focused more on public performance. Haidt and Rose-Stockwell (2019, para. 6) remind us that communication is a two-way street, but "What happens when grandstands are erected along both sides of that street and then filled with friends, acquaintances, rivals, and strangers, all passing judgment and offering commentary?" The outcome of this structure is grandstanding, which appears to encourage outrage and promote personal status. Using Twitter's "Retweet" button or Facebook's "Like" or "Share" buttons, online posts can spark contagious outrage. These types of *online firestorms* (Pfeffer, Zorbach, & Carley, 2014) can occur surrounding companies, products, political figures, the government, celebrities, movements, public policies, individual characteristics/traits and countless other topics encountered by children, adolescents and adults on a daily basis. Social media "has become a powerful accelerant for anyone who wants to start a fire" (Haidt & Rose-Stockwell, 2019, para. 19). At this moment in time, acquisition and practice of media literacy skills are paramount for users of all ages—childhood through adulthood. Furthermore, the examples above illustrate the importance of digital citizenship as a component of any media literacy paradigm. Yet, as Bulger and Davison (2018, p. 3) suggest in their assessment of media literacy efforts, the *interpretive responsibilities of the individual* form the basis of media literacy curricula. There is clearly a need for strong role models within the family as well as institutional support, whether that be local communities (e.g., school systems) or the developers of technology platforms (e.g., Facebook). We all have a part to play.

Children's and Adolescents' Perspectives on the Media Environment

Using technology affords tremendous opportunities and social connectivity carries with it multiple benefits—from maintaining personal relationships to networking with communities of interest. It is difficult to imagine a day without checking email, typing a text message, posting a comment, uploading a photo, or completing an online purchase. More recently, we can add conducting a Zoom meeting or creating a TikTok to that list. Using these tools has significantly changed how we relate to one another and has expanded our "digital footprint"—the trail of information we leave behind when using technology. More recently, the digital footprint is being replaced by the "digital tattoo" to emphasize to young people that online information is truly permanent (Ascione, 2018). This trail of information can be helpful or harmful, depending upon how we manage it, but control is becoming increasingly difficult. In his book *Filter Bubbles*, Eli Pariser (2011) describes the reality of online interactions; Internet algorithms are tracking online movements and tailoring content to suit personal preferences and search behaviors. Moreover, unwanted spam fills email boxes, virus protection software must be routinely updated, and stolen data is becoming a regular occurrence—from data breaches at favorite shopping sites to attacks on medical records. Phishing schemes (i.e., fraudulent attempts to gain access to personal information by posing as a trustworthy entity) are too commonplace. Because our online data is increasingly vulnerable, media literacy becomes invaluable.

The latter examples include the disreputable behaviors and activities of others—hackers and scammers—that are often beyond our personal control. In contrast, we have control over decisions related to our digital identity—from posting a photo to conversing online. Moreover, children's and adolescents' digital footprints begin early in life, a process that is initiated by parents. It has become routine to chronicle children's lives on social media in what has been termed "sharenting" (i.e., parents oversharing photos and other data about their children on social media.) Blum-Ross and Livingstone (2017) describe the ethical conflict between children's right to privacy and parents' need to represent their own identity as parent. These two positions are not easily resolved. Children eventually become adolescents and may express displeasure about their digital footprints. Hiniker and Schoenebeck (as cited in Dell'Antonia, 2016 and Wier, 2017) discussed their study of 249 parent-child pairs when children were ages 10–17 years-of-age. Approximately twice as many children as parents thought there should be rules about what parents shared on social media (Dell'Antonia, 2016). Teens revealed their dislike at parents' postings, asked parents to remove photos, and hid from cameras so photos of them would not be posted on Facebook. Schoenebeck suggests that parents respect children's wishes and recognize kids should have a say about what gets posted (as cited in Weir, 2017). Children and adolescents appear to be learning the importance of online safety and the longevity (even permanence) of digital identities; yet, this example suggests parents could benefit from media literacy education as well.

Despite the necessity of being connected to digital devices, children and adolescents share insights that suggest benefits of a respite from devices. Research conducted by scholars and clinicians highlights children's concerns about their parents "missing in action"; kids feel they are competing with their parents' devices for attention (Novotney, 2016; Turkle, 2011, 2015). During her explorations of young people's relationships with technology and each other, Turkle (2011) describes conflicted feelings about being constantly connected (e.g., having "no choice") and avoidance of face-to-face communication (e.g., "for later in life, I'll need to learn how to have a conversation"). Moreover, Turkle emphasizes that community means "to give among each other" (2011, p. 238) and is characterized by physical proximity, shared concerns, real consequences, and common responsibilities. She notes that online sites suggesting "community" usually fall below this mark.

Conclusions

When the Pew Research Center interviewed 1,150 technology experts, scholars, and health specialists on their perceptions of how technology (i.e., digital life) will influence individuals' overall mental and physical well-being, a mix of positive and negative opinions emerged. Among the themes suggesting beneficial outcomes included *connection* to people, education and entertainment, as well as *contentment* with improving personal and social relationships; among the themes suggesting harmful outcomes included *digital deficits* in memory and focus, as well as *digital duress* resulting from the stress of information overload (Anderson & Rainie, 2018). Among the suggested remedies for these complex effects on well-being was redesigning media literacy. "Formally educate people of all ages about the impacts of digital life on well-being and the way tech systems function, as well as encourage appropriate, healthy uses" (Anderson & Rainie, 2018, p. 3). Acquisition and practice of media and digital literacy skills have become integral to daily functioning. A productive work-life, academic achievement, engaging entertainment, social connections, identity development, and personal health and well-being all partially depend on our ability to navigate a media-rich environment. Yet, the long-term implications of constant connection to digital devices remain uncertain, particularly when these connections begin so early in life. Examining media and digital literacy within a developmental framework is a priority. It is within this context that scholars, educators, practitioners, and policy makers from diverse backgrounds and fields of study are engaging in important work to explore these issues and recommend paths forward. It is through media literacy education (both formal and informal) that we can mitigate risks of harmful effects and enhance the opportunities offered across media platforms and digital technologies.

References

Aaker, J. (1997). Dimensions of brand personality. *Journal of Marketing Research, 34,* 347–356.

Alper, M., & Herr-Stephenson, R. (2013). Transmedia play: Literacy across media. *Journal of Media Literacy Education, 5,* 366–369.

Anderson, J., & Rainie, L. (2018). *The future of well-being in a tech-saturated world.* Pew Research Center. Retrieved from https://www.pewresearch.org/internet/2018/04/17/the-future-of-well-being-in-a-tech-saturated-world/

Ascione, L. (Ed.). (2018, May 10). Digital footprint? Try digital tattoo, experts say. *eSchool News: Innovations in Educational Transformation*. Retrieved from https://www. eschoolnews.com/2018/05/10/digital-footprint-try-digital-tattoo-experts-say/?all

Aufderheide, P. (1993). *Media literacy: A report of the National Leadership Conference on media literacy*. Aspen, CO: Aspen Institute.

Banerjee, S. C., & Greene, K. (2007). Antismoking initiatives: Effects of analysis versus production media literacy interventions on smoking-related attitude, norm, and behavioral intention. *Health Communication, 22*, 37–48.

Bickham, D. S., & Slaby, R. G. (2012). Effects of a media literacy program on children's critical evaluation of unhealthy media messages about violence, smoking, and food. *Journal of Children and Media, 6*, 255–271.

Blum-Ross, A., & Livingstone, S. (2017). Sharenting: Parent blogging and the boundaries of the digital self. *Popular Communication, 15*, 110–125.

Bulger, M., & Davison, P. (2018). The promises, challenges and futures of media literacy. *Journal of Media Literacy Education, 10*, 1–21.

Common Sense Media. (n.d.) *Digital literacy and citizenship classroom curriculum*. Retrieved from https://www.commonsensemedia.org/educators/curriculum

Culver, S. H., & Redmond, T. (2019). *Snapshot 2019: The state of media literacy education in the U.S.* National Association for Media Literacy Education. Retrieved from https://namle.net/wp-content/uploads/2019/06/SOML_FINAL.pdf

Dell'Antonia, K. (2016, March 8). Don't post about me on social media, children say. *New York Times*. Retrieved from http://well.blogs.nytimes.com/2016/03/08/dont-post-about-me-on-social-media-children-say/?_r=0

DQ Institute. (2020). *What is the digital framework? Global standards for digital literacy, skills, and readiness*. Retrieved from https://www.dqinstitute.org/dq-framework/

Elea, I., & Mikos, L. (Eds.). (2017). *Young and creative: Digital technologies empowering children in everyday life*. Goteborg, Sweden: The International Clearinghouse on Children, Youth and Media.

Goldstein, D. (2019, December 6). After 10 years of hopes and setbacks, what happened to the Common Core? *New York Times*. Retrieved from https://www.nytimes.com/2019/12/06/us/common-core.html

Haidt, J., & Rose-Stockwell, T. (2019, December). The dark psychology of social networks. *The Atlantic*. Retrieved from https://www.theatlantic.com/magazine/archive/2019/12/social-media-democracy/600763/

Harrison, K., & Hefner, V. (2014). Virtually perfect: Image retouching and adolescent body image. *Media Psychology, 17*, 134–153.

Hobbs, R. (2010). *Digital and media literacy: A plan of action*. Washington, D.C.: Aspen Institute and Knight Foundation. Retrieved from https://assets.aspeninstitute.org/content/uploads/2010/11/Digital_and_Media_Literacy.pdf

Hobbs, R. (2019). Media literacy foundations. In R. Hobbs & P. Mihailidis (Eds.), *The internationalencyclopedia of media literacy* (pp. 1–19). Hoboken, NJ:Wiley-Blackwell.

Ito, M., Gutiérrez, K., Livingstone, S., Penuel, W., Rhodes, J, Salen, K., Schor, J., Sefton-Green, J., & Watkins, C. (2013). *Connected learning: An agenda for research and design.* Irvine, CA: Digital Media and Learning Research Hub. Retrieved from http://www.dmlhub.net/publications

James, C. (2014). *Disconnected: Youth, new media, and the ethics gap.* Cambridge, MA: MIT Press.

Jenkins, H., Purushotma, R., Weigel, M., Clinton, A., & Robison, A. J. (2009). *Confronting the challenges of participatory culture: Media education for the 21st century.* Cambridge, MA: MIT Press.

Kinder, M. (1991). *Playing with power in movies, television, and video games: From Muppet Babies to Teenage Mutant Ninja Turtles.* Berkeley: University of California Press.

Livingstone, S. (2014). Developing social media literacy: How children learn to interpret risky opportunities on social network sites. *Communications: The European Journal of Communication Research, 39,* 283–303.

Livingstone, S., & Blum-Ross, A. (2019). Parents' role in supporting, brokering or impeding their children's connected learning and media literacy. *Cultural Science Journal, 11,* 68–77.

Livingstone, S., Blum-Ross, A., Pavlick, J., & Ólafsson, K. (2018). In the digital home, how do parents support their children and who supports them? *Parenting for a Digital Future: Survey Report 1.* London: The London School of Economics and Political Science. Retrieved from http://www.parenting.digital

Novotney, A. (2016, February). Smartphone = not-so-smart parenting? *American Psychological Association Monitor, 47,* 52.

O'Neil, M. (2014, April 21). Confronting the myth of the 'digital native'. *The Chronicle of Higher Education.* Retrieved from http://chronicle.com/article/Confronting-the-Myth-of-the/145949/

Pariser, E. (2011). *The filter bubble: What the Internet is hiding from you.* New York: Penguin Press.

Park, Y. (2019). *DQ global standards report 2019: Common framework for digital literacy, skills and readiness.* DQ Institute. Retrieved from https://www.dqinstitute.org/wp-content/uploads/2019/11/DQGlobalStandardsReport2019.pdf

Partnership for 21st Century Learning. (n.d.) *Information, media and technology skills.* Retrieved from http://www.p21.org/about-us/p21-framework/61

Pfeffer, J., Zorbach, T., & Carley, K. M. (2014). Understanding online firestorms: Negative word-of-mouth dynamics in social media networks. *Journal of Marketing Communications, 20,* 117–128.

Pierce, D. (Ed.) (2010, February 8). Four things every student should learn … but not every school is teaching. *eSchool News: Innovations in Educational Transformation.* Retrieved from http://www.eschoolnews.com/2010/02/08/four-things-every-student-should-learn

Potter, W. J. (2019). *Media literacy* (9th ed.). Thousand Oaks, CA: SAGE Publications, Inc.

Prensky, M. (2001). Digital natives, digital immigrants part 1. *On the Horizon, 9*, 1–6.

Redmond, T. (2015). Media literacy is common sense: Bridging Common Core Standards with the media experiences of digital learners. *Middle School Journal, 46*, 10–17.

Rubin, A. M. (2002). The uses and gratifications perspective of media effects. In J. Bryant & D. Zillmann (Eds.), *Media effects: Advances in theory and research*. Mahwah, NJ: Lawrence Erlbaum Association.

Socha, T. J., Vaughan, T., Aldawoud, A., Forest, E., Kendall, C., Kurisky, B. P., Matzke-Fawcett, A., Ponthieux, J., Pruden, B., & Webb, R. (2017, April). *Managing family communication paradigm shift: Family members' cell phone use, affective responses, affective involvement, and general family functioning*. A paper presented at the annual meeting of the Southern States Communication Association, Greenville, SC.

Turkle, S. (2011). *Alone together: Why we expect more from technology and less from each other*. New York, NY: Basic Books.

Turkle, S. (2015). *Reclaiming conversation: The power of talk in a digital age*. New York, NY: Penguin Press.

Weir, K. (2017, July/August). Parents: Watch those social media posts. *American Psychological Association Monitor, 48*, 28.

Wilson, C., Grizzle, A., Tuazon, R., Akyempong, K., & Cheung, C. K. (2011). *Media and information literacy: Curriculum for teachers*. Paris, France: United Nations Educational, Scientific and Cultural Organization. Retrieved from http://unesdoc. unesco.org/images/0019/001929/192971e.pdf

12. CosmoKidz

Helping Children Make Better Social Worlds

JOHN CHETRO-SZIVOS
Assumption University and Clark University

MARIT EIKAAS HAAVIMB
Consultant, Drammen Area, Norway

KIMBERLY PEARCE
De Anza College

There is little doubt that communication patterns begin at birth and from the early weeks of life infants learn how to coordinate with caregivers to signal hunger, frustration, discomfort, and most importantly build bonds. Over a decade ago, Trevartehn and Aitken (2001) described the process of intersubjectivity as mothers and infants mutually seek communication and initiate the beginnings of attachment. Their findings showed these early attachments and coordinated acts are critical in the formation of later relationships.

Daniel Goleman's (1995, 2006) research on emotional intelligence was supporting his claim that the ability to get along with others is the glue of healthy human development. Initially we find this in the infant/caretaker relationship, but it quickly grows to include the expanding social world of peers and others. Recent longitudinal research is supporting Goleman's claim by demonstrating that the development of social skills in kindergarten correlates with their success as adults two decades later (Scelfo, 2015).

We point to a term introduced by Hillary Cottam "relational welfare" (Cottam, 2016). Relational welfare is grounded in the belief that we need new ways of addressing social change that also fosters the development of healthy relationships. This, along with the impressive work of Trevartehn, Aitken, Goleman, and others inspired us to create CosmoKidz. CosmoKidz is a series of activities designed to increase compassion and awareness so children can discover new ways of acting and being together.

The three of us are co-developers of CosmoKidz. And although the aforementioned research, not to mention our experience of being parents and grandparents, informed our thinking about CosmoKidz, our scholarly work in communication theory, and specifically our use of CMM, was the most influential lens we used. CMM invites us to subsume traditional views of communication into a larger framework.

Generally, traditional views of communication assert people use communication to express their inner purposes, attitudes, and feelings. Within a traditional view, communication is thought of as a tool to describe events, objects, and ideas. While this appears to be a straightforward and an accessible idea, scholars and practitioners of CMM feel this oversimplifies the complex act of communication and falls short of understanding what people do together. The frame of CMM asserts that what we are doing together is *always* making social worlds. It is through the process of communication we advance our sense of self, others, and larger groupings of people such as a family, community, and even our culture. More than this, CMM stresses the importance of understanding the implications and consequences of our actions. When we understand the implications of our actions and the consequences it produces, we are better equipped to participate in constructing better relationships in all spheres (Pearce, 2007). CMM provides concepts, heuristics, and models to show how particular social worlds get made and how participants can help make better social worlds (Cronen & Chetro-Szivos, 2001; Pearce, 1989, 2007; Pearce & Cronen, 1980).

For over forty years CMM has been used in a variety of contexts such as therapy, organizational development, conflict resolution, community building, and education. Within these contexts, impressive research projects have been undertaken and have yielded useful insights into the co-construction of our social worlds. The most recent research context has been our work with young children using the activities of CosmoKidz. CosmoKidz is an outgrowth of a concept developed by Barnett Pearce (1989) called "Cosmopolitan communication." Among other things, this is a form of communication that suggests everyday differences between people can be a starting place for deeper understanding, trust, and respect. The assumption underlying CosmoKidz is that children who learn how to talk together productively about their thoughts, feelings, and experiences will develop the skill set of cosmopolitan communication (empathizing with others, handling conflicts in productive ways, connecting with diverse children who are not like them, managing their strong emotions, and naming their own feelings and emotions). If these skills are reinforced over time, they become part of the repertoire for ways of acting and being in the world. Daniel Goleman would call this emotional intelligence and Hillary Cottam, relational welfare.

We also developed CosmoKidz with the recent findings in the field of Interpersonal Neurobiology (IPNB) in mind. Researchers in the field of IPNB are demonstrating that our interpersonal relationships deeply influence the structure and function of the developing brain and the formation of the maturing nervous system (Cozolino, 2006; Lewis, Amini, & Lannon, 2001; Porges, 2011; Siegel, 2007, 2011a, 2011b). What we refer to as mind or mental processes are the result of our inner neural connections as well as our interpersonal relationships. Simply put, experience modifies brain development. Teaching children how to become more aware of what they experience and not simply be reactive, creates different kinds of neurological experiences. Among other things, every scenario in the CosmoKidz activities ask children to focus their awareness on the internal state of thoughts, feelings, and their body. This is intentionally done in order for children to begin to change thoughts about a situation and find new patterns of behavior, ultimately changing a neural map. This process of interoception is accessed through basic mindful practices such as breathing, body awareness, and processing empathic feelings.

An Overview of CosmoKidz

The simple yet profound underpinning of CosmoKidz: All of us, including young children, are part of making the social worlds in which we live. We want young children to understand this and to develop the skills and abilities to help make better social worlds. How does CosmoKidz achieve this?

It begins with a set of 31 topics that comprise a young child's social world. The topics in CosmoKidz were chosen by kids themselves. We asked a variety of children to tell us what they face in their lives that they find difficult and challenging. The scenarios on each of the 31 cards in CosmoKidz represent the topics that these children expressed to us. As we were developing the questions and activities, we also piloted these activities with a variety of children in different learning contexts, different socioeconomic levels, and in two different countries. Doing this demonstrated the value of the cards in helping children name a wide range of feelings, emotions, and thoughts, as well as ways that they can act with more awareness into difficult situations to help make a better outcome

These topics include issues like making quiet time, making new friends, sharing, and bullying. Every card includes:

- a topic (in the purple bubble on the left side of the card)
- a scenario related to the topic, under the word "imagine"
- questions to help children meaningfully explore the topic
- activities to help children act more productively into a similar future situation (Act a and Act b)
- an illustration of the scenario on the reverse side of the card

An example of what each card looks like is included on the following page.

CosmoKidz also includes the acronym SOAR and a SOAR song that children can sing and dance to (the song and video can be downloaded for free at www.cmminstitute.net). SOAR stands for: Sense what's around you, Open your hands to help others, Act with kindness, Respect other people. The children below are having a short break from "traditional" class-room activities in order to recharge themselves through joint movements, music and fun.

Additionally we provided a SOAR bulletin Board for the teacher to display in the classroom and refer to throughout the school week. Teachers or other adults can refer to SOAR by asking children if their behavior is an example of SOARing behavior, and if it is not, what the children can do to SOAR.

Figure 12.1. The girl picked this card as she wants to talk about how hard it is to focus attention and be quiet in the classroom.

Figure 12.2. The flip side of illustration in Figure12.1 contains supporting questions for the teacher/adult.

Figure 12.3. Children doing a SOAR song-and-dance to re-focus energy and revive their attention in class.

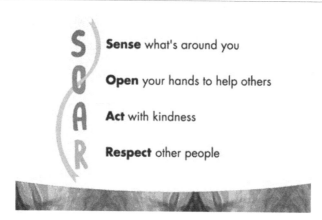

Figure 12.4. The SOAR acronym works as a short-cut to remind the children about how to act into their social worlds.

We also supplied each teacher with a male and female puppet. Each puppet has a happy face on one side and a sad face with tears on the other. Below is a sample of children play-acting and interacting with the puppets:

We invited the teachers to use the puppets to engage the children in naming emotions and emotional states as they talk about the weekly topics. Each child also has his or her own hand puppet to use during the CosmoKidz conversations.

The rest of this chapter will be devoted to the on-going two-year research project that as been conducted at Mountain Vista School in Oracle, Arizona and what we are learning about the development of children's communication skills and emotional intelligence using CosmoKidz.

Figure 12.5. Children talking about their feelings through using the CosmoKidz hand puppets.

Information about Mountain Vista School in Oracle, Arizona and Our Research Using CosmoKidz

Oracle, Arizona is a small community approximately 50 miles north of Tucson and 100 miles south of Phoenix. The median worker income is just shy of $34,000 and the poverty rate is just over 17% of the national average. Consequently, Oracle is an economically challenged community. Mountain Vista School is a K-8 public school servicing the town of Oracle. Due to budget cuts the school has eliminated or cut programs such as art, music, and physical education. And like most public schools, there are no programs designed to increase students' social skills and emotional intelligence. And yet laudably the Mountain Vista Student Pledge is based on social/emotional skills. The pledge is based on 3 Rs: "To Respect myself and others, take Responsibility for my actions and develop positive Relationships with adults and peers based on integrity." These three Rs are just as imperative as the more traditional phonetically talked about Rs of reading [w]riting, and [a]rithmetic because they serve as the bedrock of "communication and relational skills."

This is one reason why the then School Board President, Linda Thomas, the Superintendent, Dennis Blauser, and Mountain Vista's Principal, Nannette Soule, were excited about their school being the site for a research project to test the usefulness of CosmoKidz in kindergarten through second-grade classes. The research began in January, 2014 and is continuing to this day. Two kindergarten, two first-grade and two second-grade classes are involved in the research.

The teachers have been asked to use the cards daily or almost daily but in small increments. We wanted to see if CosmoKidz could be used without adding to the teacher's workload or interfering with the core subjects that must be taught. The teachers were only given minimal instructions for using CosmoKidz; we wanted the teachers to be creative in their use of the topics, scenarios, and puppets. We suggested that the teachers begin each week by choosing one of the topic areas in CosmoKidz; for example, teasing. After selecting the topic, we asked the teachers to spend about 10 minutes each day doing the following:

Monday: Announce the topic of the week and show the children the illustration that is on the card. Spend the first day asking the children to look at the illustration and invite the children to comment on what they see.

Tuesday: Remind the children of the topic. Choose one or two of the "ask" questions as a way of helping the children name and explore their own experience with the topic.

Wednesday: Remind the children of the topic. Use one or two of the "ask" questions as a way of helping the children explore how the topic may be affecting other people.

We encouraged the teachers to send home a supplemental activity sheet on the topic of the week on Wednesday (this is the day that weekly folders are sent home). Each activity sheet includes a "right brain" creative component and a "left brain" linguistic component. On the topic of teasing, for example, the activity sheet asks the child to make a drawing using colors that tell about hurtful feelings. And then to make a drawing using colors that make you feel good. Finally, to write one sentence that describes how these colors are different. We include these activity sheets to reinforce repetition and learning for the child, and to provide an opportunity for parents to talk with their child about what the child is learning that week.

Thursday: Remind the children of the topic. Choose one of the activities in the "act" section and help the children visualize positive ways of acting in a similar situation in the future.

Friday: Remind the children of the topic. Continue with the activity from Thursday or chooses the second "act."

We formulated three research questions:

Research Question 1: To what extent are children ages 5–7 able to meaningfully discuss the topics in CosmoKidz?

Research Question 2: How does the use of CosmoKidz over the course of a school year affect children's interpersonal communication skill sets and actions?

Research Question 3: How does the use of CosmoKidz over the course of a school year affect interpersonal communication skill sets and actions across contexts?

Our study was qualitative using teacher interviews and questionnaires, parent surveys and questionnaires, student recall tests, and observations as the primary means of data collection. Research Findings are based on data collected from January, 2014 to the Present (as of this writing in early 2016). Due to the limitations of space we aren't able to provide the details of our research in this chapter. Comprehensive results are available in three separate reports found on the CMM Institute website, www.cmminstitute.net/resources/documents.

Research Results

The data we have collected in the last two years has been extremely positive. We know that children as young as four years old can have useful conversations about the topics of their social world. The children at Mountain Vista have enthusiastically engaged in these daily conversations about topics such as sharing and teasing and making new friends. Some of the first kindergarten students using CosmoKidz in January, 2014 are now in second grade and they continue to stay engaged in the CosmoKidz topics.

The data is also reinforcing our hypotheses that children's interpersonal skills and actions have improved over time and across contexts (at school and at home). An interesting side-note is that the teachers are also noticing a difference in their own communication patterns after using CosmoKidz for the past two years. We have heard a version of this quote from every teacher using CosmoKidz: "Sometimes I'm upset about something and I'm now thinking what I am saying to these kids that isn't SOARing or respectful. I may be upset with something that has happened _____ (gives a few examples of contexts) so I am thinking more about how I react to them. When we are talking about SOAR, I think it makes me think more about behaviors" (kindergarten teacher).

One reason for the children's ability to apply CosmoKidz and SOAR in their daily lives is their understanding and recall of SOARing behavior. We tested the students' recall this academic year by asking the teachers to survey their students on their ability to recall what SOAR stands for and to provide an example of SOARing behavior that they demonstrated during their summer vacation. The teachers were instructed to not mention CosmoKidz or SOAR or to have any visible information about SOAR for the children to see prior to taking this survey. The results of the survey are as follows:
Current 1st grade students (last year's kindergarten students): 37 Responses.

- 69% remembered "Sense what's around you"
- 70% remembered "Open your hands to help others"
- 88% remembered "Act with kindness"
- 75% remembered "Respect other people"

Sample comments from the children: I did something nice for my brother; when my brother was crying I gave him a hug; I gave my great-grandma a card; I helped my sister when a bully pushed her; I helped my friend to climb on the monkey bars.

Current 2nd grade students (last year's first-grade students): 33 Responses

- 81% remembered "Sense what's around you"
- 97% remembered "Open your hands to help others"
- 97% remembered "Act with kindness"
- 98% remembered "Respect other people"

Sample comments from the children: My friend fell down and I helped him up; Emily fell and I helped her; I helped my cousin stand up; I helped my brother in the pool; I let my sister put her toy in my box.

Current 3rd grade students (last year's second-grade students): 42 Responses

- 80% remembered "Sense what's around you"
- 89% remembered "Open your hands to help others"
- 90% remembered "Act with kindness"
- 99% remembered "Respect other people"

Sample comments from the children: I helped my brother when he fell; I helped my sister clean up; I helped my brother swim; I helped my sister when she fell off of the monkey bars; I helped my dog get an ant off; I helped my friend who fell. I'm happy. She is too.

These survey results show that an overwhelming majority of the children remembered SOAR. The sample comments also point to the specificity with which the children can name their SOARing behavior. There were very few generic responses such as, I was nice or I was kind.

To provide a window into the teachers' experience of their students' behavior based on CosmoKidz and SOAR conversations, we are providing quotes based on teacher interviews.

A kindergarten teacher after using CosmoKidz for four months:

> In my kindergarten classroom, I have already noticed several changes with the ways that my students relate to one another and interact with each other. I think the changes can be more subtle in kindergarten because our young students are just starting the CosmoKidz program and they are at an age where they are just learning how to problem-solve, handle conflict, and manage their emotions. However, I think that the CosmoKidz program has really helped our youngest students in learning social and relational skills. Since we began the program in August, I have witnessed my students thinking through their actions and problems more successfully and I have seen them have more of an understanding of good choices versus poor choices. I have also witnessed a significant increase in the helpfulness of my students. Small children, by nature, seem to thrive on

recognition and feeling important and they seem to love to be helpful and it seems that they have been more aware of how they can reach out to help their teachers and classmates without even being asked or prompted. I was delighted to witness some of my students helping and comforting a fellow classmate who had fallen on the playground recently and their abilities worked so well that I didn't even have to intervene! CosmoKidz seems to aide our classroom in having a sense of community and togetherness! Also, I have witnessed my students become more aware of words and terminology they can use when problem-solving and, after having to be coached and guided at first, they are turning into valuable problem-solvers! Often, we just have to point out SOARing students and behaviors with very few words and behaviors have a tendency to change instantly! We still have our problems and conflicts occasionally, but this seems to be decreasing drastically as our kindergarteners strive to be CosmoKidz. The delight of being recognized as a "CosmoKid" in our weekly classroom newsletter and monthly school newsletter has definitely helped in more ways than one as well!

A first-grade teacher after using CosmoKidz for four months:

My class consists of 22 first grade students. We have had two new students in the past week. Another change is we have had one student move unexpectedly and another student leave and come back three times. These changes have been difficult for the class.

The class has embraced the language of SOAR. Students will ask another student if they are SOARing. They point out SOARing behaviors. They reference past soar cards when similar situations come up.

I continue to have a sort of spiral pattern of behaviors but when they come around again, the duration is shortened through SOAR. I may say "remember that card . . ." and what would normally be a long discussion becomes a quick reminder. We have a background of knowledge to draw from that helps repair whatever was broken down between students.

The greatest difference I have seen this year is in one student. He started the year extremely egocentric with an extreme lack of empathy. He has become amazingly aware of how he is creating his social world. When situations come up in our class he will bring up the appropriate CosmoKidz card and remind the class of our discussions around that topic. For example, when a new student arrived, he very animatedly reminded the class of the "Feeling Included" card and what we could do to make the new student feel included. He has also expanded his social circle from just one favorite friend (that no one else could play with but him) to playing with the rest of the class. He still favors his friend but not in that possessive controlling way.

A second-grade teacher after using CosmoKidz and SOAR for four months:

We were playing a game and a team of girls won. A—(student'sname) said that the girls won because girls are smarter than boys. Before I could even address it she apologized to the boys. After she said she was sorry, she looked at me and said that she apologized for saying that because that was not SOARing.

We are watching Bernstein Bears videos in class. On their own the children were commenting on the behaviors of the characters and they pointed out behaviors that were not SOARing behaviors. When the video was over they were commenting on the lesson that was being taught. They were able to catch on to the lesson being taught in the videos, which were helping others try new things and not bragging. I feel that the cards have helped the kids become more aware of "nonsoaring" behaviors as well as SOARing behaviors all on their own.

A first-grade teacher after using CosmoKidz and SOAR for an academic year:

> I have seen an increase of independent behavior. Students will attempt to use SOAR first to resolve conflict or issues. If this strategy does not work, then they will approach an authority figure.
>
> Students are much more aware of each other, other's feelings, and other's behavior. They try to help each other by correcting the behavior, pointing out feelings, and apologizing when they feel they are in the wrong. At times, this can overcompensate with some students being overly concerned with other student's behavior.
>
> When speaking to each other, I have seen a shift in word choice and a move from generalities to specifics. At the beginning of the year, it was very common for a student to use statements such as "he/she is being mean" and "He/she hurt my feelings". Now, I hear specifics such as "When you wouldn't share the ball with me I felt sad and mad." This is repairable and much less emotionally damaging then the generalized almost personal attacks.
>
> Through the SOAR conversations we have had over the year, students are identifying how they feel inside and putting words to those feelings instead of just reacting. I have seen an increase in thinking before speaking and a decrease of knee jerk reactions to situations. For example, at the beginning of the year if someone ran into someone else in line, the common reaction was to push them back. Now, I have seen a decrease in that physical behavior and an increase in discussion.
>
> At the beginning of the year, students came to me to resolve problems and even small issues. Over the year there has been a shift over from me to them. When students come to me I can remind them to use SOAR and talk to each other, they are able to do this now since we have modeled and practiced it.

We also wanted to know if parents were noticing any changes in their child's behavior. We surveyed parents at the beginning, middle, and the end of the school year. Our questions asked parents to indicate the frequency of: (1) Mentioning SOARing behavior; (2) pointing out SOARing behavior; and, (3) Exhibiting SOARing behavior. In response to the questions of exhibiting SOARing behavior, parents in all three grade levels overwhelmingly responded with "sometimes" or "frequently"; few parents responded with "never." In terms of mentioning or pointing out SOARing behavior, most parents said that their child did these things at least "sometimes" with a few parents saying "frequently" or "never." Our take-away is that most parents are seeing improvements in their child's social skills and behavior. Children are not just practicing these skills at school, they are also using these skills at home. With amusement, a parent of one of the kindergarten teachers told the teacher that she overheard her child tell her two siblings during an argument that they weren't SOARing and that they should be nice to each other. This is the kind of carry-over we hope for in the children using CosmoKidz!

Reflections on Our Learning and Future Directions

The first question an adult often asks the children when showing the picture side of a CosmoKidz card is "What do you see?" The question invites a variety of responses, depending on the number of children present as well as the adult asking more than once, "what else?" Without actively "teaching" anything at all, children are becoming aware that they may see different things, and that one child's description is no more right or wrong than another child's answer. They learn the very fundamental idea that how I perceive and manage meaning may be very different than how you make sense of the world. They learn about diversity.

Further explorations support them in recognizing and naming possible stories, as well as helping them to see that how they choose to act into every situation "makes something". These "somethings" have names like "fight", "new friend", "feeling calm", "sharing". As they are supported to explore, express and reflect on their thoughts, feelings and possible effects of different choices without being judged or corrected, they learn about how patterns of action are made and sustained. They learn about coordinating and managing meaning.

Yet CosmoKidz offers more than just reflections. It is designed to bring the reflections into action in various creative and expressive ways. Children with different learning styles get to explore possible actions in a variety of ways through, for example, role playing, use of puppets, talking about a scenario, coloring, singing and dancing. Because of this, and because of systematic work and repetitions, the likelihood of real learning happening over time is very high.

One of our curiosities as we were creating CosmoKidz, was whether this kind of learning was possible for children as young as four years old. We now know that children as young as three years old have things to say about the pictures they are looking at, even though at a "simpler" level. This makes sense in light of recent research on young children and the development of attachment theory, which shows how we are socially disposed through our bodies (Fonagy, Gergely, Jurist, &Target, 2003): In a Norwegian study (Lund, Godtfredsen, Helgeland, Nome, Kovac, & Cameron, 2015), researchers are observing how toddlers are socially interacting with each other, already growing skills of relating, coordinating and managing meaning. Interestingly, at this age, they are moving in and out through a larger group of children and adults alike. As the children turn three years old, the researchers notice a movement towards more dyadic relationships, where one friend becomes more important than others. They also notice that some children, even at this age, are less able than others to relate to their peers in ways that makes friends. The importance of learning social skills and emotional intelligence become apparent. The patterns of interacting early in life, have a tendency to carry on into the tween and teen years (Lund, 2013).

We wonder whether the importance of building relational competencies early in life has potentially preventative consequences for the experience of health and well-being later in life. What we do know is that our research shows CosmoKidz actively supports the development of such skills, even in children who initially could appear totally lacking of them. We know that the classroom climate for learning other skills improves. The children become more able to solve their own relational difficulties in school and at home. Having practiced the skills rather than just learning the content of how they should and should not act, they are largely able to transfer the skills into a variety of contexts.

We wondered how the use of CosmoKidz would affect the adults' view of social worlds. We were delighted when our research confirmed that teachers using CosmoKidz with their students became more aware of their own behavior and how it affected others. Using CMM language, the teachers gained an increased awareness of what was made, depending on how *they acted* into a situation.

As previously mentioned, the teachers in our research did not get a lot of training before using the CosmoKidz activites. They were encouraged to be creative, while making sure there was a certain level of continuity and practice over time. The results indicate it is possible for any teacher or care-giver to use CosmoKidz with little or no training. Having said that, we also think some background understanding and training is preferable, and will increase the possibilities for a preferred outcome.

The CosmoKidz activities do not offer a panacea to instantly build children's interpersonal skills, but it does represent a series of activities with wide applicability to teachers, parents, mental health professionals, and others working with children to increase the empathy and compassion of children they serve. This is one alternative to traditional ways of addressing the needs of children and it comes at a time when new ideas are needed. Moreover, these activities are grounded in the communication perspective and IPNB, which have much to offer.

We are aware of other efforts within the year to apply the CosmoKidz activities in a workshop/camp-like setting for children. We are hopeful more programs will follow and will include research on the efficacy of CosmoKidz in non-classroom contexts.

We recognize that children are not just Human Beings; they are Human Becomings (Prout, 2005). What they become—and what they make—are shaped in relationships. Through the activities of CosmoKidz and SOAR, children are becoming better equipped to meet and influence what is yet to be made.

References

Cottam, H. (2012). Relational welfare. Retrieved February 20, 2016, from http://www.participle.net/includes/downloader/MTg0NzMwNzI4NjZkMGQlMTA4MzAxMGQyZGYzNmJjYjhvy_Bkw5J5tvpI8s7ajaLKNFZZalR5VmlLam05Y2ZibHROWnE5SmFwQkx1dUV5bUM0OG9CCTVh2YjNob0VRaytLNjFxS005bS9z MTFpdk4leUpzRisrMjl6VEcye XVxRHFIZFFFEaFE9PQ

Cozolino, L. (2010). *The neuroscience of psychotheraphy: Healing the social brain* (2nd ed.). New York. W.W. Norton.

Cronen, V., & Chetro-Szivos, J. (2001). Pragmatism as a way of inquiring with special reference to a theory of communication and the general form of pragmatic social theory. In D. Perry (Ed.), *Pragmatism and communication research*. Highland, MD: Lawrence Erlbaum.

Fonagy, P., Gergely, G., Jurist, E., & Target, M. (2003). *Affect regulation, mentalization, and the development of the self.* London: Karnac Books.

Goleman, D. (1995). *Emotional intelligence: Why it can matter more than IQ.* New York: Bantam Books.

Goleman, D. (2006). *Social intelligence: The new science of social relationships.* New York: Bantam Books.

Lewis, T., Amini, F., & Lannon, R. (2001). *A general theory of love.* New York: Vintage Books.

Lund, I. (2013). Dropping out of school as a meaningful action for adolescents with social, emotional and behavioural difficulties. *Journal of Research in Special Educational Needs.* ISSN 1471–3802. 14 (2), s 96–104. doi: 10.1111/1471-3802.12003.

Lund, I., Godtfredsen, M., Helgeland, A., Nome, D. Ø, Kovac, B. V., & Cameron, D. L. (2015). *The whole child the whole way* (pp. 1–54). Oslo, Norway: University Agder.

Pearce, W. B. (1989). *Communication and the human condition.* Carbondale, IL: Southern Illinois University Press.

Pearce, W. B. (2007). *Making social worlds: A communication perspective.* Malden, MA: Blackwell Publishing.

Pearce, W. B., & Cronen, V. (1980). *Communication, action, and meaning: The creation of social realities.* New York: Prager Press.

Porges, S. (2011). *The polyvagal theory: Neurophysiological foundations of emotions, attachment, communication, and self-regulation.* New York: W.W. Norton & Company.

Prout, A. (2005). *The future of childhood: Towards the interdisciplinary study of children.* London: RoutledgeFalmer.

Scelfo, J. (2015). Retrieved from www.nytimes.com/2015/11/15/sunday-review/teaching-peace-in-elementary-schoolhtml?_r=0)

Siegel, D. (2007). *The mindful bain – Reflection and attunement in the cultivation of well-being.* New York: W.W. Norton & Company.

Siegel, D. (2011a). *Mindsight –The new science of personal transformation.* New York: Bantam Books.

Siegel, D. (2011b). *The whole brain child.* New York: Delacorte Press.

Trevarthen, C., & Aitken, K. (2001). Infant intersubjectivity: Research, theory, and clinical applications. *Journal of Child Psychiatry, 4*(1), 3–48. Cambridge University Press.

13. Lasting Impressions

Exploring Communicative Legacies of Children's Experiences in Divorced Families

JENNA R. LAFRENIERE
Texas Tech University

Divorce is a major event that occurs in many families today that forces families to redefine themselves and renegotiate their typical patterns of functioning with one another. Approximately 40–50% of all marriages end in divorce in the United States (American Psychological Association, 2020). Researchers have investigated predictors of divorce such as low income, low education level, stonewalling in conflict, and prior marriages (Gottman, 1994; Teachman, 2002). As the number of divorces has climbed, scholars have investigated the effects of divorce, both short- and long-term, on children within the family system (Amato, 2010; Cunningham & Skillingstead, 2015; Wallerstein, Lewis, & Blakeslee, 2000). As Schrodt and Afifi (2007) highlighted, most of this previous research has focused on the effects of the divorce itself rather than the communication following the divorce. Emery and Dillon (1994) labeled divorce "as the renegotiation of boundaries of intimacy and power in the relationships between members of the divorced family system" (p. 374). Hence, divorce inherently involves the development of new communication patterns, navigation of new concerns, and managing shifting family relationships.

Divorce not only alters family structure but forever changes how family members function in relation to one another (Amato, 2010; Wallerstein 1996; Wallerstein et al., 2000). Thus, it is imperative to understand what children experience regarding divorce communication within the family. Divorce leaves children with a multitude of unexpected legacies, as divorce is a profound, life-transforming event for children, influencing their childhood, adolescence, and adulthood (Wallerstein et al., 2000). Disclosures, feeling caught, and the emotional challenges that children of divorce face represent interconnected issues that not only impact one another, but continually impact children as they age. Borrowing Wallerstein and colleagues' (2000) framework of divorce legacies, the concepts covered in this chapter represent three "communication legacies" of divorce. The chapter builds on summarized research on legacies of divorce to examine these three legacies, and concludes with a proposed research agenda for further examining children's experiences in divorced families.

Legacies of Divorce

The effects of divorce endure long after the actual breakup, with children experiencing lasting legacies of their parents' decision throughout their lifetime (Wallerstein et al., 2000; Wallerstein & Lewis, 2004). Wallerstein and colleagues (2000) posited two common divorce myths: (1) Many parents believe that if their decision to divorce makes them happy, their children are resilient and will eventually approve the separation also, and (2) divorce is most harmful to children at the time of the separation. On the contrary, researchers have instead found that the divorce of one's parents has the capacity to impact a child well into adulthood (Amato, 2010). Children have little control over the numerous changes that occur in their lives following a divorce, including relocating, financial changes, parental availability, and parents' behaviors and attitudes (Wallerstein, 1996). These changes impact the way children view themselves, their families, and their worlds as they grow up.

Divorce Legacies Throughout the Lifespan

Legacies of divorce greatly transform the childhood experience, while one lasting legacy is the altered view of childhood itself. Adult children from divorced families report believing that their childhoods were more difficult than children from non-divorced families and that their childhoods had been cut short (Laumann-Billings & Emery, 2000). For example, many report feeling their childhoods were unhappy and that they felt they missed out on a normal childhood due to increased responsibilities, less play, decreased finances to pay for activities, along with enduring numerous relocations, custody scheduling, and diminished parental availability (Wallerstein & Lewis, 2004). This legacy extends far beyond the childhood years. When they grow older, many adult children of divorce report either not wishing to have children of their own as they feel unprepared to raise them or, if they do decide to have children, wishing for a vastly different childhood experience for them

(Wallerstein & Lewis, 2004). Thus, one overarching legacy of divorce is off-spring's idea that their childhoods have been fractured, altering their view of their family of origin as well as their ideas for their own families when they are older.

Another relic of divorce includes diminished parent-child relationships. After the separation, there is a shift in the parent-child bond as children face reduced contact with one or both parents as well as decreased parenting (Wallerstein & Lewis, 2004). Following a divorce, many children relocate with their primary parent to a new home, either severing contact with the noncustodial parent or significantly reducing the time spent with each parent if the children go back and forth between homes. The father-child bond may be most at risk, as many children believe their fathers are to blame for the divorce and many question their father's love for them (Laumann-Billings & Emery, 2000). As they grow older, diminished parental availability impacts children in new ways. According to Amato and Sobolewski (2001), children entering young adulthood and all its challenges with little parental support might experience amplified distress. During adolescence, children of divorce have fewer rules enforced by parents, little supervision, and often experience parenting differences between ex-spouses' households (Wallerstein & Lewis, 2004). Decreased parental availability also influences another common divorce legacy for children: their view of relationships.

Due to their parents' divorce and often their subsequent marriages, divorces, and cohabitations, another predominant legacy for children of divorce is the belief that relationships are ultimately unreliable and cannot be expected to endure (Wallerstein & Lewis, 2004). Additionally, some children of divorce grow up feeling they have no appropriate role models for their own relationships and feel skeptical that they could be part of a lasting marriage (Cunningham & Skillingstead, 2015). Children may fear becoming involved with and close to others out of fear of abandonment or being hurt after watching their parents' marriage end. As adults, children of divorce typically face a fear of loving others and being loved, struggling with conflict resolution, how to live with someone else, and working to overcome their fear of failed relationships (Wallerstein & Lewis, 2004). While there are numerous legacies of divorce, those surrounding post-divorce communication may be amongst the most challenging for families.

Communication Legacies of Divorce

Communication may prove to be one of the most important factors in divorced families as parents and children renegotiate boundaries, living situations, financial changes, and the possibility of new spouses and siblings through conversations with one another (Afifi, 2003; Emery & Dillon, 1994; Metts et al., 2013). Parents lay the foundation for post-divorce family communication from the minute they tell children of the divorce. Unfortunately, parents do not often have meaningful conversations with their children when telling them of the divorce for the first time, leaving children with few explanations and the idea that the divorce came out of nowhere (Wallerstein et al., 2000). Corroborating this point, children of divorce report that their parents have diminished communication skills compared to those from intact families (Afifi & Schrodt, 2003). The communication legacies that parents build in post-divorce families, then, are important to consider.

If effective communication following a divorce is crucial for children to develop healthy understandings of self and others, communication legacies of divorce should be examined more closely. Scholars have noted that children of divorce experience decreased behavioral and emotional adjustment as well as diminished psychological well-being (Afifi & Schrodt, 2003; Amato & Sobolewski, 2001; Jensen & Bowen, 2015). Perhaps ineffective family communication contributes to these kinds of child outcomes. Children of divorce report that their parents have diminished communication skills compared to those from intact families (Afifi & Schrodt, 2003). Moreover, Afifi and Schrodt (2003) claimed that post-divorce communication is more significant than the actual divorce. Over the last decades, scholars have highlighted the importance of investigating three facets of family communication post-divorce: disclosures, feeling caught, and emotion management (Afifi & Schrodt, 2003; Metts et al., 2013; Schrodt & Afifi, 2007). Therefore, this chapter highlights children's experiences with these three communication-focused legacies.

Examining Three Communication Legacies of Divorce

Divorce Disclosures

When parents divorce and the relationship with their now ex-spouse changes considerably, they often look for someone else with whom they can share their burdens. As parents learn to manage divorce stressors, some choose to involve their children in conversations that may be inappropriate and unwanted. Parents often find it difficult to pinpoint how much to tell their children about the divorce, when to tell them, and who should be present when engaging in the conversation (Afifi & McManus, 2010; Wallerstein, 1996). According to Afifi, Afifi, and Coho (2009), disclosures include "parents' personal statements, claims, opinions, or observations related to the topics of their relationship with the other parent, marriage (their own or in general), and divorce (their own or in general)" (p. 525). Divorce disclosures, then, cover a wide array of subjects related to the divorce. While parents in still married families also disclose to their children about their marriage (Afifi, Afifi, & Coho, 2009; Afifi, Granger, Denes, Joseph, & Aldeis, 2011), the effects of disclosures following a divorce may be more harmful long-term.

Scholars have found that when parents talk about one another or their relationship, those in divorced families communicate with more negatively valenced disclosures than parents in still married families (Afifi, Afifi, & Coho, 2009). Children of divorce, then, are placed at a higher risk to receive harmful disclosures than those whose parents are still together. While it is natural for a parent to lean on a child more around the time of divorce, parents sometimes place a heavy burden on their children, asking questions that should be reserved for a peer or significant other (e.g., what to do about dating or remarriage, where they should live, or finances) (Wallerstein & Blakeslee, 2003). When friends are not available to listen, children are often readily available and give a parent full priority (Wallerstein & Blakeslee, 2003). This relationship can be dangerous. Parents do not always recognize when their disclosures reach levels of inappropriateness (Afifi, McManus, Hutchinson, & Baker, 2007) and due to the difference in power between parent and child, children (especially younger ones) may not always alert parents to their discomfort in becoming recipients. Moreover, Wallerstein and Blakeslee (2003) noted that turning a child into a confidant might lead children to feel needed and important. Cyclically, this can bolster children's participation in the confidant role so that they receive even more disclosures. Because negatively valenced disclosures about the other parent are related to higher levels of anxiety for children from divorced rather than still married families (Afifi, Afifi, & Coho, 2009), it is necessary to more closely examine why parents make these disclosures.

Parents are motivated to disclose to children for both helpful and hurtful reasons. Some information about a divorce is helpful for children to reduce uncertainty and alleviate fears (e.g., living/visitation arrangements), but parents must decide how much and to what extent they should be revealing information (Afifi & McManus, 2010; Afifi, Schrodt, & McManus, 2009). As children work to understand their parents' relationship and make informed decisions about interacting with each parent, some information regarding the divorce is necessary, creating a space for parents to share divorce-related information for the betterment of the child. For instance, parents might wish to reduce uncertainty about the divorce through revealing information such as finances, new dating remarriages/relationships, or legal issues to their older children (Afifi, Hutchinson, & Krouse, 2006; Afifi & McManus, 2010). While children might need and even appreciate gaining more clarity about the divorce, there is a tipping point at which information about the divorce becomes inappropriate and hurtful.

Sometimes parents choose to disclose in an attempt to drive a wedge between the child and the other parent. Per Afifi and her colleagues (2007), parents may not be concerned with negatively influencing their children's view of the other parent through disclosures if the ex-spousal relationship is stressful. Some parents may even attempt to retaliate against one another through negatively valenced disclosures to their children, turning children against the other parent in a manipulative communication maneuver. Hence, maliciously harming the parent-child relationship of an ex-spouse represents one path for parents who wish to alleviate their own feelings of ill will while sacrificing the relational health of their child. Other parents are simply searching for a confidant with whom they can relate and share their thoughts.

Many parents disclose to their children purely because of their own stress and difficulties managing their emotions. Parents may reveal sensitive information to release their own feelings and emotions while not always knowing how to properly support their children who can also be hurting or confused (Afifi, Schrodt, & McManus, 2009). Although children may be struggling with the emotional fallout of the divorce and as they face new relational challenges inherent in navigating post-divorce family life, parents are not always aware that their children are also in need of support. Consequently, parents may focus on their own emotional needs rather than on their children's. Ultimately, parents may experience a sense of control when they feel they can express themselves to their children whenever they need catharsis following an emotional event (Afifi et al., 2007). When a parent is experiencing trouble reconciling the divorce or the outcomes of the divorce, he or she may gain relief from their own emotional turmoil by disclosing to their children. If parents indeed find relief in sharing the burden of their emotions with their children, they may be more likely to continue disclosing in the future when they are in search of emotional relief once again.

Regardless of the reasons parents choose to disclose information about the divorce to their children, disclosures can have serious implications for offspring. While divorce-disclosures have the ability to bring a parent and child together, children might face a simultaneous threat of mounting anxiety and a desire for relational distance in one parent-child relationship (Afifi, Schrodt, & McManus, 2009). In other words, disclosures can increase the bond in a parent-child relationship for the parent who is disclosing. Children may sense that this parent trusts them, values their opinions, and needs their help (Wallerstein & Blakeslee, 2003). However, receiving disclosures can also induce feelings of anxiety and stress as children learn more about their parents' relationship or troubled relational past. Positioning a child to become a confidant about the divorce, financial troubles, or parents' feelings of loss can place great demands on them (Afifi, 2003). The parent-child closeness resulting from divorce disclosures may lead to parentification wherein children take on a parental role in their families and become more of a peer to their disclosing parent rather than a child (Afifi & McManus, 2010; Jurkovic, Thirkeild, & Morrell, 2001). Children of divorce report increased emotional caregiving with this shift in parent-child relationships increasing feelings of maturity and independence for older children, but increasing distress for younger children (Jurkovic et al., 2001).

If a parent divulges negative information about the other parent, this could impact the relationship between the other parent and the child. Children may feel torn between parents or forced to choose sides when loyalty anxieties ensue (see Afifi, 2003; Booth & Amato, 1994; Buchanan, Maccoby, & Dornbusch, 1991). Consequently, one of the most prominent outcomes of receiving parents' divorce disclosures is feeling caught between parents.

Communication While Feeling Caught

Feeling caught between parents represents a common tension that children of divorce may experience. Following a divorce, children are often caught in loyalty conflicts and feel the need to choose sides, their conflicting feelings of loyalty typically exacerbated by parents (Emery & Dillon, 1994; Wallerstein, 1996). For some children, feelings of being caught begin to diminish as time goes on after their parents' divorce (Amato & Afifi, 2006). For other children, divorce may lead to increased feelings of triangulation as parents disclose inappropriately to their children or become engrossed in disagreements with their ex-spouse. Afifi (2003) posited that feeling caught is a consequence resulting from "communication boundaries that became enmeshed through revealing too much personal information. Inappropriate disclosures, using a child as a peer and co-parent, and using a family member as a messenger of information were ways in which the boundaries became enmeshed" (pp. 738–739). Thus, children may feel caught between parents when they become recipients of inappropriate divorce disclosures, are treated by parents as peers (i.e., parentification), or when they are asked to become messengers between ex-spouses (Afifi et al., 2011; Schrodt & Afifi, 2007; Yárnoz-Yaben & Garmendia, 2015). As parents reach out to their children for help, children sometimes give up their childhood and adolescent years to take on the responsibilities of caring for a parent post-divorce, developing feelings of being trapped and needing to rescue the parent in need (Wallerstein et al., 2000). This demands a closer examination of the communication leading to feelings of being caught.

The ways in which parents talk about one another impacts the degree to which children feel caught. After their divorce, parents naturally turn to children as confidants as they no longer have their partner to ask for advice or decision-making, glean sympathy or companionship, and have often lost members of their old social network (Wallerstein et al., 2000). When parents communicate in ways that show support or care for the other parent, children are less likely to feel caught between them (Buchanan et al., 1991). Hence, not all communication regarding the divorce or ex-spousal relationship is damaging to children. According to Afifi, Afifi, and Coho (2009), disclosures that are negatively valenced include "parental disclosures that are pessimistic and emotionally charged, derogatory, or demeaning in some way toward the other parent" (p. 520). A parent who is disturbed or hurt may convince a child to join him or her in rejecting or criticizing the other parent so that the interparental aggression eventually spills over into the parent-child relationship (Wallerstein & Blakeslee, 2003). Moreover, Wallerstein and Blakeslee (2003) noted that some children who are feeling needy or deprived may mistake the parent's attention for love. When parents reveal negative or damaging information about the ex-spouse, children may feel they should draw closer to the disclosing parent as they begin to see their other parent in a more disparaging light. In turn, this creates a closer parent-child bond with one parent while weakening the bond with the other over time.

Children are more likely to experience feelings of being caught when they believe their parents lack communication competence (McManus & Donovan, 2012). Similarly, Buchanan and colleagues (1991) found that parental relationships characterized by low levels of cooperative communication as well as high levels of hostility and discord predicted adolescents' feelings of being caught. Because parents who disclose to their children often allow themselves to reveal unnecessary or inappropriate information (Afifi et al., 2007), child recipients may perceive that the disclosing parent is a less competent communicator, once again increasing their risk of feeling caught. Therefore, parents' communication choices greatly influence the likelihood and effects of children feeling caught.

In an ideal world, parents would work to manage communication with their children in a manner that decreases the chances for children to feel caught (Afifi, 2003). However, if parents do not get along with one another following a divorce, there may be little chance of them avoiding inappropriate divorce disclosures or talking poorly about one another. The greatest predictor of children feeling caught is the co-parental relationship wherein children are less likely to feel caught if parents disengage from one another rather than continue disputing (Buchanan et al., 1991). While divorce for some families alleviates parents' arguing, for other families' divorce may only increase the chance children will get pulled into parents' disagreements through unwanted communication or inappropriate disclosures. Divorce may place legal and physical separation between parents, but if they cannot properly handle conflict, divorced parents may continue to engage in unhealthy communication patterns that entangle their children.

The effects of feeling caught vary for children of divorce. Scholars have found that feeling caught between parents is related to negative affect, increased anxiety, heightened depression, and decreased parent-child relationships (Afifi & Schrodt, 2003; Amato & Afifi, 2006; Schrodt & Afifi, 2007; Yárnoz-Yaben & Garmendia, 2015). Feeling caught, then, is harmful to children's mental well-being as well as their family relationships. Children often feel stress and guilt over wanting to please and remain close to both of their parents (Buchanan et al., 1991). For example, Buchanan et al. (1991) found that children can become fearful of what maintaining a good relationship with one parent will mean for their relationship with the other parent. After a divorce, if children want to maintain strong relationships with both parents, they may be fearful of appearing to choose sides. Hence, feeling caught between parents after a divorce creates additional tension that lies in direct contrast to their relational goals.

Children's responses to feeling caught vary. Any move toward one parent may be sensed by a child as betrayal, potentially evoking rejection and anger from the other parent (Wallerstein, 1996). Children can manage this tension in different ways. Some children, in an attempt to honor both parents, decide not to take sides but instead subject themselves to loneliness, isolation, and decreased parental support (Wallerstein, 1996). Other children may choose to align themselves with one parent, forsaking the other relationship. Booth and Amato (1994) found that when children wish to alleviate the anxiety they experience over parent loyalty conflicts, some choose to align themselves more closely with one parent. Thus, the anxiety over feeling caught between parents can be so great that children finally choose sides to ease that tension within the family, even though this choice may produce new emotional strains for those children.

Children may endure feelings of being caught throughout their adolescent and early adulthood years. Researchers have claimed that adolescents' feelings of being caught stem from a desire to protect themselves, each of their parents, and parent-child relationships (Afifi, Afifi, Morse, & Hamrick, 2008). Some adolescents protest being placed in the middle (Wallerstein, 1996) while others simply attempt to avoid conversations that will increase their feeling caught (Afifi, 2003). When young adults feel caught between parents, one of their immediate responses may include attempting to avoid the situation at hand in hopes of gaining protection from ensuing distress (Afifi, Schrodt, & McManus, 2009). If young adults believe they can better protect themselves and their parents by evading the situation (e.g., divorce disclosures or unwanted conversations), avoidance may seem like the safest option. Others may confront the issue differently. Young adults can "respond with a 'flight' response by (1) avoiding the topic and/or a 'fight' response by (2) directly confronting their parent or (3) responding with aggression" (Afifi, Schrodt, & McManus, 2009, p. 407). Some young adults are open with their parents about their feelings while others may become aggressive due to rising anxiety or anger.

Although feeling caught between parents is a major outcome of divorce communication in families, it is critical to understand other emotional experiences for children following a divorce as they will certainly face unique challenges to their emotional functioning. For instance, children must process the knowledge that their family is changing and may continue to change with possible remarriages, second divorces, and new siblings. Later on, as adolescents and emergent adults navigate life with divorced parents, they will likely encounter a variety of emotions as they face new life transitions of their own such as dating, moving away, and beginning college. Therefore, the next section reviews literature on the emotional effects of parents' divorce.

Emotional Communication Challenges

A third communication legacy for children of divorce includes emotional communication challenges. Regardless of children's age when their parents get a divorce, emotions represent one area in which they will be most impacted in both the short- and long-term (Metts et al., 2013; Wallerstein, 1996; Wallerstein & Lewis, 2004). Divorce may embody one of the greatest changes that occurs within a family system, having the capacity to impact members' emotions and emotional well-being throughout their lifetimes as parents legally separate, deal with the ensuing challenges and changes, and begin lives separate from one another yet still connected through their children. After their parents' divorce, children may feel the emotional impact of the divorce throughout their lives (Wallerstein et al., 2000; Wallerstein & Blakeslee, 2003), making it necessary to learn how to effectively navigate and manage their divorce-related emotions. For example, Marquardt (2005) found that children from divorced families report feeling that holidays and family events are stressful. Similarly, Laumann-Billings and Emery (2000) found that a prominent concern for children of divorce is the fear that both parents will one day attend major events such as graduations or weddings.

The range of divorce-related emotions may be extensive with some children experiencing relief or joy that their parents are divorced while others may instead experience apprehension, anger, or sadness as their parents grow apart and their family transitions. Children going through their parents' divorce often experience fear, loneliness, and intense worry about their future as their family system collapses (Wallerstein, 1996). Krantz (1988) also noted that children of divorce have a more negative view of life. Similarly, Baxter, Weston, and Qu (2011) found that children from divorced families typically show decreased emotional well-being when compared to children in non-divorced families. It is important, then, to understand the potential emotional troubles that children of divorce may face.

Initially, many children experience strong negative feelings when parents decide to divorce. For instance, Hetherington (1979) found that children's initial responses to divorce include feelings of depression, guilt, anger, and fear, but that those feelings begin to dissipate a year or so later. Regardless of how children reacted emotionally to the divorce originally, they continue to encounter emotion-eliciting situations related to the divorce as time goes on. Some children may never come to terms with accepting their parents' divorce. Even though there are children who eventually feel that divorce was the right decision for their families, or who recognize that divorce relieved many of the tensions felt when their parents were still married, many children never feel that the divorce freed up any of their family tensions (Laumann-Billings & Emery, 2000). Many parents continue arguing after they are separated and many bring children into their arguments as allies, messengers, or confidants (Afifi, 2003; Wallerstein & Blakeslee, 2003). In other words, family tensions may continue or even worsen following a divorce, making children emotionally vulnerable as they navigate through life with discordant, divorced parents. Amato and Sobolewski (2001) concluded that children typically experience continued discord between their parents after a divorce. Thus, communication following the divorce is an important determinant of children's emotional difficulties within their families.

Emotional communication challenges are a prominent communication legacy of divorce that begins with the emotional communication accompanying parents' announcement of their decision. Shortly after no fault divorce laws were changed in the United States, Grollman and Grollman (1977) posited that parents should announce their divorce with both spouses present and that they should allow their children to ask questions and express emotions. Wallerstein and Lewis (2004) found that, when confronted with the idea of their parents divorcing, children initially feel unhappy, shocked, angry, fearful, and confused. Children often react to a divorce announcement with fear about their family coming apart or fear about continued care and support from parents once they are separated (Grollman & Grollman, 1977). Some cry or beg for their parents to stay together, some are apprehensive or panicked, and others have delayed reactions in which they are silent for days before expressing their postponed emotions outwardly (Wallerstein, 1996). Additionally, many children withdraw into their feelings of sadness or anger, choosing to deal with their feelings alone (Wallerstein, 1996).

Although children may typically turn to parents for support during times of need, divorce represents a unique situation in which parents no longer live in the same house, one or both may be less available, and parents may be consumed with their own divorce-related issues to notice their children's needs. Additionally, parents' emotional availability for their children sometimes decreases after a divorce (Amato & Sobolewski, 2001). Specifically, children younger than seven may experience the most emotional distress when they feel their parents are unavailable since they have not yet developed ways of comforting themselves (Wallerstein & Lewis, 2004). Though younger children may not have developed means of coping with their fear or loneliness, preadolescents may manage their feelings through engaging in risky behaviors (e.g., sex or drinking), teenagers often react with bursts of anger (e.g., slamming doors or crying spells) (Wallerstein & Blakeslee, 2003), and emergent/young adults whose parents divorce must process through feelings of sadness, anger, and devastation (Jensen & Bowen, 2015).

Considering the number of emotions and potential for continued encounters with emotion-eliciting situations that follow a divorce, it is important that children know how to effectively manage their emotions. Children may have an increased chance for improved mental well-being if they learn to properly communicate and express their emotions. Overall, suppressing their feelings of grief related to the divorce may minimize the loss they are feeling for their family and become harmful to them later in life (Grollman & Grollman, 1977). Bottling up emotions can bear significant consequences. Scholars have found that those who suppress their emotions report decreased self-esteem and life satisfaction, increased depressive symptoms, and report experiencing more negative emotions (Gross & John, 2003). Although suppressing emotions dealing with parents' divorce may seem easy at the time, children may suffer in the long run if they habitually choose to muffle their feelings. Ultimately, suppressing emotions results in an inconsistent relationship between what an individual feels internally and his or her expression of those feelings to others (Gross, Richards, & John, 2006). Although choosing not to express one's emotions can be quite damaging, avoidance may be a common tool children use in facing difficult emotional situations revolving around their parents' divorce.

After parents talk badly about one another, children can feel fearful to talk about their own worry or anxiety with their parents (Afifi & McManus, 2010). For this reason, many children may not express their feelings when their parents disclose to them. They may employ avoidance when they feel they need to protect themselves or when they feel they have a decreased parent-child connection (Golish & Caughlin, 2002). It is possible that suppressing feelings may be common when it comes to handling divorce-related emotions. Gross and John (2003) found that individuals who frequently use avoidance and suppress their feelings report sharing fewer emotions (even positive emotions) with others. Continually not sharing one's emotions likely decreases the amount of support other people will offer as well as decreases the chance that those involved in the emotion-eliciting situation will know what they did that may have led to someone feeling badly. Once again, if children do not feel they can share their feelings with their parents, their parents may never consider changing their communication patterns with their children or offer help or support to them.

After a divorce, children's socio-emotional as well as psychosocial adjustment skills are partially dependent on how well they manage their stress, fear, anxiety, frustrations, and depression (Jensen & Bowen, 2015; Krantz, 1988). In their 25-year longitudinal study, Wallerstein and Lewis (2004) found that many children of divorce carry memory fragments (i.e., mental images) with them of specific moments from the time of divorce that eventually intrude into their adult relationships, affecting how they interact with and relate to close others. Considering the impact that emotion management after a divorce has on children's development and the unique emotion-eliciting situations that children of divorce face, it is critical to examine how children manage their divorce-related emotions. Therefore, the following section provides suggestions for future research to extend and further explore this topic as well as the other communication legacies discussed.

Research Agenda

After examining previous work on three communication legacies of divorce including parents' divorce disclosures, children's communication accompanying feelings of being caught, and the emotional communication challenges of divorce, this chapter concludes with an agenda for future research on these topics within the field of Communication Studies. The direction for future scholarship investigating children's communication following their parents' divorce is three-fold.

First, scholars need to further examine how children of varying ages communicate their divorce-related emotions and to whom they communicate those feelings. If parents continue to argue after their divorce, their children often become entangled in their disagreements through parent-child communication and inappropriate divorce disclosures (Afifi, Afifi, & Coho, 2009; Afifi, Schrodt, & McManus, 2009). Afifi, Afifi, and Coho (2009) suggested that researchers should work to understand how children manage arousal and anxiety over time when their parents cannot achieve a cordial relationship with each other. Hence, scholars should continue to examine not only what children feel in relation to their parents' divorce (Metts et al., 2013), but also how, if at all, they attempt to communicate their thoughts and feelings. Regardless of when the divorce occurred, children may still feel intense feelings such as fear, anger, or guilt related to the divorce well into adulthood (Maldonado, 2009).

From a lifespan perspective, children of divorce will likely encounter future situations wherein their parents' divorce will impact them in new ways (e.g., graduations, their own wedding, parents' remarriages, etc.). Over time, remarriages and blended families bring about new traditions, changing expectations, and more individuals who impact family dynamics (Wallerstein & Blakeslee, 2003). Scholars need to investigate how children of divorce manage those instances and how their navigation of their parents' divorce into adulthood impacts them in making life transitions and developing their own relationships or families. For instance, Shimkowski and Ledbetter (2018) found that feeling caught between parents predicts young adults' use of silence or changing the topic as tactics to manage their feelings when communicating with someone about their parents' divorce. Further research on managing emotions related to parents' divorce is important in helping family communication specialists.

Because adults should have better-developed cognitive and communicative skills than small children, adult children should have better control over emotionally-driven decisions and choices they make. They may choose to confront their parents, revealing their thoughts or feelings, or they may decide to suppress them and never tell anyone. To more completely understand how adult children function in divorced families, researchers need to more closely examine how they communicate during occurrences in which their parents being divorced affects them or their choices. Scholars should further investigate who adult children invite to be a part of that communication process in dealing with divorced parents and the long-term impacts of such communication. Adult children may turn to one or both parents, other family members such as siblings or stepsiblings, or to individuals outside of the family to process feelings or seek guidance. By considering not only how they communicate but also with whom they communicate, researchers can gain a clearer picture of what family members' divorce-related communication looks like in post-divorce lives.

Second, in extending our understanding of familial post-divorce relationships, scholars need to examine the effects of offspring's communication and emotion management on parent-child relationships. Researchers have previously found that parent-child relationships typically change following a divorce. For example, Laumann-Billings and Emery (2000) found that young adults often report that not only do they wish they could spend more time with their fathers after the divorce, but many young adults also report that they do not feel their fathers still love them. In examining how children and young adults communicate to manage their divorce-related emotions, it is also important to understand how parent-child relationships are affected. Perhaps one reason young adults report difficulties with their fathers (who are often the nonresidential parent following a divorce) is that they have not learned to communicate their feelings regarding the divorce with them. As Laumann-Billings and Emery (2000) also noted, children frequently blame their fathers for the divorce. Scholars, then, should consider how children might withhold their emotions from fathers based on feelings of blame for the divorce. Moreover, researchers should examine children's and young adults' overall family satisfaction as well as their satisfaction with each parent-child relationship while specifically considering the role their divorce-related emotion expression or suppression plays. While some children may feel that expressing feelings about the divorce draws them closer to their parents, others may instead feel anxiety or fear over the thought of expressing their emotions, creating more distance between them and their parents. Hence, these communication exchanges should be investigated further.

Lastly, researchers should investigate how children's post-divorce communication and emotion management impacts their own romantic relationships once they are older, potentially impacting dating, marriages, and building their own families. In considering the longitudinal effects of parents' divorce, Amato (2010) posited that the changes brought on by parents' divorce can create stressors that persist throughout one's lifetime. Based on the lasting impact of divorce, scholars need to examine how the choices children make in managing their feelings and family communication following their parents' divorce affects their own relationships. For instance, scholars have previously found that growing up with divorced parents increases the risk that off-spring's marriages will likewise end in divorce (Amato & DeBoer, 2001). One possible link that has not yet been thoroughly examined in this relationship, however, is how children of divorce learn to communicate emotions about their parents' relationship. It is possible that the more they suppress feelings about their parents' divorce, the less likely they may be to express emotions when necessary in their own romantic relationships. Moreover, if they have not properly worked through their feelings about their own family, they may feel unprepared to create a new family of their own through marriage.

Overall, scholars have agreed that divorce is a life-altering event that impacts children throughout their lifetime (Amato, 2010; Amato & DeBoer, 2001; Cunningham & Skillingstead, 2015; Wallerstein et al., 2000). Family communication through parents' divorce disclosures may increase the difficulties they feel in being members of a divorced family. Disclosures about the divorce often lead children to feel caught between their parents (Afifi, 2003; Afifi, Afifi, & Coho, 2009; Emery & Dillon, 1994; Wallerstein & Blakeslee, 2003), increasing the anxiety and distress they may already be experiencing if parents begin to rely on them as confidants or peers. Children may find it difficult, however, to fully express their feelings to their parents (Afifi & McManus, 2010; Afifi, Schrodt, & McManus, 2009), often resulting in avoidance or denial (Golish & Caughlin, 2002; Wallerstein & Blakeslee, 2003). Suppressing emotions, however, may come at a cost to children's personal and social development (Gross & John, 2003; Krantz, 1988). Thus, scholars need to examine how children communicate and regulate their divorce-related emotions within their families as well as explore the impacts of those decisions on children's personal and family lives throughout their lifetime. Children's ability to fully process their parents' divorce and navigate family life following the divorce may be greatly impacted by their effectiveness in managing and communicating their divorce-related thoughts and emotions.

References

Afifi, T. D. (2003). "Feeling caught" in stepfamilies: Managing boundary turbulence through appropriate communication privacy rules. *Journal of Social and Personal Relationships, 20,* 729–755. doi:10.1177/0265407503206002.

Afifi, T. D., Afifi, W. A., & Coho, A. (2009). Adolescents' physiological reactions to their parents' negative disclosures about the other parent in divorced and nondivorced families. *Journal of Divorce & Remarriage, 50,* 517–540. doi:10.1080/10502550902970496.

Afifi, T. D., Afifi, W. A., Morse, C. R., & Hamrick, K. K. (2008). Adolescents' avoidance tendencies and physiological reactions to discussions about their parents' relationship: Implications for postdivorce and nondivorced families. *Communication Monographs, 75,* 290–317. doi:10.1080/03637750802342308.

Afifi, T. D., Granger, D. A., Denes, A., Joseph, A., & Aldeis, D. (2011). Parents' communication skills and adolescents' salivary α–amylase and cortisol response patterns. *Communication Monographs, 78,* 273–295. doi:10.1080/03637751.2011.589460.

Afifi, T. D., Hutchinson, S., & Krouse, S. (2006). Toward a theoretical model of communal coping in postdivorce families and other naturally occurring groups. *Communication Theory, 16,* 378–409. doi:10.1111/j.1468–2885.2006.00275.x.

Afifi, T. D., & McManus, T. (2010). Divorce disclosures and adolescents' physical and mental health and parental relationship quality. *Journal of Divorce & Remarriage, 51,* 83–107. doi:10.1080/10502550903455141.

Afifi, T. D., McManus, T., Hutchinson, S., & Baker, B. (2007). Inappropriate parental divorce disclosures, the factors that prompt them, and their impact on parents' and adolescents' well–being. *Communication Monographs, 74,* 78–102. doi:10.1080/03637750701196870.

Afifi, T. D., & Schrodt, P. (2003). "Feeling caught" as a mediator of adolescents' and young adults' avoidance and satisfaction with their parents in divorced and non-divorced households. *Communication Monographs, 70,* 142–173. doi:10.1080/03637 75032000133791.

Afifi, T. D., Schrodt, P., & McManus, T. (2009). The divorce disclosure model (DDM): Why parents disclose negative information about the divorce to their children and its effects. In T. D. Afifi & W. Afifi (Eds.), *Uncertainty, information management, and disclosure decisions: Theories and applications* (pp. 403–425). New York: Routledge.

Amato, P. R. (2010). Research on divorce: Continuing trends and new developments. *Journal of Marriage and Family, 72,* 650–666. doi:10.1111/j.1741–3737.2010.00723.x.

Amato, P. R., & Afifi, T. D. (2006). Feeling caught between parents: Adult children's relations with parents and subjective well-being. *Journal of Marriage and Family, 68,* 222–235. doi:10.1111/j.1741–3737.2006.00243.x.

Amato, P. R., & DeBoer, D. (2001). The intergenerational transmission of marital instability across generations: Relationship skills of commitment to marriage? *Journal of Marriage and Family, 63,* 1038–1051. doi:10.1111/j.1741–3737.2001.01038.x.

Amato, P. R., & Sobolewski, J. M. (2001). The effects of divorce and marital discord on adult children's psychological well-being. *American Sociological Review, 66,* 900–921. doi:10.2307/3088878.

American Psychological Association. (2020). *Marriage & divorce.* https://www.apa.org/topics/divorce/

Baxter, J., Weston, R., & Qu, L. (2011). Family structure, co-parental relationship quality, post–separation paternal involvement and children's emotional wellbeing. *Journal of Family Studies, 17*, 86–109. doi:10.5172/jfs.2011.17.2.86.

Booth, A., & Amato, P. R. (1994). Parental marital quality, parental divorce, and relations with parents. *Journal of Marriage and the Family, 56*, 21–34. doi:10.2307/352698.

Buchanan, C. M., Maccoby, E. E., & Dornbusch, S. M. (1991). Caught between parents: Adolescents' experience in divorced homes. *Child Development, 62*, 1008–1029. doi:10.1111= j.1467-8624.1991.tb01586.x.

Cunningham, M., & Skillingstead, K. (2015). Narratives of socialization: Perceptions of parental influence after childhood divorce. *Journal of Divorce & Remarriage, 56*, 137–154. doi:10.1080/10502556.2014.996043.

Emery, R. E., & Dillon, P. (1994). Conceptualizing the divorce process: Renegotiating boundaries of intimacy and power in the divorced family system. *Family Relations, 43*, 374–379. doi:10.2307/585367.

Golish, T., & Caughlin, J. (2002). "I'd rather not talk about it": Adolescents' and young adults' use of topic avoidance in stepfamilies. *Journal of Applied Communication Research, 30*, 78–106. doi:10.1080/00909880216574.

Gottman, J. (1994). *What predicts divorce?* Hillsdale, NJ: Lawrence Erlbaum.

Grollman, E. A., & Grollman, S. H. (1977). How to tell children about divorce. *Journal of Clinical Child Psychology, 6*, 35–37. doi:10.1080/15374417709532759.

Gross, J. J., & John, O. P. (2003). Individual differences in two emotion regulation processes: Implications for affect, relationships, and well-being. *Journal of Personality and Social Psychology, 85*, 348–362. doi:10.1037%2F0022-3514.85.2.348.

Gross, J. J., Richards, J. M., & John, O. P. (2006). Emotion regulation in everyday life. In D. K. Snyder, J. A. Simpson, & J. N. Hughes (Eds.), *Emotion regulation in couples and families: Pathways to dysfunction and health* (pp. 13–36). Washington, D.C.: American Psychological Association.

Hetherington, E. M. (1979). Divorce: A child's perspective. *American Psychologist, 34*, 851–858. doi:10.1037//0003-066X.34.10.851.

Jensen, T. M., & Bowen, G. L. (2015). Mid-and late-life divorce and parents' perceptions of emerging adult children's emotional reactions. *Journal of Divorce & Remarriage, 56*, 409–427. doi:10.1080/10502556.2015.1046795.

Jurkovic, G. J., Thirkeild, A., & Morrell, R. (2001). Parentification of adult children of divorce: A multidimensional analysis. *Journal of Youth and Adolescence, 30*, 245–258. doi:10.1023/A:1010349925974.

Krantz, S. E. (1988). Divorce and children. In S. M. Dornbusch & M. H. Strobe (Eds.), *Feminism: Children and the new families* (pp. 249–273). New York: The Guilford Press.

Laumann–Billings, L., & Emery, R. E. (2000). Distress among young adults in divorced families. *Journal of Family Psychology, 14*, 671–687. doi:10.1037//0893-3200.14.4.671.

Maldonado, S. (2009). Taking account of children's emotions: Anger and forgiveness in "renegotiated families". *Virginia Journal of Social Policy & The Law, 16,* 443–470. www.vjspl.org

Marquardt, E. (2005). *Between two worlds: The inner lives of children of divorce.* New York: Crown Publishers.

McManus, T. G., & Donovan, S. (2012). Communication competence and feeling caught: Explaining perceived ambiguity in divorce–related communication. *Communication Quarterly, 60,* 255–277. doi:10.1080/01463373.2012.669328.

Metts, M., Braithwaite, D. O., Schrodt, P., Wang, T. R., Holman, A. J., Nuru, A. K., & Abetz, J. S. (2013). The experience and expression of stepchildren's emotions at critical events in stepfamily life. *Journal of Divorce & Remarriage, 54,* 414–437. doi:10.1080/10502556.2013.800400.

Schrodt, P., & Afifi, T. D. (2007). Communication processes that predict young adults' feelings of being caught and their associations with mental health and family satisfaction. *Communication Monographs, 74,* 200–228. doi:10.1080/03637750701390085.

Shimkowski, J. R., & Ledbetter, A. M. (2018). Parental divorce disclosures, young adults' emotion regulation strategies, and feeling caught. *Journal of Family Communication, 18,* 185–201. doi:10.1080/15267431.2018.1457033.

Teachman, J. D. (2002). Stability across cohorts in divorce risk factors. *Demography, 65,* 507–524. doi:10.1353/dem.2002.0019.

Wallerstein, J. S. (1996). *Surviving the breakup: How parents and children cope with divorce.* New York: Basic Books.

Wallerstein, J. S., & Blakeslee, S. (2003). *What about the kids? Raising your children before, during, and after divorce.* Ney York: Hyperion.

Wallerstein, J. S., & Lewis, J. M. (2004). The unexpected legacy of divorce: Report of a 25-year study. *Psychoanalytic Psychology, 21,* 353–370. doi:10.1037/0736-9735.21.3.353.

Wallerstein, J. S., Lewis, J., & Blakeslee, S. (2000). *The unexpected legacy of divorce: The 25-year landmark study.* New York: Hyperion.

Yárnoz-Yaben, S., & Garmendia, A. (2015). Parental divorce and emerging adults' subjective well-being: The role of "carrying messages". *Journal of Child and Family Studies,* doi:10.1007/s10826–015–0229–0.

14. Social (Pragmatic) Impairment

The Impact on Communication Development

Jason S. Wrench
SUNY New Paltz

Wendy Bower
SUNY New Paltz

The chapter examines the current state of research related to social (pragmatic) impairment and its relationship to children's communicative behaviors. Social pragmatic communication disorder (SCD) is a relatively new diagnosis included in the Fifth Edition of the *Diagnostic and Statistical Manual of Mental Disorders* (DSM-5, 2013) by the American Psychiatric Association. This diagnostic category was recently added and intended to clarify confusions about pragmatic disorders not included specifically in the diagnosis of autism and to recognize individuals who have significant problems in using verbal and nonverbal communication in social interactions but who are not diagnosed with an autism spectrum disorder or intellectual deficit.

Currently there is much debate about whether social pragmatic disorder is simply a part of the autism spectrum, whether it defines all children with high functioning autism, whether it characterizes many communicative disorders, or is an entirely separate condition. At the moment, much confusion surrounds the use of this terminology at the convergence of neurology, psychology, communication studies, and speech and language pathology. As noted, recent changes in the *Diagnostic and Statistics Manual* (DSM V, 2013) have resulted in a definition of Social Pragmatic Communication Disorder as a language impairment characterized by a persistent difficulty with verbal and nonverbal communication that cannot be explained by low cognitive ability. Symptoms include difficulty in the acquisition and use of spoken and written language as well as problems with inappropriate responses in conversation. The disorder limits effective communication, social relationships, academic achievement, or occupational performance (American Psychiatric Association, 2013, ¶ 1). For our purposes, we recognize that some of the behaviors that are labeled as SCD may be indicators of social (pragmatic) impairment or may be characteristics other differently diagnosed communication disorders.

A child with high levels of communication apprehension, for example, could be misinterpreted for someone who is suffering from a psychologically-based communication disorder. However, the DSM-5 tends to bundle a large range of developmental childhood communication issues together, which makes it even more difficult to differentiate among various social communicatively impaired behaviors in children. We are specifically dealing with issues that generally start in childhood. As the DSM-5 notes, "Symptoms must be present in early childhood even if they are not recognized until later when speech, language, or communication demands exceed abilities" (2013, ¶ 2). Our goal for this chapter is to present a variety of social (pragmatic) impairments that are common among children to inform readers about those childhood communication behaviors that are clearly disorders versus those behaviors that may still cause negative communication outcomes but are not "disorders" in the psychiatric sense of the term.

Defining Social Communication Disorders

Rapin and Allen originally coined the term "semantic pragmatic disorder" (SPD) in 1983 to describe children who manifested the following characteristics: unusual levels of talkativeness but deficient vocabulary, impaired ability to comprehend connected discourse, atypical choice of words, and inappropriate conversation skills (Rapin & Allen, 1983). These children were also found to exhibit additional features such as delayed language development with an assortment of contextual language errors, avoidance of eye contact, rigid habits, and a shallower range of interests than normal.

Bishop and Norbury suggested in 2002 that this disorder was not one of language alone, but of information processing and response. They found that children with "semantic pragmatic disorder," later called pragmatic language impairment, and now social pragmatic communication disorder, had expressive language that was fluent and appropriate but not appropriately used in conversation. Additionally these children so diagnosed had difficulty understanding and producing conversational discourse. In addition, their concrete and literal conversation interpretation was appropriate but nonliteral conversation such as jokes and sarcasm could not be managed, and generalization was not possible from situation to situation. (Bishop & Norbury, 2002; Drake, 2015).

Defining Pragmatics

Pragmatics involves language use to maintain a social connectedness with others. The essence of pragmatics is the ability of the speaker to effectively use and adjust communication messages for a variety of purposes with an array of communication partners within diverse circumstances. This ability is not innate, these skills develop over time and development is dependent on other factors such as joint attention, perspective taking, comprehension monitoring ability, and social interest. In this section of the chapter, specific elements of pragmatics will be defined and discussed. These elements include: communicative functions (the intent and frequency of communication; discourse management which involves keeping the conversation flowing by using turn allocation, topic initiation and maintenance, and repair of conversational break-downs; register variation (politeness and social role recognition); presupposition or perspective taking; paralinguistics including prosody, gaze, gestures and proximity; and, social behaviors including conventional gestures, facial expression and social actions (Paul, 2009; Vicker 2009a, 2009b).

Social Competence

In recent years there has also been a move to differentiate between social competence (social intelligence) and traditional perspectives of communication competence. According Han and Kemple (2006), social competence is a combination of a wide range of necessary skills to be successful in life: self-regulation, interpersonal knowledge/skills, positive self-identity, cultural competence, adopting social values, and planning and decision-making skills. This section will examine each of these factors and how social impairment can cause developmental problems with a child's ability to socialize with others. First, self-regulation includes controlling one's impulses, delaying gratification, resisting temptation and peer pressure, reflecting on ones feelings, and engaging in self-monitoring behavior, which are often difficult for individuals with social pragmatic disorders. Second, interpersonal knowledge/skills is highly related to the notion of communication competence, so we will explore these issues in a section below. Third, positive self-identity is an extremely important in the development of social competence. Many kids with either physical impairments or other communicative impairments have been shown to have lower levels of self-esteem, which impacts how they interact with others (Sebastian, Blakemore, & Charman, 2009). Fourth, cultural competence is a consistent problem for both children and parents with pragmatic disorders. Helping both sides navigate issues related to culturally competent behavioral outcomes is necessary for a child's integration into a culture. As for social values, this concept is "described as encompassing caring, equity, honesty, social justice, responsibility, healthy lifestyles and sexual attitudes, and flexibility" (Han & Kemple, 2006, p. 242). Lastly, planning and decision-making skills are important for social competence. One common problem with children with social pragmatics disorders is that their decision making and then behavioral choices make them stand out from their peers, which can lead to teasing, bullying, and social alienation.

Communication Competence. This section will explore the area of communication competence and its relationship to childhood communication. We will start by briefly overviewing the notion of communication competence and how communication competence is developed in children. As McCroskey (1982) noted:

> All domains of learning bear directly on whether learners will engage in future behavior that we deem appropriate. Some learners need to improve their competence. Some need to develop skills. Others need to alter their communicative orientations and feelings. (p. 7).

We would also argue that various impairments can also be a huge factor when examining how someone learns to be communicatively competent. For example, not unlike social pragmatic language, communicative competence may refer to a learner's ability to use language to communicate successfully. Canale and Swain (1980) defined it as composing competence in the areas of words and rules (semantics and grammar); appropriacy, cohesion and coherence, and use of communication strategies (pragmatics). The development of communicative competence involves evolving language proficiency through interactions embedded in meaningful contexts, in other words, language in authentic environments that go beyond repetition and memorization of grammatical patterns in isolation. Dell Hymes (1972) hypothesized that children acquire language typically in terms of learning not only what sentences are grammatical but also what is appropriate. [The child] acquires competence as to when to speak, when not, and as to what to talk about with whom, when, where, in what manner. In short, a child becomes able to accomplish a repertoire of speech acts, to take part in speech events ... This competence, moreover, is integral with attitudes, values, and motivations concerning language" (Gumperz & Hymes, 1972).

The section of the chapter will then focus on various issues that can impair a child's development of communication competence. Some issues that lead to impairment of communication competence include variables like family communication styles (McKay-Semmler & Kim, 2014; Schrodt, Ledbetter, Jernberg, Larson, Brown, & Glonek, 2009), physical abilities (Bat-Chava, Martin, & Imperatore, 2014; Dale, Tadić, & Sonksen, 2014; Greenberg, 1980; Hatamizadeh, Ghasemi, Saeedi, & Kazemnejad, 2008; Toe & Paatsch, 2013), and social pragmatic disorders (Christensen-Sandfort & Whinnery, 2013; Klin, Saulnier, Sparrow, Cicchetti, Volkmar, & Lord, 2007; Reichow, & Volkmar, 2010)).

Communication Apprehension. In addition to the research we have linking a wide range of impairment issues to communication competence, it is also important to realize that there are other factors that can also impact a child's perceived communication competence. McCroskey, Andersen, Richmond, and Wheeless (1981) were the first researchers to examine the impact that communication apprehension has on children, specifically within the classroom environment. Although there is relatively little research examining children and communication apprehension and credibility, research on larger adult samples have consistently shown that individuals with high levels of communication apprehension also perceive themselves as less communicatively competent (Teven, Richmond, McCroskey, & McCroskey, 2010).

Verbal Impairment

Bloom and Lahey hypothesized a framework for oral language that includes the areas of content, form and use (Bloom & Lahey, 1978). Content areas can be summarized as relating to meaning—vocabulary use and understanding, world knowledge, and semantic forms, encoding meaning. The Form aspects of language include phonological, morphological and syntactic rules and the understanding and application of these rules to construct meaningful sentences. Language Use involves pragmatic functions of language, in other words, how we use language to get things done. Each one of these modalities influences the other, and each must be present for language development to progress in a typical fashion (Owens, 2008).

Children learn to talk not by direct instruction from care-givers, but through the process of hearing language, using language and sharing language in interactions. The experience that the child receives early in development will increase his knowledge about language and contribute to listening and speaking skills. The family plays an important role in developing language skills.

It is generally agreed that SCD affects both the semantic processing of language and the pragmatics of language use. Semantics refers to encoding and decoding the meanings of words and phrases; it applies to the surface structure of the sentences, while pragmatics refers to the use and meaning of language in a social or interactional context (knowing what to say and when to say it to people); in other words, the "deep" or underlying meaning structure of an utterance. Pragmatics explores meaning of an utterance beyond the literal and considers how interlocutors construct meaning. It also focuses on implied meanings. It considers language as an instrument of interaction, what people mean when they use language, and how human beings communicate and understand each other.

Nonverbal Impairment

In addition to verbal impairments, it is also important to understand there are a wide range of nonverbal disorders to contend with as well. Nowicki and Duke (1992, 2002) were the first to categorize problems related to ability to recognize and interpret nonverbal behaviors of others, which they termed dyssemia. As a singular concept, dyssemia has not received a wealth of research. However, there has been a lot of research examining various factors related to various nonverbal communicative impairments. Love, Nowicki, and Duke (1994) categorized dyssemia into "six domains of nonverbal behavior: gaze and eye contact, posture and gesture, touch and interpersonal distance, vocal quality, facial expression, and physical appearance and personal habits" (p. 704).

Gaze and Eye Contact. Gaze and eye contact is a much valued process in Western Cultures. Unfortunately, children with social pragmatic impairments often do not know how to engage in socially appropriate eye behavior. Research has found that children with autism spectrum disorders regular suffer from the inability to gain and keep eye contact (Carbone, O'Brien, Sweeney-Kerwin, & Albert, 2013). However, children suffering from a range of different impairments, like severe brain injuries, can also have problems with oculesic behaviors (Turkstra, 2005).

Posture and Gesture. For example, according to Nichelli and Venneri (1995) nonverbal learning disorder (NLD) is characterized by children who typically have good verbal skills but lack visuospatial skills. However, it is important to note that these skills typically stem from underlying brain functions according to Schoch et al. (2014). In another study by Kidd and Holler

(2009), the researchers found that there was a strong relationship between childhood linguistic understanding and gesturing. The study started by investigating 3-year olds who were more likely to use gestures to resolve lexical ambiguity than five year olds. Furthermore, research has shown that gestures are important for learning, understanding, and creating language (Goldin-Meadow & Alibali, 2013).

Touch and Interpersonal Distance. Children with social pragmatics impairments often have issues with both touch and interpersonal distance. Some children have various responses along the hypo or hyper-responsiveness continuum when they are touched by others. With some children, they have extreme negative reactions when they are not experiencing touch; whereas, other children will have extreme negative reactions to any kind of touch (Güçlü, Tanidir, Mukaddes, & Ünal, 2007). As for interpersonal distance, learning how to appropriately manage distance socially is an extremely important skill. Unfortunately, many children with social communicative impairments do not understand space, so it is very common for these children to violate another individual's personal space (Kennedy & Adolphs, 2014).

Vocal Quality. There is a range of research examining issues related to how paralinguistics impact social development. For example, research has shown that a child's ability to recognize emotional cues from vocalics is different between children with social pragmatics disorders and children with typical development (Sauter, 2013).

Facial Expression. Another common problem among children with nonverbal communicative impairments involves facial expressions. In fact, children with social pragmatics disorders often have trouble learning how to exhibit facial expressions (Gordon, Pierce, Bartlett, & Taaka, 2014) and how to interpret facial expressions (Tell, Davidson, & Camras, 2014).

Physical Appearance and Personal Habits. Not surprisingly, with all of the other troubles that children with nonverbal communication impairments can have, their physical appearance and personal habits can also deviate from those among children with typical development. For example, McClannahan, McGee, MacDuff, and Krantz (1990) note it is not uncommon for children with SCDs often need extra regulation and instruction with regards to both personal appearance and cleanliness habits.

Outcomes of Social (Pragmatic) Impairment

Relational. Social pragmatics is usually cited as a core challenge for individuals with language issues that occur in disorders such as autism spectrum disorder (ASD). Communication is a social act and communication within a social situation involves much more than understanding the words of others. In children with high functioning autism, there is no apparent disturbance in cognitive skills, nor are there clinically significant disturbances in expressive or receptive language functioning in standardized testing. It is only in the areas of social interaction that the disorder becomes evident. (Attwood, 2006; Green et al., 2000; Wing, 1981).

Peer. The diagnostic criteria that distinguish social pragmatic impairment disorder include impairments in nonverbal behaviors such as eye contact and body language to regulate social interaction, failure to develop peer relationships appropriate to developmental level, lack of spontaneous attempts to share interests with others, lack of social or emotional reciprocity, restricted repetitive or stereotyped patterns of behavior including inflexible adherence to routine and preoccupation or intense focus on singular topics of interest. Additionally, individuals with social pragmatic disorder often have difficulty establishing frames of reference outside themselves. These difficulties are discussed in the literature as disruptions in Theory of Mind (ToM). Children with SCD or autism spectrum disorders lack the ability to make sense of others' behaviors or accurately interpret their state of mind and thus often misinterpret other people's behavior or find behaviors confusing and unpredictable. This can occur when a person says one thing but his body language or facial expression lead typical listeners to derive another meaning from these subtle cues. The ToM difficulties make sense when interpreting the social and pragmatic difficulties that children with autism or SCD often demonstrate (Baron-Cohen, 2009) and these difficulties often lead to problems initiating and maintaining peer relationships.

Play skills in a child with SPD are often very creative physically but lack any social aspect. They have difficulty pretending because they find it difficult to put themselves in others situations. This inability often leads to the child performing inappropriate actions on different objects and an inability to relate socially with same age peers (Paul, 2005, 2007, 2009; Adams & Bishop, 1989).

Academic. Because children with SPD are known to have high levels of intelligence and IQ scores within normal limits, academic intelligence is often above grade level, however motivation for learning is often an issue and the input of one-to-one support for a child with SPD in a classroom setting may be needed even though the LRE (least restrictive environment) for these children is often a mainstream classroom. Children with social pragmatic disorders may become anxious during non-structured times and may need support and encouragement to initiate social networks. In academic subjects, though a child with SPD generally understands the concepts presented in the classroom, they often struggle with handwriting, creative stories, reading comprehension and spelling. This is in part due to their lack of general understanding about appropriate language and when to use it. Additionally difficulties may be related to developing the ability for abstract thinking. For example, because of their deficits with Theory of Mind, students may misinterpret a topic as they will tend to represent in an inappropriate way or in a way that interests them from their own perspective rather than the way for which it was intended (autism.org).

References

Adams, C. (2008). Intervention for children with pragmatic language impairments. In C. F. Norbury, J. B. Tomblin, & D. V. M. Bishop (Eds.), *Understanding developmental language disorders: From theory to practice* (pp. 189–204). New York: Psychology Press.

Adams, C., & Bishop, D. V. (1989). Conversational characteristics of children with semantic-pragmatic disorder. I: Exchange structure, turntaking, repairs and cohesion. *British Journal of Disorded Communication, 24*, 211–239. Doi 10.3109/13682 828909019889. PMID: 2627544.

American Psychiatric Association. (2013). Social (pragmatic) communication disorder. Diagnostic and Statistical Manual of Mental Disorders (DSM-5). Retrieved from: http://www.dsm5.org/Documents/Social%20Communication%20Disorder%20Fact%20Sheet.pdf

Attwood, T. (2006). *The complete guide to Asperger's syndrome*. London: Jessica Kingsley.

Baron-Cohen, S. (2009). Autism: The empathizing-systemizing (E-S) theory. *Annals of New York Academy of Sciences, 1156*, 68–80. Doi 10.1111/j.1749-6632.2009. 04467.x. PMID: 19338503.

Baron-Cohen, S., Leslie, A. M., & Frith, U. (1985). Does the autistic child have a 'theory of mind'? *Cognition, 21*(1), 37–46.

Bat-Chava, Y. L., Martin, D., & Imperatore, L. (2014). Long-term improvements in oral communication skills and quality of peer relations in children with cochlear implants: Parental testimony. *Child: Care, Health & Development, 40*, 870–881.

Bishop, D. V., & Norbury, C. F. (2002). Exploring the borderlands of autistic disorder and specific language impairment: A study using standardized diagnostic instruments. *Journal of Child Psychology, Psychiatry and Allied Disciplines, 43*(7), 917–929.

Bloom, L., & Lahey, M. (1978). *Language development and language disorders*. New York: Wiley.

Canale, M., & Swain, M. (1980). Theoretical bases of communicative approaches to second language teaching and testing. *Applied Linguistics, 1*, 1–47.

Carbone, V. J., O'Brien, L., Sweeney-Kerwin, E. J., & Albert, K. M. (2013). Teaching eye contact to children with autism: A conceptual analysis and single case study. *Education & Treatment of Children, 36*, 139–159.

Christensen-Sandfort, R. B., & Whinnery, S. B. (2013). Impact of milieu teaching on communication skills of young children with autism spectrum disorder. *Topics in Early Childhood Special Education, 32,* 211–222.

Dale, N. J., Tadić, V., & Sonksen, P. (2014). Social communicative variation in 1–3-year-olds with severe visual impairment. *Child: Care, Health & Development, 40,* 158–164.

Drake, M. E. (2015). Social (Pragmatic) Communication Disorder DSM-5 315.39 (F80.89) – Retrieved from *Therapedia* http://www.theravive.com/therapedia/ Social-(Pragmatic)-Communication-Disorder-DSM--5-315.39-(F80.89) May 4, 2015.

Eriks-Brophy, A. J., Durieux-Smith, A., Olds, J., Fitzpatrick, E. M., Duquette, C., & Wittingham, J. (2012). Communication, academic, and social skills of young adults with hearing loss. *Volta Review, 112,* 5–35.

Goldin-Meadow, S. W., & Alibali, M. W. (2013). Gesture's role in speaking, learning, and creating language. *Annual Review of Psychology, 64,* 257–283.

Gordon, I., Pierce, M., Bartlett, M., & Taaka, J. (2014). Training facial expression production in children on the autism spectrum. *Journal of Autism & Developmental Disorders, 44,* 2486–2498.

Green, J., Gilchrist, A., Burton, D., & Cox, A. (2000). Social and psychiatric functioning in adolescents with Asperger syndrome. *Journal of Autism and Developmental Disorders, 30,* 279–293.

Greenberg, M. T. (1980). Social interaction between deaf preschoolers and their mothers: The effects of communication method and communication competence. *Developmental Psychology, 16,* 465–474. doi:10.1037/0012-1649.16.5.465.

Güçlü, B., Tanidir, C., Mukaddes, N. M., & Ünal, F. (2007). Tactile sensitivity of normal and autistic children. *Somatosensory & Motor Research, 24*(1/2), 21–33.

Han, H. S., & Kemple, K. M. (2006). Components of social competence and strategies of support: Considering what to teach and how. *Early Childhood Education Journal, 34,* 241–246.

Hatamizadeh, N. A., Ghasemi, M., Saeedi, A., & Kazemnejad, A. (2008). Perceived competence and school adjustment of hearing impaired children in mainstream primary school settings. *Child: Care, Health & Development, 34,* 789–794.

Hymes, D. (1972). Models of the interaction of language and social life. In J. J. Gumperz & D. Hymes (Eds.), *Directions in sociolinguistics: The ethnography of communication.* New York: Holt, Rinehart & Winston.

Kennedy, D. P., & Adolphs, R. (2014). Violations of personal space by individuals with autism spectrum disorder. *Plos ONE, 9*(8), 1–10. doi:10.1371/journal.pone.0103369.

Kidd, E. J., & Holler, J. (2009). Children's use of gesture to resolve lexical ambiguity. *Developmental Science, 12,* 903–913.

Klin, A. C., Saulnier, C. A., Sparrow, S. S., Cicchetti, D. V., Volkmar, F. R., & Lord, C. (2007). Social and communication abilities and disabilities in higher functioning individuals with autism spectrum disorders: The Vineland and the ADOS. *Journal of Autism & Developmental Disorders, 37,* 748–759.

Love, E. B., Nowicki, S., Jr., Duke, M. P. (1994). The Emory Dyssemia Index: A brief screening instrument for identification of nonverbal language deficits in elementary school children. *The Journal of Psychology, 128,* 703–705.

McClannahan, L. E., McGee, G. G., MacDuff, G. S., & Krantz, P. J. (1990). Assessing and improving child care: A personal appearance index for children with autism. *Journal of Applied Behavior Analysis, 23,* 469–482.

McCroskey, J. C. (1982). Communication competence and performance: A research and pedagogical perspective. *Communication Education, 31,* 1–7.

McCroskey, J. C., Andersen, J. F., Richmond, V. P., & Wheeless, L. R. (1981). Communication apprehension of elementary and secondary students and teachers. *Communication Education, 30,* 122–132.

McKay-Semmler, K., & Kim, Y. Y. (2014). Cross-cultural adaptation of Hispanic youth: A study of communication patterns, functional fitness, and psychological health. *Communication Monographs, 81,* 133–156. doi:10.1080/03637751.2013.870346.

Nichelli, P., & Venneri, A. (1995). Right hemisphere developmental learning disability: A case study. *Neurocase, 1,* 173–177. doi:10.1080/13554799508402360.

Nowicki, S., & Duke, M. (1992). *Helping the child who doesn't fit In.* Atlanta, GA: Peachtree Publishers.

Nowicki, S., & Duke, M. (2002). *Will I ever fit in? The breakthrough program for conquering adult dyssemia.* Riverside, NJ: Free Press, Simon & Schuster.

Owens, R. (2008). *Language development: An introduction.* Boston: Allyn & Bacon.

Paul, R. (2005). Assessing communication in autism spectrum disorders. In F. Volkmar, R. Paul, A. Klin, & D. Cohen (Eds.), *Handbook of autism and pervasive developmental disorders* (Vol. 2m, pp. 799–816). Hoboken, NJ: John Wiley and Sons.

Paul, R. (2007). *Language disorders from infancy through adolescence: Assessment and intervention.* St. Louis, MO: Mosby/Elsevier.

Paul, R. (2009). *Social skills development in school-age children with high-functioning autism spectrum disorders.* Rockville, MD: American Speech Language Hearing Association.

Rapin, I., & Allen, D. (1983). Developmental language disorders: Nosologic considerations. In U. Kirk (Ed.), *Neuropsychology of language, reading and spelling* (pp. 155–184). San Diego: Academic Press.

Reichow, B., & Volkmar, F. R. (2010). Social skills intervention for individuals with autism: Evaluation for evidence-based practices within a Best Evidence Synthesis framework. *Journal of Autism & Other Developmental Disorders, 40,* 149–166.

Sauter, D. F. (2013). Children's recognition of emotions from vocal cues. *British Journal of Developmental Psychology, 31,* 97–113.

Schoch, K. V., Harrell, W., Hooper, S. R., Ip, E. H., Saldana, S., Kwapil, T. R., & Shashi, V. (2014). Applicability of the nonverbal learning disability paradigm for children with 22q11.2 Deletion Syndrome. *Journal of Learning Disabilities, 47,* 153–166.

Schrodt, P., Ledbetter, A. M., Jernberg, K. A., Larson, L., Brown, N., & Glonek, K. (2009). Family communication patterns as mediators of communication competence in the parent-child relationship. *Journal of Social & Personal Relationships, 26*(6/7), 853–874. doi:10.1177/0265407509345649.

Sebastian, C. T., Blakemore, S. J., & Charman, T. (2009). Reactions to ostracism in adolescents with autism spectrum conditions. *Journal of Autism & Developmental Disorders, 39*, 1122–1130.

Tell, D., Davidson, D., & Camras, L. A. (2014). Recognition of emotion from facial expressions with direct or averted eye gaze and varying expression intensities in children with autism disorder and typically developing children. *Autism Research and Treatment, 2014*, 1–11. doi.10.1155/2014/816137.

Teven, J. J., Richmond, V. P., McCroskey, J. C., & McCroskey, L. L. (2010). Updating relationships between communication traits and communication competence. *Communication Research Reports, 27*, 263–270. doi:10.1080/08824096.2010.496331.

Toe, D. M., & Paatsch, L. E. (2013). The conversational skills of school-aged children with cochlear implants. *Cochlear Implants International, 14*, 67–79. doi:10.1179/1754762812Y.0000000002.

Tony Attwood: http://www.tonyattwood.com.au/

Turkstra, L. S. (2005). Looking while listening and speaking: Eye-to-face gaze in adolescents with and without traumatic brain injury. *Journal of Speech, Language & Hearing Research, 48*, 1429–1441. doi:10.1044/1092-4388(2005/099).

Vicker, B. (2009a). Meeting the challenge of social pragmatics with students on the autism spectrum. *The Reporter*, 14(2), 11–17.

Vicker, B. (2009b). *Social communication and language characteristics associated with high functioning, verbal children and adults with autism spectrum disorder.* Bloomington, IN: Indiana Resource Center for Autism.

Wing, L. (1981). Asperger's Syndrome: A clinical account. *Psychological Medicine*, 11, 115–129.

15. At the Crossroads of Prevention

Promoting Children's and Adolescents' Health

MICHELLE MILLER-DAY
Chapman University

> While humans have the propensity to develop a suite of prosocial behaviors, they are also capable of developing antisocial behavior, engaging in substance abuse, experiencing depression, and bearing children at an early age. ... Young people who develop aggressive behavior tendencies are likely to develop problems with tobacco, alcohol, and other drug use; to fail academically; to have children at an early age; and to raise children likely to have the same problems. (p. 17).
>
> —Anthony Biglan (2015)

What if there was a way to prevent drug abuse, bullying, depression and suicide among children and teens? There is a host of research indicating that nurturing prosocial behavior in children and promoting nurturing communication in families is key to preventing these problems (see for example, Chiapa, Morris, Véronneau, & Dishion, 2016; Dishion & McMahon, 1998). In the early 1960s U.S. President, John F. Kennedy, espoused the promotion of healthy youth as the foundation for a healthy future for the United States. But the science of that time had not yet caught up with its optimism. In the 21st century, we now have effective tools to prevent these problem behaviors and promote children's healthy behaviors to help them lead safe and productive lives. In 2015, President Obama signed into law the *Every Student Succeeds Act* (ESSA) calling on educational environments to help to prevent problem behaviors such as bullying and substance use by instituting behavioral interventions that "develop relationship-building skills, such as effective communication." Communication is at the center of many of the behavioral interventions being developed to prevent problem behaviors and an increasing number of communication scholars are getting involved in translating communication research and theory into prevention practices that work. As one of those scholars, I continue to ask myself, "What are some avenues available for communication research to merge with prevention science to produce evidence-based prevention efforts that benefit children?" This chapter attempts to answer that question by providing an introduction to prevention science and then discussing two promising research avenues that intersect at the crossroads of prevention and communication: social emotional learning and parent-child connectedness.

Prevention Science

What Is Prevention Science?

In the past twenty years in the United States, there has been a shift in focus from a largely treatment/recovery orientation to one which prioritizes prevention. A fundamental tenet of public health is that it is always preferable to prevent a problem from occurring than it is to address the effects of a condition once it has developed (Fallon & Zgodzinski, 2005). Prevention is the act of stopping something from happening or arising and *prevention science* and is devoted to the scientific study of the theories, research, and practices related to the prevention of social, physical, mental health, and behavioral problems and draws from a variety of disciplines, including communication, biology, psychology, human development and a variety of physical and social sciences (Robertson et al., 2015).

Prevention includes a wide range of interventions aimed at reducing risks or threats to health. Prevention interventions often focus on reducing risk factors that increase a person's vulnerability to a disorder (e.g., early aggressive behavior) and enhancing protective factors that promote one's ability to successfully cope with life situations and change (e.g., stress management skills), enhance individual's capacity for resilience, and serve to buffer the effects of risks on health outcomes. The National Research Council and Institute of Medicine (NRC) (2004) outlined three categories of prevention interventions based on risk: universal, selective, and indicated interventions. *Universal* prevention interventions are those that are targeted to a general population, without regard to risk levels of the individuals included. General health promotion is often included in this category, aimed at disseminating information about healthy behaviors and enhancing social and emotional competencies of students, such as the ability to handle adverse social situations (e.g., a school-based bullying prevention program that each child in the school receives). *Selective interventions* are provided to a specific at-risk group because of factors that increase their vulnerability to a negative outcome (e.g., a program targeting children from households with intimate partner violence). Finally, *indicated* prevention efforts are for individuals exhibiting problems or early symptoms of a disorder (e.g., a therapeutic intervention for youth with early substance use or aggressive behavior).

Epidemiology, Etiology, and the Translation of Science into Prevention Interventions

According to the World Health Organization (WHO) (2000), improving population health requires the implementation of an integrated set of evidence-based prevention interventions to affect health outcomes and an understanding of epidemiological data. Universal, selective, and indicated prevention intervention development and evaluation that is based on sound epidemiological data is central to prevention science and is at the center of the mission of the U.S. National Institutes of Health (Robertson et al., 2015). *Epidemiology* is the study and analysis of the patterns, causes, and effects of health conditions in defined populations (Porta, Greenland, Hernán, dos Santos Silva, & Last, 2014) and it is the foundation of public health, providing the keys to understanding risk and protective factors underlying health-risk disorders and mapping trajectories of these disorders (Anthony, 2010). There has been an increased worldwide focus on the epidemiology of health issues that affect children, recognizing children for who they are today as well as for their future roles in creating families, powering the workforce, and the future of humanity. This creates an important ethical, social, and economic imperative to ensure that all children are as healthy as they can be. Healthy children are more likely to become healthy adults (NRC, 2012). *Etiology* is a focus within epidemiology involving the study of causation, that is investigating causal factors of a disorder on a variety of levels such as individual, interpersonal, and environmental factors (Scheier, 2010). When considering a specific disorder such as adolescent drug abuse, etiology might identify possible causes of abuse and how a confluence of individual, social, and environmental factors interact to predict adolescent risk; whereas, the epidemiology of substance abuse takes a much wider view of substance use in a given population and studied over time. Etiological analyses have provided many of the key concepts important for understanding what kinds of interventions to develop and what outcomes are desirable in these interventions (Scheier, 2010).

The movement from conducting basic science, epidemiological, and etiologic research to the development and evaluation of *prevention interventions* is a principal function of prevention science. This process of applying scientific knowledge to the development of interventions that serve to improve human health and well-being is referred to as *translational research*. Translational research is a multi-phase process by which research-generated knowledge directly or indirectly serves the general public. There is Type 1 translation that applies discoveries generated through basic research to the development and preliminary testing of services, programs, practices and products. According to Wethington and Dunifon (2012), there is also Type 2 translation, which is aimed at enhancing the adoption, implementation and sustainability of evidence-based or scientifically-validated interventions by service systems (e.g., health care settings, community-based organizations, schools). In the field of communication, my colleagues and I have argued that 21st century scholars are obligated to find ways to bring our scientific knowledge to those who can make use of it and apply that knowledge to developing programs for those in need (Hecht & Miller-Day, 2007, 2010; Miller-Day, 2008; Petronio, 2007). There is a rich history of theory and research in the communication field that can be incorporated into the development of new interventions or enhancing existing interventions.

Once interventions are developed, their impact on targeted outcomes needs to be assessed. This evaluation and testing component is also a key component of translational research efforts. Interventions may be evaluated in a number of ways, including efficacy and effectiveness trials. Efficacy trials are defined as the assessment of an intervention's performance under ideal and controlled circumstances; whereas, effectiveness trials assess performance under 'real-world' conditions (Singal, Higgins, & Waljee, 2014). Studies of program efficacy employ methodologically sound research designs (e.g., a randomized controlled trial or quasi-experimental design) to test the impact of the intervention and its potential to transfer to real-world settings (Robertson et al., 2015). Once efficacy is established then the dissemination and implementation of the prevention intervention to the public may be warranted. Implementing prevention interventions in real-world settings introduces a variety of factors that could impact the effectiveness of the program such as the unpredictability of program settings, implementation fidelity, and other contingencies. Therefore, effectiveness trials are necessary to assess how efficacious the program is under real-world conditions and outside of controlled research conditions. Effectiveness studies often assess factors such as implementer training, fidelity of delivery, adaptations being made to the program, participant engagement, recruitment and retention of participants, and sustainability of the program. Effectiveness studies are also needed to identify what components of the program are "core" to attaining the desired effects and under what circumstances is the program most effective.

Contexts for Child and Adolescent Prevention Interventions

Child and adolescent health prevention interventions can occur in a variety of contexts and be focused on a number of target populations. Some of the most common contexts for youth interventions are family-based interventions, school-based interventions, web-based (or technology-assisted) interventions, and community-based interventions. Targets of these interventions could be any or a combination of the child or adolescent, his or her parent(s), educators, siblings or other family members, the entire family system, or others.

Family-based interventions. Family-based interventions have been developed to prevent a number of health issues such as substance use, pediatric obesity, delinquency, teenage pregnancy, and depression and suicide. These programs often include parent and/or youth training and education (e.g., on child development, communication, nutrition, stress management), counseling, dyadic or whole family activities, and may include home visits. Programs involving infants, toddlers, and young children tend to be selective programs targeted to populations at high risk (e.g., teen mothers, families living in poverty). Family-based interventions for school-aged children also tend to be indicated, targeting youth who are exhibiting behaviors that place them at risk (e.g., aggressive behavior) and trigger intervention. Referrals from schools and pediatricians most often prompt implementation of these programs, yet there are some programs that parents seek out. Other programs provide selective intervention for youth who might be in a high risk category (e.g., low socioeconomic status families). One exemplary program developed to target both a selective group of families and also a universal intervention is the Strengthening Families Program (SFP). SFP is an internationally-recognized parenting and family strengthening program targeted at high-risk and general population families. The program improves parenting skills and family relationships, reducing rates of child maltreatment, problem behaviors, delinquency and alcohol and drug abuse in children. This program also increases children's social competencies and school performance, and strengthens parent-child bonds. The original 14-session SFP targeted high-risk families with children ages-6 to 11 years (Kumpfer, DeMarsh, & Child, 1989). Culturally adapted versions and the core version of SFP have been found effective with African-American, Hispanic, Asian, Pacific Islander, and First Nations families. SFP is in 36 countries (Kumpfer, Magalhães, & Xie, 2012; Kumpfer, Pinyuchon, de Melo, & Whiteside, 2008). SFP for ages 10–14 is a seven-session universal intervention that includes activities and information that are targeted for the youth, the parent, the dyad, and the entire family (Spoth, Redmond, Mason, Schainker, & Borduin, 2015). It also includes four booster sessions one year after completing the program in order to reinforce key messages of the intervention. In order to make SFP skills available to every family, in 2011 a new low-cost SFP Home-Use DVD for ages 7–17 was developed for parents and children to watch together at home (Kumpfer, Magalhães, Whiteside, & Xie, 2015). This includes ten 30-minute SFP lessons and handouts that can be printed off the disc. Participating in the program using the DVD opened up opportunities for self-paced implementation, or implementation by a counselor or family coach (Kumpfer, 2012).

School-based interventions. Youth's behavior problems such as conduct disorders, bullying, and substance use interfere with academic success and create difficult situations for educators and other children within classrooms. Historically, schools have reacted to problem behaviors with punishments and consequences, but more recently educators see the need to prevent problem behaviors by using prevention interventions (Wilson, Gottfredson, & Najaka, 2001). Nearly all children attend schools that promote cognitive as well as social and emotional development (Robertson et al., 2015). These programs are implemented in school settings often employ scaffolding instructional techniques to move students progressively toward a goal across different developmental periods.

Prevention interventions in elementary schools often enhance teacher skill in behavioral management and reduce negative classroom behaviors (Kellam et al., 2014). Effective behavioral management promotes rewards for active learning, enhances student bonding with school, and enhance academic achievement (Iolanga, Poduska, Werthamer & Kellam, 2001). The *Incredible Years* program (Webster-Stratton, 2015) includes a s school-based intervention implemented in classroom settings to decrease disruptive behaviors, promote youth resilience, provides teacher incentives to address student's behavioral issues, and enhances positive teacher-student relationships (Boxmeyer, Lochman, Powell, & Powe, 2015). Another approach to prevention interventions that are key to preventing problem behaviors, especially in childhood, is social and emotional learning (SEL) (Collaborative for Academic, Social, and Emotional Learning (CASEL), 2015; Durlak, Domitrovich, Weissberg, & Gullotta, 2015). SEL is the process through which individuals (across the lifespan) "acquire and effectively apply the knowledge, attitudes, and skills necessary to understand and manage emotions, set and achieve positive goals, feel and show empathy for others, establish and maintain positive relationships, and make responsible decisions" (CASEL, 2015, p.1). The social and emotional competencies developed through SEL provide a foundation for future social development and reduce youth's vulnerability to risk (Durlak et al., 2015).

As youth matriculate into middle school they are at increased risk for a number of problem behaviors. The onset of problem behaviors, such as experimentation and onset of alcohol and other substance use, in early adolescence places youth at increased risk for more serious problems later in life. For example, in a nationwide survey of more than 43,000 adults, findings revealed that—relative to respondents who began drinking at 21 years or older—those who began drinking before the age of 14 were more likely to experience alcohol dependence within 10 years of first drinking (Hingson, Heeren, & Winter, 2006). Thus, prevention interventions in later childhood and early adolescence are essential within the public health prevention framework (Scheir, 2014). Longitudinal efficacy evaluation studies have had a number of impacts including reducing adolescent substance use (Tobler et al., 2000), decreasing adolescent sexual activity and pregnancies (DiCenso,, Guyatt, Willan, & Griffith, 2002), and reducing incidents of bullying (Olweus, 1993). Some programs targeting this developmental period are employed school-wide providing a "combination of schoolwide rules and sanctions, teacher training, classroom curriculum, conflict resolution training, and individual counseling" (Vreeman & Carroll, 2007) but most are classroom-based programs providing teacher training to implement a classroom curriculum.

One approach common in interventions for early adolescents is social resistance skill development. Refusal skills programs have been very effective at delaying the initiation of substance use (Griffin, Botvin, Nichols, & Doyle, 2003) and also decreasing adolescent sexual activity (Norris et al., 2014). Keepin it REAL (kiR) is social resistance skill development prevention intervention developed by communication scholars to move beyond the "just say no" approach to resisting offers of alcohol and other drugs (Hecht & Miller-Day, 2010; Miller-Day & Hecht, 2013). Initially motivated by an interest in the social processes of drug offers, a series of investigations revealed a conceptual model for the development of a communication-based drug prevention program. Guided by narrative theory as an approach to health message design and communication theory of identity, this program takes a "from kids, through kids, to kids" approach. The program prevents adolescent substance use by enhancing narrative knowledge, providing resistance skill training, enhancing communication competence, decision-making skills, risk assessment skills, and increasing awareness of social support and realistic norms surrounding adolescent substance use. The "from kids" phase of intervention development was guided by narrative theory (Fisher, 1989; Miller-Day & Hecht, 2013) and the communication theory of identity (Hecht, 1993). Narratives collected from target age youth were collected to provide descriptive data about the social experience of drug offers, refusals, and acceptance such as how offers are made, by whom and to whom, settings of offers, decision-making processes, youth identities and competencies that are involved in successful resistance. An analysis of these narratives revealed core experiences that served as a roadmap for directing prevention efforts. The "R.E.A.L." in *keepin' it REAL* stands for the four refusal strategies that emerged in student narratives: refuse, explain, avoid, and leave. The "to kids" phase of intervention involves providing the findings from the narratives (e.g., commonalities across offers, offerers, refusal strategies, settings, etc.), along with exemplar narratives from the transcripts to high school students to develop five 5-minute videos presenting the narratives and providing opportunities for the youth audience ("to kids") to model effective behaviors. The videos in all versions of the program (multicultural urban, rural, suburban, international Spanish) include an introductory overview, and a refuse, explain, avoid, and leave video. keepin' it REAL (kiR) has been proven effective for reducing drug use and establishing anti-drug attitudes and beliefs (Hecht et al., 2003; Hecht, Graham, & Elek, 2006; Warren et al., 2006). The kiR program is a curriculum taught through ten 45-minute interactive lessons by trained providers over 10 weeks, with booster sessions delivered in the following school year. kiR is identified as Substance Abuse and Mental Health Services Administration's (SAMHSA) National Registry for Evidence-Based Programs (NREPP) Model Program and the National Dropout Prevention Center Model Program. A cost effectiveness analysis suggests the kiR is among the most cost-effective programs available (Miller & Hendrie, 2008). kiR has also been adapted in recent years to be delivered by D.A.R.E., an organization that delivers prevention interventions to more than 2 million youth worldwide (D.A.R.E., 2014).

During high school, universal school prevention efforts often decrease due to challenges in scheduling and integrating such efforts into high school daily schedules. Therefore, many prevention efforts are whole-school interventions (e.g., red ribbon day). There are, however, classroom-based prevention interventions for high school youth that build on SEL principles such as effective decision making and also promote critical thinking. Media literacy programs are well-suited for high school implementation because they often require higher order analytic skills. Media literacy is defined as the ability to access, analyze, evaluate and create messages in a wide variety of media while recognizing the role and influence of media in society (Hobbs, 2004). These interventions frequently include discussion of persuasive media strategies and analysis of sample persuasive media messages to help adolescents become more aware of the socially constructed nature of messages and message design (Greene et al., 2015; Hobbs, 2004). Banerjee and Greene are both communication scholars whose work in media literacy has led to the development of REAL Media, a media literacy prevention intervention that is engaging, provides opportunities for message analysis, critical reflection, and practice in message design. There are two delivery modalities for this program. One is a classroom-based program delivered by trained teachers (Banerjee & Greene, 2007) and the other is a mobile learning program that students can complete either independently or in a web-assisted format, where a teacher can facilitate the administration of the program (Greene, Banerjee, Ray, & Hecht, in press). The ubiquitous nature of communicating using mobile devices has opened a new avenue for communicating prevention messages and Greene and her colleagues are forging new ground in the field of communication in the development of this program. REAL Media has also been adopted by D.A.R.E. for international dissemination.

Community-based interventions. At the community level, prevention interventions typically involve either strategic media communication strategies or coalitions who enlist community members to mobilize prevention efforts. Media strategies can be successful in prevention as well as reducing prevalence of certain behaviors "as long as they are theoretically derived, well executed, and based on sound scientific principles" (Robertson et al., 2015, p. 20) and attention to the messages that comprise the intervention (Harrington, Helme, & Noar, 2015). There are a number of communication scholars who have developed media campaigns to target problem behaviors include and health and risk communication programs around the U.S. are educating students on effective program development and message design. Communication researchers from the University of Kentucky were two of the first communication scholars to intersect with prevention science with their research on media interventions targeting high sensation seeking youth (see for example, Lorch et al., 1994; Palmgreen et al., 1995). These researchers developed public service announcements (PSAs) and other media in their health communication campaigns to prevent adolescent substance use. This work has made important contributions to understanding media messages, persuasion, message effects and prevention. Harrington et al. (2015) point out that prevention messages do not operate in a vacuum and are competing with a wide array of competing messages, especially with the flood of messages on social media. Yet, these health promotion and risk reduction messages can have considerable impact.

Community efforts sometimes include lobbying for, implementing, or enforcing policies to address the problem (e.g., underage drinking, HIV infection) and frequently employ community-based participatory research efforts and community coalitions. Community-based participatory research is a partnership approach to research and prevention that involves community members, organizational representatives, and researchers in all aspects of the research and the development of prevention efforts (Israel et al., 2008). The community coalitions that develop as a part of this process plan, implement, and oversee prevention activities to ensure that efforts are supported by and coordinated within the community (Fagan & Hawkins, 2015). The Communities that Care program is one example of this kind of intervention. Communities that Care (CTC) efforts begin with assessing the prevention needs of the community, forming coalitions around those needs, selecting and implementing the best evidence-based interventions, and assisting in the evaluations of those interventions. Strengths of this program are that it uses user friendly materials that translate scientific knowledge for the everyday user and is focused on selecting interventions that meet specific community needs (Fagan et al., 2015). Within the field of communication there are a number of scholar-activists that work within communities to promote change, such as Dutta and colleagues' work in the area of health care inequalities (Dutta, Anaele, & Jones, 2013); however, there are very few that are working at the intersection of prevention science and communication for the benefit of children.

At the Crossroads of Communication and Prevention: Promising Directions

The question I posed at the beginning of this chapter asked "What are some avenues available for communication research to merge with prevention science to produce evidence-based prevention efforts that benefit children?" I believe there are two promising research avenues that intersect at the crossroads of prevention and communication: promoting social and emotional learning and parent-child connectedness.

Social and Emotional Learning

Historically, the field of communication has not been highly responsive to investigating issues that directly benefit children. Miller-Day, Pezalla, and Chesnut (2013) discovered that fewer than 4% of the publications in major communication journals involved children or addressed children as communicators. Indeed, children have occupied a marginal status in the field of human communication studies. This is fortunately changing as evidenced by this current volume and other work such as Socha and Yingling (2010) and Socha and Stamp (2009). I contend that the development of children as communicators should be central to communication studies because children are active communicators in the web of human relationships, but also —as evidenced by the earlier discussion of prevention science—children's communication competence and the ability to communicatively construct positive relationships with parents, teachers, and peers serve as key protective functions in healthy child development and are central to social and emotional learning.

The past 20 years have witnessed an explosion of interest in Social and Emotional Learning (SEL) (Durlak et al., 2015) and communication competencies are at the center of this process. Intrapersonally, SEL involves application of knowledge and skills to regulate oneself and ones emotions, understand ones role in interpreting verbal and nonverbal messages, and make decisions, and interpersonally, to communicate effectively, express empathy for others and maintain positive relationships (Baverian et al., 2016). These social and emotional skills are critical to being a good student, citizen, and worker, and many risky behaviors (e.g., drug use, violence, bullying, and dropping out) can be prevented or reduced when multiyear, integrated efforts are used to develop students' social and emotional skills (Durlak et al., 2015).

Previously, approaches to prevention focused on more proximal potential causes to problem behaviors (e.g., peer pressure), but current approaches recognize that more distal skills (e.g., communication competence) may affect a wide range of behaviors, including those that are likely to promote or compromise physical health and well-being. The social competency approach suggests that youth with poor personal and social skills are not only more susceptible to influences that promote problem behaviors such as drug use, but also are motivated to participate in risky behaviors as an alternative to healthier coping strategies (Botvin, 2000). Competence enhancement approaches such as SEL emphasize teaching social competence that includes decision-making skills, interpersonal communication skills, assertiveness skills, and skills for coping with anxiety and anger. This approach is situated squarely within the realm of communication studies.

CASEL (Collaborative for Academic, Social, and Emotional Learning, see https://casel.org) is a worldwide leader in advancing SEL science, evidence-based practice, and policy. According to CASEL's (2015) guide to effective social and emotional learning programs, effective SEL programming should begin in preschool and continue through high school addressing five interrelated sets of cognitive, affective, and behavioral competencies. The five competency clusters are (CASEL, 2015, pp. 5–6):

Self-awareness: The ability to accurately recognize one's emotions and thoughts and their influence on behavior.

Self-management: The ability to regulate one's emotions, thoughts, and behaviors effectively in different situations. This includes managing stress, controlling impulses, motivating oneself, and setting and working toward achieving personal and academic goals.

Social awareness: The ability to take the perspective of and empathize with others from diverse backgrounds and cultures, to understand social and ethical norms for behavior, and to recognize family, school, and community resources and supports.

Relationship skills: The ability to establish and maintain healthy and rewarding relationships with diverse individuals and groups. This includes communicating clearly, listening actively, cooperating, resisting inappropriate social pressure, negotiating conflict constructively, and seeking and offering help when needed.

Responsible decision-making: The ability to make constructive and respectful choices about personal behavior and social interactions based on consideration of ethical standards, safety concerns, social norms, the realistic evaluation of consequences of various actions, and the well-being of self and others.

The five CASEL competencies reflect intrapersonal and interpersonal domains (National Research Council, 2012). Self-awareness and self-management are consistent with the intrapersonal domain whereas social awareness and relationship skills represent dimensions within the interpersonal domain. Responsible decision-making is both an individual and social process and therefore represents both domains.

Research reviews have appeared documenting the value of SEL programs (Durlak, Weissberg, Dymnicki, Taylor, & Schellinger, 2011). Families, schools, and communities are increasingly recognizing the importance of promoting the social and emotional competence of youth in order to prevent problem behaviors and promote healthy development (Bridgeland, Bruce, & Hariharan, 2013; Merrell & Gueldner, 2010) and SEL is integrated into many existing evidence-based prevention programs. The CASEL competency clusters are especially relevant during adolescence because youth at this stage are going through rapid physical, emotional, and cognitive changes, adolescents engage in more risky behavior than younger students, and face a variety of challenging situations, including increased independence, peer pressure, and exposure to social media (CASEL, 2015). Longitudinal studies have shown that increased social and emotional competence is related to reductions in a variety of problem behaviors including aggression, delinquency, substance use, and dropout (Durlak et al., 2015; Merrell & Gueldner, 2010). But, when we look at the developers and implementers of these programs, very few are involved in the field of communication studies. Prevention efforts guided by communication theory and constructs could make an important difference in the direction of developing effective SEL interventions. Interpersonal theories in particular, but also intercultural and family communication theories could contribute to theory building in prevention science and testing communication theory in SEL contexts.

Parent-Child Connectedness

Research has found that adolescents' perceptions of how connected they felt to parents, difficulty talking to their parents about problems, and the quality of parent-child communication is associated with compromised behavioral and emotional health (Bowlby, 1998; Biglan, 2015; Scheier & Hansen, 2014). In one study of 4746 high school students, one fourth of students felt unable to talk to their mother about their problems, and over half of girls and one third of boys felt unable to talk to their father (Ackard,, Neumark-Sztainer, Story, & Perry, 2006). These perceptions of disconnection from parents were associated with a number of poor outcomes such as unhealthy weight control, substance use, suicide attempts, body dissatisfaction, and depression (Ackard et al., 2006). Parents often assume that their role and influence diminishes as their children grow and form stronger bonds with peers. However, there is growing evidence that parents matter a great deal to their children.

There is compelling evidence from prevention science and public health that the condition of "parent-child connectedness" (PCC) serves as an important protective factor for a variety of adolescent health outcomes, including the prevention of delinquency, substance use, adolescent pregnancy, STIs, and HIV (Lezin, Rolleri, Bean, & Taylor, 2004; Scheier & Hansen, 2014). PCC has emerged in recent research as a compelling "super-protector" that may reduce children's vulnerability to the challenges and risks facing them in today's world (Lezin et al., 2004). An extensive review of over 600 publications on parent child relationships across a variety of disciplines identified PCC as a composite construct comprised of eight different components including attachment/bonding, warmth/caring, cohesion, support/involvement, communication, monitoring/behavioral control, autonomy granting, and parental characteristics (Lezin et al., 2004). Although communication is listed as a separate component, those of us in the field of communication are aware that communication processes facilitate all of the other components except parental characteristics. Lezin et al. (2004) argued that although knowledge of these different components offers many clues about how PCC works, there is a lack of theory or models explaining how PCC's various elements interact to protect children and they argue that few interventions currently exist that build on existing research and models to promote PCC in a tailored and effective way.

PCC is bidirectional, conceptualizing parents and children not just as individuals but as active players in an ongoing relationship influencing each other and receiving influence. Lezin et al (2004) indicate that PCC "is characterized by the quality of the emotional bond between parent and child and by the degree to which this bond is both mutual and sustained over time … [characterized by] mutual attachment, resilience, support, and optimism … giving both parents and children a day-to-day life relatively free of conflict and animosity, while buffering them from many kinds of adversity" (pg. 6–7). The eight different components of PCC revealed by the extensive literature review can serve as both risk and protective factor for youth. For example in the "communication" component, the review identified eight possible risk/protective factors. Parental intrusiveness (parent interrupts, dominating child's conversation) was identified as a risk factor while frequency of discussions was both a risk and protective factor. This makes sense when thinking about risk. For example, consider parent-child discussions about alcohol use where the underage child has been caught drinking alcohol. The parent might frequently bring up the topic, discussing it frequently, and dominate the conversations, interrupting the child frequently. The remaining six factors were determined to be protective factors, protecting or buffering youth against risk: use of explanation and reasoning, spending time talking together, sharing thoughts and feelings, clarity of messages about risk behaviors and values, child's comfort with discussing problems with parents, and openness was listed together with listening as the final protective factor. These protective factors are important in prevention science because interventions are designed to enhance protective factors to protect youth from risk. As with SEL, communication scholars and family communication scholars in particular are positioned to enter in the prevention conversation surrounding PCC. The communication field has a wealth of theoretical and empirical knowledge that could move the understanding of PCC and its role in prevention forward.

Going Down the Road Less Traveled

If the goal of the 21st century communication social scientist is to translate research findings into programs that can benefit society (Petronio, 2007), I believe the field of communication is poised to make a difference in the lives of children, adolescents, and families by following this path. Communication scholars have the tools to translate their research into programs for children and youth, but this may require partnerships with colleagues in prevention science. The Society for Prevention research has both national and international meetings and serves as a network to connect scholars from a variety of disciplines who have a commitment to prevention. Building partnerships with other scholars is one step in the process, but another step is to create alliances and build relationships with community organizations who might collaborate on the development of prevention interventions. Moreover, even the most effective prevention interventions will have little impact if not accessible or effectively delivered. Once programs are developed, tested for efficacy and then effectiveness, dissemination of communication programs is the next step in the process. Partnerships are central to this dissemination process. The partners should be able to work with you to make your program accessible to the target audience, conduct ongoing checks to make sure the program is delivered with fidelity, and that the quality of the program is sustained over time.

I believe that the communication scholars who have already ventured into prevention science have paved the way for the rest of the discipline to join the journey. If we are to make a strong commitment to healthy families and children, then we need to be a part of that journey, developing communication enhancement programs that are stand-alone or integral parts of other interventions. We are now at the crossroads of communication and prevention . . . which path will we take?

References

Ackard, D. M., Neumark-Sztainer, D., Story, M., & Perry, C. (2006). Parent–child connectedness and behavioral and emotional health among adolescents. *American Journal of Preventive Medicine, 30*(1), 59–66.

Anthony, J. C. (2010). Epidemiology and etiology hand in hand. In L. M. Scheier (Ed.), *Handbook of adolescent drug use prevention: Research, strategies, and practice.* (pp. 113–124). Washington, DC: American Psychological Association.

Banerjee, S. C., & Greene, K. (2007). Antismoking initiatives: Effects of analysis versus production media literacy interventions on smoking-related attitude, norm, and behavioral intention. *Health Communication, 22*(1), 37–48.

Baverian, N., Lewis, K. M., Acock, A., DuBois, D. L., Yan, Z., Vuchinich, S., . . . & Flay, B. R. (2016). Effects of a school-based social–emotional and character development program on health behaviors: A matched-pair, cluster-randomized controlled trial. *The Journal of Primary Prevention, 37*(1), 87–105.

Biglan, A. (2015). *The nurture effect: How the science of human behavior can improve our lives and our world.* Oakland, CA: New Harbinger Publications.

Botvin, G. J. (2000). Preventing drug abuse in schools: Social and competence enhancement approaches targeting individual-level etiologic factors. *Addictive Behaviors, 25*(6), 887–897.

Bowlby, J. (1998). *A secure base: Parent-child attachment and healthy human development.* New York: Basic Books.

Boxmeyer, C. L., Lochman, J. E., Powell, N. P., & Powe, C. E. (2015). Preventing conduct disorders and related problems. In L. M. Scheier (Ed.), *Handbook of adolescent drug use prevention: Research, strategies, and practice* (pp. 103–119). Washington, DC: American Psychological Association.

Bridgeland, J., Bruce, M., & Hariharan, A. (2013). The missing piece: A national teacher survey on how social and emotional learning can empower children and transform schools. *A Report for CASEL. Executive Summary.* Chicago, IL: Civic Enterprises.

Collaborative for Academic, Social, and Emotional Learning (CASEL). (2015). *Effective social and emotional learning programs: Middle and high school edition.* Chicago, IL: CASEL.

Chiapa, A., Morris, G. P., Véronneau, M. H., & Dishion, T. J. (2016). Translational research on parenting of adolescents: Linking theory to valid observation measures for family centered prevention and treatment. *Translational Behavioral Medicine, 6*, 1–15.

D.A.R.E. America (2014). *Annual report 2014: Empowering children to live safe and healthy lives.* Los Angeles, CA: Author

DiCenso, A., Guyatt, G., Willan, A., & Griffith, L. (2002). Interventions to reduce unintended pregnancies among adolescents: Systematic review of randomised controlled trials. *British Medical Journal, 324*(7351), 1–9.

Dishion, T. J., & McMahon, R. J. (1998). Parental monitoring and the prevention of child and adolescent problem behavior: A conceptual and empirical formulation. *Clinical Child and Family Psychology Review, 1*(1), 61–75.

Durlak, J. A., Domitrovich, C. E., Weissberg, R. P., & Gullotta, T. P. (Eds.). (2015). *Handbook of social and emotional learning: Research and practice.* New York: Guilford Press.

Durlak, J. A., Weissberg, R. P., Dymnicki, A. B., Taylor, R. D., & Schellinger, K. B. (2011). The impact of enhancing students' social and emotional learning: A meta-analysis of school-based universal interventions. *Child Development, 82*(1), 405–432.

Dutta, M. J., Anaele, A., & Jones, C. (2013). Voices of hunger: Addressing health disparities through the culture-centered approach. *Journal of Communication, 63*(1), 159–180.

Every Student Succeeds Act. (2015). Congressional act, Bill 114, s1177. Retrieved from https://www.congress.gov/114/bills/s1177/BILLS-114s1177enr.pdf

Fagan, A. A., Hanson, K., Hawkins, J. D., & Arthur, M. W. (2009). Translational research in action: Implementation of the Communities That Care prevention system in 12 communities. *Journal of Community Psychology, 37*(7), 809–829.

Fagan, A. A., & Hawkins, J. D. (2015). Enacting preventive interventions at the community level: The Communities that Care Prevention System. In L. M. Scheier (Ed.), *Handbook of adolescent drug use prevention: Research, strategies, and practice* (pp. 343–360). Washington, DC: American Psychological Association. doi:10.1037/14550-020.

Fallon, L. F., & Zgodzinski, E. J. (2005). *Essentials of public health management*. Jones & Bartlett Learning.

Fisher, W. R. (1989). Clarifying the narrative paradigm. *Communication Monographs, 56*, 55–58.

Greene, K., Banerjee, S. C., Ray, A., & Hecht, M. L. (in press). Active involvement interventions in health and risk messaging. In R. L. Parrott (Ed.), *Oxford encyclopedia of health and risk message design and processing* (pp. 1–36). New York, NY: Oxford University Press.

Greene, K., Yanovitzky, I., Carpenter, A., Banerjee, S. C., Magsamen-Conrad, K., Hecht, M. L., & Elek, E. (2015). A theory-grounded measure of adolescents' response to media literacy interventions. *Journal of Media Literacy Education, 7*(2), 35–49.

Griffin, K. W., Botvin, G. J., Nichols, T. R., & Doyle, M. M. (2003). Effectiveness of a universal drug abuse prevention approach for youth at high risk for substance use initiation. *Preventive Medicine, 36*(1), 1–7.

Harrington, N. G., Helme, D. W., & Noar, S. M. (2015). Message design approaches to health risk behavior prevention. In L. M. Scheier (Ed.), *Handbook of adolescent drug use prevention: Research, strategies, and practice* (pp. 381–396). Washington, DC: American Psychological Association.

Hecht, M. L. (1993). 2002—a research odyssey: Toward the development of a communication theory of identity. *Communications Monographs, 60*(1), 76–82.

Hecht, M. L., Graham, J. W., & Elek, E. (2006). The drug resistance strategies intervention: Program effects on substance use. *Health Communication, 20*(3), 267–276.

Hecht, M. L., Marsiglia, F. F., Elek, E., Wagstaff, D. A., Kulis, S., Dustman, P., & Miller-Day, M. (2003). Culturally grounded substance use prevention: An evaluation of the keepin'it REAL curriculum. *Prevention Science, 4*(4), 233–248.

Hecht, M. L., & Miller-Day, M. (2007). The drug resistance strategies project as translational research. *Journal of Applied Communication Research, 35*(4), 343–349.

Hecht, M. L., & Miller-Day, M. A. (2010). "Applied" aspects of the drug resistance strategies project. *Journal of Applied Communication Research, 38*(3), 215–229.

Hingson, R. W., & Winter, M. R. (2006). Age at drinking onset and alcohol dependence: Age at onset, duration, and severity. *Archives of Pediatrics & Adolescent Medicine, 160*(7), 739–746.

Hobbs, R. (2004). A review of school-based initiatives in media literacy education. *American Behavioral Scientist, 48*(1), 42–59.

Ialongo, N., Poduska, J., Werthamer, L., & Kellam, S. (2001). The distal impact of two first-grade preventive interventions on conduct problems and disorder in early adolescence. *Journal of Emotional and Behavioral Disorders, 9*(3), 146–160.

Israel, B. A., Schulz, A. J., Parker, E. A., Becker, A. B., Allen, A., & Guzman, J. R. (2008). Critical issues in developing and following CBPR Principles. In M. Minkler & N. Wallerstein (Eds.), *Community-based participatory research for health: From process to outcomes* (2nd ed., pp. 47–66). San Francisco: Jossey-Bass.

Kellam, S. G., Wang, W., Mackenzie, A. C., Brown, C. H., Ompad, D. C., Or, F., . . . & Windham, A. (2014). The impact of the Good Behavior Game, a universal classroom-based preventive intervention in first and second grades, on high-risk sexual behaviors and drug abuse and dependence disorders into young adulthood. *Prevention Science, 15*(1), 6–18.

Kumpfer, K. (2012). *Strengthening families program.* Retrieved from http://www.strengtheningfamiliesprogram.org/

Kumpfer, K. L., DeMarsh, J. P., & Child, W. (1989). *Strengthening families program: Children's skills training curriculum manual, parent training manual, children's skill training manual, and family skills training manual. Prevention Services to Children of Substance-abusing Parents.* Salt Lake City: Social Research Institute, Graduate School of Social Work, University of Utah.

Kumpfer, K. L., Magalhães, C., Whiteside & JingXie, H. (2015). Strengthening families for middle/late childhood. In M. J. Van Ryzin, K. L. Kumpfer, G. M. Fosco, M. T. Greenberg (Ed.), *Family-based prevention programs for children and adolescents: Theory, research, and large-scale dissemination* (pp. 68–85). New York, NY: Psychology Press.

Kumpfer, K. L., Magalhães, C., & Xie, J. (2012). Cultural adaptations of evidence-based family interventions to strengthen families and improve children's developmental outcomes. *European Journal of Developmental Psychology, 9*(1), 104–116.

Kumpfer, K. L., Pinyuchon, M., de Melo, A. T., & Whiteside, H. O. (2008). Cultural adaptation process for international dissemination of the Strengthening Families Program. *Evaluation & the Health Professions, 31*(2), 226–239.

Lezin, N., Rolleri, L., Bean, S., & Taylor, J. (2004). *Parent-child connectedness: Implications for research, interventions and positive impacts on adolescent health.* Santa Cruz, CA: ETR Associates.

Lorch, E. P., Palmgreen, P., Donohew, L., Helm, D., Baer, S. A., & Dsilva, M. U. (1994). Program context, sensation seeking, and attention to televised anti-drug public service announcements. *Human Communication Research, 20*(3), 390–412.

Merrell, K. W., & Gueldner, B. A. (2010). *Social and emotional learning in the classroom: Promoting mental health and academic success.* New York: Guilford Press.

Miller, T., & Hendrie, D. (2008). *Substance abuse prevention dollars and cents: A cost-benefit analysis,* DHHS Pub. No. (SMA) 07-4298. Rockville, MD: Center for Substance Abuse Prevention, Substance Abuse and Mental Health Services Administration.

Miller-Day, M. (2008, May), Translational oerformances: Toward relevant, engaging, and empowering social science. *Forum Qualitative Sozialforschung / Forum: Qualitative Social Research, 9*(2), artcle 52. doi:http://dx.doi.org/10.17169/fqs-9.2.402.

Miller-Day, M., & Hecht, M. L. (2013). Narrative means to preventative ends: A narrative engagement framework for designing prevention interventions. *Health Communication, 28*(7), 657–670.

Miller-Day, M., Pezalla, A., & Chesnut, R. (2013). Children are in families too! The presence of children in communication research. *Journal of Family Communication, 13*(2), 150–165.

National Research Council. (2012). Education for life and work: Developing transferable knowledge and skills in the 21st century. Committee on Defining Deeper Learning and 21st Century Skills. In J. W. Pellegrino & M. L. Hilton (Eds.), *Board on testing and assessment and board on science education, division of behavioral and social sciences and education.* Washington, DC: The National Academies Press.

National Research Council; Institute of Medicine. (2004). *Children's health, the nation's wealth: Assessing and improving child health.* Washington, DC: National Academy of Sciences Press. doi:10.17226/10886.

Norris, A. E., Pettigrew, J., Miller-Day, M., Hecht, M. L., Hutchison, J., & Campoe, K. (2014). Resisting pressure from peers to engage in sexual behavior what communication strategies do early adolescent Latina girls use? *The Journal of Early Adolescence, 35*(4), 562–580.

Olweus, D. (1993). Victimization by peers: Antecedents and long-term outcomes. In K. H. Rubin & J. B. Asendorpf (Eds.), *Social withdrawal, inhibition, and shyness in childhood* (pp. 315–341). New York: Psychology Press.

Palmgreen, P., Lorch, E. P., Donohew, L., Harrington, N. G., Dsilva, M., & Helm, D. (1995). Reaching at-risk populations in a mass media drug abuse prevention campaign: Sensation seeking as a targeting variable. *Drugs & Society, 8*(3–4), 29–45.

Petronio, S. (2007). JACR commentaries on translating research into practice: Introduction. *Journal of Applied Communication Research, 35*(3), 215–217.

Porta, M., Greenland, S., Hernán, M., dos Santos Silva, I., & Last, J. M. (2014). *A Dictionary of epidemiology* (6th ed.). New York: Oxford University Press, USA. ISBN 978-0-19-997673-7.

Robertson, E. B., Perl, H. I., Reider, E. E., Sims, B. E., Crump, A. D., & Compton, W. M. (2015). Drug use prevention: Definitions and terminology. In L. M. Scheier (Ed.), *Handbook of adolescent drug use prevention: Research, strategies, and practice* (pp. 11–29). Washington, DC: American Psychological Association.

Singal, A. G., Higgins, P. D., & Waljee, A. K. (2014). A primer on effectiveness and efficacy trials. *Clinical and Translational Gastroenterology, 5*(1), e45.

Scheier, L. M. (Ed.). (2010). *Handbook of drug use etiology: Theory, methods, and empirical findings.* Washington, DC: American Psychological Association.

Scheier, L. M. (Ed.). (2014). *Handbook of adolescent drug use prevention: Research, strategies, and practice.* Washington, DC: American Psychological Association.

Scheier, L. M., & Hansen, W. B. (Eds.). (2014). *Parenting and teen drug use: The most recent findings from research, prevention, and treatment.* Oxford University Press.

Socha, T. J., & Stamp, G. H. (2009). A new frontier for family communication studies: Parent-child-societal communication. In T. J. Socha, & G. H. Stamp (Eds.),
*Parents and children communicating with society: Managing relationships outside of
the home* (pp. 1–16). New York, NY: Routledge.

Socha, T. J., & Yingling, J. (2010). *Families communicating with children.* Cambridge,
UK: Polity Press.

Spoth, R., Redmond, C., Mason, W. A., Schainker, L., & Borduin, L. (2015). Research
on the strengthening families program for parents and youth 10–14: Long-term
effects, mechanisms, translation to public health, PROSPER partnership scale up. In
L. M. Scheier (Ed.), *Handbook of adolescent drug use prevention: Research, strategies,
and practice* (pp. 267–292). Washington, DC: American Psychological Association.

Tobler, N. S., Roona, M. R., Ochshorn, P., Marshall, D. G., Streke, A. V., & Stackpole,
K. M. (2000). School-based adolescent drug prevention programs: 1998 meta-analysis. *Journal of Primary Prevention, 20*(4), 275–336.

Vreeman, R. C., & Carroll, A. E. (2007). A systematic review of school-based interventions
to prevent bullying. *Archives of Pediatrics & Adolescent Medicine, 161*(1), 78–88.

Warren, J. R., Hecht, M. L., Wagstaff, D. A., Elek, E., Ndiaye, K., Dustman, P., &
Marsiglia, F. F. (2006). Communicating prevention: The effects of the keepin'it
REAL classroom videotapes and televised PSAs on middle-school students' sub-
stance use. *Journal of Applied Communication Research, 34*(2), 209–227.

Webster-Stratton, C. (2015). THE INCREDIBLE YEARS® SERIES. In M. J. Van
Ryzin, K. L. Kumpfer, G. M. Fosco, & M. T. Greenberg (Eds.), *Family-based prevention programs for children and adolescents: Theory, research, and large-scale dissemination* (pp. 42–65). New York, NY: Psychology Press.

Wethington, E., & Dunifon, R. E. (2012). *Reach for the public good: Applying the methods of translational research to improve human health and well-being.* Washington,
DC: American Psychological Association.

Wilson, D. B., Gottfredson, D. C., & Najaka, S. S. (2001). School-based prevention
of problem behaviors: A meta-analysis. *Journal of Quantitative Criminology, 17*(3),
247–272.

World Health Organization. (2000). *The world health report 2000—health systems: Improving performance.* Geneva, Switzerland: World Health Organization.

Coda

The Urgent Need for Global, Inclusive and Comprehensive Lifespan Communication

THOMAS J. SOCHA
Old Dominion University

NARISSRA MARIA PUNYANUNT-CARTER
Texas Tech University

Recent fervor in the field of communication brings to the forefront the pressing need for the field to become far more inclusive than in its past. All communicators should be able to read the communication research literature, read communication textbooks, as well as take communication classes, and be able to see themselves in its pages and in its lessons. In short, no communicator should ever be left out. This volume joins and supports the scholars of transformation and inclusion with the unambiguous message that all children and indeed communicators of all ages must be included in communication.

The *National Communication Association* (NCA) is currently organized into 49 divisions, 7 sections, and 6 caucuses (*National Communication Association*, 2020a). Of its 49 divisions, there are no divisions that specifically focus on children or adolescents and only one section that does (Elementary and Secondary Education Section). According to this NCA section's website:

> The Elementary and Secondary Section welcomes membership from all academic levels. We seek to be at the forefront of curricular change and development in the areas of speaking, listening, and media literacy on the elementary and secondary levels. ... To us, it is important that elementary and secondary students receive the best preparation possible in speaking, listening, and media literacy. While we strongly prefer that these subjects be taught by communication specialists, we realize that many universities and colleges no longer offer certification in communication but place it all within language arts. ...

Therefore, we actively seek to incorporate the latest research and knowledge from areas of communication theory, instructional practices, technology, argumentation, and debate, interpersonal, listening, and other specialties within our discipline to inform and improve our work. Thus, we encourage the membership of colleagues from all areas of our discipline. (*National Communication Association*, 2020b)

This Section's mission statement should be a prominent part of NCA's larger mission statement and should become a visible priority for all of its divisions, sections, and caucuses. Indeed, remedying invisibility is an important part of the solution for children and adolescents being included in the communication.

For the past 15 years, for example, the first author has been a member of the Praxis II Speech Communication Examination Committee of the Educational Testing Services (see Educational Testing Services, 2020) that includes writing many examination items appearing in the current test. This exam is a general communication knowledge test that concludes the education of those pursuing certification to teach speech communication in secondary education. Few in communication know about the test. Few states require it. And only a few states offer secondary education teaching licensure in communication (e.g., see Certificates in Pennsylvania Types and Codes, 2020). For example, in the Commonwealth of Virginia, licensure in speech communication is only available as an add-on endorsement to a Secondary Teacher License in an approved subject area such as English (Virginia Department of Education, 2020). Because communication instruction is currently not labeled as a separate and specific content area of elementary school curricula, it is also not an area of teaching licensure and certification. However, this does not mean that communication is not being taught in primary grades. Listening, speaking, reading, and writing, although currently labeled "language arts" are really better labeled, "communication arts" and are indeed being taught in schools today. Further, it is critically important that communication arts should also include digital media literacy as well as relational communication. Making communication arts a central part of elementary school curricula and teacher licensure will go a long way to increase communication's role in US educational systems.

In order to raise the visibility of the communication field in education, one starting place is working towards all 50 states requiring formal instruction and demonstrated communication competencies (e.g., presentational, relational, and media literacy) in at least at the middle and high school levels. And in those states that do not already offer this, lobby state boards of education in support of required communication arts education in middle and high schools and the accompanying teacher certifications in communication at these levels. Not only will this go a long way to raising communication's visibility and equipping today's students with much needed communication competencies but will add jobs for those majoring in communication.

As mentioned in earlier chapters, communication education occurs not only in schools but in the nation's preschools and homes. Thus, going forward, family communication and communication education should be considered together as components of a continuous process of lifespan communication education and not as completely separate and distinct. Journals like *Communication Education* (that currently focus primarily on classroom communication) and the *Journal of Family Communication* can and should focus conjointly on their roles in lifespan communication education.

University textbooks in all the areas covered by NCA's 49 divisions should systematically consider the age of communicators and the role of communication development in their topic areas. For example, imagine NCA's Peace and Conflict Division adopting a lifespan focus and featuring the development of theories, methods, and pedagogy of communication in service of peace and effective conflict management for 3-year-olds to the end of life. Or, the Activism and Social Justice Division working on teaching advocacy skills to first graders as well as seniors. Each and every one of NCA's 49 divisions can be enriched by being age-inclusive including those whose mission and purpose is inclusion itself.

Going forward, it should also be the policy of all communication associations and journals that all studies accepted for publication or for presentation at conferences, similar to what is now required at the NIH, must somehow include and consider children, adolescents, as well as early-, middle-, and later life-, adults in their conceptualization, operationalization, and samples, or least report reasons why they are excluding children, adolescents, and the elderly from their study. Although to some this may seem like a radical notion, for many topic areas like family communication, media studies, communication and aging, and more children are already there and just need to be more visible.

Communication has always and will always begin with children. It is our collective hope that this volume will help the field of communication recognize this and to begin to move the field forward to become the most inclusive of all the social sciences and humanities from first words to final conversations.

References

Educational Testing Services. (2020). *Speech communication content knowledge.* https://www.ets.org/praxis/prepare/materials/5221.

National Communication Association. (2020a). *NCA interest groups.* https://www.nat-com.org/about-nca/membership-and-interest-groups/nca-interest-groups.

National Communication Association (2020b). *Elementary and secondary education section.* https://www.natcom.org/about-nca/membership-and-interest-groups/nca-interest-groups.

Virginia Department of Education. (2020). *Teacher licensure and assessment.* http://www.doe.virginia.gov/teaching/licensure/#assessment

About the Co-editors

Narissra Maria Punyanunt-Carter (Ph.D., Kent State University, 2002) is an Assistant Dean of international affairs for the College of Media and Communication. She is a Full Professor in the department of communication studies at Texas Tech University. She was just elected as Vice Chair-Elect of the Elementary and Secondary Education Section and is currently the past chair of the Mass Communication Division and "The Family Communication Division" of the *National Communication Association*. She was elected to serve on NCA's Nominating Committee and appointed to serve on NCA's Doctoral Program Committee. She was just awarded Texas Tech University's 2018 Professing Excellence Award. Dr. Punyanunt-Carter's research interests include romantic relationships, computer-mediated communication, father-daughter communication, and mass media portrayals of romance. She has published 12 book chapters and 70+ journal articles. She has been listed as a lead article many times, is a consultant for several book publishers, and has published many articles, which have been featured in *Cyberpsychology, Behavior, & Social Networking, Southern Communication Journal, Howard Journal of Communication, Communication Research Reports, and Communication Quarterly.* She has devoted an extraordinary amount of work towards her discipline, department, the university, and the community of Lubbock. She has served as a permanent or ad-hoc reviewer for ten different peer-reviewed journals. In 2020 for the Eastern Communication Association conference, she has received two top paper awards. She has won numerous teaching and advising awards.

Thomas J. Socha (Ph.D., University of Iowa, 1988) is University Professor of Communication, in the Department of Communication & Theatre Arts at Old Dominion University, Norfolk, Virginia. He has served as the

Founding Editor of the *Journal of Family Communication*, Founding Editor of the *Lifespan Communication: Children, Family and Aging* book series (Peter Academic Lang Publishing), and the Founding Graduate Program Director, MA in Lifespan & Digital Communication (Old Dominion University). He has received numerous awards for his teaching (e.g., ODU University Professor designee, ODU's *Robert L. Stern Award* for Excellence in Teaching, and *State Council of Higher Education in Virginia Faculty Award* Finalist), research [e.g., *National Communication Association's* (NCA), *Bernard J. Brommel Award for Outstanding Research in Family Communication*, ODU's *Charles & Elizabeth Burgess Award for Faculty Research*], as well as advising and mentoring [e.g., National Association of Academic Advisors (NACADA), Finalist for *National Faculty Advisor of the Year*; Joel S. Lewis Award for Academic Mentoring]. He has published nine co-authored/co-edited books/special journal issues, 45+ articles/chapters, and presented over 75 papers at professional association meetings. His research and teaching focuses on lifespan communication (wellness; food/ nutrition; Blue Zones; aging, resilience, & relocation), family communication (ethnic culture, race, smartphone use, health & wellness), children's communication (e.g., positive communication development, behavioral regulation, moral development, early childhood bullying, humor development), positive communication (e.g., theories, models, peak communication). He is a Past President of the Southern States Communication Association (SSCA), Past Chair of the Family Communication Division (*National Communication Association*), Interpersonal Communication Division (SSCA), and Applied Communication Division (SSCA).

About the Authors

Fashina Alade, Ph.D. Candidate, Media, Technology and Society Doctoral Program, Northwestern University

Gary A. Beck, Ph.D., Associate Professor of Communication and Graduate Program Director, Old Dominion University, Norfolk, Virginia

Wendy Bower, Ph.D., Graduate Coordinator, Communication Disorders Department, SUNY, New Paltz

Kristen Carr, Ph.D., Associate Professor, Department of Communication, Texas Christian University

John Chetro-Szivoc, Ph.D. Associate Dean, School of Professional Studies, Clark University, Worcester, MA

Melinda J. Colwell, Ph.D., Professor, Human Development and Family Studies, Texas Tech University

Sydney Cox, BA, Teacher - Carrollton-Farmers Branch ISD, Carrollton, Texas

Robin Duffee, Ph.D. Candidate, Communication Arts & Sciences, Penn State University

Marit Eikaas Haavimb, MA BPSS, Consultant, Drammen Norway

Danyella Jones, M.A., Lifespan & Digital Communication, Department of Communication & Theatre Arts, Old Dominion University, Norfolk, Virginia

Jenna LaFreniere, Ph.D., Assistant Professor, Communication Studies, Texas Tech University

Alexis R. Lauricella, Ph.D., Associate Director, Center on Media and Human Development, Northwestern University

Andrea McCourt, Ph.D., Instructor in Humanities and Psychology, South Plains College

Michelle Miller-Day, Ph.D., Professor of Communication Studies, School of Communication, Chapman University, Orange, CA

Kimberly Pearce, Professor of Communication, De Anza College and the Public Dialogue Consortium and Pearce Associates

Ronda Scantlin, Ph.D. Associate Professor, Communication, University of Dayton

Elizabeth Trejos-Castillo, Ph.D., Associate Professor, Human Development and Family Studies, Texas Tech University

Paula S. Tompkins, Ph.D., Professor Emeritus, Department of Communication Studies, St. Cloud State University

Ellen Wartella, Ph.D., Sheikh Hamad bin Khalifa Al-Thani Professor of Communication, Professor of Psychology, Professor of Human Development and Social Policy, Communication Studies Department, Northwestern University

Jason Wrench, Ed.D., Professor of Communication, Department of Communication, SUNY, New Paltz

Jill Yarbrough, Ph.D., Clinical Assistant & Virginia Engler Professor of Business Management, West Texas A&M University

Author Index

Subject Index

LIFESPAN COMMUNICATION

Children, Families, and Aging

Thomas J. Socha, *General Editor*

From first words to final conversations, communication plays an integral and significant role in all aspects of human development and everyday living. The Lifespan Communication: Children, Families, and Aging series seeks to publish authored and edited scholarly volumes that focus on relational and group communication as they develop over the lifespan (infancy through later life). The series will include volumes on the communication development of children and adolescents, family communication, peer-group communication (among age cohorts), inter-generational communication, and later-life communication, as well as longitudinal studies of lifespan communication development, communication during lifespan transitions, and lifespan communication research methods. The series includes college textbooks as well as books for use in upper-level undergraduate and graduate courses.

Thomas J. Socha, Series Editor | *tsocha@odu.edu*

To order other books in this series, please contact our Customer Service Department at:

peterlang@presswarehouse.com (within the U.S.)
orders@peterlang.com (outside the U.S.)

Or browse online by series at www.peterlang.com